Successful
Transition Programs

2 edition

2 edition

Successful
Transition Programs

Pathways for Students With
Intellectual and Developmental Disabilities

John McDonnell | Michael L. Hardman

University of Utah | *University of Utah*

Los Angeles • London • New Delhi • Singapore • Washington DC

For information:

SAGE Publications, Inc.
2455 Teller Road
Thousand Oaks, California 91320
E-mail: order@sagepub.com

SAGE Publications Ltd.
1 Oliver's Yard
55 City Road
London EC1Y 1SP
United Kingdom

SAGE Publications India Pvt. Ltd.
B 1/I 1 Mohan Cooperative Industrial Area
Mathura Road, New Delhi 110 044
India

SAGE Publications Asia-Pacific Pte. Ltd.
33 Pekin Street #02-01
Far East Square
Singapore 048763

Printed in the United States of America

Library of Congress Cataloging-in-Publication Data

McDonnell, John, 1954-
Successful transition programs: Pathways for students with intellectual and developmental disabilities/ John McDonnell, Michael L. Hardman. — 2nd ed.
    p. cm.
Rev. ed. of: Transition programs for students with moderate/severe disabilities. Pacific Grove, Calif.: Brooks/Cole Pub. Co., © 1996.
Includes bibliographical references and index.
ISBN 978-1-4129-6021-2 (pbk.)
    1. Students with disabilities—United States. 2. School-to-work transition—United States.
I. Hardman, Michael L. II. McDonnell, John, 1954– Transition programs for students with moderate/severe disabilities. III. Title.

LC4019.M34 2009
371.9—dc22   2008038981

Printed on acid-free paper.

    12   13   10 9   8   7   6   5   4   3   2

Acquiring Editor:	Diane McDaniel
Editorial Assistant:	Ashley Conlon
Production Editor:	Sarah K. Quesenberry
Copy Editor:	Melinda Masson
Proofreader:	Scott Oney
Indexer:	Wendy Allex
Typesetter:	C&M Digitals (P) Ltd.
Cover Designer:	Candice Harman
Marketing Manager:	Christy Guilbault

Brief Contents

Detailed Contents

SECTION III: INSTRUCTION AND EDUCATIONAL SUPPORTS

Chapter 8. Inclusion in General Education Classes   149

Chapter 9. Instruction in Community Settings   173

Preface

The reauthorization of the Individuals with Disabilities Education Act of 1997 (IDEA) mandated for the first time that state and local education agencies provide comprehensive transition services to students with disabilities. Subsequent amendments to IDEA in 2004 strengthened these mandates and focused the transition planning process on achieving measurable postschool goals that are based on each student's educational needs and preferences. School districts must provide a coordinated set of transition services that will enable the student to achieve his or her goals, and they must work collaboratively with appropriate agencies to ensure that students have access to needed postschool services. These mandates have dramatically expanded the role of secondary programs in supporting the transition of students with disabilities from school to work, community life, and postsecondary education.

This book discusses transition services, supports, and programs for individuals with intellectual and developmental disabilities in America's schools, including historical perspectives, current evidence-based practices, and future directions. Research over the last 2 decades has led to the development and validation of a number of strategies that can improve postschool outcomes for students with intellectual and developmental disabilities. The purpose of this text is to prepare new and practicing professionals with the knowledge and skills necessary to provide effective transition programs to these individuals. We believe that transition programs should be designed to cumulatively build every student's capacity to actively and successfully participate in postsecondary education, employment, community living, and citizenship.

Organization of the Text

The text is organized into five sections that address critical issues related to the successful implementation of transition programs for students with intellectual and developmental disabilities.

Section I addresses the foundations of transition programs. Chapter 1 discusses the development of transition programs and provides an overview of legislation that affects the provision of transition services. Chapter 2 addresses the outcomes that are important to achieve for students in secondary programs and the contemporary principles underlying effective transition services. Chapter 3 provides an overview of the strategies that increase the effectiveness of transition programs and discusses how these strategies can be successfully implemented at the middle school, high school, and post-high school levels.

Section II focuses on the design of curricula in secondary programs and key issues related to carrying out student-centered transition planning. Chapter 4 addresses the structure of general education and ecological curricula. The Individuals with Disabilities Education Improvement Act of 2004 requires that students with disabilities have equal access to the general education curriculum in order to achieve their desired postschool outcomes. This chapter reviews the common structure of the general education curriculum nationally and discusses how states have attempted to make the curriculum accessible to students with disabilities. The chapter also discusses various ecological curricula models for secondary students. Strategies for blending general education and ecological curricula to meet the transition needs of each student are also introduced and discussed. Chapter 5 addresses strategies for developing a student-centered and student-directed individualized education program (IEP) that includes a transition plan. Chapter 6 reviews the research on developing self-determination skills for students with intellectual disabilities and strategies for promoting self-determination during transition planning. Chapter 7 focuses on the roles of parents and families in transition planning and how professionals can work with parents and family members to ensure they participate more effectively in the planning process.

Section III outlines strategies for carrying out effective instruction for students in general education classes and community settings. Chapter 8 reviews the research on effective instructional and social supports for students who are participating in general education classes. It also describes a process that teachers can use to design and implement effective instruction in these settings. Chapter 9 discusses strategies needed to instruct students in community settings, including how to design and implement instructional programs. The chapter concludes with an overview of common logistical issues that teachers face in the implementation of community-based instruction.

Section IV addresses four program areas that are critical to preparing students for their transition to work and community living. Chapter 10 focuses on home and community living. The principles that should be considered in selecting IEP and transition planning goals, approaches to carrying out instruction, and the development of alternative performance strategies are introduced and analyzed. Chapter 11 deals with issues related to developing appropriate leisure and recreational alternatives for students, including advantages and disadvantages of various models of leisure and recreation training, the considerations that should guide the selection of goals, and the decisions that teachers face in providing instruction. Chapter 12 focuses on the design of employment training for middle and high school students. It describes the important role that employment training plays in helping the student, his or her family, and school staff develop a clear understanding of the student's work interests, strengths, and support needs. Common approaches in the implementation of employment training are addressed, as are several key issues that affect successful implementation. Chapter 13 describes the process for helping post-high school students obtain paid employment prior to graduation. Specific recommendations on job development, training, and follow-along activities are addressed.

Section V concludes the text with a discussion on postschool alternatives for secondary students with intellectual and developmental disabilities. Chapter 14 describes residential options for adults with intellectual and developmental disabilities. Emphasis is placed on supported living and personal assistance options and the federal programs needed to support each individual's access to them. Chapter 15 reviews the history and structure of employment programs for adults with disabilities. Supported and customized employment models that are designed to improve career and work outcomes for adults are introduced. The chapter concludes with several key federal work incentive programs that can support young adults in obtaining paid employment. Chapter 16, the final chapter in the text, discusses the issues related to the participation of young adults with intellectual and developmental disabilities in postsecondary education. The chapter describes legislation that affects the participation of students in these programs and the current models being used to support students in these settings. Considerations for preparing students for postsecondary education are discussed.

Acknowledgments

We would like to thank the students, parents, families, and professionals with whom we have had the pleasure to work over the years. Their insights and wisdom have informed our professional and personal development, and they have helped us become more effective advocates for people with intellectual and developmental disabilities. This book draws heavily from *Transition Programs for Students With Moderate/Severe Disabilities*, written by John McDonnell, Connie Mathot-Buckner, and Brad Ferguson, and *Secondary Programs for Students With Developmental Disabilities*, written by John McDonnell, Barbara Wilcox, and Michael Hardman.

Although Connie, Brad, and Barbara have moved on in their careers, we thank them for their continuing friendship and support. We would also like to acknowledge the important contributions of the contributors to this text. Writing a book is without a doubt a daunting task, but their professionalism and strict adherence to timelines made it a rich and rewarding experience. Finally, we would like to thank Andrea and Monica for their love, support, and everlasting patience.

We gratefully acknowledge the contributions of the following reviewers.

Elizabeth Ankeny, St. Cloud State University

Susan M. Bruce, Boston College

Patricia Edwards, Ashland University

Yeunjoo Lee, California State University–Bakersfield

Jerry G. Petroff, The College of New Jersey

Janice J. Seabrooks, University of North Florida

About the Authors

John McDonnell (PhD) is a professor and program coordinator in severe disabilities in the Department of Special Education at the University of Utah. His research interests include curriculum and instruction, secondary/transition programs for students with severe disabilities, and inclusive education.

Michael L. Hardman (PhD) is dean of the College of Education at the University of Utah. He also serves as chair of the Department of Teaching and Learning, professor in the Department of Special Education, and university coordinator for the Eunice Kennedy Shriver National Center for Community of Caring. His research interests include educational policy and reform, developmental disabilities, professional development, inclusive education, transition from school to adult life, and preparing tomorrow's leaders in special education.

About the Contributors

Brigid E. Brown (MEd) is completing her doctorate at the University of Utah. Her research has been in the areas of inclusion at the secondary education level, functional literacy for students with severe disabilities, and providing appropriate services for English language learners with severe disabilities.

Margaret Collier (MS) is completing her doctorate at the University of Utah. Her research has been in the areas of transition at secondary and postsecondary levels, literacy for English language learners and struggling readers, and response to intervention (RTI).

Margret A. Crockett (PhD) is adjunct faculty in the Department of Special Education at the University of Utah. Her research interests include the provision of services to English language learners with severe disabilities, multicultural education, and the inclusion of students with disabilities in general education classrooms.

Shirley Ann Dawson (MS) is a doctoral candidate in the Department of Special Education at the University of Utah and has taught general and special education for 25 years. Her professional interests include special education law and policy.

J. Matt Jameson (PhD) is a clinical assistant professor in special education at the University of Utah. He has worked as a classroom teacher for middle school students with intellectual and developmental disabilities, a teacher of preschoolers with autism, and a specialist in a residential program for adults with intellectual and developmental disabilities. His primary research interests include instructional strategies and inclusive educational procedures for students with severe intellectual disabilities.

Sharlene A. Kiuhara (MEd) is a doctoral candidate and an adjunct instructor in the Department of Special Education at the University of Utah. Her experience as a special educator for 6 years at the secondary level has laid the groundwork for her higher education teaching and research agenda. Her areas of interest include transition, literacy, and policy issues for students with mild to moderate disabilities in secondary and in higher education settings.

Andrea P. McDonnell (PhD) is a professor and chair of the Department of Special Education at the University of Utah. Her areas of interest include embedded instruction in inclusive, developmentally appropriate preschool programs; family-professional partnerships; interdisciplinary personnel and leadership preparation; and preparation of culturally competent educators.

Jayne McGuire (PhD) is an assistant professor in the special education credential program at Humboldt State University. Beyond her scholarly work, McGuire's professional experiences have included teaching high school special education and nonprofit leadership focused on accessible recreation and community inclusion for people of all abilities. Her current research has focused on self-determination and the impact of recreation programming on people with disabilities.

Catherine Nelson (PhD) is an assistant professor and program coordinator in early childhood special education in the Department of Special Education at the University of Utah. Nelson teaches in the areas of severe disabilities, early childhood special education, and deafblindness. In addition, she consults worldwide in programs serving children and youth who are deafblind. Her current research interests include assessment of individuals with severe multiple disabilities and the use of visual strategies to facilitate social communication in young children with autism.

Shamby Polychronis (PhD) is an assistant professor in the special education program at Westminster College in Salt Lake City, Utah. She has experience teaching students with severe disabilities in post-high school programs with an emphasis on community-based education. Polychronis has served on multiple grant projects, coauthored several articles and textbooks, and presented at state and national conferences. Her scholarly interests include secondary education, individual rights for people with disabilities, postschool outcomes for students with disabilities, family support services, and teacher education.

Tim Riesen (PhD) is the director of the Utah Supported Employment Training Project at the University of Utah's Department of Special Education. The project is designed to provide training and technical assistance to state, education, and nonprofit agencies involved in providing community employment services to people with disabilities. Riesen has also worked as a secondary special educator and as a specialist in residential programs for individuals with autism and severe disabilities.

Tessie Rose (PhD) is a research analyst at the American Institutes for Research (AIR) specializing in transition and data-based decision making. She currently has technical assistance and evaluation responsibilities for AIR's National Center on Response to Intervention. Prior to joining AIR, Rose served as principal investigator and project coordinator on several grant and contract projects, including model demonstration sites in progress monitoring and community-based transition programs for youth with low-incidence disabilities. She is a former assistant professor of special education with an emphasis on mental retardation at the University of Nevada–Las Vegas, where she provided technical assistance and expert support for several state transition and RTI initiatives. She served on the Nevada Autism Task Force for Transition, Community Inclusion, and Employment and the Nevada Transition Advisory Council while in Nevada. Rose is the author of numerous publications and has given numerous national presentations on school models, model components, and sustained practice implementation to improve student outcomes.

Section I

FOUNDATIONS OF TRANSITION PROGRAMS

CHAPTER 1

Historical and Legislative Foundations

MICHAEL L. HARDMAN

SHIRLEY ANN DAWSON

Each year, more than 3 million students graduate from high school in the United States (U.S. Department of Education, 2008). For many, graduation is a time of celebration—a rite of passage into independence and adult life. Unfortunately, this is often not the case for students with intellectual and developmental disabilities. For these students and their families, the transition from school to adult life may be a time of uncertainty and concern about the future (Bambara, Wilson, & McKenzie, 2007; Larkin & Turnbull, 2005). Students with intellectual and developmental disabilities lack the myriad opportunities and choices for postsecondary education, community living, and employment that are commonly available to their peers who are not disabled (Bambara et al., 2007; Wagner, Newman, Cameto, & Levine, 2005). They are often unable to participate in community employment and remain isolated from the community, lacking critical access to services and supports necessary for active participation in adult living (Houtenville, 2002; National Organization on Disability, Harris, & Associates, 2004).

Although 2 decades have passed since Congress mandated that transition planning be included in federal law and though new advances in instructional technology have taken place, access to meaningful transition programs is at best "inconsistent" within schools. As such, the intended outcomes of comprehensive transition planning and services for all students with disabilities have yet to be fully realized. However, the critical goal of improving the quality of adult life for students with disabilities remains as important today as when the federal transition mandate was initially passed by Congress in 1990. Future opportunities for greater independence and full participation in the community remain highly dependent on the development and implementation of effective practices in transition planning and secondary programs.

This book examines the purpose, scope, content, and results of school-based transition planning and secondary programs for students with intellectual and developmental disabilities. To begin, several terms used throughout the text are defined below.

Individuals with intellectual and developmental disabilities are those who, because of the nature of their intellectual, physical, and/or sensory disabilities, require ongoing and intensive support from family, education, and community agencies in order to fully participate in adult life.

Transition refers to the passage from adolescence to adulthood, wherein each individual is faced with a number of life choices.

Transition planning is the process during which an individual, his or her parents, his or her educators, and adult service professionals come together to create an adaptive fit between the student's abilities, needs, and preferences and the requirements of the environment in which he or she will live as an adult. The process involves accommodating a change status from the interdependence of being a student to taking on more independent adult roles within and external to the family. These roles include employment, participation in postsecondary education, residential living, and developing personal relationships.

Transition services include a coordinated set of activities designed to facilitate disabled students' move out of school and into community living, employment, postschool education, or more independent living. A more in-depth definition of transition services as mandated in the Individuals with Disabilities Education Act (IDEA 2004, Public Law 108–446) will be discussed in the next section of this chapter.

This book is written for those who are seeking careers in the fields of education and social services, as well as for professionals from many disciplines who want to know more about evidence-based transition services for people with intellectual and developmental disabilities. Chapter 1 begins with an overview of the history and scope of federal legislation and the impact of educational reform on secondary education and transition planning in America's schools. We conclude with a discussion of the evolution of transition models during the past 20 years.

The Federal Mandate for Transition Services

Focus Question 1	Identify the components of the transition amendments in IDEA.

The year 2010 marks the 35th anniversary of the passage of Public Law 94–142, now IDEA 2004. Since the law's original passage, Congress has made significant changes to the legislation five times, including the 1990 amendments, which mandated the provision of comprehensive transition planning for all adolescents with disabilities aged 16 years and older, and the 2004 amendments, which defined transition services as follows:

> The term "transition services" means a coordinated set of activities for a child with a disability that—
>
> (A) is designed to be within a results-oriented process, that is focused on improving the academic and functional achievement of the child with a disability to facilitate the child's movement from school to post-school activities, including post-secondary education, vocational education, integrated employment (including supported employment), continuing adult education, adult services, independent living, or community participation;
>
> (B) is based on the individual child's needs, taking into account the child's strengths, preferences, and interests; and
>
> (C) includes instruction, related services, community experiences, the development of employment and other post-school adult living objectives, and, when appropriate, acquisition of daily living skills and functional vocational evaluation. (Sec. 602[34])

IDEA 2004 states that transition planning services are to begin no later than the first Individualized Education Program (IEP) that is in effect when the child is 16 years of age and must be updated annually thereafter (Sec. 614[d][VIII]). IEP teams, which include the student, his or her parents and educators, and other professionals as appropriate, have some discretion if transition planning and services are needed at an earlier age. Although initiating transition services at age 16 may be appropriate for students with mild or moderate disabilities, the needs of most students with intellectual and developmental disabilities will necessitate the planning and implementation of services and supports at an earlier age (Steere, Rose, & Cavaiuolo, 2007).

The requirements of IDEA 2004 are intended to help students who are leaving school make a successful transition to living and working in the community. This mandate specifically requires state and local education agencies to

1. Provide transition services for every child with a disability.

2. Develop a "coordinated set of activities" for students with disabilities. These activities must be focused on achieving individualized postschool employment or vocational training and community living goals for each student.

3. Coordinate transition activities with community service agencies to make needed services more readily available to graduates.

4. Consider individual needs, strengths, preferences, and interests.

IDEA further requires schools to take an active role in preparing students for life after graduation. Schools can no longer assume that students, their families, and community service programs are solely responsible for graduates' postschool adjustment. Achieving the goal of the transition mandate will have a far-reaching impact on the way secondary programs are designed and implemented (see Window 1.1).

Window 1-1

Eric

Before I graduated from high school, I was very nervous. I had questions in my head: What will my future hold? What will I be doing in 5 years? I was nervous because I was leaving high school and moving to a new transition school, South Valley. I was very sad to leave all my friends behind, but I knew I would make new friends. All of my friends were going to a different college. I was staying behind and was sad that my friends were leaving.

While at South Valley, I have learned to ride the UTA bus. I have had lots of job sites at South Valley. My first jobs were at elementary schools. I cleaned tables, vacuumed carpets, put books away, and dusted shelves. I also worked at Sam's Club where I put cardboard in the crusher and put go-backs away. This year, I have worked at a car dealership, a bookstore, and a movie theater. I put order forms in numerical order, clean, and take tickets. I have two volunteer jobs. I put books away at the library, and I file papers and get folders out for the next day at the Neurobehavior HOME Program at the University of Utah.

I had questions about the life design program I would move to in South Valley: What will my job be like? Who will help me? What will my future hold? My dreams for the future are becoming a basketball manager for the university and working at the movie theater. My fears are being in a bus wreck and being late for work.

—Eric

Transitions are difficult for each one of us as we move through life, but as a parent of a child with autism, my angst over transitions was sometimes greater than my son's. Educators in both the middle school and the high school had been trying to prepare us for the transition after high school for many years. The question that would have jolted me into reality was "What will Eric do all day long each day when you are at work and the school bus doesn't stop to pick him up each morning?"

The year after Eric left high school, he saw several of his friends at the grocery store. When he came home, he told me he was a "little embarrassed." When I asked why, he said, "Everyone else was going to college, and I was embarrassed to tell my friends where I was going to school." It was then that I fully realized what people had been trying to guide me toward for several years—Eric needed to have meaningful experiences that he could take pride in, and to a greater degree these experiences needed to more closely mirror the experiences of his peers.

My initial thoughts about building a plan of activities for Eric centered on activities for a person with autism (although, to this day, I am not certain what those activities are). I have transitioned my thinking to ensure that his life will provide the same activities that each of us see in our daily lives to provide a feeling of self-worth: independence, community service, social activities, continuing education, religious activities, employment, and family. It is also important that Eric takes an active part in the decision-making process and, just like any other individual at the age of 20 years, believes that the world holds numerous possibilities, choices, and opportunities. This is not the last transition we face; my hope for the future is that, as we continue along the way, we will continue to have guides for the journey.

—Karla, Eric's mom

Successful implementation of this mandate raises several important issues for schools. For example, how does the development of transition services for students with disabilities fit within the broader context of educational reform? What outcomes should be used to evaluate the ultimate effectiveness of these services?

Transition Services in Secondary Schools and Educational Reform

Focus Question 2	Identify the major elements of educational reform in schools and their impact on transition planning for students with intellectual and developmental disabilities.

In today's schools, improved student performance—*results*—has become the critical indicator in determining the effectiveness of an educational program. Although federal mandates over the past 35 years have been successful in ensuring students with disabilities *access* to a free and appropriate education, Congress noted in 1997 and in 2004 that the implementation of federal legislation had been impeded by low expectations and an insufficient focus on applying research on proven methods of teaching and learning for children with disabilities. Follow-up studies of special education graduates in the 1990s (e.g., Hasazi, Furney, & Destefano, 1999; Wagner & Blackorby, 1996) suggested high levels of unemployment rates, low access rates for postsecondary education, and few comprehensive support networks. However, in 2005, the National Longitudinal Transition Study-2 reported improvement in such areas as high school completion, employment rates, postschool education, social involvement, and living accommodations (Wagner et al., 2005). Yet, in spite of this improvement, the National Organization on Disability suggests that the educational possibilities granted by federal legislation have not been fully realized by many special education graduates as they participate in the social and economic mainstream of their local communities (National Organization on Disability et al., 2004).

Window 1-2

A Snapshot of Young Adults With Disabilities: 1985 and 2001

Two studies commissioned by the U.S. Department of Education have documented changes experienced by young adults with disabilities 2 years after they exited high school. The 1987 National Longitudinal Transition Study (NLTS) followed up on students with disabilities who had been receiving special education services in 1985, and the 2003 National Longitudinal Transition Study-2 (NLTS2) assessed the status of young adults with disabilities who exited high school in 2001. Below are some highlights of the results of comparing these two studies.

School Completion

- The school completion rate of young adults with disabilities increased and the dropout rate decreased by 17% between 1987 and 2003. With these changes, 70% of the young adults with disabilities from the 2003 study completed high school.

Community Living and Social Activities

- The living arrangement of young adults with disabilities has been stable over time. Two years after exiting high school, approximately 75% of young adults with disabilities from both studies lived with their parents; 1 in 8 lived independently; and 3% lived in a residential facility or institution.
- Ninety percent of young adults with disabilities from the 1987 and 2003 studies were single. However, membership in organized community groups (e.g., hobby clubs, community sports, performing groups) more than doubled so that 28% of young adults with disabilities from the 2003 study belonged to a group.
- There was a large increase in adults with disabilities ever having been subject to disciplinary action at school, fired from a job, or arrested between 1987 and 2003. More than 50% of the young adults with disabilities from the 2003 study had negative consequences for their behavior, compared with 33% from the 1987 study.

Engagement in School, Work, or Preparation for Work

- Overall engagement in school, work, and job training increased only slightly (70% to 75%) from 1987 to 2003. Although disabled students' overall rate of engagement in these activities did not increase markedly over time, the modes of engagement did change.
- Engagement in the combination of postsecondary education and paid employment nearly quadrupled to 22% for students in the 2003 study.
- There was a significant increase in employment (11%) from 1987 to 2003, and 44% of the young adults in the 2003 study had been employed since high school.

Employment

- In 2003, 70% of young adults with disabilities who had been out of school up to 2 years had worked for pay at some time since leaving high school; only 55% had done so in 1987. However, 18% of young adults in the 2003 study were less likely than those in the 1987 study to be working full-time in their current job. Approximately 39% of the young adults in the 2003 study were employed full-time.
- Over time, considerably more young adults with disabilities earned above the federal minimum wage (70% in 1987 vs. 85% in 2003). Yet the average hourly wage did not increase when adjusted for inflation; earning averaged $7.30 per hour in 2003.

Note. From "Transition from High School to Work or College: How Special Education Students Fare," by M. Wagner and J. Blackorby, 1996, *Special Education for Students with Disabilities*, 6(1), pp. 103–120, and *Changes Over Time in the Early Postschool Outcomes of Youth with Disabilities*, a report from the National Longitudinal Transition Study (NLTS) and the National Longitudinal Transition Study-2 (NLTS2), Menlo Park, CA: SRI International. Adapted with permission.

Historically, federal legislation has been the driving force behind changes in special education services in the United States. The original tenets of the Education for All Handicapped Children Act (EHCA) in 1975 were strengthened in IDEA 2004 to ensure that students with disabilities are provided opportunities for academic growth and long-term success. EHCA did not include specific provisions for transition services but did state that all children with disabilities must have access to the same programs and services that are available to children without disabilities. The initial federal mandate and subsequent parent and professional advocacy initiatives on behalf of students with disabilities expanded the national discussion from accessing education to ensuring results and accountability for all students in public schools (Hardman & Mulder, 2003).

In the next section, we examine the federal role in public education reform over the past 2 decades and its impact on transition planning education of students with disabilities. Federal reform initiatives are addressed in the context of the standards movement, high-stakes accountability, and the eventual passage of the reauthorization of the Elementary and Secondary Education Act (ESEA) in 2001 (renamed the No Child Left Behind Act [NCLB]). The evolution of IDEA is addressed in light of general education reform and its proposed alignment with NCLB.

A Nation at Risk

In 1983, the National Commission on Excellence in Education issued a report card on the status of America's schools titled *A Nation at Risk.* The phrase "needs improvement" was written on nearly every page of the document. Using strong and sometimes provocative language, the report sparked national debate and set forth recommendations that focused on the need to "fix" America's schools, including the need for more subject matter content, high standards and expectations for student learning, increased time for learning, quality teaching, and more effective leadership and fiscal support. The recommendations were based on the premise that everyone can learn and that public education is responsible for providing students with the requisite skills for postsecondary education, future careers, and civic engagement. Six years after the release of *A Nation at Risk,* governors from across the country met in a national summit to transform the commission's recommendations into the National Education Goals and establish a framework for educational reform (Vinovskis, 1999). However, it took another decade for the educational needs of students with disabilities to be specifically addressed within the educational reform movement and eventually within federal legislation.

Goals 2000 and the Improving America's Schools Act

In 1994, the National Education Goals were codified into federal law in Goals 2000: Educate America Act, and performance, content, and opportunity-to-learn standards were defined at the national level. At the core of Goals 2000 was the belief that *all* students, including those with disabilities, must achieve at higher academic levels. In order to receive federal financial assistance under Goals 2000, states had to describe how the lowest-performing students (including those with disabilities, those living in poverty, and English language learners) would gain access to instruction and a rigorous curriculum. The ultimate goal of this federal legislation was to develop "a broad national consensus for American education reform" (Sec. 2[4][A]). To make this objective a reality, the states were to voluntarily develop core curriculum standards and assessments (Table 1.1).

In 1994, Congress also reauthorized ESEA and renamed it the Improving America's Schools Act (IASA). IASA reiterated the premise that *all* children can achieve high standards and recommended that states voluntarily develop content and student performance standards. Students with disabilities were included under Title I of the act, which is the largest and most recognized program in federal education legislation, serving millions of disadvantaged children to ensure their "fair, equal, and significant opportunity to obtain a high-quality education and reach, at a minimum, proficiency on challenging state academic achievement standards and state academic assessments" (Sec. 1001).

The government-mandated reforms under Goals 2000 and IASA proposed standardization in testing, teaching, and curriculum in response to declining academic performance in America's schools. These reforms eventually resulted in every student, including those with disabilities, taking more standardized tests than ever before; increased graduation requirements; and greater state accountability for student learning.

The No Child Left Behind Act

The era of standards-based reform and accountability at the federal level hit its peak in 2001 with the passage of the No Child Left Behind Act. NCLB not only strengthened the standards approach to education; it also sent a clear message: *In spite of some state efforts to establish an accountability system, there is no confidence that student performance will be improved on a consistent basis without a stronger federal role.* As such, NCLB expanded the federal role from assisting states in setting standards and improving local performance to fiscal sanctions and corrective action for both states and schools that fail to meet set criteria.

Table 1.1 Initiatives Under the First Wave of Federal Education Reform

A Nation at Risk Recommendations	The National Education Goals	Standards Definitions
• Strengthen content requirements in high schools • Adopt rigorous and measurable state standards and higher expectations for student performance and conduct • Use school time more effectively and lengthen the school day • Increase leadership and fiscal support to reform public education • Improve teacher preparation • *Source:* National Commission on Excellence in Education (1983)	• Every student will start school ready to learn • Graduation rates will be increased to at least 90% • Students will achieve in challenging subject matter • The United States will be first in the world in math and science • All adults will be literate with skills for a global economy • Teacher education and professional development will be strengthened • All schools will be free of drugs and violence • Parental participation will be increased • *Source:* Vinovskis (1999)	• Content standards: Broad descriptions of the knowledge and skills students should acquire in a particular subject area • Performance standards: Concrete examples and explicit definitions of what students have to know and be able to do to demonstrate that they are proficient in the skills and knowledge framed by content standards • Opportunity-to-learn standards are the criteria for, and the basis of, assessing the sufficiency or quality of the resources, practices, and conditions necessary at each level of the education system (schools, local educational agencies, and states) to provide all students with an opportunity to learn the material in voluntary national content standards or state content standards (Sec. 3[a]) • *Source:* Goals 2000: Educate America Act (1994)

Continuing the theme of the past 2 decades that all students can learn, NCLB specifically addressed the need for states to be accountable for the reading, math, and science achievement of all students, including those with disabilities, those from culturally and linguistically diverse backgrounds (English language learners), and those living in poverty. Whereas ESEA, when it was originally passed into law in 1965, emphasized the *opportunity* for disadvantaged students to learn, NCLB *required* schools to be account-able for increased academic learning (Hardman & Mulder, 2003; Hunt & McDonnell, 2007). The premise for an increased emphasis on school accountability and inclusion of students with intellectual and developmental disabilities is "the promise for increased consideration of these students in school and state policy decisions, as well as enhanced educational expectations, greater access to the general education curriculum, and improved instructional programs for this population of students" (Hunt & McDonnell, 2007, p. 275).

The four principles of school accountability under NCLB are the following:

1. Focus on student achievement as the primary measure of school success.

2. Emphasis on challenging academic standards that specify the knowl-edge skills that students should achieve and the levels at which mas-tery of the knowledge should be demonstrated.

3. Expectation that all students can and will learn more if high expecta-tions are required.

4. Heavy reliance on achievement testing to ensure compliance and mon-itoring of student achievement (U.S. Department of Education, 2008).

These principles form the core of a standards-based system to ensure that schools make genuine progress in closing persistent achievement gaps between disabled and disadvantaged students and their peers. A standards-based education emphasizes prespecified mastery of the curriculum. School progress in closing this gap is measured by annual yearly progress in read-ing, math, and science and must be the same for all students regardless of academic ability, English language acquisition, or socioeconomic disadvan-tage. The unprecedented focus on accountability and a standards approach (one size fits all) to student achievement has created concern and many unanswered questions for educators, students with disabilities, and the stu-dents' parents. For example, are the characteristics of evidence-based spe-cial education instruction compatible with a standards-based approach to education? Will the participation of students with disabilities in a standards-based curriculum result in higher academic achievement or inevitable fail-ure? How should special and general education teachers be prepared to ensure adequate training in working with students in a standards-based edu-cational system?

Evolution of School-to-Work Transition Policy

Focus Question 3	How has federal legislation evolved to include individuals with disabilities in planning for the transition from school to the workplace and community?

A broad range of federal legislation has been enacted over the last 3 decades to support the long-term and complex nature of the transition from school to adult life. The purpose of these programs and services is to support young adults with disabilities as they transition to postsecondary school, employment, or community living. Anchoring employment transition, in addition to IDEA and NCLB, are five pieces of federal legislation: the Vocational Rehabilitation Act of 1973 and subsequent amendments, the Americans with Disabilities Act (ADA) of 1990, the Workforce Investment Act (WIA) of 1998, the Ticket to Work and Work Incentives Improvement Act (TWWIIA) of 1999, and the School-to-Work Opportunities Act (STWOA) of 1994. The Carnegie Council on Adolescent Development stated in 1995 that school-to-work programs should help all students, especially those with disabilities, address the full range of issues they will confront as they leave school. Each of these acts addresses specific transition and employment needs of individuals with disabilities throughout the life span.

The Vocational Rehabilitation Act of 1973

The Vocational Rehabilitation Act of 1973 specifically prohibits discrimination against people with disabilities and provides funding and the opportunity to gain employment and living assistance as needed. Section 504 of the act "focuses on the needs of adults and youth transitioning into employment settings and ensures the development and implementation of a comprehensive and coordinated program of vocational assistance for individuals with disabilities thereby supporting independent living and maximizing employability and integration into the community" (Larkin & Turnbull, 2005, p. 68).

Key provisions of the Vocational Rehabilitation Act as amended in 1998 are "a coordinated set of activities for a student, designed within an outcome-oriented process, which promotes movement from school to post-school activities, including:

- Postsecondary education
- Vocational training
- Integrated employment (including supported employment)
- Continuing and adult education
- Adult services

- Independent living
- Community participation" (Larkin & Turnbull, 2005, p. 68)

The Americans with Disabilities Act of 1990

ADA is a civil rights act that mandates protections for people with disabilities in public- and private-sector employment, all public services and public accommodations, transportation, and telecommunications. The U.S. Department of Justice is charged with the responsibility of ensuring that these provisions are enforced on behalf of all people with disabilities. The intent of ADA is to create a fair and level playing field by ending discrimination against citizens with disabilities by requiring reasonable accommodations. Reasonable accommodations take into account each person's needs resulting from his or her disability. As defined in the act, the principal test for a reasonable accommodation is its effectiveness: Does the accommodation provide an opportunity for a person with a disability to achieve the same level of performance and to enjoy benefits equal to those of an average, similarly situated person without a disability? ADA federal regulations banned discrimination and ensured accessibility in workplaces, community facilities, public transportation, government services, and telecommunications.

The Workforce Investment Act of 1998

WIA consolidated a variety of federally funded programs as part of the first major reform of the nation's job training and employment services for individuals with disabilities. Key elements of the WIA include

1. Streamlined service via a one-stop delivery system of information and job training services.

2. Universal access to essential services.

3. State and local requirements for a workforce investment system that fully includes and accommodates the needs of persons with disabilities.

4. Improved youth programs (Mank, 2007).

The Ticket to Work and Work Incentives Improvement Act of 1999

The purpose of TWWIIA is to support the employment of adults with disabilities without costing them Medicare or Medicaid coverage. Prior to this legislation, many individuals with disabilities faced the prospect of losing federal benefits if they went to work. Persons with disabilities were then forced to choose between employment and access to medical care that was vital to sustain life. TWWIIA provides health care support for people with severe disabilities by allowing states the option to establish a Medicaid state-plan buy-in option for those who are eligible, to offer premium-free extended Medicare coverage, to provide grants to states to develop state infrastructures to support working individuals with disabilities, and to offer statewide demonstrations to provide health care coverage to individuals with potentially disabling conditions who work to test the hypothesis that the provision of health care and related supports will prolong independence and employment and reduce dependency on disability income support programs (Centers for Medicare & Medicaid Services, 2008).

The School-to-Work Opportunities Act of 1994

The major tenets of STWOA (Public Law 103–239) are based on several studies that criticized students' lack of preparation for transitioning from school to competitive employment. A joint initiative between the U.S. Department of Education and the U.S. Department of Labor, STWOA was part of a national initiative for comprehensive educational reform in 1994. The purpose of STWOA, similar to the Goals 2000 legislation, was to establish a national framework within which all states could create statewide school-to-work systems. The primary goal of this act was to "offer opportunities to all students to participate in a performance-based education and training programs that will enable them to earn portable credits, prepare for first jobs in high-skill high-wage careers and increase their opportunities for further education" (Sec. 3[a]). The result would be an expanded workforce. STWOA comprised a variety of school-based learning, work-based learning, and connected opportunities throughout high school to achieve this goal, including (a) career exploration and counseling, (b) academic and occupational instruction that was integrating and focused on high standards of achievement, and (c) various structured work experiences that taught broad transferable workplace skills.

STWOA also made several specific references to students with disabilities. As further referenced within the statute, additional purposes of the act were "to motivate all youths, including low-achieving youths, school dropouts, and youth with disabilities, to stay in or return to school or a classroom setting and strive to succeed, by providing enriched learning experiences and assistance in obtaining good jobs and continuing their education in postsecondary educational institutions" and "to increase opportunities for minorities, women, and individuals with disabilities, by enabling individuals to prepare for careers that are not traditional for their race, gender, or disability" (Sec. 3).

The Evolution of Models for Transition Planning and Services

Focus Question 4	What are the components of an effective transition planning system?

Since the mid-1980s, a number of transition planning and service models for students with disabilities have been developed and implemented. While each emphasizes different aspects of the transition process, there is general agreement that an effective system of transition services must include (a) education programs designed to prepare students to live and work in the community, (b) access to postsecondary education and/or adult services that will support a lifestyle that reflects the needs and preferences of each student, and (c) a coordinated system of planning that promotes opportunities for educational and community service agencies to work collaboratively in achieving desired postschool goals.

Bridges From School to Working Life

The Bridges From School to Working Life Model focuses primarily on successful transition from school to employment for students with disabilities (Will, 1985). Bridges emphasizes the importance of improving every student's access to needed services and supports during the period of transition (ages 14 to 22) from school to competitive employment. The model is based on three underlying assumptions: (a) the complexity of postschool services and competition for those services, (b) a focus on students with disabilities and their needs rather than the type or severity of disability, and (c) the goal of sustained and paid employment either immediately after school or after a period of postschool training or vocational services.

In 1985, Madeleine Will, then assistant secretary of the Office of Special Education and Rehabilitative Services and the parent of a child with a disability, first described transition as a bridge that "requires both a solid span and a secure foundation at either end" (p. 4). A transition planning system for students with disabilities is most effective when schools and adult service agencies work together in supporting students' needs while they are in school.

Coordinated transition planning and services are grouped into five components that become the bridges reflecting the necessary level of support.

1. High School Foundation: The school security and structure forms this foundation. Curriculum content and instructional procedures in high school determine whether or not students leave school with entry-level job skills, social interaction skills, and academic skills.

2. Transition Without Special Services: This bridge is shared by many individuals with and without disabilities. The resources needed for a successful transition to working life are those that are available to all citizens in general modes.

3. Transition With Time-Limited Services: The second bridge comprises temporary services that lead to permanent employment. Some individuals may require time-limited specialized services like vocational rehabilitation, postschool education, or other job training before entering employment. Access to these services is generally restricted to individuals who will continue to be successful when the support or service is withdrawn.

4. Transition With Ongoing Services: The third bridge consists of sustained support that enables the individual to maintain employment. This bridge is designed for individuals with the most severe disabilities who will always need supportive assistance.

5. Employment Foundation: This foundation represents the work opportunities in adult life. Regardless of which bridge is used or the strength of the high school foundation, successful transition depends on available employment options. Work opportunities are influenced by family and neighborhood networks, the economy, perceptions about individuals with disabilities, business incentives, and cooperative relationships among educational and government agencies (Will, 1985).

The Halpern Model

The model proposed by Andrew Halpern (1985) is perhaps the most comprehensive of the various approaches to transition planning because it addresses the full range of services and supports necessary for students with disabilities. The model includes all three components that define a comprehensive transition planning program while simultaneously addressing the range of services and supports needed for a student to successfully move from school to adult life.

The first component of the model comprises the areas of adult life that are critical to community adjustment. These areas include employment, residential living, and social and interpersonal relationships. Halpern argues that schools must comprehensively address all three areas if they are to succeed in supporting a student's transition from school to community. As suggested by Halpern, the quality of our lives is multidimensional. We gain pleasure and satisfaction from our work, our homes, and our families and friends. Consequently, transition services must be designed to address all areas of community adjustment.

The school provides the foundation for a successful transition. Its role is to provide the training and support necessary to support students and their families in achieving their own postschool goals and objectives. These supports not only include instruction on critical goals and objectives but also may include education of the student and family about postschool options, development of linkages with local businesses and service vendors, and coordination of service delivery with state community service agencies.

The second component of Halpern's model is the type of support (or services) that will be needed for a student to move smoothly and successfully from school into community life in one of three possible avenues:

1. Students may enter community life with the assistance and support of the generic services available to all individuals. These services include, but are not limited to, counseling and advising services provided by the high school and adult service agencies available to individuals without disabilities (such as job agencies), as well as the natural supports that students receive from friends and family.

2. Students may enter community life with time-limited support. In this situation, a community agency may provide temporary support. Such services might include postsecondary vocational training programs designed to place the individual in an entry-level job or temporary support to assist the individual in obtaining residential living (such as an apartment or a home).

3. Finally, students may make the transition into community life with ongoing supports. In this situation, students receive "lifelong" support to facilitate their adjustment to community life. The intensity of this support will vary significantly based on the needs and desires of particular students.

It is important to understand that these three avenues are not mutually exclusive. Often, students must tap into all three levels of services and supports to make a successful transition to adult living.

Systematic planning that leads to valued transition outcomes is at the core of the Halpern model. Halpern argues that in order to effectively prepare students for community life, schools must use IEPs as the vehicle to develop educational experiences that will meet each student's postschool needs and as a mechanism to promote collaboration between education and adult service programs. The decisions that students and their families face in the transition process include not only where the students will work and live but also how the students will be supported in achieving these outcomes.

POINT/COUNTERPOINT 1.1

NCLB, IDEA 2004, and Students With Intellectual and Developmental Disabilities: Increased Academic Achievement or Inevitable Failure

Standards-based reform in the No Child Left Behind Act is based on the premise that improving student performance is highly correlated with standards system and high-stakes accountability. However, the issue has engendered considerable debate. In this Point/Counterpoint, we examine contrasting perspectives on including students with severe disabilities in a standards-driven system with high-stakes accountability.

POINT

Proponents of including students with intellectual and developmental disabilities in a standards-driven system argue that it will enable these students to experience a wider variety of subjects at a deeper level. This would give students with intellectual and developmental disabilities exposure to higher-order thinking skills, such as problem solving, and enable them to develop collaborative skills and engender a sense of responsibility and self-esteem (McLaughlin & Tilstone, 2000). A standards-driven system also promotes more collaboration among special and general educators, requiring them to develop more challenging learner goals and raise expectations for students with disabilities.

Traditionally, students with intellectual and developmental disabilities have not been held accountable for the achievement of IEP goals. This has resulted in a lowering of individual expectations and failure to learn essential skills. As a corollary, special educators

COUNTERPOINT

Opponents of the standards-based approach as espoused in NCLB and IDEA 2004 raise several concerns. First, failure is inevitable because there is insufficient instructional time and resources to meet the instructional needs of students with intellectual and developmental disabilities. Second, there is no evidence that a standards-driven system will actually lead to sustained higher levels of achievement among students with intellectual and developmental disabilities and "whether the skills gained through this curriculum are the ones that will prove necessary for successful transition from school" (McLaughlin & Tilstone, 2000, p. 62).

It can be argued that establishing content standards for students with intellectual and developmental disabilities at the state level is inconsistent with the concept of individualization and not in the best interests of students with intellectual and developmental disabilities or their peers

(Point continued)

were not held accountable for the poor performance of their students, and they largely regarded the IEP as paper compliance rather than an accountability tool (Sebba, Thurlow, & Goertz, 2000). Including students with intellectual and developmental disabilities in a standards-driven system forces teachers to use the IEP as an accountability blueprint, altering goals and objectives as necessary to ensure student progress in the general curriculum.

Some educators, while accepting the premise that standards-based reform should apply to all students, are uneasy about including students with intellectual and developmental disabilities in the accountability system and its corresponding impact on teachers. Teachers and principals may become anxious about the consequences of published low scores. General education teachers may be concerned that students with intellectual and developmental disabilities will negatively affect publicly available scores and that schools would blame them.

(Counterpoint continued)

without disabilities. There is a fear that if all students are expected to reach the same standard, the bar will be lowered to accommodate those with less ability. If the bar isn't lowered, students with disabilities will routinely fail to meet the standard. Teachers may feel powerless because they believe it is not possible for all students to reach the required standards.

Some educators have concerns that inclusion in a standards-driven system will damage the self-esteem of students with disabilities if they do not perform well. Valuable instruction time would be spent teaching content in academic areas rather than concentrating on the acquisition of critical, functional life skills. In order to facilitate a student's mastery of academic skills, teachers could be forced to remove students from the general education class, thus compromising the inclusion of students with their same-aged peers. While there is no denying the need to improve results in both general and special education, students with disabilities will never catch up with their peers who are not disabled. In fact, they may fall even farther behind.

Note. Major portions of this debate forum are drawn from "Critical Issues in Public Education: Federal Reform and the Impact on Students With Disabilities," by M. Hardman and M. Mulder, in L. M. Bullock and R. A. Gable (Eds.), *Quality personnel preparation in emotional/behavior disorders* (pp. 12–36), Dallas, TX: Institute for Behavioral and Learning Differences. Adapted with permission.

Halpern's model highlights several important issues about the transition process. Secondary programs must comprehensively address the community adjustment needs of students. Schools can and do play a critical role in ensuring that these needs are met. Successful transition is a challenge not just for schools but also for family, friends, and education and community service agencies. Effective transition requires not only improving how students are prepared for community life but also ensuring that all possible personal and public resources are focused on achieving students' postschool goals.

The Kohler Model

Paula Kohler's (1996) model, "A Taxonomy for Transition Programming," acknowledges that transition planning encompasses all aspects of education and includes a basis for planning transition, evaluating content, and program effectiveness. Based on the premise that all secondary schooling is education for transition, the taxonomy views transition planning as the foundation for education rather than as an additional activity or requirement. Operationally, this requires (a) identifying postschool goals based on student abilities, needs, interests, and preferences; (b) development of instructional activities and educational experiences to prepare students for postschool goals; and (c) collaboration and cooperation among the student, his or her family, and professionals to identify and develop the goals and activities (Kohler, 1996). Components of the taxonomy can be divided into five categories:

1. Student-focused planning, which consists of IEP development, student participation, and planning strategies.

2. Student development, which includes life skills instruction, career and vocational curricula, structured work experience, assessment, and support services.

3. Interagency and interdisciplinary collaboration made up of a collaborative framework and collaborative service delivery.

4. Family involvement, which includes family training, participation, and empowerment.

5. Program structure, including program philosophy, program policy, strategic planning, program evaluation, resource allocation, and human resource development (Kohler, Field, Izzo, & Johnson, 1999).

Summary

Federal legislative initiatives of the past 2 decades have laid the foundation for improved postschool outcomes for individuals with intellectual and developmental disabilities as they transition from school to adult life. The long-term effectiveness of the various pieces of federal legislation will be gauged by the success students and their families experience in achieving these valued outcomes over time. From the high school transition years through adult life, the challenges of providing quality services and supports for people with disabilities are ever changing, varied, and complex. With the information in Chapter 1 providing the foundation, our discussion now moves into a more in-depth discussion of expected outcomes and emerging values in transition planning for students with intellectual and developmental disabilities for the 21st century.

Focus Question Review

Focus Question 1: Identify the components of the transition amendments in IDEA.

- Develop a "coordinated set of activities" for students that promotes successful movement from school to postschool activities. These activities must focus on achieving individualized postschool employment and community living goals for students.
- Coordinate transition activities with community service agencies to increase the availability of needed services to graduates after leaving school.
- Base specific services on transitions included in each student's IEP.

Focus Question 2: Identify the major elements of educational reform in schools and their impact on transition planning for students with intellectual and developmental disabilities.

- NCLB and IDEA require that students with intellectual and developmental disabilities have access to the general curriculum and be included in the state's accountability system for measuring student performance.
- During the past 2 decades, federal legislation has expanded its focus from access to public education for students with disabilities to improving student achievement within the general education curriculum.
- Schools must be accountable for the achievement of all students, including those with intellectual and developmental disabilities.

Focus Question 3: How has federal legislation evolved to include individuals with disabilities in planning for the transition from school to the workplace and community?

- Several federal initiatives (i.e., the Vocational Rehabilitation Act of 1973, ADA, TWWIIA, and STWOA) have focused specifically on meeting the transition needs of students with disabilities.

- Federal legislation seeks to protect individuals with severe disabilities from discrimination in employment, transportation, and communication and to ensure accessibility to facilities, government programs, and health care.

Focus Question 4: What are the components of an effective transition planning system?

- Education programs must be designed to prepare students to live and work in the community.
- Postsecondary services must be available to provide the opportunity for each individual to develop and achieve a lifestyle that reflects his or her own needs and preferences.
- A coordinated system of planning must be in place that requires education and community service agencies to work collaboratively in achieving valued postschool outcomes for each student with a disability.

CHAPTER 2

Expected Outcomes and Emerging Values

MARGRET A. CROCKETT

MICHAEL L. HARDMAN

Historically, "educational outcomes" for students with intellectual and developmental disabilities have primarily focused on "access to instruction" or the skills learned and applied within a classroom setting. The emphasis on access to instruction and classroom-based learning failed to provide these students with the skills needed to achieve valued postschool outcomes, including personal independence, employment, and community/family participation. As a result, a number of researchers have suggested that the expected outcomes of educational programs for students with intellectual and developmental disabilities should be defined more broadly to reflect the actual demands of living successfully in the community (Baer, Flexer, & Dennis, 2007; McDonnell, Hardman, & McDonnell, 2003; Neubert & Moon, 2006; Wehman, 2006). Achieving these broad outcomes for students also requires a fundamental shift in the values on which services for students are based. This chapter discusses the expected outcomes and the values that should drive the design, implementation, and evaluation of secondary and transition programs for students with intellectual and developmental disabilities.

Window 2-1

Frank

Frank is 24 years old and has a job, an apartment he shares with a friend, and an active life. Frank is also a person with an intellectual disability. Although he is able to speak, many people have difficulty understanding him. He has limited academic skills and some-times has difficulty adapting to changes in his life. Despite these challenges, his life is very similar to that of many people without disabilities.

Frank works at a convenience store making sandwiches, restocking shelves, and doing light custodial tasks. He earns $6.15 an hour and has a health and dental plan. Frank's boss says he is an excellent employee whose hard work has been rewarded with four different pay raises over the last 3 years. Frank is considered a reliable and responsible member of the staff. He eats lunch with his friends, goes to staff parties, and on Fridays joins others in celebrating the end of the workweek.

Frank shares an apartment with Josh, who works for the Metropolitan Transit Authority cleaning busses. Josh also has an intellectual disability. Frank and Josh share the responsibilities of cleaning the apartment and preparing their own meals. They often have friends over for dinner, to watch movies, or to play video games. Frank has joined a health club and works out or goes swimming a couple of times a week. He also sees his parents and brothers about once a week. Frank would like to buy a better stereo system and maybe take an out-of-town vacation this summer. Frank enjoys his life but also wants to improve it. He takes pride in his independence and his contribution to the community.

Frank is a person whose life exemplifies what parents, advocates, and professionals would like to see for all adults with intellectual and developmental disabilities as they transition from school to community living. Frank works where he chooses and sees his job as making an important contribution, lives with whom he wants, and makes his own decisions about how he spends his free time. Frank's life reflects his own personal preferences and values.

Expected Outcomes for Transition Programs

Focus Question 1	Identify outcomes of transition programs for students with intellectual and developmental disabilities that will enhance access to valued postschool community living and employment.

Although successful community living is a broad concept that can mean many different things, professionals and advocates agree that four general outcomes are universally critical (McDonnell et al., 2003; Wehman, 2006):

1. Establishing a network of friends and acquaintances.

2. Developing the skills to use community resources as a component of daily living.

3. Securing a paid job that supports the use of community resources and interaction with peers.

4. Establishing independence and autonomy in making lifestyle choices.

Friends and Acquaintances

A network of friends and acquaintances is essential to enhancing the quality of life for all people, including those with intellectual and developmental disabilities. Friendship provides individuals with the support needed to meet day-to-day needs, provides them with companionship, and gives them understanding and emotional support during stressful times (Berndt, 2002; Rubin, 2004). A lack of close friends can result in lowered self-esteem, a lack of self-confidence, and greater vulnerability to the influences of others. For students without disabilities, research has indicated that the development of stable and ongoing friendships helps individuals adjust to the transition from school to community life (Berndt, 2004). The same holds true for students with disabilities. Researchers have found that friendships play an important role in job performance and job satisfaction (Test, Carver, Ewers, Haddad, & Person, 2000; West, Wehman, & Wehman, 2005), successful employment (Phelps & Hanley-Maxwell, 1997; Test et al., 2000), independent living (Walker, 1999), and participation in recreational activities (Rynders, Schleien, & Matson, 2003; Terman, Larner, Stevenson, & Behrman, 1996). Consequently, effective transition programs must help students establish and maintain a support network of friends and family. This is more likely to occur if students with intellectual and developmental disabilities are provided with the opportunity to interact with peers without disabilities and are provided with the skills to initiate and maintain social interactions. The development of friendships for students can be encouraged through the use of peer buddy programs, peer support committees, and friendship circles (Miller, Cooke, Test, & White, 2003). A key goal of these different approaches is to develop respectful, reciprocal relationships between individuals with disabilities and their peers without disabilities.

Participating in the Life of the Community

To actively participate in the life of a community, each individual must have ongoing access to multiple resources, such as grocery stores, restaurants, theaters, mass transit systems, and banks. The more competent the individual is in accessing these resources, the more options and choices each person has in shaping his or her quality of life. For example, the ability to access different types of stores (grocery, department, pharmacy, etc.) influences our health and nutrition, as well as our personal appearance and hygiene. Access to community resources also affects how each individual is perceived and accepted as a member of the community. The competence of each individual directly affects the perception of others, and for better or worse, the more an individual is seen as dependent, the more negative the perception. As such, it is important for transition programs to be structured to ensure that each individual with intellectual or developmental disabilities has the skills to meet basic personal management and leisure activities in home, school, and community settings.

Window 2-2

The Nine Values of High-Quality Supported Employment Programs

A critical goal of supported employment is to support people with intellectual and developmental disabilities to be successful in paid community employment. Community employment is considered to be a very important component of how people define the quality of their life. To accomplish the goal of successful community employment, high-quality supported employment programs must have the following values:

1. Presumption of employment: Quality supported employment programs should assert that all people have the capacity to do a job and the right to have a job, regardless of the severity or type of their disability.

2. Competitive employment: Another value of high-quality supported employment programs is the belief that employment for individuals with intellectual and developmental disabilities should be in regular community businesses instead of in segregated work settings.

3. Self-determination: Individuals with intellectual and developmental disabilities participating in high-quality supported employment programs should be able to determine the employment supports and services that are best suited to their unique needs and preferences.

4. Commensurate wages and benefits: Individuals with intellectual and developmental disabilities must be provided with wages and benefits that are equal to those of their coworkers without disabilities who are performing the same job.

5. Focus on capabilities: Programs should focus on the abilities, strengths, and interests of individuals with intellectual and developmental disabilities rather than on their disabilities or limitations.

6. Importance of relationships: Acceptance of and mutual respect between individuals with intellectual and developmental disabilities and their coworkers without disabilities is enhanced in supported employment programs that foster community relationships both at work and away from work.

7. Power of supports: Individuals with intellectual and developmental disabilities in quality supported employment programs should be able to determine their own goals and receive the support that is appropriate for them to meet their goals.

8. Systems change: Traditional systems of supported employment should be changed to ensure that individuals with intellectual and developmental disabilities have greater control over their employment.

9. Importance of community: Individuals with intellectual and developmental disabilities must be connected to formal and informal supports within their community in order to facilitate acceptance.

Note. From "Competitive Employment: Has It Become the 'First Choice' Yet?" by P. Wehman, W. G. Revell, and V. Brooke, 2003, *Journal of Disability Policy Studies,* 14, pp. 163–173. Adapted with permission.

Community Employment

Community employment is one of the single most important factors influencing how most people define the quality of their life (Kraemer, McIntyre, & Blacher, 2003). First, the money earned from employment allows the person to access goods and services that enhance his or her standard of living. Most adults agree that the ability to do things like buy a new jacket or stereo or pay someone to clean the house can make life happier and more satisfying. Second, employment provides an important source for the development of social relationships. The friendships that adults establish with coworkers provide support in dealing with the stress of a job and create opportunities for involvement in social and leisure activities after the workday. Third, employment provides the resources necessary to increase personal independence and to reduce reliance on others. Employment allows people to make choices about where they live, whom they see, what they do in their free time, and so on. Finally, employment plays an important role in defining the identity of adults in the community. An individual who has a good job is often perceived more positively than a person who is unemployed. The level of acceptance that society has for an individual is related directly to the role he or she plays in supporting the economy of the community.

Postschool adjustment of individuals with intellectual and developmental disabilities correlates directly with successful employment (West et al., 2005; White & Weiner, 2004). People who obtain paid employment have greater financial security, are less dependent on family, and have more control over their own life choices (West et al., 2005). If individuals can obtain and maintain paid employment, their level of community participation and interaction with peers will improve dramatically. Transition programs must be structured to ensure that graduates have paid community employment upon leaving school (Kohler & Field, 2003; White & Weiner, 2004). Components of effective transition programs should include opportunities for students to receive employment training in community settings prior to graduation, employment training focused on opportunities present in the local community, a shift in focus to specific job training as students near graduation, and continuing interagency collaboration (Martin, Woods, Sylvester, & Gardner, 2005).

Independence and Autonomy

Successful participation in community living requires that adults be able to make choices regarding whom they spend time with, where they live, where they work, and what leisure activities they prefer. In order to make choices, individuals must have the opportunity to understand and choose from a variety of living, work, and leisure options. The planning and instructional procedures adopted by secondary programs must be designed to empower students to make these choices and select the services that they will need to meet their goals. In many respects, the effectiveness of secondary programs is determined by their responsiveness to the values and beliefs of students in shaping their educational programs and whether the students are prepared to continue to make choices for themselves after they leave school.

Emerging Values of Secondary Programs

Focus Question 2	Identify the emerging values that are driving the development of effective transition programs for students with intellectual and developmental disabilities.

Window 2-3

Loretta

Loretta's opportunities following school were strongly influenced by her secondary school program. From the time she was 16 years old, most of her school day focused on learning to complete employment, leisure, and personal management activities in community settings. Loretta's training for employment included 3 years of sampling various jobs in the local community in an effort to match her interests and abilities with the demands of various employment opportunities. These experiences included direct instruction and support from teachers and school support staff, vocational education personnel, and vocational rehabilitation counselors. At age 19, as a part of her individualized transition plan, Loretta was hired at the city airport, where she received support from her coworkers as well as school personnel until she was 22 years old. In addition, Loretta also learned to access various community settings, such as parks, theaters, stores, and restaurants. Personal management instruction focused on many different areas, including hygiene, developing and using her own personal schedule, and a time management system.

While a clear description of instructional outcomes for students with intellectual and developmental disabilities is critical to a successful educational experience, parents, professionals, advocates, and policymakers have begun to articulate the underlying values to guide the development of services and supports for the future (Kohler & Field, 2003; Test et al., 2004). These values stress the importance of creating an adaptive fit between individual needs and preferences and the demands of community, employment, and family environment. As suggested by Hardman, Drew, and Egan (2007), adaptive fit involves learning and applying various strategies that will facilitate the ability of each individual to meet the expectations of a given environment. The individual may find that the requirements for success within the environment (e.g., employment) are beyond his or her adaptive capabilities and that the system is unwilling to accommodate academic, behavioral, physical, sensory, or communicative differences. As a result, the individual may develop negative attitudes toward the environment. However, transition programs and adult services based on the value of creating an adaptive fit between the individual and the environment have strengthened collaborative efforts among the individual, the family, and the network of supports available in the community. Among these values are self-determination, full inclusion in all aspects of community and family life, a shift to greater reliance on natural supports, and the development of participant-driven school and community programs.

Self-Determination

Self-determination focuses on a person's ability to consider options and make appropriate decisions and to exercise free will, independence, and individual responsibility (University of Illinois at Chicago National Research and Training Center, 2003). An essential component of self-determination is understanding an individual's strengths and limitations along with believing that the individual is able to participate in making choices about his or her own life. The development of self-determination skills enables students to play a major role in determining and achieving valued postschool goals and to advocate on their own behalf. Educational programs must be structured to ensure that students learn to make informed decisions about their postschool lifestyle and that they are directly involved in the selection of service programs that will support those choices (Kohler & Field, 2003; Test et al., 2004). This can be accomplished by encouraging the active participation of students in individualized education planning, providing frequent opportunities to make personal and life choices, and providing the supports necessary to meet specific student needs (Field & Hoffman, 2002).

Window 2-4

Key Elements of Self-Determination

Self-determination skills enable students with intellectual and developmental disabilities to advocate for their own needs, preferences, and interests in order to achieve valued postschool outcomes. Students are able to make more informed decisions about where and with whom they will live, how they will spend their time, how they will participate in the community, and what supports they need and prefer. The following are some key components of self-determination skills.

Choice-Making Skills

The ability to make choices is an essential component of self-determination. Students must be provided with the opportunity to make choices in order to identify and communicate their needs and preferences. Some ways this can be accomplished include providing students with their choice of activities, location of activities, academic assignments, and the order of completion of assignments.

Problem-Solving Skills

Instruction on problem-solving skills should include teaching students to identify problems, analyze a problem and determine potential solutions, and resolve a problem using the most appropriate solution. Students should be provided with the support and accommodations to increase their capacity to solve problems in their everyday lives.

Decision-Making Skills

Decision making involves coming to a conclusion about which potential solution is best under different circumstances and understanding the consequences of different solutions. Key to teaching decision-making skills is the teaching of choice-making skills.

Goal-Setting and -Attainment Skills

Goal setting and attainment involves teaching students how to define a goal, determine where they are currently in relation to the goal, develop a plan of action, and evaluate their progress toward the attainment of the goal. Goal-setting skills can be very useful in helping students become more responsible for their own learning.

Self-Management Skills

Self-management skills comprise self-monitoring, self-evaluation, and self-reinforcement. Self-monitoring teaches students to assess, observe, and record their behavior. Self-evaluation teaches students to track and evaluate their progress on different activities. Self-reinforcement teaches students to deliver consequences based on their behavior.

Self-Advocacy and Leadership Skills

Self-advocacy skills provide students with the ability to advocate on their own behalf. Teaching self-advocacy and leadership skills includes teaching students about their rights and responsibilities, how to advocate for themselves, how to communicate in large and small groups, and how to negotiate.

Self-Efficacy

Self-efficacy is the belief that one is capable of performing or attaining certain goals. Self-efficacy may not be directly taught but may be enhanced through successful experiences in applying other self-determination skills.

Self-Awareness or Self-Knowledge

Self-awareness or self-knowledge refers to an individual's ability to understand his or her strengths or abilities and his or her weaknesses or limitations. Teaching self-awareness or self-knowledge includes teaching students to use their attributes in influencing their quality of life and to understand how their actions influence those around them.

Note. Adapted from "Self-Determination and Quality of Life: Implications for Special Education Services and Support," by M. L. Wehmeyer and R. L. Schalock, 2001, *Focus on Exceptional Children, 33*(8), pp. 1–20, and "Promoting Student Self-Determination Skills in IEP Planning," by W. M. Wood, M. Karvonen, D. W. Test, D. Browder, and B. Algozzine, 2004, *Teaching Exceptional Children, 36*(3), pp. 8–16. Adapted with permission.

The principle of self-determination states that individuals with disabilities, not service providers, have the right to determine where and with whom they will live, how they will spend their time, how they will take part in the community, and what services they need and prefer. Historically, individuals with more significant disabilities have had limited input on the decisions that are made in their lives because it is often assumed that they do not possess the ability to make these choices. However, research has demonstrated that individuals with a variety of disabilities can be taught self-determination skills that enable them to have greater control over their lives and their postschool outcomes (Test et al., 2004). Researchers have also suggested that self-determination increases the ability of an individual with intellectual and developmental disabilities to take responsibility for his or her own life and to transition effectively from school to community life (Test et al.).

Effective transition programs must provide students with the necessary tools to assume some role in making choices as they transition out of school and into adult life. This can be accomplished by infusing self-determination into the curriculum, encouraging students with disabilities to actively participate in the development of their individual education programs and individualized transition plans, providing students with numerous opportunities to make choices, providing the supports and accommodations necessary for students to meet their goals, and providing students with ongoing opportunities to advocate for themselves (Field & Hoffman, 2002).

Wehmeyer and Schalock (2001) and Wood, Karvonen, Test, Browder, and Algozzine (2004) outlined several key components of self-determination skills. First, students must be provided with the opportunity to make choices in order to identify and communicate their preferences. Within the classroom, this can be accomplished by providing students with a choice of activities, a choice of the location of activities, a choice of academic assignments to be completed, and a choice of the order of completion of assignments. Second, students should be provided with instruction on problem-solving skills, including how to identify problems, how to analyze a problem and determine potential solutions, and how to resolve a problem using the most appropriate solution. Students must also receive instruction in decision-making skills, which involve the ability to come to a conclusion about which potential solutions are best under different circumstances and to understand the consequences of different solutions. Students should be taught how to define a goal, how to determine where they are currently in relation to the goal, how to develop a plan of action, and how to evaluate their progress toward the attainment of the goal. Another component of self-determination is self-management, which includes self-monitoring, self-evaluation, and self-reinforcement. Students should be given instruction on self-advocacy skills in order to provide them with the ability to advocate on their own behalf. Finally, students should be taught self-awareness or self-knowledge in order to understand their strengths or abilities and their weaknesses or limitations so they are better able to influence their quality of life and to understand how their actions influence those around them. The development of self-determination skills will enhance access to valued postschool outcomes for students with intellectual and developmental disabilities.

Full Inclusion

One of the most significant changes in educational and community programs for persons with intellectual and developmental disabilities is the move toward full inclusion. Historically, the educational and community service system was based on the concept of a continuum of placements (Hardman et al., 2007). The continuum was conceived as a hierarchy of placements and was designed to move individuals incrementally toward a more "normal" lifestyle as they developed the skills professionals believed were necessary to function competently in more inclusive school and community settings. Service programs at the first level in the continuum were designed to provide the most intensive training and support and thus were the least inclusive. The intensity of support was gradually reduced as participants "graduated" to the next program in the hierarchy with the ultimate goal of being fully included in all aspects of school and community life. Historically, for the vast majority of people with intellectual and developmental disabilities, this goal was never met. Although many professionals and parents believed that the continuum would ultimately result in the movement of persons with intellectual and developmental disabilities into the mainstream of school and community life, the reality is that most persons with intellectual and developmental disabilities remained in more restrictive and segregated settings. Bellamy, Rhodes, Borbeau, and Mank (1986), using data from the U.S. Department of Labor, examined the average length of time that individuals with disabilities required to move from one program to another in the employment continuum. Based on this information, the researchers found that if individuals with intellectual and developmental disabilities were placed in a work activity center (the most restricted placement within the continuum) at age 22, they would not reach competitive employment in the community (the most inclusive placement within the continuum) until age 64. The inability of individuals with intellectual and developmental disabilities to move through the continuum from restrictive to inclusive placements is reflected in the growth of more segregated programs. Rusch and Braddock (2004) found that the growth of segregated employment services, such as day programs and sheltered workshops, continues to outpace the growth of supported employment. In practice, the continuum of placements has become a significant barrier to developing services and supports that would promote the inclusion of persons with intellectual and developmental disabilities in community life.

In recent years, alternative service and support models have been developed based on the *value* of full inclusion. Rather than placing individuals with intellectual and developmental disabilities in segregated environments, these programs are designed to bring needed supports to individuals in home, school, work, and community settings. In addition, support is provided on an individualized and ongoing basis to ensure individuals' success (Hughes & Carter, 2000). For example, supported employment programs, based on the concept of adaptive fit, are designed to help individuals find community employment that matches their personal interests and needs, promotes acquisition of critical employment skills, and provides ongoing support on the job. This ongoing support may include additional training and monitoring of an individual's performance, working with supervisors and coworkers to provide an individual with more effective supports, or any other services and supports necessary to ensure success. Research in the area of employment suggests that, compared with people in the continuum-of-employment programs, people enrolled in supported employment programs earn significantly higher wages, engage in more remunerative work, have more frequent social interactions with coworkers without disabilities during the workday, have more frequent social interactions with individuals without disabilities after the workday, and use community services to a greater extent (West et al., 2005; White & Weiner, 2004). Similar positive benefits exist for supported living (Stancliffe, Abery, & Smith, 2000) and supported inclusive educational programs (Downing & Peckham-Hardin, 2007).

The value of full inclusion is having a significant impact on the development of secondary programs for students with intellectual and developmental disabilities. A commitment to full inclusion means that students have equal access to the educational opportunities available to peers without disabilities. In middle school and high school programs, this means opportunities for participation in the range of academic and employment preparation experiences included in the school's general education curriculum, as well as opportunities for educational experiences that anchor instruction to the demands of working and living in the community. For older students, inclusive programs create access to the same opportunities for employment training available to young adults without disabilities in postsecondary programs.

Natural Supports

Most individuals with intellectual and developmental disabilities will require continuous support to partially or fully participate in home, school, work, and community settings. However, the best source of this support may not always be paid staff or direct care workers. A number of researchers have raised concerns about the overreliance on paid staff to support the participation of persons with intellectual and developmental disabilities in home, school, work, and community settings (Causton-Theoharis & Malmgren, 2005; Giangreco & Broer, 2005; Mautz, Storey, & Certo, 2001). Rather than promoting inclusion, the presence of paid staff may actually interfere with the acceptance of individuals and prevent access to the natural supports available from peers. For students in inclusive school settings, the presence of a paid paraprofessional may negatively impact their ability to develop social relationships with their peers without disabilities (Giangreco & Broer, 2005).

The use of natural supports is an alternative to relying *solely* on formal supports, such as paid paraprofessionals. Natural supports include family members, classmates, coworkers, and neighbors, in home, school, work, and community settings. Research indicates that, if they are provided with adequate support, peers can develop the skills necessary to support the training and behavioral needs of persons with intellectual and developmental disabilities (McDonnell, Mathot-Buckner, Thorson, & Fister, 2001). In inclusive school environments, peers can be used to provide students with support that ranges in level of intensity from very occasional exchanges of support (for example, asking for clarification of an assignment) to ongoing relationships formed expressly to promote students' success in class activities (for example, student work groups). In employment settings, coworkers can be used to support individuals with intellectual and developmental disabilities. This can be facilitated by providing coworkers with training on how to interact with, communicate with, and support the individual with a disability. Natural supports should be a primary source of support when students participate in inclusive school and community environments. Paid staff should be used primarily to supplement the support provided by family, friends, classmates, coworkers, and other community members.

Person-Centered School and Community Programs

Another component of effective transition services is the development of person-centered school and community programs. Traditionally, planning in both school and community programs for persons with intellectual and developmental disabilities has been based on a diagnostic-prescriptive model (Meyer, Peck, & Brown, 1991). In this model, the specific deficits of an individual are identified, and then a specialized set of services is developed that will reduce or eliminate those deficits. Consequently, education and community programs are often more concerned with ameliorating the differences between individuals with disabilities and individuals without disabilities than with improving their overall quality of life.

A number of professionals, parents, and advocates recommend that the planning processes adopted by education and community service agencies focus directly on the personal goals and needs of students instead of on their skill deficits (Holburn, Jacobson, Vietze, Schwartz, & Sersen, 2000; Kim & Turnbull, 2004; Menchetti & Garcia, 2003). Such planning approaches assume that individuals with intellectual and developmental disabilities do not have to "earn" membership in their schools, neighborhoods, and communities. Given this assumption, the goals and objectives included with a student services and supports plan are structured to meet personal preferences for participation in these settings. Furthermore, these goals and objectives not only address what is immediately attainable but also take into account each person's goals for the future.

Person-centered planning addresses what each person will learn to do, the level of support necessary to ensure success, where the learning will occur, and who (formal and natural support network) will be involved. Given that these personal and structural supports may come from a number of sources, the planning team must include many different individuals, including friends, family members, classmates, coworkers, teachers, and representatives of community service agencies. The adoption of person-centered planning has shifted the focus of transition planning away from *what* services a student will have available in a community setting and toward identifying the adaptive fit between the individual and the supports needed to enhance his or her quality of life following school.

Window 2–5

Principles of Person-Centered Planning

Person-centered planning has shifted the focus of transition planning away from what services a student will need and toward identifying the adaptive fit between the individual and the supports needed to enhance the quality of life following school. Schwartz, Holburn, and Jacobson (2000, p. 238) identified the following eight principles of person-centered planning:

1. The person's activities, services, and supports are based on his or her dreams, interests, preferences, strengths, and capacities.

2. The person and people important to him or her are included in lifestyle planning and have the opportunity to exercise control and make informed decisions.

3. The person has meaningful choices with decisions based on his or her experiences.

4. The person uses, when possible, natural and community supports.

5. Activities, supports, and services foster skills to achieve personal relationships, community inclusion, dignity, and respect.

6. The person's opportunities and experiences are maximized and flexibility is enhanced within existing regulatory and funding constraints.

7. Planning is collaborative and recurring and involves an ongoing commitment to the person.

8. The person is satisfied with his or her relationships, home, and daily routine.

Summary

The instructional technology and program models necessary to support the transition of persons with intellectual and developmental disabilities from school to community life have improved dramatically over the last decade. Schools, family members, and adult services know much more about the type and extent of the supports needed to fully include these individuals in home, school, work, and community settings. Equally important is the fact that the improvements in instructional technology have occurred simultaneously with the enactment of laws and policies that more clearly articulate the expected outcomes of educational programs and values that should drive the design of services and supports. Together, these technologies have opened the door to meaningful access to opportunities that enhance the quality of life for persons with intellectual and developmental disabilities. Educational and community service programs play an important role in achieving this outcome. In the following chapters, we discuss how these changes in philosophy and technology can be pragmatically applied in educational programs for students with intellectual and developmental disabilities as such students transition from school to community living.

POINT/COUNTERPOINT 2.1

Person-Centered Planning, or a Continuum of Placements

The practice of *person-centered planning* is changing how people view the future for individuals with intellectual and developmental disabilities. Person-centered planning addresses what the individual wants and needs to learn, the level of support necessary to ensure success, where the learning will occur, and who (formal and natural support network) will be involved. This represents a shift away from what has traditionally been viewed as a more *system-centered* approach and toward planning that focuses more on the services provided by the system to individuals with intellectual and developmental disabilities than on the abilities and preferences of each person. However, there is still considerable debate about the effectiveness of these two approaches. In this Point/Counterpoint, we consider the differing perspectives on the provision of services for individuals with intellectual and developmental disabilities.

POINT

Advocates of person-centered planning for individuals with intellectual and developmental disabilities assert that the use of this approach empowers people to choose a life that is consistent with their individual abilities and values. Advocates of person-centered planning assert that system-centered approaches have left individuals with intellectual and developmental disabilities with limited or no real choices regarding the services that are provided to them (Schaller, Yang, & Chien-Huey Chang, 2004). The continuum of placements is viewed as a system that has historically placed individuals in predetermined "slots" in schools, social agencies, and rehabilitation agencies based on availability of services (Garner & Dietz, 1996). This has created a system that is largely inflexible and not able to meet the unique needs and preferences of the individual. Despite federal legislation guaranteeing the provision of a free and appropriate public education in the least restrictive environment, placement decisions within the continuum are

COUNTERPOINT

Critics of person-centered planning for individuals with intellectual and developmental disabilities have asserted that while it sounds like a "panacea," the implementation and use of person-centered planning is impractical (Schaller et al., 2004). Critics suggest that family members, an integral part of the person-centered planning team, may not have the resources or the desire to assist in the planning process (Schaller et al.). It is also possible that there may be members of the team who have little knowledge of the individual involved in the planning process. The result is the inability of the planning team to adequately address the needs of the individual, resulting in greater difficulty meeting his or her needs.

Another concern raised by critics of person-centered planning is that the process is too time-consuming to be practical (Schaller et al., 2004). As a result, planning teams often fail to follow through with all of the essential components of person-centered planning and thus do not

(Point continued)

based on the services currently available within the system and the professionals trained to deliver these services rather than the needs of the individual (Schaller et al., 2004). The result is the continued placement of individuals with intellectual and developmental disabilities in more restrictive, segregated settings.

In contrast, person-centered planning focuses on identifying the needs, preferences, and dreams of individuals with intellectual and developmental disabilities in order to create truly individualized supports that will help them achieve their goals. The person-centered planning team includes many different individuals, including friends, family members, classmates, coworkers, teachers, and representatives of community service agencies, as well as the individual. The goal is to determine the adaptive fit between the individual and the supports needed to enhance the quality of life following school instead of merely identifying what services a student will have available in a community setting. The result is enhanced career planning and decision making and a greater overall sense of empowerment of people with intellectual and developmental disabilities (Menchetti & Garcia, 2003).

(Counterpoint continued)

address the many needs of each individual. Thus, the team ends up with a poorly conceived plan that does not provide the supports needed by the individual to achieve his or her desired outcomes. In contrast, the continuum-of-placements approach includes professionals who can act as case managers to ensure that individuals receive appropriate services within a system that has a number of service delivery options available.

Focus Question Review

Focus Question 1: Identify outcomes of transition programs for students with intellectual and developmental disabilities that will enhance access to valued post-school community living and employment.

- Establish a network of friends and acquaintances.
- Develop the ability to use community resources on a regular basis.
- Secure a paid job that supports use of community resources and interaction with peers.
- Establish independence and autonomy in making lifestyle choices.

Focus Question 2: Identify the emerging values that are driving the development of effective transition programs for students with intellectual and developmental disabilities.

- Self-determination and empowerment.
- Full inclusion in educational and community settings.
- Reliance on family members, same-age peers, neighbors, and friends in educational and community settings, rather than on paid staff, to provide support.
- School and community programs that are person-centered.

CHAPTER 3

The Role of Secondary Education in Transition

MARGRET A. CROCKETT

MICHAEL L. HARDMAN

As discussed in Chapter 1, contemporary transition models emphasize the important role that secondary programs play for students with intellectual and developmental disabilities in supporting their transition to community life. This has led advocates and professionals to suggest that secondary education be conceptualized as a longitudinal process that cumulatively develops life skills, creates access to needed resources, and provides personal supports necessary for successful adjustment to employment and independent living (Baer, Flexer, & Dennis, 2007; Bambara, Wilson, & McKenzie, 2007; McDonnell, 2003; Neubert & Moon, 2006; Rusch & Millar, 1998; Wehman, 2006a). It has also been suggested that to be successful the transition process must begin no later than middle or junior high school and continue in adulthood. However, envisioning transition as a longitudinal process requires curriculum, instruction, and programs that are aligned across content domains within secondary programs. This represents a significant shift in secondary education for students with intellectual and developmental disabilities.

Window 3-1

David

David, an 18-year-old senior at Valley High School, has Down syndrome. His IEP includes goals that focus on his participation in general education classes and community-based instruction. His teacher worked with the school counselor to schedule David's general education classes in the morning. Following lunch, he leaves school to receive instruction on his community-based goals.

David's schedule fits right in with that of his peers without disabilities. A large number of students split their classes between those at Valley and concurrent enrollment classes at the local community college. Many of David's peers also participate in service learning classes and school-to-work programs.

On Monday, Wednesday, and Friday afternoons, David goes to his work experience placement at the neighborhood public library. He has a number of jobs, including sorting returned books, replacing the computer bar codes on the books that track when they are checked out and checked in, and checking DVD cases to make sure the discs have been returned with the case. A paraprofessional from Valley provides him with training and support. His instruction is focused on riding the bus to and from work, completing his assigned jobs, and promoting social interactions with his coworkers. David has made a significant amount of progress, and the paraprofessional expects him to be nearly independent before the end of the semester.

On Tuesday and Thursday afternoons, David practices swimming or uses the exercise equipment at the local community recreation center. With the assistance of Steve, a peer tutor, he chooses the activities that he wants to complete, uses the locker room to dress appropriately for the activity, and is learning to use the equipment correctly. David and Steve have become good friends, and they have begun to spend time together after school and on the weekends. David's teacher showed Steve how to implement the career-based intervention program, and she regularly monitors him to make sure that he is providing David with appropriate prompts, reinforcers, and error correction.

Defining Secondary Programs

The term *secondary program* encompasses educational services for students between the ages of 12 and 22. This includes middle or junior high school, comprehensive high school, and post-high school programs. Middle and junior high school programs typically serve students between the ages of 12 and 15, high school programs typically serve students between the ages of 15 or 16 and 18, and post-high school programs typically serve students who are 19 and older. We will use these terms and age levels throughout the text when referring to programs for students with intellectual and developmental disabilities.

As we have noted, effective transition services in the schools require that curriculum and instruction be aligned across age levels. However, the structure of secondary programs should also reflect the diverse developmental needs of students at each age level. Unfortunately, in many school districts, the educational programs of middle school, high school, and post-high school students are nearly identical. For example, it is not uncommon for students to receive instruction on isolated developmental and academic skills through graduation. A number of authors have argued that the focus of the educational program should shift away from basic skills and toward employment and community-living skills as students get older (Baer et al., 2007; Bambara et al., 2007; McDonnell, 2003; Neubert & Moon, 2006; Rusch & Millar, 1998; Wehman, 2006b).

Focus Question 1	Why is it important to understand typical adolescent development in designing and implementing secondary programs for students with intellectual and developmental disabilities?

Before we outline the functions of secondary programs in preparing students for community life, a brief discussion of the developmental needs of students at each age level is necessary. Understanding the development of adolescents and young adults provides an important frame of reference for aligning curriculum and instruction across middle school, high school, and post-high school programs.

The middle school years for most children are a time of significant physical, intellectual, and psychosocial growth (Arnett, 2000; Lichtenstein, 1998; Williams & Downing, 1998). During this time, young adolescents begin to focus on social relationships as an important part of their identity. Peer acceptance becomes a critical factor in shaping a child's social and intellectual development. In addition, children seek to break away from dependence on adult supervision and support and increase their independence. Cognitively, children acquire an emerging ability to see themselves as part of a larger social network, and their responsibilities within this network emerge. Students begin to think more abstractly and to make moral decisions and are increasingly able to see things from another person's point of view.

Social development and participation in social networks remain critical aspects of the development of high school students. However, high school is also a time when students explore potential employment and living alternatives, develop an understanding of their individual strengths and weaknesses, and establish general goals for adulthood (Arnett, 2000; Lichtenstein, 1998). In American society, much of this development is accomplished through the educational experiences provided by schools and through the interactions that students have with same-age peers and adult mentors in the community (Mortimer, 2003). These experiences provide students and their families with the information necessary to make wise decisions about the future.

At around age 18, most young adults begin to turn their attention to establishing lifestyle goals and initiating the specific activities necessary to achieve those goals (Arnett, 2000; Lichtenstein, 1998). For example, an individual may no longer talk in terms of getting a job in the art field but rather begin a postsecondary training program to become a graphic artist. Other students may seek employment to buy a car or get their own apartment. It is during this time when students begin to establish themselves as members of the adult community.

Researchers have long recognized the need for age-appropriate programs for students between the ages of 19 and 22 who have intellectual and developmental disabilities (Grigal, Neubert, & Moon, 2002). These programs must be structured to provide students with educational experiences that will allow them to get a job that is emotionally and financially satisfying, to live in their own home, to establish social routines with friends, and to establish control over their own lives. It has become clear that alternative program structures that allow access to regional vocational education centers, community colleges, 4-year colleges, and community-based training programs will be necessary if the unique educational needs of this group of students are going to be addressed (Grigal et al., 2002).

Between the ages of 12 and 22, children experience phenomenal growth and development. However, this development is a cumulative process in which a student's perceptions of personal identity and self-worth, responsibility, independence, and autonomy evolve simultaneously with the development of cognitive and social skills. Researchers have recognized that to effectively prepare students for their ultimate transition into adulthood, school programs must reflect this reality. School districts face a significant challenge in developing programs that both align the curriculum across secondary programs and meet the unique developmental needs of adolescents and young adults.

One way to approach this problem is to think in terms of the functions of secondary programs in meeting the needs of students. That is, what are the common organizational and pedagogical foundations that should undergird educational programs for middle or junior high school, high school, and post-high school students? Ideally, these foundations will reflect factors known to be associated with successful postschool adjustment of students with intellectual and developmental disabilities. Once the foundations have been identified, the issue becomes what strategies or methods can be used to ensure that schools and teachers provide educational experiences that adhere to the identified foundations and meet the unique needs of students at various age levels. The following sections of this chapter articulate what we believe should be the common foundations of effective transition programs and the implications for middle or junior high school, high school, and post-high school programs.

Foundations of Effective Transition Programs

It seems obvious that school districts concerned with developing effective transition services for students with intellectual and developmental disabilities should base the organization of programs on those variables that research has shown to be predictive of successful postschool adjustment. These variables should then serve as the foundation of the educational process for students. In general, research has suggested that the following variables are associated with students' successful transition to community life: (a) promoting self-determination, (b) systematic transition planning, (c) supporting the inclusion of students in school and community settings, (d) anchoring curriculum and instruction to the demands of adulthood, (e) providing career awareness and employment preparation programs, and (f) developing social competence (Bambara et al., 2007; Flexer, Simmons, Luft, & Baer, 2001; McDonnell, Hardman, & McGuire, 2007; Sitlington, Clark, & Kolstoe, 2000; Wehman, 2006a).

Focus Question 2	Identify factors associated with the successful transition of students with intellectual and developmental disabilities from school to community life.

Self-Determination

Self-determination has been defined as "a combination of skills, knowledge, and beliefs that enable a person to engage in goal-directed, self-regulated, autonomous behavior" (Field, Martin, Miller, Ward, & Wehmeyer, 1998, p. 2). The principle of self-determination states that individuals with disabilities have the right to determine where and with whom they will live, how they will spend their time, how they will take part in the community, and what services they require. While secondary programs must teach students the skills they will need to achieve their goals in the areas of employment, personal management, leisure, and community access, they must also provide students with instruction on how to make choices based on their own preferences, how to evaluate the outcomes of their choices, and how to come up with solutions when problems arise. Students who are taught these self-determination skills are able to have greater control over their lives and their postschool outcomes and are better able to adjust to community life (Test et al., 2004).

Field and Hoffman (2002) assert that there are a number of strategies that schools can employ to improve the self-determination skills of their students. Programs must be designed to infuse self-determination skills and attitudes throughout the curriculum, family support programs, and staff development, and these skills should be modeled throughout the school environment. These programs must ensure that students, parents, and staff are actively involved in the IEP planning process and that they are provided with choices throughout the school environment. Programs must also make sure that there are predictable consequences for the choices that are made. Effective programs must encourage students, faculty, and staff to take appropriate risks, encourage the development of supportive relationships, and provide the opportunity to be heard. Successful programs will provide the accommodations and supports necessary to meet the individual needs of their students.

Systematic Transition Planning

Few people ever achieve their goals without planning. The process of identifying how we want to live and what we hope to accomplish in our lives affects the decisions we make about our education, job, home, and personal relationships. This is no less true for students with intellectual and developmental disabilities. Comprehensive transition planning provides a framework for cumulatively developing the skills, resources, and supports necessary to achieve a student's desired goals.

Transition planning brings together students, parents, and professionals to identify and develop the skills and resources necessary to ensure successful postschool adjustment. An effective planning process begins early in the student's educational program that cumulatively builds the skills and supports necessary for postschool adjustment, focusing planning activities on specific postschool outcomes rather than general skill development, emphasizing the preferences and needs of the student rather than the resources that may be available in the local community, and involving both education and community service programs in the planning process.

Inclusive Education

One of the most powerful predictors of postschool adjustment by students with intellectual and developmental disabilities is the opportunity to participate in general education classes and extracurricular activities with peers without disabilities (Baker, Wang, & Walberg, 1994–1995; Benz, Lindstrom, & Yovanoff, 2000; Phelps & Hanley-Maxwell, 1997; Salend & Garrick-Duhaney, 1999). These experiences allow students with disabilities to learn the social and communication skills necessary to live in the community and provide opportunities to develop the social relationships that are critical to a high quality of life (Carter & Hughes, 2005; Downing & Peckham-Hardin, 2007).

Inclusion of students with disabilities in general education classes also has significant benefits for students without disabilities. These include developing more positive attitudes about persons with disabilities, learning strategies for positively supporting students with disabilities in school and community settings, and developing friendships with peers with disabilities (Carter & Hughes, 2006; Cole, Waldron, & Majd, 2004; Copeland et al., 2004). Development of these attitudes and skills will help young adults without disabilities accept individuals with disabilities in future work and community settings. If the ultimate goal of transition is to ensure the full participation of individuals with disabilities in the community, secondary education clearly must be structured to promote regular interactions between students with disabilities and students without them.

Anchoring Curriculum and Instruction to Valued Postschool Outcomes

One of the most important functions of secondary programs is to teach students the skills to successfully participate in home, school, work, and community settings (Bouck, 2004; McDonnell, 2003; Patton, Cronin, & Jarriels, 1997). A student is unlikely to adjust successfully to adulthood if he or she does not have the skills to use the resources of the community. Consequently, secondary programs must anchor the curriculum to the actual demands of community life. Students must have opportunities to learn skills that are relevant in our changing economy and society.

The development of capacity is not simply demonstrating the mastery of curriculum content; it includes the ability to apply skills in real-life contexts and settings. Developing effective transition services will require schools to make a commitment to pedagogy that promotes the connection between skills learned in school and performance in home and community settings. To achieve this, secondary programs will need to expand the typical instructional methods used by teachers to include the use of "situated" teaching models, community-based evaluation and instruction, and the integration of traditional "academic" and "vocational" curriculum through apprenticeship programs.

Curriculum and instruction in secondary programs should focus on developing academic and social skills, performing age-appropriate personal management and leisure activities, and acquiring work and work-related skills. The educational program should anchor instruction to the employment and living options available to all adults who live in a particular community. Furthermore, instruction should require students to demonstrate mastery and application of skills in actual performance settings. Achieving these outcomes will require secondary programs to adopt a broad array of strategies and methods.

Window 3-2

Characteristics of Effective Inclusive Schools

One of the most powerful predictors of postschool adjustment by students with intellectual and developmental disabilities is equal access to the educational opportunities available to peers without disabilities. In middle school and high school programs, this means opportunities for participation in the range of academic and employment preparation experiences included in the school's general education curriculum. Effective inclusive schools have the following characteristics:

1. High expectations for student learning that are associated with a clear mission.

2. Strong instructional leadership that views special education as part of general education classroom services that should be available to meet the needs of all children and includes frequent monitoring of student progress.

3. Promotion of the values of diversity and belonging. Programs must establish a sense of community where all students feel welcomed and accepted.

4. Formal and natural supports in the general education setting. Formal supports provide students with important instruction, while natural supports promote inclusion and the development of friendships.

5. Services and supports that are provided in age-appropriate classrooms in neighborhood schools. This allows students to participate in general education classes and develop social networks with their same-age peers.

6. Access to the general education curriculum while meeting the unique needs of every student. Meaningful participation of all students requires the use of effective strategies, including differentiated instruction, cooperative learning, and assistive technology.

7. School-wide support systems that use general and special education resources to meet the needs of all students.

Note. Adapted from *Human Exceptionality: School, Family, and Community* (9th ed.), by M. L. Hardman, C. J. Drew, and M. W. Egan, 2007, Boston: Houghton Mifflin. Adapted with permission.

Career Awareness and Employment Preparation

Another variable associated with the successful transition of students with intellectual and developmental disabilities from school to community life is the provision of career awareness and employment preparation programs (Benz et al., 2000; Phelps & Hanley-Maxwell, 1997). Programs must assess the needs and strengths of students, assist students in developing realistic goals, and provide students with the skills they will need to find a career that fits with their desired postschool outcomes (McDonnell, Mathot-Buckner, & Ferguson, 1996; Sitlington et al., 2000; Wehman, 2006a). This can be accomplished using career education programs that focus on helping students understand their various career choices, explore different career opportunities, and develop the attitudes and work habits that will be appropriate for their career choice.

Developing Social Competence

Research has suggested that for students with disabilities, friendships play an important role in their job performance and job satisfaction (West, Wehman, & Wehman, 2005), their successful employment (Phelps & Hanley-Maxwell, 1997), their independent living (Walker, 1999), and their participation in recreation activities (Terman, Larner, Stevenson, & Behrman, 1996). Therefore, effective programs must be designed to help students establish and maintain a network of friends and acquaintances. This can be accomplished by providing students with social skills instruction in inclusive environments rather than in isolation as they will be better able to generalize their skills (Fisher & Meyer, 2002). Students must also be provided with frequent opportunities to use their skills when interacting with their peers without disabilities. This will enable them to become socially competent in home, school, employment, and community settings.

Secondary education should be structured to maximize the participation of students in the natural social networks of the school, the neighborhood, and the community. At the same time, the opportunities that students receive to develop friendships must reflect their chronological age. For example, the primary source of friendships for young adolescents is their school. In contrast, for many young adults, the primary source of friendships is their job. Secondary programs must be structured to reflect the differences in how friendships and social networks evolve for students at various ages.

Implications for Secondary Programs Across Age Levels

Although the variables described above provide a framework for developing cohesive educational programs for secondary-age students, how these variables are implemented at each age level must be sensitive to the developmental needs of students. The following sections briefly discuss the implications of these variables in middle and junior high schools, in high schools, and in post-high school programs.

The Middle or Junior High School Years

Focus Question 3	Why are age-appropriate and neighborhood school programs during the middle or junior high school years important to the development of effective transition planning and services?

The middle school years can be a time of great change for students, including those with intellectual and developmental disabilities. It is during these years that many children seek to increase their independence at home and in school. This is an ideal time to focus on teaching students self-determination skills to foster their newfound independence. Effective programs should focus on providing students with self-determination skills instruction early on and should include frequent opportunities for students to make choices regarding their activities and school career (Test et al., 2004). For example, students can be given the opportunity to choose whom to work with on group projects, how they will approach school projects, and how they will complete homework assignments (Test et al.). Students can also be encouraged to be active participants in the development and planning of their IEP goals. Families should be encouraged to give children increased freedom to make choices about whom they spend time with, where they go, and what they do. Families should also give middle school children increased responsibility in meeting the needs of the family and household. In addition, programs should assist parents and families in beginning to examine their hopes and fears about their child's participation in the community as an adult. Students and their parents should begin to discuss long-term expectations and goals. School programs should support this exploration by providing information to parents about work and living alternatives.

For students between the ages of 12 and 15, transition planning should maximize their participation in age-appropriate school and community activities and increase their responsibility for managing their own day-to-day activities. While long-term employment and living goals should serve as a reference point in educational planning, the primary focus should be on enhancing a student's immediate participation in home, school, and neighborhood settings. Programs should emphasize identifying and developing the natural sources of support that may be available in these settings, including peers, family, and other community members.

Schools can support the inclusion of middle school students through a variety of strategies. Perhaps one of the most critical issues is to provide educational services in the student's neighborhood school, promoting the participation of students with disabilities in general education classes and in the extracurricular activities of the school. A number of authors have argued that students should attend the school that they would go to if they were not disabled (McDonnell, 2003; Williams & Downing, 1998). One reason for the development of neighborhood school programs is related to the capacity of schools to provide inclusive education. Centralized school programs that serve large numbers of students with disabilities may create conditions that are counter to inclusive education even when there is a strong commitment by staff to this outcome (McDonnell, 2003). Inclusive education is most effective when the number of students with disabilities matches the natural proportion of children with disabilities to those without disabilities in the general population. In these contexts, the level of accommodation and support required for students with intense educational needs is well within the resources of most schools. By contrast, centralization of services for students with disabilities often creates excessive demands on the materials and human resources of the school. General education teachers find themselves attempting to meet the needs of large numbers of children with disabilities. Consequently, it is not uncommon in such schools for teachers to become wary of and resistant to inclusive education.

Perhaps the most important reason for neighborhood school programs is that they provide a direct link between students and their peers. Students who do not attend their neighborhood schools typically have fewer interactions with peers outside of school hours than students who do (McDonnell, Hardman, Hightower, & O'Donnell, 1991). Social interactions for these students tend to be restricted to the 6-hour school day. In contrast, students who attend their neighborhood schools enjoy frequent interactions with peers after school hours. The social networks in our neighborhoods provide us with important sources of emotional and logistical support. Neighborhood school programs facilitate the development of these linkages for middle school students with intellectual and developmental disabilities.

Once they are introduced into the neighborhood school, educational programs should be structured to maximize participation of students with disabilities in general education classes and extracurricular activities. An increasing number of strategies are available to assist teachers in supporting students in these contexts (Hunt & McDonnell, 2007). Participation in general education classes and extracurricular activities provides numerous opportunities to teach critical academic and social skills to students. Equally important, participation of students in these classes and activities creates the conditions necessary to promote the development of friendships and a viable social network.

In middle schools, the focus of curriculum and instruction should be on achieving individual student goals and objectives within the context of the school's core curriculum. Strategies for supporting disabled students' participation in the general education curriculum include, for example, adaptation of the curriculum and instructional strategies used by the class-room teacher (Downing, 2002; Udvari-Solner, Villa, & Thousand, 2002), the use of differentiated instruction (Lewis & Batts, 2005; Tomlinson, 1999), cooperative learning (Putnam, 1994; Sapon-Shevin, Ayres, & Duncan, 1994), and embedded skill instruction (McDonnell, Johnson, & McQuivey, 2008). Participation in general education classes not only provides students with a more normative way of learning critical academic skills; it also provides opportunities for students to develop social relationships that will support their participation in the school, the neighborhood, and the community.

In middle schools, the focus of employment preparation programs should focus on career awareness and career exploration (McDonnell et al., 1996; Wehman, 2006b). These programs should provide students with information about what work is and what part they will play in the world of work. Students must be given the opportunity to explore their interests and their abilities to determine potential employment options once they leave school. They must also be provided with the work habits and social skills that they will need to have in order to obtain and maintain employment once they leave school.

Effective middle and junior high school programs should be designed to help students establish and maintain a network of friends and acquaintances. This can be accomplished using a variety of approaches, including circles of friends, peer buddies, and peer supports (Carter & Kennedy, 2006; Hunt & McDonnell, 2007; Miller, Cooke, Test, & White, 2003). Because friendships have been shown to play an important role in the job performance and job satisfaction, successful employment, independent living, and participation in recreational activities of individuals with intellectual and developmental disabilities, effective programs must be designed to help students establish and maintain a network of friends and acquaintances.

The High School Years

Focus Question 4	What is the focus of inclusion in high school and post-high school settings for students with intellectual and developmental disabilities?

High school programs must be developed to teach students with intellectual and developmental disabilities the skills they will need to achieve their goals in the areas of employment, personal management, leisure, and community access. The self-determination skills of these students may be increased by the direct involvement of these students in the development of their IEPs (Field & Hoffman, 2002; Test et al., 2004). High schools should also be structured to serve students in their neighborhood schools and to promote each student's participation in general education classes and the extracurricular activities of the school. The benefits of these strategies for high school students are the same as for middle school students. However, we believe that high school programs must ensure that students are able to develop and maintain social relationships with same-age peers as well as older peers who may be present in employment or other community settings. This is important because the nature of the social interactions that high school students have with friends is dramatically different from that of the relationships they have with older community members. For most students, these relationships have been mediated previously by their parents or other family members. High school is the time when most youths begin to learn the skills necessary to function successfully in diverse social contexts (Arnett, 2000; Lichtenstein, 1998). Experience in interacting with older adult peers will be critical to a student's ultimate adjustment to work and other aspects of community life (Mortimer, 2003). Consequently, high school programs need to ensure that students have educational experiences that promote the inclusion of students in community settings. As stated earlier, this may be accomplished through general education classes by anchoring instruction to real work and community living contexts or through direct instruction in community settings. Whatever instructional approaches are used to meet the educational goals of students, they must promote the development of both academic and social competence.

In high school, the curriculum and instructional methods used by teachers should be designed to provide a more direct link between school learning and performance in community settings. Participation in general education classes that "situate" learning activities in real-life contexts is a useful and important tool in meeting the educational needs of high school students. As students get older, however, the emphasis of their educational program may need to shift away from participation in general education classes and toward direct experiences in work and community settings (see Chapter 9). Community-based instruction is consistent with the recommendations of educational reformers concerned with secondary education for students without disabilities (Darling-Hammond, Rustique-Forrester, & Pecheone, 2005; DiMartino & Castaneda, 2007; Herman, 1997). These recommendations are based on research that questions the ability of students without disabilities to "transfer" the skills learned in school to work, home, and community settings. It appears that effectively preparing students for their transition to adulthood requires high schools to adopt curricular and instructional methods that include direct instruction in work and community settings.

There is a general consensus that at age 18 the educational programs of students with intellectual and developmental disabilities should be focused on the immediate postschool goals of the student (Kohler & Field, 2003; Neubert & Moon, 2006; Neubert, Moon, & Grigal, 2002). Curriculum and instruction should be designed to establish the specific daily routines that will make up the student's life in the community after school. This process should build on the educational experiences that the student had during middle school and high school. For example, employment training during high school may have "sampled" various jobs and work settings, but the transition program should focus on developing a paid job for the student that matches personal preferences and needs. The educational experiences that students receive during high school will assist in identifying and developing an appropriate paid job for them prior to graduation. Similarly, in the area of leisure, transition programs should develop alternatives that can become a routine part of the student's lifestyle. A number of instructional strategies will be important in achieving these outcomes, including instruction in actual performance settings, emphasis on functional performance rather than development of "prerequisite" academic or social skills, and redesign of work, personal management, and leisure activities to maximize a student's participation.

Post-High School Programs

When students with disabilities are between the ages of 19 and 22, inclusive education and community-based programs should ensure that they have equal access to all of the opportunities and options available to young adults without disabilities. These include access to meaningful and satisfying employment or postsecondary training programs, a home, and use of the generic resources and services of the community. The focus of inclusion is on the broader community in which the student lives rather than the school. Post-high school programs should promote each student's acceptance and participation in these settings.

Post-high school programs should seek to establish strong collaborative relationships with local community service providers. This should include procedures for sharing information, defining the roles of educational and community service agencies in transition planning, and seeking ways to pool or jointly use resources at the local level to support each student's transition to community life (Grigal et al., 2002; Neubert & Moon, 2006; Neubert et al., 2002). A well-defined, person-centered transition planning process encourages development of structural supports that will promote rather than impede students' participation in the community.

Transition planning in post-high school programs must ensure that all available sources of support necessary for a student's life in the community are established prior to graduation. These available supports must be balanced to ensure that the student has maximum control over his or her life and to minimize reliance on community service programs. Necessary community services should be designed to supplement rather than supplant the natural support that the individual receives from friends, family, and other community members. Furthermore, rather than adjusting the student's goals to available services, these services should be designed around the student's personal goals.

During the last several years of school, it is critical for families to clarify their role in supporting the student in community life (Kohler & Field, 2003). Students and families must address a number of emotional issues, including where the student will live, where he or she will work, how much control the individual will have over lifestyle choices, and so on. As noted earlier, parents and families play a significant role in supporting the transition of many students to community life. Consequently, it is imperative that transition programs be structured to help parents define the role they will play in supporting their son or daughter as an adult. A couple of strategies that have proven effective in addressing these issues are to provide workshops for families to promote a critical examination of these issues and to create opportunities for families to obtain support from each other in addressing the needs of the student.

POINT/COUNTERPOINT 3.1

The Value of the High School Diploma: Single or Multiple Diploma Options for Students With Disabilities

Receiving a high school diploma is for many students an important rite of passage into adulthood that represents the successful completion of high school. The diploma is often regarded as a requirement for acceptance into college, the military, and higher-paying careers (O'Neill, 2001). However, for many students with disabilities, especially those with intellectual and developmental disabilities, the traditional high school diploma remains an elusive goal. In some cases, an alternate form of the diploma is a more viable option for this population of students. However, some contend that multiple diploma options cause too much confusion. In this Point/Counterpoint, we consider the differing perspectives on the single versus multiple diploma options for students with disabilities.

POINT

The traditional single diploma is meant to convey to colleges, potential employers, and others in society that an individual has acquired a certain level of knowledge and a set of skills that will enable him or her to leave school and participate in post-secondary education or the workforce (Hardman, Drew, & Egan, 2007). The intended consequences of a single diploma option for all students include high expectations for all students, including those with disabilities; consistency in the meaning of the requirements associated with the diploma; and a sense of equity in that all students are given the same options and tested on the same standards (Johnson, Thurlow, & Stout, 2007). Multiple diploma options cause confusion for institutions of higher education and employers who need to understand a graduate's qualifications and actually hinder students with disabilities because they can create confusion about what the student has accomplished (Johnson, Thurlow, Cosio, & Bremer, 2005).

COUNTERPOINT

The standard single diploma option frustrates the ability of students with disabilities to communicate the knowledge and skills they have acquired during high school. This option harms students with disabilities because they may not be able to meet all of the requirements for a standard diploma, which may result in more students with disabilities opting to drop out of school (Johnson et al., 2005). This may place them at a greater disadvantage in terms of post-secondary education, career options, and self-esteem. Multiple diploma options, including standard diplomas, certificates of completion or achievement, special education diplomas, and occupational diplomas, provide school districts with greater flexibility in addressing and accommodating the diversity in student abilities (Johnson et al., 2005). Multiple diploma options are a way to maintain high standards for the standard diploma because they reduce the pressure on schools to make the standard diploma attainable by more students while still increasing graduation rates (Johnson et al., 2007).

Summary

This chapter has outlined the roles of middle school, high school, and transition programs in preparing students with intellectual and developmental disabilities for community life. We have argued that all secondary programs should adopt organizational goals that are based on variables known to be associated with successful postschool adjustment. These goals provide the necessary framework to align curriculum, instruction, and planning across middle school, high school, and transition programs. The strategies that teachers use to meet these organizational goals for students should change across age levels. These strategies should be designed to reflect the chronological age of the student.

Focus Question Review

Focus Question 1: Why is it important to understand typical adolescent development in designing and implementing secondary programs for students with intellectual and developmental disabilities?

- Secondary programs must adopt curriculum and instructional approaches that reflect the developmental needs of students at various age levels. This perspective allows school districts to align educational programs so that students develop cumulatively the skills they need for successful adjustment to community life.

Focus Question 2: Identify factors associated with the successful transition of students with intellectual and developmental disabilities from school to community life.

- Six factors are important in supporting the transition of students with intellectual and developmental disabilities from school to community life. These are self-determination, systematic planning, inclusion in school and community settings, anchoring curriculum and instruction to the demands of adulthood, career awareness and employment preparation programs, and the development of social competence.

Focus Question 3: Why are age-appropriate and neighborhood school programs during the middle or junior high school years important to the development of effective transition planning and services?

- Age-appropriate school programs provide students with opportunities to participate in general education classes, develop social networks with their same-age peers, and participate in the extracurricular activities of the school.
- Neighborhood schools provide a direct link between a student and his or her community. In these programs, students have opportunities to develop important social relationships with peers and to learn to use the community resources that are available on a day-to-day basis.

Focus Question 4: What is the focus of inclusion in high school and post-high school settings for students with intellectual and developmental disabilities?

- The focus of inclusion in high school settings is on the participation of students in general education classes and the extracurricular activities of the school, as well as community-based instruction that will enable students to adjust to work and other aspects of community life.
- The focus of inclusion in post-high school settings is on the broader community in which the student lives rather than the school. Post-high school programs should promote each student's acceptance and participation in these settings.

Section II

CURRICULUM AND TRANSITION PLANNING

CHAPTER 4

Curriculum

JOHN MCDONNELL

C urriculum for students with intellectual and developmental disabilities has changed significantly over the last several decades. During the 1960s and 1970s, the content of students' educational programs was typically drawn from preacademic or elementary academic skill sequences (e.g., reading, math, writing), developmental skill sequences (e.g., cognitive, communication, motor), or analyses of functional living skills (Bellamy, Wilcox, Rose, & McDonnell, 1985; Brown et al., 1988). Advocates and researchers began to raise questions about the utility of these curricula in improving the quality of life of students based on the poor transition outcomes that were realized by the first cohorts of students exiting public school following the passage of the Education for All Handicapped Children Act (Hasazi, Gordon, & Roe, 1985; Wilcox & Bellamy, 1982). Their concerns ranged from the age-appropriateness of some skills, especially for older students (e.g., teaching a 17-year-old to match colors), to the lack of generalization of skills taught in classrooms to actual performance environments (e.g., being able to count money in the classroom but not when purchasing items in grocery stores).

These issues prompted a shift in focus for curriculum during the 1980s and 1990s away from teaching isolated skills and toward developing students' performance of employment, personal management, and leisure activities that enabled them to participate more fully in community life (Falvey, 1989; Ford et al., 1989; Neel & Billingsley, 1989; Wilcox & Bellamy, 1987). The content of students' educational programs was derived from the demands that students faced in home, school, work, and community settings. These "ecological" curricula were referenced to the activities

completed by similar-age peers and the opportunities available within students' communities. Instruction moved out of the classroom and into the
community settings that students would be expected to use on a daily basis.

The notion of what should constitute the curriculum for students with
intellectual and developmental disabilities has recently been affected by the
standards-based reform movement (see Chapter 1). The focus of this movement is to establish universal content standards for all students (including
students with disabilities) and to develop accountability systems that allow
for comprehensive assessment of students' proficiency (McGregor, 2003;
McLaughlin & Tilstone, 2000). Standards-based reform has been driven in
large part by federal legislation (e.g., Goals 2000, IAS, NCLB, and IDEA). This
legislation has several purposes: (a) to establish high expectations for all
students; (b) to ensure equal access to the general education curriculum
by students who are at risk of school failure and by those with disabilities;
(c) to provide a framework for linking curriculum, assessment, and instruction; and (d) to promote more efficient allocation of resources within
schools to maximize learning for all students.

The standards-based reform movement has forced the field of special
education to once again examine its expectations for students. A primary
assertion of this movement is that all students, including those with intellectual and developmental disabilities, can learn challenging academic
content if they are provided with effective instruction and supports. At this
point, the impact of students' participation in the general education curriculum on their achievement during school or their adjustment to community life after school is not known; however, it seems clear that federal
mandates requiring students to access and progress in the general education curriculum will remain in place for the foreseeable future.

This chapter will discuss the structure of the general education and ecological curricula and how they can be used to meet the full range of education needs for students with intellectual and developmental disabilities.
The implications of both curriculum approaches on the development of
students' IEPs and transition plans are also addressed.

General Education Curriculum

Structure of the General Education Curriculum

The structure of general education curricula in all states reflects the
current requirements of the No Child Left Behind Act of 2001. NCLB presumes that there should be alignment among what students are taught,
the assessments used to determine if they have mastered the content, and
instruction. Consequently, NCLB mandates that states establish academic

content standards and academic achievement standards within their general education curriculum in the areas of reading/language arts, math, and science. The academic content standards "specify what all students are expected to know and be able to do; contain coherent and rigorous content; and encourage the teaching of advanced skills" (U.S. Department of Education, 2007b, p. 2). Academic achievement standards "must include at least two levels of achievement (proficient and advanced) that reflect mastery of the material in the State's academic content standards, and a third level of achievement (basic) to provide information of the progress of lower-achieving students toward mastering the proficient and advanced levels of achievement" (U.S. Department of Education, 2007b, pp. 2–3). Achievement standards provide the basis for the development of states' assessment systems, and the systems must specify the "cut-off scores" that students must obtain at each level of proficiency. In addition, the states' assessments must be designed to allow for the determination of students' "Adequate Yearly Progress (AYP)" toward achieving the academic achievement standards.

IDEA 2004 reinforces the NCLB mandates on curriculum and assessment by requiring IEP teams to address how students will participate and progress in the general education curriculum. In addition, it requires that students with disabilities participate in the state's assessment system, or an alternate assessment, that documents students' AYP toward meeting the academic achievement standards. Under the regulations of NCLB, states are allowed to develop one or more alternate assessments that would track students' AYP, including (a) alternate assessments based on alternate achievement standards and (b) alternate assessments based on modified grade-level achievement standards (U.S. Department of Education, 2007b).

Focus Question 1   What is the difference between an alternate assessment based on alternate performance standards and an alternate assessment based on modified assessment standards?

All states have developed and begun implementing alternate assessments based on alternate achievement standards for students with the most significant cognitive disabilities. Regulations require that these assessments be aligned to the state's content standards but that they establish a different set of expectations for students. The content of the alternate assessments must be "clearly related to grade-level content, although it may be restricted in scope or complexity or take the form of introductory or pre-requisite skills" (U.S. Department of Education, 2005, p. 26). This is accomplished by "adapting or 'extending' those content standards to reflect instructional activities appropriate for this group of students" (U.S. Department of

Education, 2005, p. 26). The number of students within a district or state taking alternate assessments based on alternate achievement standards may not exceed 1% of all of the students in the grades tested.

Alternate assessments based on modified achievement standards are focused on students "whose progress in response to appropriate instruction, including special education and related services designed to address the students' individual needs, is such that, even if significant growth occurs, the students' IEP teams are reasonably certain that the students will not achieve grade-level proficiency within the year covered by their IEP" (U.S. Department of Education, 2007b, p. 17). NCLB requires that alternate assessments based on modified achievement standards address the same grade-level content as the general assessment (U.S. Department of Education, 2007a). In other words, the assessments may change the level of difficulty of the questions on the assessment but not the content that is assessed at each grade level. The number of students who may take an alternate assessment based on modified achievement standards may not exceed 2% of all students in the grades assessed by the district and/or the state. In addition, the regulations require that the IEPs of students participating in alternate assessments based on modified achievement standards include goals that directly address grade-level content standards. The intent of this requirement is to ensure that students receive instruction that will allow them to progress in the general education curriculum. At the time this chapter was written, the regulations on alternate assessments based on modified achievement standards had just been finalized, and it was not clear how many (if any) states would choose to establish this assessment option (M. J. McLaughlin, personal communication, February 25, 2008). Consequently, the impact of these assessments on students' educational programs is not known.

Focus Question 2	How are most states' academic content and achievement standards organized?

Most states have organized their academic content and achievement standards into three levels (Nolette & McLaughlin, 2005). Table 4.1 illustrates the typical organizational framework. The first level is a broad standard that identifies a general skill or area of knowledge that all students are expected to master. The second level describes knowledge and skill benchmarks that are specific to each grade level. Finally, the third level lays out the specific indicators that are designed to demonstrate that students have mastered the grade-level benchmarks. Kohl, McLaughlin, and Nagle (2006) conducted a study examining the structure of alternate assessments based on alternate achievement standards in 16 states. They did a comprehensive review of each state's content standards and alternate assessments. In addition, they interviewed state representatives who were directly involved in the implementation of the alternate assessment program. Representatives from 12 of the 16 states reported that students with the most significant disabilities were held to the general content standards. However, they found that states made several common adjustments to the standards at the second and third levels. Typically, these adjustments included (a) expanding or extending the indicators, (b) providing alternate or modified performance indicators, or (c) providing functional performance indicators (Table 4.2).

Table 4.1   Common Structure of Academic Content Standards

Element	Example
Standard:	Students will understand the world in spatial terms.
Benchmark/Objective:	Use maps and other geographic tools to acquire information from a spatial perspective.
Indicator:	Explain the differences between major types of map projections.

Table 4.2   Common Adjustments to Standards, Benchmarks, or Indicators

	Extended
Standard:	The student will develop an understanding of the structure of atoms, compounds, chemical reactions, and the interactions of energy and matter.
Benchmark:	The student will understand the relationship between force and motion.
Indicator:	The student understands Newton's laws, and the variables of time, position, velocity, and acceleration can be used to describe the position and motion of particles.
Extended Indicator:	The student manipulates and/or describes the movement of objects.
	Alternate
Standard:	Students will develop an understanding of personal and community health.
Benchmark:	None.
Indicator:	Investigate and describe the effect of nutritional balance on growth, development, and personal well-being.

(Continued)

Table 4.2 (Continued)

Alternate Standard:	Students will, using their primary mode of communication, demonstrate an understanding of personal and community health.

Functional

Standard:	Under the process of scientific investigation and design, conduct, communicate about, and evaluate such investigations.
Benchmark:	Communicate and evaluate scientific thinking that leads to particular conclusions.
Indicator:	Identify and use evidence to support a particular conclusion.
Functional Indicator:	Provide descriptive information about what is seen/heard/felt.

Research to date suggests that states are struggling to achieve significant alignment between state content standards and alternate assessments. For example, researchers have found (a) weak links between the content standards and alternate assessments in many states (Browder et al., 2004; Kohl et al., 2006), (b) that alternate assessments are frequently focused on a narrowed range and depth of academic content standards (Flowers, Browder, & Ahlgrim-Delzell, 2006) and often do not reflect a logical sequenced curriculum across grade levels (Kohl et al.), (c) that alternate assessments in many states are focused on significantly less complex indicators of performance (Kohl et al.), and (d) that there is significant variability in the reliability and validity of the measurement procedures used in many alternate assessments (Browder et al., 2005; Kohl et al.).

There is a general consensus that students with intellectual and developmental disabilities benefit from access to and participating in the general education curriculum (Hunt & McDonnell, 2007). However, the research suggests that the field faces a number of challenges in effectively assessing students' achievement in the general education curriculum. Alternate assessments are a reality for students, teachers, and administrators, but the utility of such assessments in helping IEP teams make evidenced-based decisions in designing students' educational programs is questionable at this point in time (Lowrey, Drasgow, Renzaglia, & Chezan, 2007). The utility of alternate assessments for making informed decisions for students is diminished by a fluid regulatory context that requires states to continuously modify and fine-tune their alternate assessments (Kohl et al., 2006).

In spite of these challenges, teachers must adopt educational planning procedures that will ensure that students' participation in the general

---

POINT/COUNTERPOINT 4.1

Assessing Students on State Content Standards

POINT	COUNTERPOINT
"Is assessing students with developmental disabilities on state academic content standards sound policy? Given that there is some evidence, albeit limited by the scope of educators' past priorities, it seems equitable to offer students with developmental disabilities the opportunity to acquire academic content.... Withholding academic instruction places a ceiling of achievement on students with developmental disabilities" (Wakeman, Browder, Meier, & McColl, 2007, p. 147).	"Alternate assessment focused solely on general education standards may unintentionally change the curricula of students with the most significant disabilities by creating a focus on instruction that is driven by the assessment rather than by what is individually appropriate and necessary for success as an adult. Individuals with severe disabilities may not achieve future independence or partial independence as adults if we teach and measure only an academically focused curriculum" (Lowery, Drasgow, Renzaglia, & Chezan, 2007, p. 249).

---

education curriculum contributes to their postschool goals (Bambara, Wilson, & McKenzie, 2007). Fortunately, several authors have recommended strategies that can help IEP teams align the instruction that students receive with their particular state's academic content standards (Browder, Ahlgrim-Delzell, Courtade-Little, & Snell, 2006; Ford, Davern, & Schnorr, 2001; McGregor, 2003). The following section will describe the steps that teachers can use to achieve this outcome for students.

Aligning Content Standards With Postschool Outcomes and Instruction

Most of the proposed strategies for aligning content standards and instruction are based on three common planning steps (Browder et al., 2006; Ford et al., 2001; Kleinert & Thurlow, 2001; McGregor, 2003; Thompson, Quenemoen, Thurlow, & Ysseldyke, 2001):

1. *Identify priority content standards.* The general education curriculum is commonly divided into broad areas of knowledge and skills, such as social studies. These broad areas are further divided into subdisciplines or strands, such as American history, geography, and world

civilizations. Content standards are identified within each strand, and these standards represent the "big ideas" that students are expected to master within a particular strand.

Browder and colleagues (2006) suggest that one way of identifying specific content standards that are appropriate for a student is to ask the general education teacher to identify the top three "big ideas" from the list of content standards that he or she would like all students in the class to master. For example, in geography, this might include a content standard like "Students will understand the world in spatial terms." It is also helpful to identify specific benchmarks or objectives that a student might be accountable for within the content standard. Continuing with the geography example, a priority benchmark for a student might include "Use maps and other geographic tools to acquire information."

2. *Identify alternate achievement targets.* In this step, teachers and other members of the IEP/transition planning team should focus on identifying alternate ways that a student can demonstrate mastery of the content. As discussed above, some states have developed extended or adapted achievement standards for students who are taking the alternate assessment, but many have not. If these extended or adapted achievement standards have not been identified, Kleinert and Thurlow (2001) suggest that teachers focus on the critical function of the standard or benchmark to develop an alternate achievement target. For example, the essential functions of the benchmark "Use maps and other geographic tools to acquire information" are to use maps to learn more about other places and to travel more independently. So instead of focusing on such achievement indicators as "Explain the differences among major types of map projections," teachers and IEP/transition planning team members might establish an achievement standard that allows a student to demonstrate the critical function of the standard or benchmark using alternate means, such as selecting the correct type of map (e.g., bus route map, street map) to plan how to get to various locations in the community and then using the map to get to a selected location.

3. *Assess the alignment between the content and achievement targets and students' expected postschool outcomes.* In order to maximize the benefits of a student's participation in the general education curriculum, it is recommended that teachers and the IEP/transition

planning team review each of the content standards and achievement targets to ensure that they promote meaningful postschool outcomes (Bambara et al., 2007). In the previous example, the ability of a student to get a job, take care of his or her home, or engage in meaningful leisure activities would be enhanced from the ability to use maps to get around his or her community.

Ecological Curricula

Structure of Ecological Curricula

As discussed previously, during the 1960s and 1970s, educational content for students was often selected from preacademic or elementary academic skill sequences, developmental skill sequences, or analyses of functional daily living skills. Instruction typically occurred in classroom or school settings, and students were rarely required to show that they could use these skills in actual settings. It was simply assumed that the acquisition of these skills would lead to successful performance at home, in school, or in the community. But research has consistently shown that students with intellectual and developmental disabilities require systematic instruction in actual settings in order to promote the generalization of isolated skills (Horner, McDonnell, & Bellamy, 1986; Rosenthal-Malek & Bloom, 1998). So while students learned many different skills in school, this learning frequently did not lead to tangible improvements in the quality of their lives or in their ability to adjust to work and independent living after school (Brown, Branston, et al., 1979; Brown, Branston-McClean, et al., 1979; Wilcox & Bellamy, 1982).

Focus Question 3	What are the primary instructional targets within an ecological curriculum?

In response, researchers developed a number of "ecological" curricula that were based on the actual demands that secondary students would face in home, school, and community settings (Falvey, 1989; Ford et al., 1989; Neel & Billingsley, 1989; Wilcox & Bellamy, 1987). Although their structure varies, ecological curricula have a number of common features. First, they are organized into domains that reflect the typical demands of adult life, such as work, personal management, and leisure (Wilcox & Bellamy, 1987). These domains emphasized the need for students' educational programs to focus instruction on preparing them for what they will be expected to do as adults. Second, the primary instructional targets within these curricula are referred to as "activities." Wilcox and Bellamy (1982, 1987) defined activities as having three characteristics:

- Activities are chains of behavior that reflect logical units of performance in home, school, and community settings.
- Completion of an activity produces a meaningful outcome that improves a student's ability to live independently and participate in the community.
- The behaviors that make up an activity are completed in a predictable and regular sequence that reflects natural performance demands.

For example, a common activity included in ecological curricula is "shopping for groceries." It meets the definition of an activity because (a) it is regularly done by adults living in the community, (b) it produces meaningful outcomes for students because it allows them to meet their nutritional needs and enhances choice and autonomy over what they eat every day, and (c) the basic sequence of responses necessary to shop for groceries is predictable and occurs in essentially the same order for everyone who does it (e.g., enter the store, get a cart, locate items, pay for items, and exit the store). In contrast, a skill like counting coins does not meet the definition of an activity because being able to count coin combinations does not in and of itself produce a meaningful outcome for students. In fact, this skill needs to be combined with a number of other academic and developmental skills in order for a student to complete an activity like shopping for groceries.

The third feature of ecological curricula is that the activities included therein are selected based on a cataloging of local opportunities within a neighborhood and community. This is done in order to ensure that the activities that are taught to students reflect real demands. For example, the employment opportunities available to adults in a rural community often vary significantly from those available to adults who live in an urban area. Similarly, the leisure opportunities across rural and urban communities will be different. In addition, activities included in the curricula are selected based on what typical adolescents and adults within a particular neighborhood or community are expected to do. This is done to ensure that the activities that are selected for instruction reflect age-appropriate performance for students. The result is the development of a list or "catalog" of activities that reflect the typical demands placed on adolescents and adults living in a particular community. The content of students' educational programs is selected from this catalog of activities. Table 4.3 provides an illustrative list of activities that might be included in each domain in an ecological curriculum.

Some researchers have suggested that activities will need to be combined into "routines" in order for them to be functional for a student (McDonnell, Mathot-Buckner, & Ferguson, 1996). For example, shopping for groceries could be considered part of the routine of meal planning. In order to complete this routine, students would need to be able to complete a number of activities, including developing a menu, developing a grocery list, traveling to the store, shopping for the groceries, traveling home, and putting away the food. This kind of routine might be done by students on the weekend in order to avoid having to go to the grocery store every day. Similarly, the routine of doing laundry might include the activities of sorting clothes, washing clothes, drying clothes, and folding clothes and putting them away.

Finally, the academic and developmental skills taught to students are those that are necessary for successful performance of a routine or an activity. These skills are selected based on the actual performance demands. For example, in order to shop for groceries, students might need to read food sight words, count out the number of items being purchased, determine more or less, or count money. Ecological curricula do not diminish the importance of teaching academic and developmental skills but require that the skills that are taught have immediate application and utility for students' performance in home, school, and community settings.

McDonnell and colleagues (1996) suggested that the relationships among routines, activities, and skills can provide an effective framework for selecting goals and objectives for students' IEPs/transition plans and to support the cumulative development of students' skills across their educational careers. For

Table 4.3 Illustrative List of Activities

Domain	Home	School	Community
Personal Management	Washing Dishes	Dressing for PE	Shopping for Groceries
	Paying Bills	Eating Lunch	Using an ATM
	Dressing	Using Locker	Eating at a Restaurant
Leisure	Playing Video Games	Reading a Book	Swimming
	Scrapbooking	Shooting Baskets	Going to a Movie
	Gardening	Talking With Friends	Attending Club Meetings
Work	Doing Chores	Participating in a Service Learning Project	Job Sampling at a Business

middle or junior high school students, the focus of their IEPs/transition plans would be placed on teaching important academic and developmental skills. These skills would then be anchored to an activity or a routine that students could complete regularly in home, school, and community settings in order to promote the generalization. For high school students, the focus would shift to teaching activities that would increase their independence in home, school, and community settings. In addition, the planning team would target academic and developmental skills for instruction that students need to complete the routines and activities successfully. Finally, educational programs for students about to exit school would focus on establishing performance of routines that will be critical for their adjustment to adult life following school. Figure 4.1 illustrates the relationships among a routine, activities, and skills.

Figure 4.1   Relationships Among a Routine, Activities, and Skills

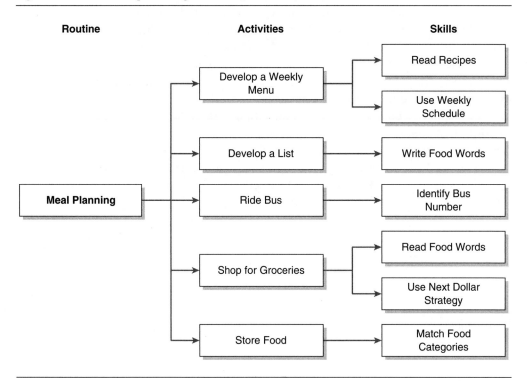

Aligning Ecological Curricula With Postschool Outcomes and Instruction

The benefits of ecological curricula for secondary students are maximized when they are used to improve students' immediate and long-term quality of life. Consequently, the curricula must be used to align the content of students' educational programs to obtain their expected postschool outcomes. Several simple steps can help students and other IEP/transition planning team members ensure that this alignment occurs in students' educational programs:

1. *Identify priority routines and activities.* Decisions regarding what routines and activities students will learn from an ecological curriculum are not driven by prescribed sequences but rather through an interactive process that requires students and the other members of the planning team to consider a number of factors:

• *Impact.* The first consideration in using an ecological curriculum is to evaluate the impact that the routine or activity will have on a student's quality of life. A critical aspect of this decision is whether or not the student has, or will have, the opportunity to actually complete the routine or activity on a regular basis. Teaching a student to complete an activity like shopping for groceries or riding the bus to work often requires a significant investment of staff resources and time. The focus should be on selecting routines and activities that will enhance a student's participation in home, school, and community settings over the long term.

• *Comprehensiveness.* Successful postschool adjustment requires that a student participate fully in all aspects of community living. This means that he or she must have the opportunity to make a contribution to the community, manage his or her own needs and household, and engage in leisure/recreational activities that are enjoyable. In selecting priority routines and activities, members of the educational planning team must look holistically at a student's current and future life in the community in order to ensure that all of his or her needs are met.

• *Self-determination.* The routines and activities selected for a student's educational plans should be chosen to increase the student's control over his or her life. This means not only teaching multiple activities that give him or her more choices (e.g., using a stationary bike, doing yoga, lifting weights) but also selecting routines and activities that will help him or her learn to make more effective choices, advocate for his or her own needs, and increase his or her autonomy in planning for his or her future.

• *Inclusion.* The routines and activities selected for a student should promote his or her participation in the school and community settings and his or her interactions with peers without disabilities. A student cannot become socially competent without regular and frequent opportunities to interact with other people. Further, a student cannot develop the friendships that are crucial to ensuring a high quality of life unless he or she has opportunities to become part of the natural social networks at school, at work, and in the neighborhood.

• *Age-appropriateness.* The success of secondary and transition programs hinges on their ability to cumulatively develop the capacity of a student to work and live in the community. This means that a student must be expected to become increasingly independent and assume more responsibility for his or her life as he or she gets closer to leaving school. Obviously, we would have significantly different expectations for a 15-year-old student than we would for a 20-year-old. The routines and activities selected for students' educational plans must be referenced to the expectations that we would typically have for same-age peers.

• *Safety and security.* As we build a student's capacity for increased independence and autonomy, there is also increased risk for potential injury or harm. There is inherent risk in anything that we do as adults, and none of us can be completely protected from it. However, as Perske (1972) argued, there is also a dignity of risk that comes with increased independence and participation in the community. If we prevent individuals with intellectual and developmental disabilities from becoming more independent based on our fears of injury or harm, we run the risk of unnecessarily segregating and isolating them within the community. Consequently, educational planning teams must balance students' safety and security with the need to maximize their participation in community life.

2. *Determine a student's method of performance.* All routines and activities require an individual to use a variety of academic and developmental skills. The extent to which secondary school students with intellectual and developmental disabilities have developed these skills will vary significantly. One of the decisions facing students and their educational planning teams is whether instructional time should be dedicated to teaching these skills or whether alternate performance strategies will be taught to students to allow them to successfully complete the routine or activity. Alternate performance strategies are "nontypical ways of performing normal functions" (McDonnell & Wilcox, 1987, p. 49). They are designed to simplify the cognitive, language, physical, or academic demands of routines and activities so that individuals who do not have these skills can still participate in home, school, and community activities. For example, an individual who cannot read could use pictures to locate items in the grocery store, or someone who does not have clear verbal communication could use a communication device to express his or her desires or needs.

3. *Assess the alignment between priority routines and activities and students' expected postschool outcomes.* An educational planning team must evaluate the potential impact of priority routines and activities on students'

future quality of life. For example, planning teams will need to ask themselves whether learning to shop for groceries, ride the bus, or use an ATM benefits students after school and improves the likelihood that they will achieve their goals.

Implications for Educational Planning

The educational programs for most students with intellectual and developmental disabilities will need to blend content from the general education curriculum with content from ecological curricula. The balance of content from these curricula will need to be tailored to the needs of students and be based on a long-term vision of their life after school. Articulating a clear vision for students requires an interactive process that allows them to weigh the advantages and disadvantages of their decisions with their family, their friends, their teachers, and other important people in their lives. In addition, students will need to make a decision about the educational path that they will pursue to achieve their vision. Specifically, students must decide whether they will pursue a traditional high school diploma or whether they will seek an alternate diploma or certificate of attendance.

Focus Question 4	How can person-centered planning support the balancing of the general education and ecological curricula within the IEP/transition plan?

It has been suggested that the most effective way to make these decisions is through a person-centered planning process (Keyes & Owens-Johnson, 2003; McDonnell et al., 1996; Wehman, 2001). Most person-centered planning strategies are designed to take into account a student's choices, preferences, and strengths in developing his or her vision. These strategies are also structured to result in a specific action plan that lays out the steps necessary to achieve his or her vision. If done correctly, the person-centered plan should provide a basis for the development of the student's IEP/transition plan (Figure 4.2).

While the person-centered plan should address all of the areas that will impact students' immediate and future quality of life, it is particularly important to identify postschool outcomes in several key areas. These outcomes typically include the type of career or job students want, where they will live after exiting school, and how they will spend their free time. The person-centered plan should also result in a decision regarding students' participation in general education and ecological curricula.

Figure 4.2   Process for Aligning General Education and Ecological Curricula With Postschool Outcomes

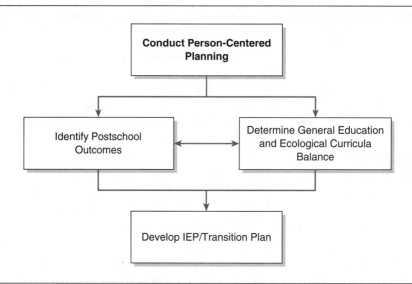

Students pursuing a traditional high school diploma will obviously need to be fully included in the course of study required by the school district to obtain a diploma. Students pursuing an alternate diploma or certificate of attendance will have much more flexibility in selecting courses from the general education curriculum and targeting specific content standards within courses. While participation in the general education curriculum is desirable for all students, most students with intellectual and developmental disabilities will also need access to curricula that will prepare them to work and live independently following school (Bouck, 2004; Johnson, Stodden, Emanuel, Luecking, & Mack, 2002; Patton, Cronin, & Jarriels, 1997; Sitlington, 2003). Ecological curricula provide the necessary structure for students and their planning teams to identify the routines, activities, and skills that will be necessary for them to navigate the demands of community living. The challenge facing students and their planning teams is determining the optimal balance between the two curricula in achieving students' expected postschool outcomes.

The decisions made in the person-centered planning process can lay the groundwork for meeting the requirements for transition planning with IDEA 2004. The information included in a person-centered plan can support the development of measurable postschool goals for students, identification of needed transition services, creation of IEP goals that ensure that students receive instruction on content drawn from the general education and ecological curricula, and development of linkages with community service agencies necessary to support students' transition into community life. The specific steps required to develop a comprehensive and effective IEP/transition plan are described in Chapter 5.

Summary

This chapter describes curriculum options for students with intellectual and developmental disabilities. Current federal legislation requires that students participate and progress in the general education curriculum and participate in district- and statewide assessments or alternate assessments that are directly linked to state content standards. The general education curriculum can provide students with a number of educational opportunities that will enhance their ability to work and live independently in the community. The key to making sure that these opportunities are meaningful is to align the content and achievement standards with students' expected postschool outcomes. Although students with disabilities can benefit from participating in the general education, they will often need access to ecological curricula that focus on the development of routines and activities that will directly enhance their performance in home, school, and community settings. The challenge facing students and their planning teams is how to blend these two curriculum approaches into an educational plan that enhances students' postschool adjustment. Person-centered planning is an effective strategy for exploring students' expected postschool outcomes and developing an action plan that builds on their preferences and strengths. The person-centered plan includes critical information that can serve as a framework for the development of students' IEPs/transition plans.

Focus Question Review

Focus Question 1: What is the difference between an alternate assessment based on alternate performance standards and an alternate assessment based on modified assessment standards?

- Alternate assessments based on alternate performance standards must be related to content standards but may have extended, alternate, or functional indicators.

- Alternate assessments based on modified performance standards must assess the same academic content standards as the district- or statewide assessment, but the questions included in the assessment may be complex.

Focus Question 2: **How are most states' academic content and achievement standards organized?**

- Standards that identify a skill or general area of knowledge that all students are expected to master.
- Benchmarks that describe the knowledge and skills that are specific to each grade level.
- Indicators that denote what students must do to demonstrate mastery of the grade-level benchmarks.

Focus Question 3: **What are the primary instructional targets within an ecological curriculum?**

- Routines, activities, and skills.

Focus Question 4: **How can person-centered planning support the balancing of the general education and ecological curricula within the IEP/transition plan?**

- The planning process creates a forum for identifying students' expected postschool outcomes and the ways that content from the general education and ecological curricula can contribute to obtaining those outcomes.
- Results in an action plan can provide the information necessary to establish measurable postschool goals, identify needed transition services, develop IEP goals that blend content from each curriculum, and establish linkages with community service agencies.

CHAPTER 5

Developing IEPs/ Transition Plans

SHAMBY POLYCHRONIS

JOHN MCDONNELL

T he Individuals with Disabilities Education Improvement Act of 2004 requires educators to develop a comprehensive transition plan as part of each student's Individualized Education Program beginning at age 16. The focus of transition planning is on facilitating the student's successful movement to postschool activities that are based on specific and measurable postschool goals. These activities may include postsecondary education; vocational education; integrated employment, including supported employment; continuing and adult education; adult services; independent living; or community participation. Under IDEA, schools are required to provide transition services as part of the IEP that will allow the student to achieve his or her postschool goals. For a more in-depth definition of transition services, as detailed in IDEA 2004, refer to Chapter 1.

Obviously, the transition planning mandate in IDEA has important implications for how the IEP process is structured, ranging from who is invited to participate in the planning meeting to the time frame that is used to plan a student's education program. This chapter addresses the process for developing comprehensive IEPs and transition plans that incorporate the practices that are most predictive of postschool success.

Window 5-1

How Can We Design a Road Map for My Future?

Ella is a 15-year-old student at Mountain High School. The school is located in a small rural community and has approximately 210 students. Ella gets very excited when discussing her future plans for adulthood because she has wanted to become an actress since she was a small child.

When Ella was 4 years old, she had a near-drowning incident that resulted in a traumatic brain injury. Ella enjoys school but often struggles to understand instructions given to her by teachers and has difficulty concentrating for long periods. The special education team is committed to supporting Ella in the general education curriculum and helping her develop her coping skills when she feels overwhelmed and frustrated.

Ella will be 16 years old at the beginning of next year and has begun preparing for her first transition planning meeting. She sits down with Mr. Allen, the special educator, and discusses her personal vision for her future, as well as possible accommodations that she feels will help her succeed. Ella has a strong interest in moving to the city when she graduates and enrolling at a small acting school.

Mr. Allen calls a preplanning meeting with Ella and her parents to discuss possible goals that will help prepare Ella for her intended postschool activities. During the planning session, Ella's parents note concerns regarding her judgment of new people, as well as her problem-solving skills in dealing with stressful situations. Because of these concerns, her parents are apprehensive about Ella's ideas to live on her own in an apartment in the city and attend an acting school. They also mention that they plan on renovating their basement to make a small apartment for Ella when she graduates and think she can help out by providing child care services for her sister's children since she enjoys being around family.

The planning team (Ella, her parents, and the special educator) work together to discuss possible coordinated activities that will prepare Ella for the transition to adulthood and help her work toward her personal goals. They each commit to further explore some of the issues that were discussed in the meeting so they can prepare for the transition planning meeting in the fall. For the remainder of the school year, Mr. Allen and Ella work to complete various skill inventories and assessments to gather more information about her needs and interests. Over the summer, Ella and her parents attend a recruitment event at the acting college and look into various living arrangements and support services in the city.

When school begins in the fall, the planning team is able to correspond via e-mail and telephone to relate information and discuss additional ideas and concerns. Mr. Allen works with the school faculty to determine which general educators will be teaching the classes that Ella will be taking so they may attend the meeting. When the transition planning meeting is held, the entire team is able to use the report from the planning team to establish a coordinated set of activities and support services that will lead Ella to achieving the postschool goals she envisioned for herself!

Critical Elements of Educational Planning

Person-Centered Planning

Several studies suggest that transition planning that is driven by the needs and preferences of the student results in better postschool student outcomes (Benz, Lindstrom, & Yovanoff, 2000; Frank & Sitlington, 2000; Merchant & Gajar, 1997) and higher levels of student and parent satisfaction with the educational program (Collet-Klingenberg, 1998; Miner & Bates, 1997). In spite of this, students often do not attend IEP and transition planning meetings with school personnel (Grigal, Test, Beattie, & Wood, 1997; Test et al., 2004; Trach & Shelden, 2000). Even when students are present, the amount of input they have in defining their postschool goals and selecting the transition services necessary to achieve their desired postschool outcomes is limited (Abery & Stancliffe, 1996; Collett-Klingenberg, 1998; Cooney, 2002; Johnson & Sharpe, 2000; Thoma, Rogan, & Baker, 2001).

A number of studies suggest that if they are provided with adequate training and support, students can develop the capacity to be active participants in the IEP/transition planning process (Test et al., 2004; see Chapter 6). Recommended strategies include student training on person-centered transition planning, creating preplanning documents and procedures to encourage students and their families to weigh various postschool options, and turning control of the planning process over to the students and their parents (deFur, Todd-Allen, & Getzel, 2001; Hasazi, Furney, & Destefano, 1999).

Focus Question 1	Why is family participation in the IEP/transition planning process so important for students with intellectual and developmental disabilities?

Family Involvement

Families play an important role in supporting the transition of students from school to community life (Kim & Morningstar, 2005). For example, research suggests that the characteristics and structure of a student's family play a significant role in the career and employment decisions made by young adults with disabilities (Lindstrom, Doren, Metheny, Johnson, & Zane, 2007). In addition, the majority of young adults with intellectual and developmental disabilities live with their parents or another adult family member and receive ongoing financial support from family members after leaving school (Wagner, Newman, Cameto, & Levine, 2005). These data highlight the need for parents and other family members to be active participants in the IEP and transition planning process (Turnbull & Turnbull, 2001).

However, research also suggests that parents and other family members often do not believe that they have sufficient information to actively participate in transition planning (Chambers, Hughes, & Carter, 2004). The IEP/transition planning process needs to be designed so that students become more knowledgeable about the decisions they must make during school to prepare for community living and learn about the types of adult and community services and programs available to support them after school and so that parents become more knowledgeable about how to effectively advocate for their adult child (McDonnell, Mathot-Buckner, & Ferguson, 1996; Turnbull & Turnbull, 2001; Wehman, 2006). Secondary school programs can help educate students and families about transition issues through a variety of means, including developing a transition planning handbook for students and parents, hosting "agency" fairs at adult and community service agencies to share information about their programs, connecting families to parent training and information centers, and developing family-to-family support groups (Aspel, Bettis, Quinn, Test, & Wood, 1999; Johnson, Stodden, Emanuel, Lueking, & Mack, 2002; Rueda, Monzo, Shapiro, Gomez, & Blacher, 2005).

Secondary schools can also encourage higher levels of family involvement during the transition process by working with a student's family to develop appropriate roles in helping the student achieve his or her goals. For example, parents can take a lead role in helping their student transition to college by coordinating college tours while the special educator works with the student to strengthen the necessary skills for successful college participation. Parents can also take a lead role in employment preparation by engaging in community service activities with their adolescents that can help them develop skills that will translate to employment. Activities may include volunteering at the local soup kitchen to develop similar skills to those necessary in a restaurant or working with the local animal shelter to develop skills that provide exploration into the possible career of veterinary assistance. These kinds of experiences can provide parents and other family members with opportunities to develop a more comprehensive understanding of a student's preferences and needs and foster the development of realistic expectations for the student's future.

Cumulatively Developing
Student Capacity for Adult Life

Transition planning is not a one-time event; rather, it must be viewed as an ongoing, coordinated process beginning no later than a student's 16th year of life and continuing through graduation. Each IEP/transition plan should be directly linked to a student's postschool goals and should be designed to cumulatively build the student's knowledge and skills and develop the supports necessary for him or her to work and live independently in the community. Although IDEA only requires schools to conduct transition planning at age 16, it is widely recommended that transition planning begin much earlier for students with intellectual and developmental disabilities (Baer, 2008; Wehman, 2006).

Developing IEPs and Transition Plans

Figure 5.1 presents the general steps required to develop IEPs/transition plans for students. The steps of the process are the same across middle or junior high school, high school, and post-high school programs. However, the transition services included with the IEP/transition plan and content of the IEP goals and objectives will vary based on the student's age and specific postschool goals.

Figure 5.1   Steps of the IEP/Transition Planning Process

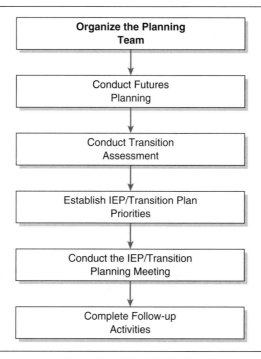

Window 5-2

Planning for Robert's Future

Robert is a 19-year-old student with severe intellectual disabilities who is attending a post-high school program at City Community College. Robert is able to communicate, but his articulation sometimes makes it difficult to understand him. He is a big guy and is very strong. Robert is currently completing a work experience program at the Canyon Market. He has been working as a bagger and as an assistant to the produce manager. Robert also attends several classes at the community college. He particularly enjoys his weight lifting class that he attends with his friend Zack.

Last spring, Robert; his parents; Ms. Rowley, his special education teacher from Valley High School; and Mr. Sebastian from the post-high school program met to develop a futures plan. The meeting was also attended by his friend Zack, who had worked with Robert as a peer tutor; his older sister Allison; and Ms. Irvin, who was the paraprofessional in Ms. Rowley's program. The meeting was focused on identifying Robert's postschool goals. Robert had completed several work experience placements in different businesses during his junior and senior years. He particularly enjoyed working at the grocery store, and he expressed an interest in getting a job in a similar setting. He also wanted to move out of his parents' house and live with a friend. All of the members of the planning team agreed that these were realistic goals for Robert and that he would have very good support from his family and friends to achieve them.

In September, Robert, his parents, Mr. Sebastian, and Ms. Heath, the school district transition specialist, met to develop an IEP/transition plan. Mr. Sebastian reviewed the results of the futures planning meeting conducted the previous spring and summarized the results of the ecological assessments that he had conducted with Robert and his parents, who were asked to present their priorities for the plan. These priorities included getting a job working in a grocery store in the produce section, learning how to ride the bus, and participating in several classes at the community college. Robert specifically asked to enroll in a weight lifting class with Zack. Mr. Sebastian and Ms. Heath had developed similar recommendations but had also included learning how to use a self-management system, learning how to use an ATM, and learning to call his parents, school staff, and employer. After some discussion, Robert's parents agreed to get him a cell phone. Mr. Sebastian agreed to help Robert learn how to use the speed-dial and message functions. They also agreed that Robert would be initially placed in a work experience site to allow Mr. Sebastian to get to know his work strengths and needs a little better and that Mr. Sebastian would begin to work on finding Robert a job working in a store in his neighborhood. Ms. Heath indicated that she would contact vocational rehabilitation and mental retardation/developmental counselors assigned to the post-high school program to invite them to attend Robert's next IEP/transition planning meeting.

Organize the Planning Team

Planning for a student's future requires the perspectives of multiple people who are vested in the student's life. IDEA 2004 requires that the planning team include the parents; at least one general education teacher (if the student is, or may be, participating in general education classes); the special educator who works with the student; a representative of the school district; an individual who can interpret the instructional implications of evaluation results and who may also be one of the other listed members; and (at the discretion of the parent or agency) any other individuals who have knowledge or special expertise regarding the student, including related service personnel. Furthermore, in accordance with 34 CFR 300.321(a)(7), the school must invite the student to attend the IEP/transition planning team meeting if a purpose of the meeting is to consider postsecondary goals and the transition services needed to assist the student in reaching those goals. The language in the law is very clear in stating that every attempt must be made to ensure that students participate meaningfully in their own transition planning. If a student does not attend the meeting, IDEA regulations require schools to involve the student in the planning process to the maximum extent possible, as well as to ensure that the student's preferences and interests are considered in writing the goals and objectives.

When the purpose of the IEP includes the development of a transition plan, families must also be advised so they can become empowered to help guide the educational program for their children. Educators can help families prepare for their role in the process by engaging them in preplanning activities to explore their own thoughts and feelings about the transition process and their vision for their child's future. Family involvement in the transition planning process is important because family members have intimate knowledge of the student and play a key role when connecting to adult service systems.

As mentioned previously, the IEP/transition planning team should include other members as appropriate to meet the student's needs. Guidance counselors, related service providers, vocational educators, and administrators can participate in transition planning depending on the needs of the student (deFur, 1999). Furthermore, adult service organizations that may provide or pay for transition services must also be invited to participate in the development of the transition plan. Such interagency collaboration allows the school to work with adult service agencies to maximize the level of services available to the student when he or she leaves school and to reduce operational costs for providing these services (Johnson, Zorn, Tam, LaMontagne, & Johnson, 2003).

One of the challenges facing secondary programs is how to best organize the planning team to maximize the effectiveness and efficiency of the planning process. Researchers have generally recommended the use of collaborative teams to plan the educational programs for students with intellectual and developmental disabilities (Hunt, Soto, Maier, & Doering, 2003; Rainforth & York-Barr, 1997; Thousand & Villa, 2000). This approach to educational planning allows each team member to develop a shared knowledge and understanding of the student's learning characteristics and needs, become aware of the student's postschool goals and the content of the student's IEP/transition plan, and become familiar with the most effective instructional approaches and supports for the student. Collaborative teams are not only required for developing the student's IEP/transition plan; they are also responsible for design, implementation, and evaluation of instruction.

Focus Question 2	How can collaborative teams be organized so that they maximize the involvement of key individuals and the efficiency of planning?

Although collaborative teams have a number of advantages for students, the large number of individuals participating in the planning process can sometimes make it unwieldy. One way to deal with this problem is to develop both core and extended planning teams (Rainforth & York-Barr, 1997). The core team comprises the individuals who are directly involved in the day-to-day delivery of services to the student. Typically, this includes the student, his or her parents, his or her special education teacher, his or her general education teacher(s), related service staff, and a school district representative. The core team assumes primary responsibility for the development, implementation, and evaluation of the IEP/transition plan. The expanded team includes the members of the core team plus individuals who may have a vested interest in the outcomes of the student's educational program. This might include the student's friends or family members, other members of the school faculty, or representatives of adult and community service agencies. The expanded team is directly involved in the futures planning process and IEP/transition planning as needed to ensure the success of the student's educational program. The composition of the core and expanded teams will change across time based on the needs of the student and as the student gets closer to leaving school.

Conduct Futures Planning

IDEA requires that the IEP/transition plan be based on a student's postschool goals. This requires that the planning team identify the student's preferences and interests, his or her experiences in education and employment activities, and the resources that are available to support his or her participation in community life. It is recommended that this discussion be guided through formal futures planning. A few of the most commonly used tools for carrying out futures planning are discussed below.

Personal Futures Planning. Personal futures planning was developed by Mount and Zwernick in 1988 and has led to the present-day understanding of person-centered planning. The concept of person-centered planning was a paradigm shift for its time: replace system-centered services with those that respond to the unique needs of each individual. The process includes forms to develop a personal profile, processes for discovering what the community has to offer, and a pathway for helping individual students take over their own action plans.

McGill Action Planning System (MAPS). MAPS is a person-centered planning process that is used extensively to support effective transition planning for students with intellectual and developmental disabilities (Falvey, Forest, Pearpoint, & Rosenberg, 1993; Forest, Pearpoint, and Snow, 1992; Vandercook, York, & Forest, 1989). The futures plan is developed by key individuals who will be important to supporting the student's successful transition to community life. The process is driven by a number of questions that focus on the personal history and educational experience of the student, his or her dreams and desires, his or her strengths and preferences, and the supports that he or she will need to be successful after school. This information is used to develop an action plan that can help inform the development of the IEP/transition plan.

Big-Picture Planning. Big-picture planning was developed to involve the student, as well as the individuals most important in his or her life, in planning for the future (McDonnell et al., 1996). The tool can be utilized early in the student's school career and allows educators to consider the student's interests and needed supports, as well as the natural supports available within his or her family and support network. Figure 5.2 is a summary of the information gathered during the big-picture planning process for Robert.

Figure 5.2   Big Picture for Robert

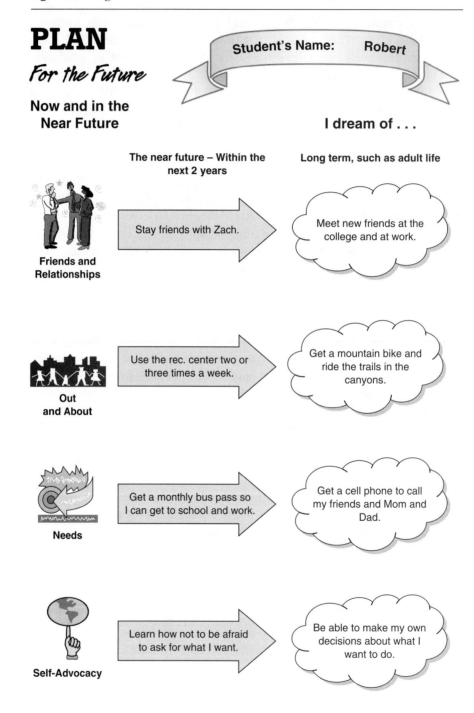

PLAN

For the Future

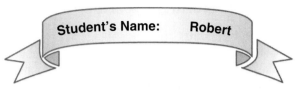

Student's Name: Robert

Now and in the Near Future

I dream of . . .

The near future – Within the next 2 years

Long term, such as adult life

My Home

Live with Mom and Dad until I finish school.

Get my own apartment with a friend.

My Resources

Get my own checking account.

Start a savings account to buy the things I want.

Schools and Work

Go to the community college and get a job and take some classes.

Work at a store in the produce section.

Getting Around

Learn to ride the bus to the college and my job.

Be able to ride the bus to where I want to go. Be able to ride the bus up the canyons.

Conduct Student Assessment

IDEA requires the use of age-appropriate transition assessments to establish a student's measurable postschool goals and guide the provision of transition services. The transition assessment information gathered by teachers must (a) be valid for the student's disability and functioning level, (b) be linked to the student's current and projected postschool environments, (c) be focused on the student's strengths, and (d) support a person-centered approach to establishing the student's postschool goals. Unfortunately, neither the statute nor the subsequent regulations defines transition assessment. The decisions regarding the selection of assessments are left up to the IEP/transition planning team.

It is generally recommended that the transition assessment process include a wide array of formal and informal measures (Miller, Lombard, & Corbey, 2007; Sitlington, Neubert, Begun, LeConte, & Lombard, 1996). These may include assessments of career development, self-determination and self-advocacy skills, and functional life skills. However, a number of researchers have cautioned against overreliance on standardized assessments because they often lack validity for students with intellectual and developmental disabilities and do not take into account the contextual factors that may influence a student's performance (Brown, Snell, & Lehr, 2006; Craddock & Scherer, 2002). A preferred approach, especially for students with more significant disabilities, is the use of ecological inventories and interviews that are focused on the student's performance in home, community, and work settings (Browder, 2001; McDonnell et al., 1996).

For many students, the effectiveness of the planning process can be improved through the use of instruments that provide general assessment of their transition skills. Three of the most widely used instruments include the Transition Skills Inventory, or TSI (Halpern, Herr, Doren, & Wolf, 2000); the Transition Planning Inventory, or TPI (Clark & Patton, 2007); and the Life-Centered Career Education (LCCE) Program (Brolin, 1997). The TSI (Halpern et al., 2000) is a self-report inventory that is completed by the student, his or her parents, and his or her teacher. It assesses the student's knowledge and perceived level of performance in a number of areas, including his or her personal life, jobs, education and training, and living on his or her own. The student's, his or her parents', and his or her teacher's responses on the TSI are triangulated to identify strengths and weaknesses that can be used to guide the identification of postschool goals and provision of transition services.

The TPI (Clark & Patton, 2007) is similar in structure and is designed to provide an assessment of the student's capabilities in the areas of employment, education, daily living, leisure, community participation, health, self-determination, communication, and interpersonal relationships. The instrument also includes several open-ended questions that are designed to determine the student's general preferences and interests. The assessment is completed by the student, his or her parents, and his or her teacher in order to identify common areas of need that can assist in the selection of transition services for the student and provide a basis for the development of his or her IEP goals and objectives.

Finally, the LCCE (Brolin, 1997) is a comprehensive curriculum program, and it also provides related assessment instruments that are anchored to the curriculum domains. The curriculum includes three curriculum-based measures: the LCCE knowledge battery, the LCCE performance battery, and the competency rating scale. There are two versions of these assessments: one designed for students with mild disabilities and the other designed for students with moderate disabilities.

As discussed above, ecological assessments and inventories are often more appropriate for students with more significant disabilities (Browder, 2001; McDonnell et al., 1996). Typically, these instruments are completed during an interview with the student, his or her parents, and other key individuals who are knowledgeable about the student's performance in home, community, and work settings. Figure 5.3 presents an example of an ecological inventory in the area of leisure and recreation (Browder, 2001). The form is designed to (a) determine what skills the student currently has and what activities the student currently completes and (b) identify the student's level of performance on each skill and activity. It is also useful to gather information during the interview on how frequently the student completes activities in home and community settings. In addition, new activities that the student needs to learn should be identified. This information is used to help identify IEP goals and objectives that would contribute to the student achieving his or her postschool goals and improving the immediate quality of his or her life.

Establishing IEP/Transition Priorities

The information gathered during the transition assessment should provide the basis for describing the student's present level of academic and functional performance in home, school, community, and employment settings. The present level of performance allows the IEP/transition planning team to establish goals and objectives that are logically linked to the student's current abilities and postschool goals. In addition, it allows the team to systematically evaluate the effectiveness of the student's educational program in improving his or her performance.

Figure 5.3   Checklist for Leisure Skills for Fitness

Activities	Mastery	Partial Mastery	Not Tried Yet
Jumping rope			
Yoga			
Dancing			
Tennis			
Hockey			
Softball, baseball			
Basketball			
Soccer			
Swimming			
Riding a bike			
Walking, hiking			
Roller skating or in-line skating			
Running, jogging			
Weight lifting			
Other (specify)			
Other (specify)			

Note. Adapted from *Curriculum and Assessment for Students with Moderate and Severe Disabilities,* by D. M. Browder, 2001, New York: Guilford. Adapted with permission.

McDonnell and colleagues (1996) suggested that the planning process is more effective when members of the core planning team discuss the student's postschool goals and use this information to identify goal priorities before the IEP/transition planning meeting. The student and his or her family should be asked to independently identify transition services and important routine and activities goals that will be necessary for the student to achieve his or her postschool goals. School staff members who are on the core team also must identify their priorities for the student. This information is brought to the IEP/transition planning meeting and is discussed by the entire team.

Conduct the IEP/Transition Planning Meeting

The purpose of the IEP/transition planning meeting is to develop a comprehensive educational program that will allow the student to meet his or her postschool goals and improve the quality of his or her life. It is recommended that the IEP/transition plan follow a standard agenda that is designed to ensure that the student's goals, preferences, and needs are honored and addressed. A sample meeting agenda is presented in Figure 5.4.

First, the team should discuss the student's postschool goals in order to provide a context for the identification of needed transition services and the development of goals and objectives. The discussion should focus on clearly articulating measurable postschool goals that match the student's preferences in the areas of employment, community participation, recreation and leisure, postsecondary education, and community living. Next, school staff should summarize the student's present level of academic and functional performance based on the results of the transition assessments.

In the next step of the process, the student and his or her parents should present their priorities for needed transition services and IEP goals. The student should be encouraged to take the lead role in presenting these priorities and why they are important to achieving his or her postschool goals. The student's priorities should be listed on a sheet of paper, a flip chart, or a blackboard for future reference. The school staff members should present their priorities for the student and explain why they believe that the services and goal priorities will assist the student in achieving his or her postschool goals. The staff's priorities should be listed beside the student's on the paper, chart, or board so that they can be compared and discussed. The aim is to identify a list of transition services and goals and objectives that directly contribute to achieving the student's postschool goals and that are acceptable to all members of the IEP/transition planning team. In addition, the team should identify the logistical activities

Figure 5.4   Sample IEP/Transition Planning Meeting Agenda

1. Welcome and introductions.

2. Discuss the student's postschool goals based on his or her preferences and interests for employment, community participation, recreation and leisure, postsecondary education, and community living.

3. Discuss the student's present levels of educational performance related to his or her postschool goals. Emphasize the student's strengths as well as needs.

4. The student and his or her parents present their IEP/transition plan priorities.

5. The teacher presents school staff's IEP/transition plan priorities.

6. Identify needed transition services and IEP goals and objectives.

7. Develop a statement of needed transition services. This should incorporate a coordinated set of activities, including
   a. Interagency linkages and responsibilities.
   b. Movement from school to postschool goals.
   c. Instruction related to community experience, employment, daily living skills, and postschool training.

that will be necessary to ensure that the IEP/transition plan can be successfully implemented. This might include such things as getting a student a bus pass so he or she can travel to and from his or her job site, developing specific accommodations or adaptations to allow him or her to participate in general education classes, or applying for the Supplemental Security Income program.

The IEP goal and objectives identified by the team should be prioritized in order of importance to the student and his or her family. This will allow the school staff to ensure that instructional resources are allocated to address the student's most important needs first. Finally, the team should determine how each transition service provided to the student will be used to help him or her meet his or her goals and objectives.

Complete IEP/Transition Planning Meeting Follow-up Activities

Following the IEP/transition planning meeting, the teacher should finalize the IEP/transition plan (Figure 5.5). This includes ensuring that all of the regulatory requirements for developing the transition plan are noted on the IEP and developing comprehensive annual goals and short-term objective statements. The IEP/transition plan should be distributed to all team members for final review. Minor changes in the wording of goals or objectives can be completed by the teacher. Only substantive changes in the content of the IEP/transition plan require that the team reconvene.

Once the IEP/transition plan has been developed, progress toward meeting those goals must be monitored by the team according to the measurement statement in the IEP/transition plan (20 U.S.C. § 1414[d][1][A]). Progress monitoring is essential to determine if the programming decisions being utilized are effective in making progress toward meeting IEP goals. However, in a review of recent legal decisions stemming from schools being sued over failure to provide appropriate services, Etscheidt (2006) concluded that "there is less compliance with this component [progress monitoring] of the IEP than any other" (p. 56).

Progress monitoring provides educators with an ongoing way to measure expected student progress with the actual level of student achievement. This process helps educators provide more appropriate instruction based on students' needs and progress, make informed programming decisions, document students' progress for accountability purposes, and share more detailed information with families and other professionals. Progress monitoring allows special educators to collaborate more effectively with general and vocational educators in addressing the learning needs and instructional programs of students. The information gathered

Figure 5.5   Sample Transition Plan for Robert

Student: Robert Brown

Date: September 15, 2007

Graduation Date: June 2010

IEP/Transition Planning Team Members: Robert, Mr. and Mrs. Brown, George Sebastian, and Renee Heath

Transition Planning Area: Employment

Postschool Goal: Robert would like to work as a produce stocker in a grocery store.

Present Levels of Academic and Functional Performance: Robert has held several work experience placements, including one in a grocery store. His work accuracy and rate is good. He needs to learn to use a self-management checklist to complete assigned work tasks. He also needs to learn to ride the bus independently to get to and from his job.

Needed Transition Services: Robert will require job placement, training, and follow-along services from the post-high school program. He will also require community-based instruction on learning to ride the bus.

Annual Goal: Robert will work as a bagger and produce assistant at Canyon Market completing all assigned tasks without assistance on five consecutive weekly performance probes.

Short-Term Objectives:

1. When given his bus pass, Robert will ride the Number 5 outbound bus to Stop 15 without teacher assistance on five consecutive daily probes.
2. When given his bus pass, Robert will ride the Number 12 outbound bus to Stop 23 without teacher assistance on five consecutive daily probes.
3. When given a self-management checklist listing assigned tasks, Robert will initiate all tasks without prompts on five consecutive daily probes.
4. During his break, Robert will purchase a drink and snack from the deli without prompts on five consecutive daily probes.

Follow-up Activities/Person/Date:

1. Obtain a monthly bus pass for Robert/Mr. Brown/September 20, 2007.
2. Schedule Robert for an employee orientation meeting/Mr. Sebastian/September 30, 2007.
3. Invite vocational rehabilitation and MR/DD counselors to Robert's next IEP/transition planning meeting/Ms. Heath/August 1, 2008.

can be provided to determine upcoming service needs of students for strategic planning purposes. With the appropriate authorization from students and their families, the progress monitoring assessment information can be provided to relevant community agencies.

Collaboration with community agencies is an important part of delivering effective services needed to meet transition goals. However, interagency collaboration has been identified as one of the primary challenges facing secondary education and transition services (Johnson et al., 2002). Interagency collaboration was identified because of issues related to the difficulty of sharing information and providing follow-up data to improve services, inadequate attention to adult-related issues, and ineffective interagency agreements. In an analysis of effective interagency collaborations, Johnson and colleagues (2003) found seven factors that were related to successful collaborations: commitment, communication, strong leadership from key decision makers, understanding the culture of collaborating agencies, engaging in serious preplanning, providing adequate resources for collaboration, and minimizing turf issues. By interacting effectively with community service providers, educators can work to identify and address students' service and support needs.

Summary of Performance

IDEA 2004 changed the requirements for schools to conduct a comprehensive evaluation of students' eligibility for special education prior to graduation. The intent of the evaluation was to provide students and their families with documentation of a disability and the supports students would need to access postschool services and programs. Instead of an evaluation, in IDEA 2004 Congress included language that required secondary schools to provide a Summary of Performance (SOP) for each student graduating from high school or exiting the school system based on age:

> [T]he local education agency shall provide the child with a summary of the child's academic and functional performance, which shall include recommendations on how to assist the child in meeting the child's postsecondary goals. (Sec. 614c[5])

Focus Question 3	What are the recommended components of a Summary of Performance?

The statute and the subsequent regulations provided no additional definition or guidance on the content or structure of the SOP for states and local school districts. It is generally accepted that the SOP should include (a) a statement of the student's postschool goals; (b) a summary of the student's academic performance in such areas as reading, math, and writing; (c) a summary of the student's functional performance in such areas as social skills and behaviors, independent living skills, self-determination, and career or employment skills; (d) recommendations for accommodations, modifications, or supports that will be necessary for the student to achieve his or her postschool goals; and (e) statements from the student that articulate his or her perceptions of how his or her disability affected his or her performance in school, the accommodations and modifications that worked the best for him or her, and his or her strengths (Kochhar-Bryant & Izzo, 2006). In addition, the information included in the SOP should be sufficiently specific to meet the disability documentation requirements under federal laws, such as the Americans with Disabilities Act and Section 504 of the Vocational Rehabilitation Act. This can be facilitated by attaching assessment protocols and reports to the SOP that provide documentation of the student's disability or functional limitations with the consent of the student or his or her parents. Most states have developed policies and procedures to help educators develop SOPs.

Although the impact of the SOP on students' postschool adjustment is unknown at this point, the SOP offers a number of potential advantages to students and their families in facilitating a successful transition to community life. These include providing a comprehensive description of students' present level of performance that can assist in selecting appropriate services and programs, reducing the time necessary to determine eligibility for adult and community services, facilitating the identification accommodations and modifications for students as they enter postsecondary education institutions, and helping students be more effective in advocating for themselves.

Summary

Recent changes in federal regulations have had a significant impact on the development of students' IEPs/transition plans. These changes have sought to increase the control that students have in establishing their postschool goals and accessing the services necessary to achieve these goals. By definition, IEP/transition planning is a value-laden process. Consequently, it must be driven by the student's values, preferences, and needs. In order to honor the student's choices, educators and other school staff must be willing to release some control and empower the student and his or her family to lead the planning process whenever possible. In addition, the IEP/transition planning process must not be viewed as a one-time event. Rather, it should be structured as a cumulative process that gradually prepares the student to work and live successfully in the community. Finally, the process should be structured to educate the student and his or her family about the challenges that lie ahead and to help them develop the skills necessary to advocate for needed services and supports.

Focus Question Review

Focus Question 1: Why is family participation in the IEP/transition planning process so important for students with intellectual and developmental disabilities?

- Parents and families are often the primary source of support for young adults following school.
- Students often live with their parents after exiting school.

Focus Question 2: How can collaborative teams be organized so that they maximize the involvement of key individuals and the efficiency of planning?

- Establish a core team comprising individuals who have day-to-day responsibilities for implementing the student's IEP/transition plan.
- Establish an extended team comprising important individuals in the student's life who can participate in futures planning and as needed in the development of the IEP/transition plan.

Focus Question 3: What are the recommended components of a Summary of Performance?

- Statement of the student's postschool goals.
- Summary of the student's academic performance.
- Summary of the student's functional performance.
- Recommendations to enhance the student's access to and participation in postschool activities.

CHAPTER 6

Promoting Self-Determination

JAYNE MCGUIRE

T ransition planning is an essential step in preparing students with disabilities for adult life. The transition-related requirements included in the Individuals with Disabilities Education Act stipulate that all students aged 16 years and older must be invited to the Individualized Education Program meeting. Additionally, the student should be at the center of the planning process with a focus on his or her specific needs, preferences, and values. One way to ensure that students are central in the transition planning process is to encourage their active involvement, including goal identification and development. The skills and behaviors required for students to be active participants in the transition planning process are at the core of self-determination.

This chapter will define self-determination and discuss its importance in supporting students' transition to community life. In addition, strategies for promoting self-determined behavior during the IEP/transition planning process will be addressed. Finally, methods for infusing opportunities for students to learn self-determination skills in home, school, and community settings will be addressed.

Window 6-1

It's My Future—Don't I Have a Say?

Clay, a junior at an inclusive high school, has some strong ideas about what he wants to do as an adult. He wants to work with police officers or firefighters; he wants to earn his driver's license; he wants to live in an apartment with friends; he wants to play recreational basketball; and he wants to be respected as a valuable member of his community. Clay has an intellectual disability, and although his goals are similar to those of many of his schoolmates, he will likely need more support to realize them. Together with his teacher and family, he has identified his strengths and interests and used those as a guide to develop his transition plan. Clay and his planning team have also focused on identifying the areas where he will need support. Clay's transition plan, which was crafted collaboratively with him, focuses on helping him gain the skills he will need to be as independent as possible in his chosen path.

Self-Determination

Self-determination refers to a combination of skills, knowledge, and beliefs that enable a person to engage in self-directed, self-regulated, autonomous behavior (Field, Martin, Miller, Ward, & Wehmeyer, 1998). A student's actions are considered self-determined when they reflect a positive use of knowledge and understanding about his or her own strengths and limitations. Additionally, a self-determined student sets realistic goals, makes decisions, sees options, solves problems, acts as a self-advocate, and understands what supports are needed for success. According to Wehmeyer, Palmer, Agran, Mithaug, and Martin (2000), self-determination is often misinterpreted as a student doing everything for him- or herself. Instead, self-determination should be viewed through the lens of causal agency. This involves seeing the student as a catalyst for making things happen, without implying that he or she should be solely responsible for goal implementation or provision of supports needed.

Focus Question 1	What are the four characteristics of self-determined behavior?

Characteristics of Self-Determination

According to Wehmeyer, Agran, and Hughes (1998), there are four main characteristics of self-determined behavior. The first characteristic focuses on a student's ability to make decisions and choices as needed. This relates to acting anonymously or free from external influence or interference. The second characteristic, self-regulation, is demonstrated when a student implements some personal control over his or her actions. A third characteristic of self-determined behavior is psychological empowerment, which simply means that one acts in way that reflects his or her feelings of being capable and competent. The final characteristic, self-regulation, refers to an understanding of the effects of one's actions.

The characteristics of self-determination are supported by a set of skills that can be taught directly and tend to build over the course of one's life. These skills include choice making, decision making, problem solving, goal setting, self-observation, self-evaluation, self-reinforcement, self-instruction, self-advocacy, and self-awareness (Wehmeyer et al., 1998). As students grow in their ability to utilize these skills, they become increasingly self-determined.

Self-Determination and Transition

Self-determination and its effect on the adult outcomes for individuals with disabilities has been a primary focal point in special education for the past decade (Wehmeyer et al., 1998). Further, it is no coincidence that the self-determination movement within special education emerged in conjunction with the transition mandates (Wehmeyer, Palmer, Soukup, Garner, & Lawrence, 2007). Emerging evidence suggests that self-determination skills are positively correlated with adult outcomes and an individual's perception of his or her quality of life. Students with disabilities who behave in self-determined ways have a greater likelihood of being successful in adult life, including employment and community independence (Wehmeyer & Palmer, 2003). It has become best practice for transition teams to focus on promoting and enhancing self-determination as a means to improve outcomes for students with disabilities.

Self-determination contributes not only to adult outcomes but also to student involvement in the transition planning process. A recent study by Wehmeyer and colleagues (2007) reconfirmed the importance of self-determination in transition planning for students with intellectual and developmental disabilities. Their study demonstrated that self-determination as a whole and, particularly, student self-regulation and -realization were the most important contributors to student transition planning knowledge and skill. This relationship further supports the importance not only of involving students in transition planning but also of promoting self-determination as a means to promote more effective participation. Self-determination is improved by interventions that promote student involvement. Conversely, promoting self-determination can increase student capacity to effectively participate in educational planning.

Enhancing the capacity of students to be more self-determined includes promoting the development of decision-making, problem-solving, goal-setting, and self-management skills and self-advocacy. As a result, students who develop and practice skills related to self-determination become better able to plan for their futures, make meaningful decisions about their lives, take reasonable risks, and evaluate and make changes to their life circumstances.

Focus Question 2	Why is self-determination best learned in a "real-world" or community setting?

Learning Self-Determined Behavior

The promotion of self-determination is a complex process that necessitates a variety of educational activities across students' educational experiences. These activities include specific instruction in the component elements of self-determination, student involvement in educational planning and decision making, and opportunities to express preferences, make choices, and learn about individual strengths and limitations (Wehmeyer et al., 2000). Individualized skill instruction can increase a student's repertoire of behavioral and goal-related options. Interaction within supportive environments can provide students with opportunities to develop and support self-determined behaviors. Working with students to identify and develop support systems and accommodations can also lead to the development of self-determination. As students become self-determined, they increasingly make decisions, solve problems, advocate for themselves, and set and achieve personal goals.

Evidence supports the notion that the skills necessary for self-determination are best learned in social settings because they have a greater likelihood of generalizing than skills learned out of these contexts (Langone, Clees, & Oxford, 1995). This means that skills necessary for self-determination are best learned through real-world experiences. These experiences enable students to set goals, make choices, evaluate the outcome, and reflect on the process. The variations that occur in community-based settings provide a more ideal venue for students to engage in self-determined behavior than does the controlled environment of the traditional classroom.

A review of published literature on instructional strategies for self-determination found that instruction is enhanced through an ecological approach, self-determination emerges as an individual interacts with the environment, and the development of self-determination is enhanced by the advocacy of others (Malian & Nevin, 2002). Participation in real-world settings contributes to the psychological aspects of self-determination, as well as to developing specific skills. Supporting a student in becoming self-determined is about more than just community access, however. It involves providing structured opportunities for students to practice self-determined behavior, gain an awareness of options, and make meaningful decisions about their own futures.

In order for students to make meaningful contributions to their transition plans, they need to know themselves and understand how their disability affects their learning, relationships, employment, participation in their communities, and need for supports. This knowledge empowers students to develop plans, make decisions, and advocate for the supports that will be needed for adult success.

Promoting Self-Determination During Transition Planning

Self-determination is a broad construct made up of several subskills, behaviors, and beliefs. In their effort to support students in the transition process, teachers need to support the development of self-determined skills and beliefs, guide the process of goal setting, provide students with an understanding of the transition process, and build a supportive and comprehensive transition plan. Mason, Field, and Sawilowsky (2004) collected survey responses from special education teachers, administrators, and related service professionals regarding student participation in IEPs. They found that although teachers highly valued student involvement, only 28% indicated that they provided any instructional strategies to support student involvement prior to the IEP meeting.

Instructional Strategies to Increase Self-Determination

Self-determination is best taught through an ecological approach that looks at ways to embed opportunities for self-determination within other transition planning activities (Sands & Wehmeyer, 1996). In addition, embedding instruction on self-determination skills within routines and activities creates a wealth of opportunities for students to practice these skills in real-life contexts and situations.

An initial step in promoting the development of self-determination is teaching students to make choices. Teachers can do this through creating option-rich environments with several acceptable choices available to students. This allows them the freedom of choice within a slate of options that are specifically selected to support their specific needs. Some examples of areas of choice include the schedule of daily activities, lunch options, community activities, free-time activities, and extracurricular options. Teachers should create a slate of options based on the strengths and interests of their students. Students should be encouraged to exercise their right to choose and explore the reasons for the choices. When discussing choices with students, teachers should emphasize the role each student took in making the choice so they can encourage a sense of empowerment in making choices in the future. Following choice making, students should be encouraged to evaluate the outcome of their choices. The process of self-evaluation allows students to develop the characteristics of self-determined behavior, self-realization, self-advocacy, self-regulation, and autonomy.

Specific instructional models have been developed to support teachers in augmenting student self-determination. One such model is the Self-Determined Learning Model of Instruction, which was developed to help teachers promote self-regulated problem solving and enhance self-determination (Wehmeyer et al., 2000). The model provides teachers with a structure through which they can help students learn how to advocate for themselves. The model consists of a three-phase instructional process that involves students in answering a series of questions and includes a list of educational supports that can be used by teachers to support student self-directed learning (Table 6.1).

Table 6.1   Self-Determined Learning Model of Instruction

Phase 1

Set a Goal: What is my goal?

Student Question 1: What do I want to learn?
- Teacher Objectives:
  - Enable students to identify specific strengths and instructional needs.
  - Enable students to communicate preferences, interests, beliefs, and values.
  - Teach students to prioritize needs.

Student Question 2: What do I know about it now?
- Teacher Objectives:
  - Enable students to identify their current status in relation to the instructional need.
  - Help students gather information about opportunities and barriers in their environments.

Student Question 3: What must change for me to learn what I don't know?
- Teacher Objectives:
  - Enable students to decide if action will be focused on capacity building, modifying the environment, or both.
  - Support students to choose a need to address from a prioritized list.

Student Question 4: What can I do to make this happen?
- Teacher Objective:
  - Teach students to state a goal and identify criteria for achieving that goal.

Phase 2

Take Action: What is my plan?

Student Question 5: What can I do to learn what I don't know?
- Teacher Objective:
  - Enable students to self-evaluate current status and self-identify goal status.

Student Question 6: What could keep me from taking action?
- Teacher Objective:
  - Enable students to determine a plan of action to bridge the gap between self-evaluated current status and self-identified goal status.

Student Question 7: What can I do to remove these barriers?
- Teacher Objectives:
  - Collaborate with students to identify the most appropriate instructional strategies.
  - Teach students needed student-directed learning strategies.
  - Support students to implement student-directed learning strategies.
  - Provide mutually agreed-upon teacher-directed instruction.

Student Question 8: When will I take action?
- Teacher Objectives:
  - Enable students to determine the schedule for their action plan.
  - Enable students to implement their action plan.
  - Enable students to self-monitor their progress.

Phase 3

Adjust Goal of Plan: What have I learned?

Student Question 9: What actions have I taken?
- Teacher Objective:
  - Enable students to self-evaluate their progress toward goal achievement.

Student Question 10: What barriers have been removed?
- Teacher Objective:
  - Collaborate with students to compare progress with desired outcomes.

Student Question 11: What has changed about what I don't know?
- Teacher Objectives:
  - Support students to reevaluate their goal if progress is insufficient.
  - Help students decide if their goal remains the same or changes.
  - Collaborate with students to identify if an action is adequate or inadequate given their revised or retained goal.
  - Help students change their action plan if necessary.

Student Question 12: Do I know what I want to know?
- Teacher Objective:
  - Enable students to decide if progress is adequate or inadequate or if the goal has been achieved.

Self-determination and self-advocacy are closely related skills that enhance the capacity of students with disabilities to assume responsibility for their lives and transition effectively from school to community life. Recently, Test, Fowler, Wood, Brewer, and Eddy (2005) developed a conceptual framework for self-advocacy that includes four components: (a) knowledge of self, (b) knowledge of rights, (c) communication, and (d) leadership. In order for students to advocate for themselves, they must have an awareness of their rights, an awareness of their strengths and needs, and the ability to communicate those strengths and needs with others. Izzo and Lamb (2002) noted that just as students with disabilities need direct instruction in learning strategies, they also need instruction and modeling in self-advocacy. Teachers can promote self-advocacy by encouraging communication and self-representation with their students. Opportunities to speak in the classroom, school, and community provide students with a supported environment to develop the communication skills needed to be a self-advocate. Identification of strengths and needs is a critical component of self-advocacy and is the outcome of increased self-awareness (Wood, Karvonen, Test, Browder, & Algozzine, 2004). Students need to understand their strengths and needs in order to make achievable goals for their futures. Some teachers find it challenging to discuss the subject of disability with their students. Table 6.2 offers some strategies for talking with students about their disabilities.

Table 6.2 Strategies for Discussing Disability Issues With Students

- Focus on students' strengths and abilities while talking about specific disabilities.
- Help students understand that disability-specific terms are used for federal funding.
- Include famous people with disabilities in your discussion.
- Convey empowering messages like "Even though you have a disability, you can achieve realistic goals that you set for yourself."

The exploration of options available to students can be embedded within many settings. When students are aware of the options available, they are better able to make choices, evaluate the outcome, and set realistic goals. Along with an awareness of options, students benefit when they are able to apply problem-solving strategies to real-world situations. Problem-solving skills should be explicitly taught using situations that are relevant to the students. Problems or situations can be diagrammed to help students understand the possible outcomes. A problem-solving diagram that offers a sequential representation, illustrating options and outcomes, is useful when teaching problem-solving skills (Figure 6.1).

Figure 6.1   Illustration of a Problem-Solving Diagram

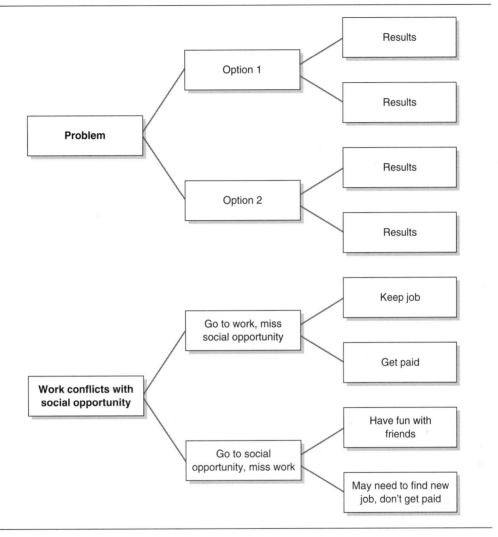

Involving Students in the
IEP/Transition Planning Process

Given the student-centered focus of IDEA, it is surprising that many students continue to be excluded from this important process (Agran & Hughes, 2008; Mason, Field, & Sawilowsky, 2004). Konrad (2008) suggests that students be directly involved in all stages of the IEP/transition planning process, including (a) developing background knowledge, (b) planning for the IEP/transition plan, (c) drafting postschool goals, (d) conducting the meeting, and (e) implementing the plan. She suggests a number of simple strategies that teachers can use to help students participate effectively in each phase (Table 6.3).

Table 6.3 Strategies for Prompting Student-Directed Transition Planning

Developing Background Knowledge

- Help students gain awareness about their disability through books, Web resources, and open discussions.
- Spend time with students reviewing their previous IEPs.
- Invite students to evaluate their IEPs to determine if they contain all of the sections required by law.

Planning for the IEP

- Help students develop vision statements for themselves, such as "After high school, I plan to live _____, learn _____, work_____, and play _____."
- Involve students in preparing for the meeting by writing.

Drafting the IEP

- Have students prepare a paragraph about their strengths and needs.
- Help them turn needs into "I will . . ." statements.
- Encourage students to bring home a draft to share with parents.

Meeting to Develop the IEP

- Keep in mind the range of options for student involvement. These can include attendance, greeter, agenda keeper, presenter, or any combination.
- Provide students with opportunities to rehearse for the meeting.

Implementing the IEP

- Help students create a fact sheet that summarizes their IEP for general education teachers and that includes their disability, strengths, needs, services, and accommodations.
- Teach students to self-monitor and self-evaluate their progress in meeting IEP goals.
- Have students develop progress reports to share with parents and their IEP team.

Research has suggested that several factors may lead to students' lack of involvement in their IEP process, including not understanding the purpose of the IEP/transition plan, not knowing how to become involved in the discussion, and feeling as if none of the adult participants listen to them when they talk (Agran & Hughes, 2008; Martin, Van Dycke, Christensen, et al., 2006). These findings support the importance of an increased focus on specifically teaching students how to participate in transition discussions. There are several commercial programs available to support student involvement in the IEP process. One such program is the Self-Directed IEP Instructional Model (Martin, Marshall, Maxson, & Jerman, 1997), an instructional tool for helping students learn how to advocate for themselves through participation in IEP planning meetings. The Self-Directed IEP Instructional Model is a multimedia lesson package that includes 11 instructional components, video segments depicting students involved in the lesson, a teacher's manual, and a student workbook, which has been found to be useful for increasing active student participation (Martin, Van Dycke, Christensen, et al., 2006). Successful application of the Self-Directed IEP Instructional Model has been shown to lead to improved student understanding and participation in IEP meetings (Arndt, Konrad, & Test, 2006). Whether teachers choose a packaged instructional program or develop a program to meet their students' specific needs, emphasis should be placed on helping students learn how to choose appropriate postschool outcomes, develop measurable goals, and advocate for themselves in planning and carrying out their IEP meetings.

Choosing Postschool Outcomes. Postschool outcomes need to be based on the student's strengths, preferences, and interests. Self-determination and advocacy skills are the key to ensuring a student-centered focus. It is critical that teachers and families support students in identifying postschool goals and the steps needed to achieve their goals through ongoing discussions, assessment, and instruction. This can be accomplished through regular futures planning with the student and the members of his or her extended planning team (see Chapter 5).

Developing Measurable Goals. Transition goals should target selected outcomes while considering present levels of academic achievement and functional performance. The student can contribute information about his or her strengths and present level of performance by stating his or her disability, strengths, and needed accommodations. Family members, teachers, and other members of the transition team may include additional information in this section.

The goals developed in the transition plan will take students from where they are currently (present level of performance) to where they want to be as adults (postschool outcomes). Students may need support in developing attainable goals with realistic timelines for their transition plans. The transition team can support students by discussing possible benchmarks that lead to goal attainment. Charting benchmarks onto a timeline provides a pictorial representation that can lead to increased student understanding.

Focus Question 3	What are the steps involved in student-directed IEP meetings?

Student-Directed IEP/Transition Planning Meetings. Prior to initiating student-directed IEP/transition planning meetings, teachers should obtain administrative support (Mason, McGahee-Kovac, & Johnson, 2004). Schools and school districts across the country have significantly different infrastructures and protocols. To obtain administrative approval, teachers may need to talk to any or all of the following individuals: department chairs, principals, and special education directors or other supervisory staff.

In order for students to be actively involved in their IEP/transition planning meetings, they first need to have some knowledge of the purpose of an IEP/transition plan, the rationale, and the main sections of the document (McGahee, Mason, Wallace, & Jones, 2001). To help students understand the purpose of an IEP/transition plan, teachers should begin by explaining that not all students have the benefit of having an individualized plan with direct focus on their unique strengths and needs. It should also be explained that the IEP/transition plan is a benefit to the students and they have the right and responsibility to be involved with its development. Students can learn about the various sections of the document by taking a teacher-narrated tour of their own IEP/transition plan. Typically, the most important sections to concentrate on, particularly in the beginning, are those that describe the nature of the student's disability; current levels of academic achievement; and need for positive behavioral supports, goals and objectives, accommodations, modifications, or other supports.

Students with disabilities, with support from other members of the IEP/transition planning team, are actively participating in their meetings. Students may participate in the preparations for the meeting, as well as the actual meeting itself. Preparation for the meeting may include assistance with the draft of the IEP/transition plan, development of a meeting agenda, creation of a portfolio to share at the meeting, development of the guest list, and creation and delivery of invitations. A meeting template or agenda is an excellent way to provide structure to the planning process and to ensure that all essential components are included in the meeting (Mason, McGahee-Kovac, et al., 2004). Teachers can support student readiness by initiating class discussions about their feelings regarding the meetings and by role-playing student-directed IEP/transition planning meetings in the classroom. Additionally, students and teachers can develop strategies or prompts to be used during the meeting to guide students' focus.

Students participate in IEP/transition planning meetings at several different levels. The entry level of student direction in the process involves students attending the meeting and sharing preselected information. At this level, students are considered full members of the team with an expectation of contribution. The second level of student direction involves coleadership or presentation at the meeting. The student shares responsibility for presenting information with the team leader. Students could read or present information that should be incorporated into the IEP/transition plan. This level of participation is most effective when there is a clear delineation of responsibilities prior to the meeting. The highest level of student direction involves students in a primary leadership role. The student greets everyone, makes introductions, shares the meeting agenda, and directs the conversation throughout the meeting. It is important to encourage students to participate to the greatest extent possible. That extent will vary with each student's understanding of the process and level of preparation. Once all the preparation is complete, it is time to host the meeting and support the student's leadership.

Summary

Student involvement in transition planning is an essential step in preparing students with disabilities for adult life. IDEA supports student involvement by requiring that the transition plan be developed around the student's strengths, preferences, and interests and by requiring students aged 16 years or older to be invited to the meeting. We know that increased levels of self-determination lead to improved adult outcomes for students with disabilities. Additionally, it is clear that student self-determination is improved by interventions that promote student involvement in the transition process. Teachers can support their students by teaching instructional strategies focused specifically on self-determination in relation to transition planning, by involving students in the transition planning process, and by giving students an opportunity to be actively involved in the IEP/transition planning meeting.

Focus Question Review

Focus Question 1: What are the four characteristics of self-determined behavior?
- Autonomous behavior
- Self-regulation

- Self-realizations
- Psychological empowerment

Focus Question 2: Why is self-determination best learned in a "real-world" or community setting?

- Community provides an opportunity for variability and risk taking.
- A real-world setting leads to greater generalization.
- Self-determination emerges as a student interacts with his or her environment.

Focus Question 3: What are the steps involved in student-directed IEP meetings?

- Obtain administrative approval.
- Teach students the meaning, purpose, and sections of the IEP.
- Prepare students for the IEP meeting.
- Determine level of student leadership.
- Support students during the meeting.

CHAPTER 7

Parent and Family Involvement

ANDREA P. MCDONNELL

CATHERINE NELSON

A dolescence, or the developmental stage between childhood and adulthood, is often identified as one of the most challenging phases for parenting (Turnbull, Turnbull, Erwin, & Soodak, 2006) and is marked by a number of major changes for both the adolescents and their families (Hanley-Maxwell, Pogoloff, & Whitney-Thomas, 1998; Kim & Turnbull, 2004; Lichtenstein, 1998). Adolescence is often viewed as beginning with puberty and continuing into young adulthood (Elliott & Feldman, 1990; Levinson, Darrow, Klein, Levinson, & McKee, 1978). Historically, the length of adolescence has expanded substantially, especially in societies where secondary and postsecondary education is common (Lichtenstein, 1998). It is not unusual for parents or other family members to continue to provide adolescents with financial support, as well as emotional support and guidance, well into young adulthood, while at the same time trying to encourage increasing autonomy and independence on the part of the young adult.

Beliefs about the age or life event(s) that signify becoming an adult, the rituals or celebrations that mark these events, and the expected roles of families in supporting adolescent family members vary widely from family to family and across various religious and cultural traditions (Dehyle & LeCompte, 1994; Preto, 1999). Gender, socioeconomic class, and decisions about participation in postsecondary education are additional factors that influence the timing and process of the transition from adolescence to adulthood (Koenigsburg, Garet, & Rosenbaum, 1994; Lichtenstein, 1998). Clearly, the transition from adolescence and school to adult life is a major life change for both young adults and their families, and different adolescents and families will approach this transition with different values, expectations, and ideas of how to make the transition successful.

Focus Question 1	How does transition affect families, and what are some of the barriers to actively involving families in transition planning, implementation, and evaluation?

If a young adult has an intellectual or a developmental disability, evidence suggests that the school-to-adult transition is often significantly more stressful for both the young adult and his or her family (Ferguson & Ferguson, 2000; Jordan & Dunlap, 2001). In addition to all of the changes and decisions usually related to this transition, young adults with disabilities and their families face (a) the end of the entitlement to familiar school-based special education services and (b) the need to identify, apply for, and coordinate services and informal supports across a wide array of life functions, with the preferred adult services often not being available at the time the family and young adult would choose to access them (Sheehey & Sheehey, 2007; Turnbull et al., 2006).

Families have been defined in a variety of ways—for example, as two or more individuals who are related by birth, marriage, or adoption and who live together (Turnbull et al., 2006). Within this chapter, we will use a broader definition of *family*. "Families include two or more people who regard themselves as a family and who carry out the functions that families typically perform. These people may or may not be related by blood or marriage and may or may not usually live together" (Turnbull et al., 2006, p. 7). Families play an important role in supporting an adolescent's transition to adult life and provide "both foundation and the context for the decisions made during the transition-time period" (Hanley-Maxwell et al., 1998, p. 235). This chapter will provide an overview of issues affecting parents and families during transition, key roles for family members, and strategies for encouraging and supporting parent and family participation in the design, implementation, and evaluation of the adolescent's transition to adult life.

Issues Affecting Parent and Family Involvement in Transition Planning

Importance of Parent and Family Involvement

There is consistent evidence from more than 3 decades of research that family members' involvement in their children's education results in improved student outcomes, including more consistent attendance and retention (Falbo, Lein, & Amador, 2001; Henderson & Berla, 1994), improved behavior in school (Gonzalez, 2002), improved homework completion rates (Balli, Demo, & Wedman, 1998; Callahan, Rademacher, & Hildreth, 1998; Cooper, Lindsay, & Nye, 2000), and improved academic performance (Chavkin, Gonzalez, & Rader, 2002; Finn, 1998; Keith et al., 1998; Shaver & Walls, 1998). In spite of the consistency of research findings concerning the importance of parent involvement for a variety of student outcomes, many of the studies do not include families and students with disabilities, and family involvement has been studied more frequently for elementary students than for secondary students (SRI International, 2005). However, recent research indicates that family involvement improves educational behaviors and outcomes for secondary students as well as for children from a variety of backgrounds and income levels (Turnbull et al., 2006).

Families of children with disabilities have been instrumental in the development of disability law, policy, educational services, and community services (SRI International, 2005; Turnbull et al., 2006). Although the research base is somewhat limited regarding students with disabilities and their families, there is every reason to believe that family participation is at least as important in the attainment of a variety of outcomes for students with disabilities (Council for Exceptional Children, 2001). Available research suggests that parental participation is very important to successful transition outcomes, including the identification and maintenance of employment (Luft, 2008). Family participation and involvement in transition planning may be especially crucial in determining ongoing adult quality of life for individuals with intellectual and developmental disabilities, for whom complete independence in all areas of adult life may not be a realistic goal. Many young adults with intellectual or developmental disabilities will continue to live at home with their families for a number of years, making an interrelated quality of life even more evident and important to consider (Kim & Turnbull, 2004).

However valuable education and social services are to their children with disabilities, it is beyond argument that social support and friendships are the ultimate safety nets for the children and their families. Special education is important, and the benefits that come from various federal and state programs are important. But without the support of family and friends, especially those in school and work, the programs are unlikely to provide the kind of life that everyone wants to have. (Turnbull et al., 2006, p. 276)

Challenges and Barriers to Family Participation

In spite of the importance of family members' participation during an adolescent's transition, there are a number of challenges and barriers to their active involvement. Research studies demonstrate that parents' participation at IEP meetings and in school activities tends to decrease as their child with disabilities gets older (Smith, Gartin, Murdick, & Hilton, 2006), although a recent national survey of parents of secondary students with disabilities found that nearly 9 out of 10 parents report participating in at least one IEP in the current or prior school year, and their overall participation in school-based activities indicated they were more involved than parents of secondary students in the general population (SRI International, 2005). However, families of students with disabilities whose children were placed away from their neighborhood school to receive special education services had decreased family participation in school programs (SRI International, 2005). Some barriers to family participation may be primarily logistical, such as work scheduling conflicts, transportation problems, or needing child care for younger children in the family. Other barriers may be based on a lack of knowledge about the transition process and future program and support options, a breakdown in communication with school personnel, or an orientation to the present that makes future planning seem too difficult or even undesirable. A recent summary of barriers to family participation in the transition planning process included

- Lack of thought given to child's future
- Assumption that the school system would continue to provide for their child
- Fear of the future
- Lack of knowledge of adult service agencies
- Conflicting aspirations of the parents and child
- Assumption that professionals know best and should lead the planning process
- Lack of information about what the transition planning process entails
- Expectations that are not challenging enough for the student (too low)

- Expectations that may not be attainable (excessively high)
- Lack of time and energy to devote to planning
- A focus on day-to-day concerns and not on the long-term future (Steere, Rose, & Cavaiuolo, 2007, p. 63)

Although research studies have had somewhat mixed results and have frequently been confounded by such factors as socioeconomic status, it nevertheless appears that many families from culturally and linguistically diverse backgrounds are less involved in educational decision making for their children with disabilities than are parents who are more a part of the mainstream culture (Kalyanpur & Harry, 1999). A variety of factors may contribute, including cultural traditions of deferring to experts or those in authority (Greene, 1996; Lynch & Hanson, 2004), a lack of knowledge about their rights and options for their child, and prior negative experiences with professionals in education or other agencies, including a deficit view of families and an underestimation of parents' actual participation in the transition planning process (Harry, 2008).

> Parents who do not believe that they can challenge school authorities are likely to withdraw from participation. Out of a traditional respect for authority, however, they may continue to defer to professionals, yet fail to cooperate with professional recommendations or even to respond to an invitation to participate. (Harry, 1992, p. 475)

Misunderstandings can easily arise from different expectations of the roles of families and professionals in the transition planning process, and it is important to continue to listen to families and not to interpret their level or type of participation as an evaluation of the transition team, the transition planning process, or their level of support for their adolescent or young adult child.

Family Systems Model and Transition Planning

In order to understand how to develop partnerships during transition for individuals with intellectual and developmental disabilities, it is helpful to develop a better understanding of the strengths and challenges of individual families and how this may influence participation, needed support, and decision making during the transition planning process. One comprehensive model for understanding families, the complexity and interaction of factors influencing family members, and considerations for partnerships is Family Systems Theory or the Family Systems Approach (Turnbull,

Summers, & Brotherson, 1984, 1986; Turnbull et al., 2006). Systems theory (Whitechurch & Constantine, 1993) and Family Systems Theory are based on three assumptions. The first assumption is that characteristics serve as "inputs" into the system. Within the Family Systems framework, these inputs include characteristics of the family as a whole (e.g., size, membership, socioeconomic status); characteristics of individual members, including family member(s) with disabilities; and any special challenges faced by one or more family members (e.g., homelessness or substance abuse) (Turnbull, Summers, et al., 1984, 1986; Turnbull, Turnbull, et al., 2006). The second assumption of systems theory and Family Systems Theory is that the system can be understood only as a whole, not as one or more of its parts. The third assumption of systems theory and Family Systems Theory is that boundaries will develop among family members and also between family members and outside relationships and influences, based on previous and ongoing inter-actions. As a high school teacher, a transition coordinator, or another service provider, you may encounter many of these changing boundaries.

All of the preceding components affect the "outputs" of a family, or how well the family meets various family functions, including the need of family members for (a) affection, (b) self-esteem, (c) spirituality, (d) economic sup-port, (e) daily physical care and health needs (e.g., cooking, laundry, and transportation), (f) socialization, (g) recreation, and (h) education (Turnbull, Summers, et al., 1984, 1986; Turnbull, Turnbull, et al., 2006). These family functions may overlap (cooking may be daily physical care, recreation, and socialization); however, for teachers, it is well worth considering how difficult it is to balance these various needs across family members and over time. It is especially important to consider the time demands already placed on fam-ily members as we partner with families during transition planning and to recognize that what might be optimal for an individual with intellectual or developmental disabilities may also create tensions or problems for family members. The life cycle stage of a family will often have significant impli-cations for the varying demands and joys of a family supporting an adoles-cent or a young adult in the transition process. If this is the last child at home, if an aging grandparent is in need of caregiving and support, or if young children are still being raised in the family, this will inevitably affect the transition planning process.

One of the key recognitions of Family Systems Theory and recent research on families is that individuals with disabilities may make positive, negative, and neutral contributions to their families over time, as is true for all family members (Turnbull et al., 2006). Consequently, although it is impor-tant to be aware of the many challenges that families face during the transi-tion process, it is equally important to recognize the many contributions an adolescent or a young adult with intellectual or developmental disabilities may be making to his or her family during this time.

Family Diversity and Possible Influences on Transition Planning

> When a person names particular children and families as being cultur-ally diverse, that individual must simultaneously name himself or her-self as being diverse from them. Calling "them" diverse without also calling oneself culturally diverse fails to recognize the relational aspect of diversity. It implicitly assumes a hierarchy of power within which only the namer has the privilege of setting the norm and naming the other(s) in reference to that norm. (Barrera & Corso, 2003, p. 7)

The United States is one of the most culturally and linguistically diverse countries in the world (Vaughn, Bos, & Schumm, 1997), and this diversity is increasing (Luft, 2008). For example, only about 12% of the U.S. population was identified as "nonwhite" in the 1970 Census. By 2000, nearly 30% of the U.S. population was identified as such (U.S. Census Bureau, 2000), and pop-ulation growth is higher for minority population groups, including African Americans, American Indians/Alaska Natives, Asians, and Hispanic or Latino populations (Luft, 2008; U.S. Census Bureau, 2004). As the previous quote from Barrera and Corso (2003) indicates, diversity is referenced to a norm, and depending on the point of reference, everyone is from a diverse cultural background or differs in many ways from others in the larger community. Individuals identified as "minorities" within the U.S. Census, or other larger groups within society, may in fact be the majority in a number of urban and rural communities. Another important insight in the quote from Barrera and Corso is the uneven power relationship and the ability to set the "norms." The transition from adolescence to adulthood is heavily culturally influ-enced, and IDEA and other disability laws and policies in the United States are heavily based on "mainstream" European-American cultural perspectives and values (Harry, 2008). This can create issues for families and teachers who come from differing or diverse backgrounds as they approach transi-tion planning together.

Luft (2008) identified four "essential elements" in which this predom-inance of mainstream cultural ideas is related to the transition process within the framework of IDEA. First, "consideration of the student's needs, strengths, interests, and preferences" (p. 54) is mandated. However, many cultural groups will consider the needs of the group or interdependence among group members as more important or taking precedence over such values as individual needs and preferences, self-reliance, or independence (Harry, 1992; Joe & Malach, 2004; Lynch & Hanson, 2004). The second essential element is the "outcome (results) oriented process" (Luft, 2008, p. 54). However, a goal-driven orientation and the desired outcomes may vary a great deal across cultures (Nieto, 2000), and it is important for transition team members not to impose their outcomes or the process of working toward outcomes in opposition to family and young adult values. The third essential element of transition planning is a "coordinated set of activities" (Luft, 2008, p. 54). In fact, IDEA requires teachers and other school personnel to invite individuals from community and adult service agencies who may provide assistance to the young adult with intellectual disabilities and his or her family in the future to participate in transition planning. However, in many cultures, there may be a preference for meeting future needs within the family or immediate community, and asking for help from a large team of professionals may be especially difficult (Luft, 2008). The fourth essential element of transition is "movement from school to postschool activities" (Luft, 2008, p. 56). Again, culture heavily influences what may be viewed as desirable "postschool" activities. Is this living at home as part of a loving extended family or living in a supported living arrangement in the community? Is this postsecondary education, employment, or helping the family with caregiving and other activities? Values and the way they influence transition planning may differ as much across families within the "same" cultural group as they do across cultural perspectives (Lynch & Hanson, 2004), so it would be inappropriate to develop assumptions about how families from Hmong, Guatemalan, or other cultural backgrounds will approach transition planning. However, it is important to consider these essential elements of transition planning and possible cultural differences as we work in partnership with families and young adults (see Point/Counterpoint 7.1).

POINT/COUNTERPOINT 7.1

Differing Dreams for Estella

There are times in transition planning when conflicts arise between service providers and parents in what they see as future needs for an individual with disabilities. Differences in cultural values can arise and cause such conflict. In this Point/Counterpoint, we look at how cultural values clash between a family from Mexico who values providing for its daughter at home and teachers who see work placement and supported living as preferred options for an individual with severe disabilities.

POINT

Estella is a 19-year-old who has multiple disabilities, including cerebral palsy and a severe visual impairment. She is able to walk with the help of a walker and communicate basic needs using enlarged picture symbols. She lives at home with her parents and five younger brothers and sisters. Her mother, Gloria, came to the United States from Mexico with her husband 20 years ago. She has always planned for Estella to stay at home after finishing school. Throughout Estella's life, Gloria has taken care of her and says it would be shameful to have her live outside of the home. She does not feel Estella needs a job because the family can provide for her needs and is thus not interested in transition planning with her daughter's teachers. She says that Estella loves being at home with her family and is always happy there. Her brothers and sisters have promised to always take care of her. Gloria is grateful for all the teachers have done but feels that as Estella leaves the school, it is time for the family to take over.

COUNTERPOINT

Estella's IEP and transition team suggested to Gloria that she sign Estella up for adult services, including respite care and supported living. There is a long waiting list for services, and they feel that she should get on the list. Gloria has repeatedly said that she is not interested in any of the services. The classroom teacher would like to explore work options, but Gloria has refused to look at any possible work sites. Estella's teacher is frustrated and is worried that Estella will be sitting home with nothing to do after she finishes school. She thinks it is unfair that her siblings are being asked to do so much to take care of her and wishes that Gloria would at least look at the options available that would encourage Estella's independence.

| **Focus Question 2** | What are key roles for parents and other family members during the transition? |

Key Roles for Parents and Families in Transition

Continuity and Support of Young Adolescents Through Young Adulthood

Transitions in the lives of families of individuals with intellectual and developmental disabilities are many and frequent. Families often are faced with a transition from hospital care to home, from early intervention services to preschool, from preschool to elementary school, from elementary school to secondary school, and from secondary school to work and adult services. Families are also involved in transitions from infancy to childhood, from childhood to adolescence, and from adolescence to young adulthood (Smith et al., 2006; Turnbull et al., 2006). Each transition involves a reevaluation and readjustment of family roles, needs, and resources. Successful transitions begin early and keep an eye to the future.

For the majority of young adolescents moving toward young adulthood, families are the primary source of support and guidance. Teachers and adult service providers fulfill important roles, but it is family support that is most likely to be constant and enduring across time (Smith et al., 2006). Beginning in childhood, families of children with and without disabilities set expectations and provide work experiences. Families can provide a safe base from which children and young adults reach out to the outside world and prepare to make the transitions that await them. The role of providing support while letting go is an important one as students prepare to leave school for the workplace, as well as one home for another.

Window 7-1

Roots and Wings

I can still remember looking at our daughter 30 years ago as she lay on the floor, staring at the bright lights in the ceiling and making strange noises. I wondered: "What does the future hold for her?" She was almost two, did not walk and did not appear to have much going for her.

I would reflect on such questions as: "Would she be able to attend school? If so what kind? Would she be able to talk? How would we communicate with her? What would she do all day? Would she still be scooting on her back when she was 20 years old?" My wife and I did not have any answers but did have a basic philosophy which stated that we need to give all our children "roots and wings." By "roots" we mean those basics in life on which we build in order to do life reasonably well. "Roots" ought to be established by the time children are between 18 and 20. Then they need to start flapping their "wings" so they can move out and on.

This philosophy also included our daughter with dual sensory impairments, mild cerebral palsy and epilepsy. An extremely important "root" for our three daughters was a work ethic. This was not easy for someone like our daughter with special needs. But whatever her abilities were, we needed to start with the basics, such as:

Sharing Household Responsibilities

She had chores, very simple ones such as picking up toys, putting her dirty clothes in the laundry basket, taking her dishes from the table to the sink. (Yes, we lost a fair number of dishes.) As she became older the responsibilities and scope of work were increased. Carrying dishes to the sink translated into washing the dishes. (Yes, still more broken dishes.)

Meeting Time Lines

The tasks to which she was assigned had to be finished by a certain time. Did this cause problems? You bet! Sometimes I would think: "It would be a lot easier to do it myself!" But would our daughter learn anything by doing the task for her? Obviously not! But she did learn from suffering the consequences. (No TV that evening. Or, go to bed earlier. Or, no dessert.)

Attitude

Most of the time our daughter did not really want to follow through with her responsibilities and would develop a negative attitude. Inevitably this would be counterproductive to her doing a good job. We tried to overcome this by suggesting that if we developed a negative attitude about all the things we do for her (meals, laundry, chauffeuring, on and on) it would not be a very pleasant home. Eventually she received the message that a lousy attitude would only be another handicap for her.

Do Your Best the First Time

This was probably one of the more difficult work ethics to instill. Her "best" did not always meet our standards of "best" and sometimes her vision prevented her from seeing details. When she was a teenager we assigned her a car to clean every Saturday. Because she knew that she was never going to drive a car she was not very interested in maintaining one and at first tried to do a minimal job. But she discovered that she had to do it over until she did it right. At first, we encountered a great deal of resistance but then she caught on: "Do it right the first time and then I'm finished."

Work Equals Money and Money Means Power

Her two sisters learned this through baby-sitting but in Heidi's early teenage years she was not baby-sitting material. However, there were other jobs she could do for extra money and [she] soon learned that doing jobs for money gave her spending power to buy some of the things she wanted.

Was it easy to teach her a work ethic? Not at all! She resisted much of the time. Other times she did such a lousy job that we wondered if it was worth it, but we knew that we had to give her the tools. Too many times we parents have a tendency to "baby" our children with special needs and allow them not to learn a work ethic.

My wife and I had many a "discussion" about this issue. She often felt I was too demanding and I would complain that she was too soft. Eventually we learned to compromise and both took more of a middle position. And eventually Heidi developed a work ethic which allowed her to enter the work-a-day world and be successful.

—Bill Aulenbach, Father

Family Specialist, CDBS

Note. From "Roots and Wings," by B. Aulenbach, 1997, *reSources* 9(1), p. 1. Reprinted with permission. The California Deaf-Blind Services *reSources* newsletters are supported in whole or in part by the U.S. Department of Education, Office of Special Education Programs (Award No. H32c030017). However, the opinions expressed therein do not necessarily reflect the policy or position of the U.S. Department of Education, Office of Special Education Programs, and no official endorsement by the department should be inferred. The URL for the complete edition of *reSources* (Vol. 9, No. 1) is http://www.sfsu.edu/~cadbs/Winter97.html.

As educators support transitions from school to work, it is important that they enlist the help of families in identifying and obtaining employment opportunities (Ferguson, Ferguson, Jeanchild, Olson, & Lucyshyn, 1993). Families know their children and their abilities and interests and have knowledge of many community resources. Families often have many opportunities to observe their children doing home tasks that may relate to future job placements, and they know if potential jobs will fit within their values and culture. They can use their social networks to help identify employment opportunities (Westling & Fox, 2008). Research also tells us that if families are not involved in employment selection, the chances of that employment being maintained are lessened (Buckley, Mank, & Sandow, 1990; Salomone, 1996).

While postschool employment is important, it is just one piece of the transition package. Community participation with leisure and socialization opportunities is also important. Again, families can help identify resources that can broaden opportunities. They can identify peers who have been friendly and after-school social activities that have been successful, and they can identify favored social, leisure, and recreational opportunities (Westling & Fox, 2008). Strategies and opportunities that have been successful can be built upon to create more opportunities and a larger social network.

Wehmeyer, Morningstar, and Husted (1999) suggest that "during transition, families should be dreamers, expect to contribute by talking, ask school personnel to be clear and specific, support the student's efforts to be a self-advocate, keep the focus on the student's strengths rather than deficits, and support the school's efforts to provide vocational training and career development" (pp. 39–40).

Balancing Family Needs and Supports While Understanding the Individual Within Broader Community and Service Contexts

At the same time we recognize the importance of family involvement in the transition process, it is also important to recognize that families face difficult dilemmas as they support their adolescents in this time of major transition (Thorin, Yovanoff, & Irvin, 1996). Family involvement when it comes to adolescents without disabilities typically decreases as they prepare to transition out of the home, but families of adolescents with disabilities often must have increased intensive involvement as the transition approaches (Thorin et al., 1996). Families may be very involved in the transition but are often pessimistic about their children's future in the work environment (Kraemer & Blacher, 2001). A qualitative study of nine students with severe disabilities by Cooney (2002) found that as families attempt to support their young adult children, there is often a discrepancy between what they want and expect in terms of adult services and what is actually available. Cooney also looked at the goals of parents and found they wanted their adolescent children to be able to use their talents and abilities and contribute to their communities. However, another finding of the study was that transition meetings rarely provided meaningful opportunities for participation by either family members or the student. In another study that utilized focus groups and interviews, parents expressed frustration at an often complex and inconsistent adult service system (Timmons, Whitney-Thomas, McIntyre, Butterworth, & Allen, 2004). The study also found that families in rural environments faced increased challenges because of lack of availability of postschool options.

Person-Family Interdependent Planning

In response to the need to support individuals with intellectual and developmental disabilities and their families during often stressful transitions, two positive approaches to individualized support and planning emerged. The first evolved from the quality-of-life movement and involves person-centered planning (Kim & Turnbull, 2004). Several strategic processes exemplify person-centered planning (Hanley-Maxwell et al., 1998). These include the Lifestyle Planning Process (O'Brien & Lyle, 1987), the McGill Action Planning System (Vandercock, York, & Forest, 1989), and Personal Futures Planning (Mount, 1992, 1995). Common to all of these approaches is the focus on the individual's talents, strengths, preferences, and dreams; the importance of planning occurring within a group format; and finally the development of goals with subsequent identification of resources, supports, and action steps (Butterworth et al., 1993). The strategies are based on the assumptions that individuals with disabilities have rights to a community presence and community participation and that they be considered competent, have valued community roles, and have choices about both everyday matters and those that will have a greater life impact (O'Brien & Lovett, 1992).

The second approach, family-centered planning, emerged from the field of early intervention and involves a focus on family members as active decision makers and the development and provision of services and goals that meet the needs of the family of the child with disabilities (Kim & Turnbull, 2004). In this model, families are viewed as the ultimate decision makers (Bailey et al., 1998). Central to this approach is the tenet that every family has strengths as well as needs, preferences, resources, and visions (Saleebey, 1996).

However, as individuals with intellectual and developmental disabilities approach the transition from school to adulthood, there is a need to combine the strengths of both approaches into what Kim and Turnbull (2004) term a Person-Family Interdependent Planning Approach. This holistic model is important when one looks at transition as affecting not only the individual with disabilities but rather the family as a whole. The entire family is affected by the approaching transition as its members face often limited adult services (Ferguson & Ferguson, 2000; Kraemer & Blacher, 2001). Although self-determination is fundamental to successful transitions and quality of life (Wehmeyer & Schalock, 2001), young adults with severe disabilities may continue to need to rely on the support of those who have their best interest at heart, and such individuals are often family members (Jordan & Dunlap, 2001; Turnbull & Turnbull, 2001). In addition, planning for quality of life must include, and be colored by, the family's interpretation of the meaning of "quality of life" (Bailey et al., 1998). Therefore, transition planning that utilizes a Person-Family Interdependent Planning Approach takes into account the culture and values of the family, as well as family members' need to be a continuing source of support and advocacy in the lives of their adult children.

Person-Centered Interdependent Planning in Action

There are times when families find that their role in transition goes beyond that of support. When desired community services do not exist, the family may be in a position of advocate as well as broker and creator of new services.

Window 7-2

James, Joe, and Risa's House

Three years ago, I was involved in the creation of a living arrangement for my son Joe, and two friends, Risa and James (JRJ). Joe is tall, handsome, and if one is not seeking a conversationalist, a soul-mate. Risa and Joe were an "item" at the time. They remain affectionate friends. Risa has another guy (or two) in her life. Joe, incidentally, is dating Risa's ex-roommate. James has a great smile and loves to be with his Mom and Dad. He also enjoys riding a tandem bicycle, shooting hoops, riding horses, dancing, and dates two local girls he went to school with. Joe likes to jog, and enjoys bicycling as well.

We were attracted to several supported living principles. Our regional center, however, wanted the place to be licensed. So, we set out to personalize the living arrangement within rules of Community-Care Licensing and the Department of Developmental Services. We are proud of several innovations that we put into place:

- Extensive, up-front use of person-centered planning;
- Separation of housing from services;
- Ownership of the home by interested family members;
- Individual lease agreements with sharing of utilities;
- Greater control by JRJ of their own financial affairs;
- Establishment of a microboard, a non-profit society of family and friends;
- James, Joe, and Risa being employees of those who provide paid support;
- Involvement of volunteers; and
- Use of quality-of-life mapping.

Early on, we had three separate planning meetings, one for each person, using PATH (Planning Alternative Tomorrows with Hope). Our goal was simply to see how the lives of the three might continue to intersect. They had been playing on the same baseball team for two years. Each wanted or needed a different living arrangement. In the process, we discovered common aspirations as well as unique needs. The possibility (indeed, desirability) of JRJ living together evolved from those gatherings.

James and Joe's fathers talked with our local housing authority, but Section 8 Rental Assistance was ruled out, because our housing authority doesn't use the "shared housing" option for unrelated adults. We learned more about preferences (e.g., "life in the neighborhood"; adequate backyard) as we looked at homes and apartments. Ultimately, for investment, life planning, stability, and other reasons, six of us decided to buy a suitable house. The Willis Drive Partnership was formed to hold the property, with one of the mothers agreeing to collect rents and perform other property management functions (e.g., repairs, end-of-year accounting for tax purposes, etc.).

While Options3, Inc., our microboard, holds the license on the house, and our Treasurer (Joe's aunt) deposits and writes checks, we decided to recycle some of the money. Each month, the Treasurer sends each of the three a check for $500. James, Joe and Risa deposit their checks in their checking accounts at a local bank, and each month they pay their rent ($275 each) and split utilities (PG&E, garbage, cable TV, and the common telephone) four ways with their paid housemate. Options3, Inc., pays $325 in rent on behalf of the paid housemate. Estimated utilities are $75 per month each. If JRJ are careful (e.g., turning off lights, setting the thermostat low), they have about $150 per month each for discretionary outlays. Food at home is funded separately to encourage family-style main meals.

The microboard concept is growing in popularity in British Columbia and elsewhere, where Individual Funding (e.g., personal budgets) and service brokerage have taken hold. A microboard is like an incorporated Circle of Friends, a group of people who agree to stand beside and support each other. As a group, we commit to James, Joe, and Risa, wherever life takes each of them, whether Options3, Inc. is the service delivery vehicle or not. Our microboard is a newly-formed, California, non-profit, public benefit corporation. It holds the residential license. We asked Risa to be President. She declined, but accepted the vice-presidency.

(Continued)

(Continued)

A critically important feature of the home is having JRJ as employers of the people who provide paid support. Risa speaks for herself. James and Joe have limited conservators-of-the-person, who function as Personal Advocates, assisting James and Joe in making employment decisions. Family and friends screen applicants, who are always interviewed by JRJ and their support team. Licensed homes for three are financially tricky. JRJ's home has a designated service level of 4G, which means that it must provide 55 hours a week of a second person on-duty. For those hours, the effective staff ratio is 2:1 or 1:1, and this permits considerable individualization. It works financially, only because seven family members and friends, as volunteers, have divvied up various administrative and coordinative functions. Because biking (and, for Joe, running) are favorite activities, we sought a "paid volunteer" to share those interests. We found a wonderful young man through a health club in town. He runs (or bikes) with the guys fifteen times a month, and receives a small stipend to cover mileage and other expenses.

In Level 4 homes that are licensed, it is traditional to "take data," and to file quarterly reports with the regional center. At an early planning meeting, James's mother asked why, if her son were the employer, he would ask an employee to "take data." Good point. We suggested, and our regional center approved, an alternative called quality-of-life mapping. The individual, family, and friends identify "success indicators" and get together in small groups to plot on a ten-point scale where the person would be if everything were going well, and where he/she actually is. If these two diverge by much, the group brainstorms ways to bringing the two scores closer together. In my son's case, he quickly put on 35 pounds when he moved into his own home. The recruitment of a paid volunteer, beyond its social dimension, was part of a plan to redress the balance between calories in and calories out.

Because we were creating a living arrangement from scratch, we had a wonderful opportunity to be creative. It was, of course, a lot of work. We don't believe in models (or templates), but would encourage anyone to take from our experience anything that makes sense for those they love and support.

—John Shea, Parent Advocate

Allen, Shea & Associates

Note. From "James, Joe and Risa's House," by J. Shea, 1998, reSources 10(3), p. 1. Reprinted with permission. The California Deaf-Blind Services reSources newsletters are supported in whole or in part by the U.S. Department of Education, Office of Special Education Programs (Award No. H32c030017). However, the opinions expressed therein do not necessarily reflect the policy or position of the U.S. Department of Education, Office of Special Education Programs, and no official endorsement by the department should be inferred. The complete edition of reSources (Vol. 10, No. 3) is available from http://www.sfsu.edu/~cadbs/News.html.

Many communities offer participant direction of funding and support. This allows family members to broker services based on person-centered planning or person-centered interdependent planning (Beach Center on Disability, 2008). The first step in this process is to convene a person-centered planning team and develop a plan that focuses on the dream or vision that both the individual and his or her "allies" have for his or her life. The team then decides what supports are needed in order to achieve this lifestyle vision, and financial resources are gathered. A fiscal intermediary is identified to manage funds, and human supports, such as housemates, job coaches, and personal assistants, are identified. A budget is then developed based on identified needs, and the vision becomes a reality. Finally, the plan is revisited frequently both to ensure its continued success and to meet legal requirements. Reports must be filed with state and local agencies to ensure that public monies are well spent and the individual's needs are actually being met. Such a process is obviously time- and resource-intensive but may meet the needs of some families and individuals with disabilities to develop new and individualized services that reflect family and person-centered planning.

Guardianship and Families

Another role that families of individuals with disabilities will need to consider as they approach the postschool transition is that of guardian. When children reach the age of 18 years, the law presumes that they are able and competent to make all of their own decisions unless it is proven otherwise. If parents wish to continue to have authority after their children turn 18, they must file for guardianship (Resource Foundation for Children with Challenges, 2000; Varnet, 2006). There are five main types of guardianship: guardianship of person, guardianship of property, full guardianship, limited guardianship, and temporary guardianship. These are described in Point/Counterpoint 7.2, and it is important that teachers and others who support families during this transition help them understand each type. Once considered a necessity, the role of guardianship is now questioned as intrusive and counterproductive to self-determination (Harris, 2005; Hoyle, 2005). Payne-Christiansen and Sitlington (2008) recommend the issue of guardianship be an integral part of the transition planning process and that it be based on ongoing assessments of "the student's strengths, needs, preferences, and interests" (p. 17). The transfer of rights should be seen as a pivotal point in transition planning rather than used as a warning or a threat (Payne-Christiansen & Sitlington, 2008).

POINT/COUNTERPOINT 7.2

Guardianship

Guardianship is a legal means of protecting individuals who are unable to make decisions in their own best interests, take care of themselves, or handle their own assets. Many parents assume that they will be their children's guardians throughout their lives; however, legally an adult is presumed competent unless deemed otherwise. After a child reaches the age of 18, regardless of disability, parents are no longer the child's legal guardian unless they go through the legal process to have the individual declared incompetent and in need of a guardian. The disability itself is not reason enough to declare an individual incompetent; rather it is the incapacity of the individual to make his or her own decisions. Recently, advocacy groups for individuals with disabilities, such as TASH, have called for a curtailment of the pervasive use of guardianship (Hoyle, 2005). In this Point/Counterpoint, we look at issues of guardianship from both the perspective of it being important for individuals with disabilities (Point) and the perspective that it should be used only as a last resort (Counterpoint).

POINT

Parents are usually very involved in the medical and personal care of their children with severe disabilities, and such needs do not automatically change at age 18. Individuals with severe disabilities are a vulnerable population and should not be at the mercy of people who are less than scrupulous. Parents need to ensure that their adult children are not taken advantage of financially, personally, or sexually. Guardianship laws currently have provisions to ensure that guardianship is not used lightly. The laws of every state require due process and that an adult child has a representative called a guardian *ad litem* at the guardianship hearing.

Most states have several levels of guardianship, including (a) guardian of person, wherein an individual needs assistance with personal issues, such as consent for medical treatment and where to live; (b) guardian of property, in which the guardian has power over the individual's property or

COUNTERPOINT

Guardianship of individuals with disabilities is pervasive in our society yet is seldom needed and severely impinges on the rights of individuals with disabilities. It goes against the principles of self-determination and removes constitutional rights of individuals, including where to live, what kind of work to do, how to spend money, and whom to spend time with (Harris, 2005).

School professionals far too often recommend that parents seek guardianship without understanding the many alternatives to guardianship that exist. Parents are unduly frightened into believing that they won't have access to their child's educational or health records. Yet, when parents file for guardianship, they are bringing a third party into what was a two-party relationship; the government or the court now has the authority to replace the parent as guardian if it so chooses (Hoyle, 2005).

(Point continued)	(Counterpoint continued)
assets but not personal issues; (c) full guardianship that includes power over an individual's person and property; (d) limited guardianship, in which the individual retains as many rights as possible and the guardian only has decision-making power over areas where there is evidence the individual is not competent to make decisions; and (e) temporary guardianship. Guardianship is typically given to a person who plays a significant role in the life of the individual. If a parent is the guardian, consideration should be given to what will happen upon the parent's death (Resource Foundation for Children with Challenges, 2000).	Individuals with disabilities often do need help to make decisions, but such decision-making support can be accomplished without resorting to taking away rights. Support circles and person-centered planning processes can be pivotal in avoiding guardianship. The support circle can help the individual with disabilities make decisions that fully take into account the individual's preferences. Other alternatives include (a) the use of durable powers of attorney, which allows individuals to give power of attorney to a designee and also to take back that power if they are unhappy with decisions made; (b) a representative payee designated to receive and disburse public funds that an individual with disabilities might receive; (c) joint banking accounts; and (d) financial trusts that can specify that someone periodically visit to make sure living situations and supports exist at a satisfactory level (Harris, 2005).

Focus Question 3 What strategies support successful communication with families and their participation in transition planning?

Strategies for Supporting Family Participation in Transition Planning

Listen to Family Members and Honor Differences

How often do we meet with family members of individuals with intellectual or developmental disabilities and tell them what we think they need to know about transition? How often do we unintentionally offend or alienate family members by expressing (a) our values and our dreams for their son or daughter or brother or sister, rather than listening to theirs; (b) our recommendations for how to achieve these dreams, rather than listening to theirs; and (c) our concerns regarding the future of their family member with intellectual or developmental disabilities, rather than listening to theirs? How often have many of the families of adolescents or young adults involved in transition encountered professionals who have shared their expertise but have not known how to really listen and learn from families? How often do we attempt to build partnerships with families who feel that assumptions have been made about them by other professionals who have shown a lack of respect or blame for the parent, as well as undervalued the parent's expertise about his or her own child?

"Listening is the language of acceptance" (Turnbull et al., 2006, p. 142) and essential to building partnerships with families, especially where discord, distance, or distrust may have been a part of their experience in interacting with professionals concerning their family member with intellectual or developmental disabilities. A failure to listen may escalate conflicts and even result in mediation or due process hearings (Lake & Billingsley, 2000). Listening to families does not signal agreement with their views; approval of their comments, values, or lifestyle; or approval of the decisions they wish to make, but it does form a basis for building a respectful partnership and further communication.

> The first thing is to LISTEN to us. Because we know our kids better than anybody, ya know, they're our kids. They're part of us! And, ya know, you go to some of those places and they just fill a form, ya know, and that's it. (Blue-Banning, Summers, Frankland, Nelson, & Beegle, 2004, p. 175)

Harry (1997) identified four areas of beliefs and values where dissonance may occur between families and professionals. These include the meaning and cause of disability, parenting style, educational goal setting, and beliefs about groups of people. Culturally sensitive programs *honor and respect* differing interpersonal styles, attitudes, behaviors, and beliefs (Roberts et al., 1990), and listening is a critical part of demonstrating honor and respect.

Increase Your Understanding of Effective Family-Professional Partnerships

> For as long as there has been a law regulating the relationships among students, their families, teachers, and administrators, there has been a distinction between "law on the books" and "law on the streets." Law on the books is the law as written in statutes, regulations, and court decisions. Law on the streets is the practice of the written law. It is what students, families, teachers, and school administrators do when they try to implement the law, especially as partners with each other. . . . No law can create genuine partnerships.

All the law can do is to provide rights, impose responsibilities, and create the structures within which parents, students, teachers, and administrators can relate to each other. Beyond these essential roles, the law is relatively powerless to foster partnerships. It is up to people to breathe life into the written law, to ensure that their practice on the streets is wholesome for each other and a model for others who struggle and prevail to be authentic partners. (Turnbull et al., 2006, pp. 139–140)

Effective family-professional partnerships are based on the common interest of doing what is best for the individual with disabilities and the realization that partnerships are beneficial to everyone (Smith et al., 2006). Themes or principles that characterize effective family-professional partnerships described by Blue-Banning et al. (2004), Smith et al. (2006), and Turnbull et al. (2006) include the following:

- Communication that is positive, understandable, coordinated, and of sufficient quality and frequency to accomplish partnership goals.
- Commitment, including a willingness to be available and go above and beyond to accomplish goals of the child and family.
- Equality, including shared power and decision making and fostering empowerment or the ability of all partners to have control over their own lives.
- Skills, or competence, including a willingness to learn from each other and from new sources of knowledge and professional practice.
- Trust, including being reliable and dependable, using sound judgment, and maintaining confidentiality.
- Respect, including demonstrating esteem through communication and actions and affirming strengths.

The value of family-professional partnerships and that of family participation are widely acknowledged. Teachers, transition coordinators, and other team members may have to show persistence to achieve partnerships that will support improved student outcomes.

Increase Your Cultural Competence

"Culture is not just something that someone else has. All of us have a cultural, ethnic, racial, linguistic, and religious (or nonreligious) heritage that influences our current beliefs, values, and behaviors" (Lynch, 2004, p. 76). Culture is a complex and dynamic concept. Consider these key understandings of culture:

- Culture is composed of the socially generated and socially sanctioned ways of perceiving, believing, evaluating, and behaving shared by members of particular communities and transmitted across generations.
- The aspects of culture most easily perceived (e.g., food, behavior) are only the surface level of culture and are inextricably tied to and generated from deeper values, beliefs, and worldviews, which form culture's primary level.
- Culture functions to set parameters that both connect and separate people and communities and to transmit from one generation to another ways of perceiving, believing, evaluating, and behaving deemed to be critical to personal and group survival.
- Everyone's ways of perceiving, believing, evaluating, and behaving, come from somewhere. That is, everyone participates in one or more cultures, some of which may be identified by ethnic labels, some by other labels, and others that may have no easy labels. (Barrera & Kramer, 1997, p. 222)

Most individuals belong to a number of different microcultures, which provide varying levels of influence across time and within different contexts (Gollnick & Chinn, 2002). For example, young adults with intellectual or developmental disabilities may share the race, ethnicity, and religion of one or both of their parents. However, the difference in age, recreational interests, and participation in a self-advocacy organization for people with disabilities may provide them with a number of experiences, interactions, and ways of viewing the world that also shape their cultural perspectives. Another consideration in interactions with culturally and linguistically diverse families is the level of acculturation of family members to mainstream European American cultural beliefs and values. This is believed to be influenced by a number of variables, such as urban or rural background, U.S. or foreign place of birth, English proficiency, residence in immigrant enclaves, educational attainment, and length of time a family has been in the United States (Pachter, 1994). However, although these factors are influential, "research indicates that acculturation is a selective process" (Sturm & Gahagan, 1999, p. 353), and different levels of acculturation occur among people with similar demographic characteristics, including family members.

Many recent immigrants to the United States have survived very adverse economic or political circumstances in the areas from which they have emigrated (e.g., Africa, Eastern Europe, Southern Asia). High levels of stress, repeated loss, social isolation, and financial hardship often result (Sturm & Gahagan, 1999). These factors and the numerous adjustments to a new country may produce ongoing struggles and intense hardships for some young adults with intellectual and developmental disabilities and their families as they are involved in transition planning. It is well worth considering if we are sometimes too critical of families who are struggling to survive and adjust. A similar consideration is whether we are unconsciously more affirming and supportive of families who have chosen to assimilate to mainstream culture, values, and language as rapidly as possible, compared with families who have chosen to retain more traditional cultural values, beliefs, and lifestyles (McDonnell & Hardman, 2003). Regardless, great variation among individual and family values, beliefs, and behaviors will occur within and across cultures, and it is critical that we approach each family and family member without making assumptions based on cultural group membership (Lynch & Hanson, 2004). However, accessing culture-specific information can be useful in expanding knowledge, understanding issues that need to be considered, thinking about questions, and making it evident that a teacher is making a sincere effort to work respectfully and effectively within cross-cultural communications with each family and family member (Lynch & Hanson, 2004).

Cultural competence is often used as a framework for approaching multicultural interactions. Cultural competence has been described as "the ability to think, feel, and act in ways that acknowledge, respect, and build upon [social,] cultural, and linguistic diversity" (Lynch & Hanson, 1993, p. 50) and as "the skillful, creative, and sometimes intuitive application of knowledge and skills to determine the source of cultural and linguistic dissonance and re-establish the desired communication and learning" (Barrera & Kramer, 1997, p. 225). "Competence also implies skills which help to translate beliefs, attitudes, and orientation into action and behavior" (Roberts et al., 1990, p. 1). A key step in becoming more culturally competent is examining your own cultural background, beliefs, values, and biases and their impact on how you interpret and relate to cultural differences (e.g., Harry, 1992; Lynch & Hanson, 2004).

Another important way to increase cultural competence is to expand your understanding of the extent to which the emphasis in how we communicate differs across cultures in ways that may be much more subtle than speaking different languages. In some cultures, most information is communicated through words; in others, the context of the exchange, the relationship between the individuals who are communicating, and other communication cues, such as facial expressions and body language, play more of a role (Hall, 1976; Lynch, 1998). Hecht, Andersen, and Ribeau (1989) noted that "facial expressions, tensions, movements, speed of interaction, location of the interaction, and other subtle 'vibes' are likely to be perceived by and have more meaning for people from high-context cultures" (p. 177).

High-context cultural communicators include many Arab, Asian, American Indian, and Latino cultures (Lynch, 2004). Perhaps the best way of understanding high-context communication is to note how close colleagues, best friends, or family members may be able to communicate a great deal based on their shared past and the immediate context without needing to verbally fill each other in on all the details, sometimes without saying anything at all (Lynch, 2004). Low-context communication is usually verbal, direct, logical, and precise, and low-context communicators may become impatient with others who can't "get to the point" quickly (Hecht et al., 1989; Lynch, 2004). Examples of low-context cultural communicators include many European Americans, Germans, and Scandinavians (Hecht et al., 1989). Low-context communicators are often less adept at reading nonverbal or situation-specific communication cues (Lynch, 2004).

> When families and service providers differ in the level of context that they use in communication, misunderstandings may arise. On the one hand, lots of talking, clearly specified verbal directions, and detailed demonstrations may seem insensitive and mechanistic to individuals from high-context cultures. They may feel that the talking is proof that the other individual does not truly understand them and cannot, therefore, be of help. On the other hand, members of low-context cultures may be uncomfortable with long pauses and silences, cryptic sentences, and indirect modes of communication such as storytelling. They may feel that these are time wasters or are signs of resistance. These interactions are further complicated by the fact that under pressure or when confronted with a communication style that they do not understand, people rely on patterns of behavior that reflect their own zone of comfort. Thus, low-context communicators talk more, speak more rapidly, and often raise their voices; whereas high-context communicators say less, make less eye contact, and withdraw from interaction. (Lynch, 2004, p. 62)

A young adult with intellectual or developmental disabilities who has attended school for a number of years may demonstrate an ability to use either or both communication styles, and teachers and other transition team members may be somewhat unprepared for communicating with parents or extended family members who may communicate in a manner more traditional for their culture. It is critical that team members take time to build rapport and communicate effectively with families throughout the transition process.

Take Time to Build Rapport and Communicate Effectively

Teachers may have a long-standing and positive partnership with the family of an adolescent or a young adult prior to beginning transition planning. However, unfamiliar potential adult service providers, siblings or extended family members, and others may become involved as a part of the transition planning process, and it may take time to build rapport with new team members before planning can proceed effectively. Professionals on transition teams may also be working with families who have had negative interactions and confrontations with professionals in other settings, and building trust with these families will take additional time. Although it may be difficult for teachers to "take the time," it is well worth considering how much can really be accomplished if rapport with the family has not been established prior to discussion of transition planning. Joe and Malach (2004) provide a number of guidelines for teachers and other service providers who are working with American Indian families. Many of their guidelines are also helpful suggestions for establishing rapport and working with families from a variety of cultural backgrounds during the transition planning process. Here are some of their key guidelines:

- *Ask parents whom they want to include in meetings. . . .* Explain to the parents that all family . . . they choose to include are welcome.
- *When extended family members participate in a meeting, communication should be directed to the entire group, not just to the parents, interpreter, or spokesperson for the family.* This shows respect for the entire family.
- *Always show respect for and provide emotional support to the family.* This can be practiced by listening to the family's ideas, acknowledging their concerns and feelings, and including interested family members. . . .
- *When first establishing contact with a family, proceed at a pace that is comfortable for the family members.* Take some time at the beginning of each visit for "small talk." Ask how they are, comment on the weather, talk about road conditions, share an appropriate personal experience (e.g., you were glad to have rain for your own garden), or find things you have in common. This time provides an opportunity for the family to get to know you as a person, and it forms a foundation for developing rapport with the family.
- *When you need to ask a lot of questions . . . first explain to the family that you will be asking them questions, tell them about the types of questions, and inform them as to how the information will help*

you to serve their child. Tell the family that it is okay for them to ask you for clarification by asking you questions at any time they do not understand your question or do not understand why you are asking it. Let them know it is okay if they need to discuss a question with other family members before they answer. Ask them to tell you if they want to think about a question or to discuss it with other family members before they answer. (Joe & Malach, 2004, pp. 129–130)

When working with culturally and linguistically diverse families, cultural mediators and interpreters may be an important part of preparing for communication with a family, and they may also be of assistance during meetings or other conversations with family members, including transition planning (Ohtake, Santos, & Fowler, 2000). Interpreters provide the translation of spoken language between family members and school or agency personnel, and translators provide the translation of written documents or communication, such as transition plans or e-mail communication between a family member and a transition coordinator. Cultural mediators may serve as interpreters or translators but may also become involved in facilitating communication between family members and teachers who speak the same language but have different cultural backgrounds and understandings. The role of a cultural mediator includes making two cultures or languages understandable to each other, a broader role than the translation of written or spoken language (Barrera, 2000).

Skillful interpreters can make a tremendous difference in the effectiveness of involving families in transition planning. Characteristics of effective interpreters include (a) proficiency in the language of both the family and the service provider(s), (b) an understanding of cross-cultural communication and the role and principles of serving as an interpreter, (c) education in a relevant professional discipline, and (d) an ability to respect and appreciate both cultures and communicate tactfully and with sensitivity about cultural nuances (Lynch, 2004). Although well-trained and experienced interpreters with all of these characteristics cannot always be identified within the needed time frame, caution should be used in asking family members or members of the family's immediate cultural community to serve in this role (Lynch, 2004). It may be difficult to use an interpreter whom a family knows through business, church, or similar contacts, especially if there is any sense of embarrassment about having a child with disabilities or if sensitive topics need to be discussed. The use of family members is also potentially problematic as they may have their own agendas or may try to protect other family members by softening what has been said by rephrasing or omitting part of the original message.

Some additional suggestions for the use of an interpreter include the following:

- Introduce yourself and the interpreter, describe your respective roles, and clarify mutual expectations and the purpose of the encounter. . . .
- During the interaction, address your remarks and questions directly to the family (not the interpreter); look at and listen to family members as they speak, and observe their nonverbal communication.
- Avoid body language or gestures that may be offensive or misunderstood.
- Use a positive tone of voice and facial expressions that convey sincere respect and interest in the family. Address the family in a calm, unhurried manner.
- Speak clearly and somewhat more slowly but more loudly. . . .
- Avoid technical jargon, colloquialisms, idioms, slang, and abstractions.
- Avoid oversimplification and condensing important explanations.
- Give instructions in a clear, logical sequence; emphasize key words or points; and offer reasons for specific recommendations.
- Periodically check on the family's understanding and the accuracy of the translation . . . but avoid literally asking, "Do you understand?"
- When possible, reinforce verbal information with materials written in the family's language and visual aids or behavioral modeling, if appropriate. . . .
- Be patient, be prepared, and plan for the additional time that will inevitably be required for careful interpretation. (Lynch, 2004, pp. 71–72)

Assist Families in Seeing the Possibilities

In an interview of parents and siblings of students with severe disabilities, Chambers, Hughes, and Carter (2004) found that parents and siblings felt they lacked knowledge of postschool options and were not optimistic about the future of their family member with disabilities. Most believed that the individual would work in a segregated setting and would continue to live at home. The National Longitudinal Transition Study-2 (SRI International, 2005) found that 36% of families of individuals with mental retardation did not expect their children to graduate from high school or attend post-secondary school. This was true of 48% of parents of children with autism and 52% of parents of children with multiple disabilities. Forty-two percent of parents of children with mental retardation said that their children would definitely or probably not live independently, and 41% said they would likely not live independently with supervision either. These percentages increased with parents of children with autism and multiple disabilities. Almost 63% of parents of children with autism and 64% of parents of children with multiple disabilities did not envision their children living independently, and 32% of parents of children with autism and 45% of parents of children with multiple disabilities believed their children would not live independently with supervision.

Family interview formats have been developed that can help families see options and possibilities and yield important information for goal setting and transition planning (e.g., Giangreco, Cloninger, & Iverson, 1998; Hutchins & Renzaglia, 1998). Refer to Chapter 5 for examples of these approaches.

Assist Families in Receiving Accurate and Understandable Information

Once families see the possibilities and begin to formulate a vision, it is important that they receive accurate and understandable information about the transition process and possible resources. School personnel should work closely with families and recognize and respond to their unique concerns. Information about possible employment options, as well as community living and participation, should be in a format that is understandable to families and up to date. Here again, it is important to reiterate that "family education" is not the purpose; rather, we are striving for a reciprocal process in which there is an exchange of information, resources, and learning (Hanley-Maxwell et al., 1998).

Barriers to successful communication with families that have been identified include the use of jargon, a lack of rapport with the family, limited time to facilitate communication, and a perception by family members that they are being spoken to in a condescending manner by professionals (Hanline, 1993). It is also very frustrating for families when information provided by transition team members is out of date. Too often, resource lists include agencies that no longer exist or phone numbers or e-mail addresses that have changed since the list was developed.

Assume That Information Needs to Be Shared More Than Once and That Needs Change

Have you ever been given route directions and then realized you forgot them when you began your trip? Have you been given instructions by your doctor and then failed to remember his or her exact direction? Families face similar difficulties as they are confronted with a great deal of information in a short amount of time. Those involved in transition planning teams need to ensure that information does not get shared in just one meeting but rather is heard many times and is provided in more than one way. Repetition is important for all of us as we learn new information. Transition personnel should look for a variety of methods to provide information to families. Some families will want to read brochures, articles, and books on transition, and other families may want to attend meetings at the school or watch videotapes, while other families may find it helpful to be connected with another family who has experienced a successful transition (Westling & Fox, 2008). Communication about transition can be in the form of handbooks, handouts, and newsletters. It can be accomplished via letters, notes, and dialogue journals or by telephone, Internet, or meeting with families (Turnbull et al., 2006).

Transition is never a discreet activity or event, and family and individual needs inevitably change over time. With changing needs come requirements for different or expanded information. Again, it is important to maintain an ongoing and trusting relationship to recognize when needs have changed and when it is appropriate to provide new information. Although influenced by the dynamics of individual families, societal contexts, and cultural influences, one of the goals of working in partnership with families during the transition process is to facilitate the development of positive and sustainable adult relationships among family members, including the individual with intellectual or developmental disabilities. As parents age and siblings become adolescents or adults with increasing responsibilities and choices about their lives, both may benefit from receiving more information about the potential impacts of having a family member with intellectual or developmental disabilities. Research results are inconsistent but suggest that while many siblings benefit from having a brother or sister with a disability, some siblings also experience a variety of problems or negative outcomes (Turnbull et al., 2006), including difficulties in coping with feelings of anger, guilt, and embarrassment and with making decisions about careers, what to tell others, whether or not to have children, and how they want to be involved in decisions and day-to-day support of their adult sibling with a disability (McHugh, 2003).

Summary

In conclusion, one of the most important understandings for teachers and other team members who support adolescents or young adults with intellectual disabilities and their families during the school-to-postschool transition is the acknowledgment that changing needs, dreams, and circumstances will inevitably lead to changes in the transition plan and the specific strategies needed to support implementation. Transition team members can support individuals with intellectual and developmental disabilities and their families throughout the school-to-adult transition by assisting families in coordinating services across agencies and natural supports, facilitating practical problem solving as challenges or barriers arise, facilitating long-term planning and the growth of new interests and pursuits, and providing information and support that may enhance the development of adult family relationships. *"Huli man daw at magaling, ay naihahabol din* (Worthwhile things even when presented late can still be included.)—Pilipino saying" (Santos & Chan, 2004, p. 298).

Focus Question Review

Focus Question 1: How does transition affect families, and what are some of the barriers to actively involving families in transition planning, implementation, and evaluation?

- All families face challenges during adolescence and the transition to young adulthood.
- Families of adolescents and young adults with intellectual and developmental disabilities also have added challenges and stress during this transition.
- Family involvement during transition influences outcomes in a variety of important ways.
- Barriers to family participation in the transition process include transportation, conflicting work schedules, a lack of knowledge about the transition process and future program and support options, and a breakdown in communication with school personnel.

Focus Question 2: What are key roles for parents and other family members during the transition?

- Providing continuity and support of young adolescents through young adulthood.
- Balancing family needs and supports while understanding the individual within broader community and service contexts.
- Participating in person-family interdependent planning for individuals with intellectual and developmental disabilities.
- Exploring options related to guardianship.

Focus Question 3: What strategies support successful communication with families and their participation in transition planning?

- Listening to family members and honoring differences.
- Increasing your understanding of effective family-professional partnerships.
- Increasing your cultural competence.
- Taking time to build rapport and communicate effectively with families.
- Assisting families in seeing the possibilities for their son or daughter.
- Assisting families in receiving accurate and understandable information.
- Assuming information needs to be shared with families more than once and that needs will change.

Section III

INSTRUCTION AND EDUCATIONAL SUPPORTS

CHAPTER 8

Inclusion in General Education Classes

JOHN MCDONNELL

BRIGID E. BROWN

I n the 1980s, recommended practice for high school students with intellectual and developmental disabilities focused on providing educational experiences that would directly prepare them for successful community living (Brown et al., 1979; Wilcox & Bellamy, 1982). Curricula focused on teaching employment, personal management, and leisure activities that reflected the expectations of adulthood (Ford et al., 1989; Neel & Billingsley, 1989; Wilcox & Bellamy, 1987). Teachers were encouraged to move instruction out of the classroom and into community settings in order to ensure that students developed the skills necessary to obtain paid jobs, use the resources of the community, and live independently prior to graduation (Horner, McDonnell, & Bellamy, 1986; Sailor et al., 1987).

Although community-based curriculum and instruction are still critical elements of secondary programs, there is a growing agreement that students also benefit educationally and socially from participating in the general high school curriculum and in content-area classes (Fisher, Sax, & Pumpian, 1999; Wehmeyer & Sailor, 2004). There is clear empirical evidence that shows that inclusive educational programs are as effective, if not more effective, than segregated alternatives on a number of measures for students with intellectual and developmental disabilities (Hunt & McDonnell, 2007). In addition, research suggests that students who participate in general education classes have better postschool adjustment than peers who do not have these opportunities

(Baker, Wang, & Walberg, 1994–1995; Benz, Lindstrom, & Yovanoff, 2000; Phelps & Hanley-Maxwell, 1997; Salend & Garrick-Duhaney, 1999).

In spite of the positive impacts of inclusive education, meeting the unique educational needs of students with intellectual and developmental disabilities in typical high school classes remains a challenge for teachers and administrators (Harrower, 1999; McDonnell, 1998). Fortunately, research on strategies for supporting students' participation in the instructional activities and social networks of general education classes has increased significantly over the last decade (Hunt & McDonnell, 2007; Snell, 2007). This chapter will summarize the research on how to effectively support students in the general education curriculum and content-area classes. In addition, the recommended steps for designing effective inclusive educational programs for students will be presented.

POINT/COUNTERPOINT 8.1

Participation in the General Education Curriculum

POINT

"It is possible for students with disabilities to learn from the regular education curriculum. That the barrier to this happening isn't the student's ability, but often it is our own. We know that 'no man is an island,' but without modifications and supports, sometimes students with disabilities in regular classrooms can be. We know the difference between alternative and modified. That 'being in' isn't the same thing as 'being with.' And that ultimately we need to stop talking about curriculum modification and start talking about inclusive curriculum design" (Shapiro-Barnard et al., 2005, p. 197).

COUNTERPOINT

"Equally problematic is the general education curriculum's lack of focus on functional and vocational skills. Curricular demands as early as first grade do not match the educational needs of many students with disabilities. Even with an infinite amount of planning, the educational interests of some students with disabilities cannot be met through modifications to the general education curriculum" (Chesley & Calaluce, 2005, p. 202).

Importance of Inclusive Secondary Education

The term *inclusive education* describes an approach in which students go to the school that they would attend if they did not have a disability and in which they participate in chronologically age-appropriate general education classes and community sites (McDonnell, Hardman, & McDonnell, 2003). In addition, inclusive educational programs share a number of other characteristics, including school policies and procedures that encourage the development of classroom and school communities in which all students are valued members, natural proportions of students with disabilities in classes and on the school site, a policy of zero rejection so that no student is excluded from typical educational experiences based on type or severity of disability, staff and fiscal resources that are allocated within the school so the educational needs of all students are met, and effective and high-quality instruction designed to promote learning (Giangreco, Cloninger, & Iverson, 1998; Halvorsen & Neary, 2001; Hunt & McDonnell, 2007).

The early expansion of inclusive education for students with developmental disabilities was driven in large part by federal legislation (e.g., the Individuals with Disabilities Education Act) designed to ensure students' equal access to appropriate publicly funded education and by calls from individuals with disabilities and their families demanding their full participation in all aspects of our society and community (Lipsky & Gartner, 1997). Increasingly, however, support for inclusive education is based on its demonstrated effectiveness in improving the quality of life of students both during and following school. For example, some of the documented benefits of including secondary students in content-area classes are

- Increased opportunities to participate in the extracurricular activities of the school (Wagner, Newman, Cameto, Levine, & Marder, 2003).
- Improved social interactions and relationships with peers without disabilities, especially when appropriate contextual arrangements and supports are provided (Carter & Kennedy, 2006; Schwartz, Staub, Peck, & Gallucci, 2006).
- Increased access to the general education curriculum (Wehmeyer, Lattin, Lapp-Rincker, & Agran, 2003).
- Improved performance on alternate assessments tied to the mandates of IDEA 2004 and the No Child Left Behind Act (Roach & Elliot, 2006).
- Improved postschool adjustment to employment, especially if students have taken general vocational education classes (Benz et al., 2000; Phelps & Hanley-Maxwell, 1997).

| **Focus Question 1** | What factors improve educational benefits for students enrolled in content-area classes? |

The potential benefits of including students in content-area classes are enhanced when their participation is based on several key principles. First, as discussed in Chapters 4 and 5, the content-area class is selected to increase the likelihood that students will be able to achieve their stated postschool outcomes (Bambara, Wilson, & McKenzie, 2007). IDEA 2004 requires that students' Individualized Education Program/transition plan teams identify the students' expected postschool outcomes and then select specific transition services that will allow them to achieve their goals. Participation in the general education curriculum is one of the possible services that students can use to achieve expected outcomes. The potential advantages of participating in content-area classes will be improved if the goals and objectives included in students' IEPs/transition plans are anchored to their postschool outcomes and aligned with the content standards covered in the class. Second, teachers use strategies that promote students' interaction with the general education curriculum and provide instruction that is tailored to students' unique learning needs (Dymond et al., 2006). Finally, teachers build on the natural social supports available in the class to promote students' participation in instructional activities and to create frequent opportunities for students to interact with peers without disabilities (Carter & Kennedy, 2006). The remaining sections of this chapter will discuss the specific strategies that teachers can use to successfully implement these principles.

Effective Instructional Strategies

The benefits of students participating in content-area classes are enhanced when teachers employ a combination of student-level interventions designed to meet the students' unique needs and classroom interventions that enhance their ability to participate in the instructional activities of the class (Hunt & McDonnell, 2007; Snell, 2007).

Student-Level Interventions

A primary tenet of special education is that instruction is individualized to meet the unique needs of students. The discrepancy between students' ability and the complexity of knowledge and skills addressed in secondary content-area classes often requires teachers to use multiple strategies to effectively promote learning. A number of possible student-level interventions have been discussed in the literature, but three have received significant attention. These strategies include the use of modifications and adaptations (Lee et al., 2006), student-direct learning

(Wehmeyer, Field, Doren, Jones, & Mason, 2004), and embedded instruction (McDonnell, Johnson, & McQuivey, 2008).

Modifications and Adaptations. The use of curriculum accommodations and modifications as part of larger intervention packages has been shown to be very effective in supporting students in general education classes (Coots, Bishop, & Grenot-Scheyer, 1998; Fisher & Frey, 2001; Janney & Snell, 1997; McDonnell, Mathot-Buckner, Thorson, & Fister, 2001; Ryndak, Morrison, & Sommerstein, 1999; Udvari-Solner, 1996). One study that examined the unique contributions of curriculum accommodations and modifications to student learning and participation in general education classes was conducted by Fisher and Frey (2001). They examined the ways that an elementary school, a middle school, and a high school student accessed the general education curriculum through the design and implementation of accommodations and modifications. Data were gathered through direct observations of students in their general education classes and through interviews with parents, general education teachers, special education teachers, and peers without disabilities. The researchers found that all three students were provided with a number of individualized accommodations and modifications to participate in the instructional activities of their general education classes. The adaptations ranged from reducing the number of items presented to students to the use of curriculum overlapping. They also found that collaboration between special education and general education teachers was essential to developing effective accommodations and modifications for students. In addition, they observed that peers without disabilities had significant insights into how curriculum and instruction could be adapted or modified to increase the students' success. Finally, the researchers noted that the most effective accommodations were those that were specifically designed for the class and the instructional tasks completed by the students.

Focus Question 2	Why are self-directed learning strategies important to improving students' participation in content-area classes?

Student-Directed Learning. The purposes of student-directed learning strategies are to increase students' autonomy in participating in classroom activities and thereby reduce the level of assistance they need from special and general educators to be successful. Student-directed learning encompasses a number of different skills, including problem solving, study planning, goal setting, and self-monitoring (Agran et al., 2005; Gilberts, Agran, Hughes, & Wehmeyer, 2001; Hughes et al., 2002; King-Sears, 1999; Koegel, Harrower, & Koegel, 1999; Wehmeyer, Yeager, Bolding, Agran, & Hughes, 2003).

Agran and colleagues (2005) examined the impact of a self-monitoring strategy on the ability of six middle school students with developmental disabilities to follow their general education teachers' directions. The students were taught to nod their heads or verbally affirm that they had been given a direction by their teacher, complete the direction, and self-monitor whether they followed the direction correctly or incorrectly. The results showed that all the students quickly learned the self-monitoring procedures and significantly increased their completion of the directions given by their teacher. In addition, the students were able to maintain their use of the self-monitoring strategy across time.

Embedded Instruction. The term *embedded instruction* (EI) commonly refers to explicit, systematic instruction that is designed to distribute instructional trials within the ongoing routines and activities of the performance environment (Rule, Losardo, Dinnebeil, Kaiser, & Rowland, 1998; McDonnell et al., 2008; Schepis, Reid, Ownbey, & Parsons, 2001; Wolery, Ault, & Doyle, 1992). The specific instructional procedures used during embedded instruction vary based on the needs of individual students, the skills being taught, and the contexts in which instruction is being provided. In the last decade, embedded instruction has increasingly been recommended as a potential strategy for meeting the needs of students participating in general education classes (Harrower, 1999; McDonnell, 1998).

For example, McDonnell, Johnson, Polychronis, and Ricsen (2002) used embedded instruction to teach four junior high school students with developmental disabilities to read or define words that were included in vocabulary lists of a food and nutrition class, a health class, and a computer class. The study was also designed to examine whether paraprofessional staff could successfully implement EI as part of their responsibilities in supporting the participation of students in the class. The results indicated that embedded instruction led to the acquisition and maintenance of the target skills. The paraprofessionals implemented the embedded instruction procedures in general education classes with high levels of procedural fidelity. The students' general education teachers and the paraprofessionals reported that EI was an effective and acceptable strategy for supporting their participation in the general education curriculum.

Part of the utility of embedded instruction is that it can be implemented by peers. In a study conducted by Jameson, McDonnell, Polychronis, and Riesen (2008), three junior high school students without disabilities were taught to deliver EI to three peers with developmental disabilities in an arts and crafts class and a health class. The students were taught to define key concepts drawn from the lessons being presented to students without disabilities enrolled in the classes. Students without disabilities were taught to implement EI in a 30-min training session prior to the implementation of the study and were provided with ongoing feedback about their implementation of EI on one set of concepts throughout the study. The results showed that students with developmental disabilities learned the target skills when receiving instruction from peers without disabilities and that the peers could implement EI with a high degree of procedural fidelity. Finally, the students without disabilities and their general education teachers reported that EI was an effective and acceptable strategy for providing instruction to students within the ongoing routines of the general education classes.

Classroom-Level Strategies

Several classroom-level interventions have also been proposed to support students in secondary content-area classes. Based on the available research, four strategies in particular hold promise: professional teaming, universal design, cooperative learning, and peer-mediated instruction.

Professional Teaming. There is general agreement that inclusive education programs can be successful only if special and general educators work together as a team to support students (Downing, 1996; Rainforth & England, 1997). While most of what has been written on professional teaming has focused on collaboration at the elementary level, the case studies and qualitative studies that have been conducted at the secondary level have confirmed the importance of teaming to the long-term success of inclusive education for middle or junior high school students and high school students (Fisher et al., 1999; Jorgensen, 1998; Park, Hoffman, Whaley, & Gonsier-Gerdin, 2001; Wallace, Anderson, & Bartholomay, 2002).

For example, Wallace and colleagues (2002) examined the collaboration and communication strategies in four high schools that had been identified as successfully including students with disabilities, including students with intellectual and developmental disabilities, in content-area classes. They used interviews with teachers, focus groups, and surveys to identify the school and classroom variables that were associated with successful collaboration between special education and general education teachers. The results suggested that having adequate planning time was key to successful teaming. In addition, the findings emphasized the importance of teachers from different departments working together to support students, planning lessons together, sharing their knowledge and materials, and attending professional development activities together in order to establish a unified vision of inclusion and to develop the relationships necessary to make teaming successful.

Universal Design. The concept of universal design emerged in the field of architecture more than 30 years ago (McGuire, Scott, & Shaw, 2006). It focused on the proactive design of physical settings to accommodate the needs of all individuals (i.e., the elderly, tall and short individuals, and people with disabilities). Most of us understand the concept of universal design as it is applied to home, school, and community environments (e.g., curb cuts for wheelchairs, ramps), but its application to curriculum and instruction to improve educational outcomes for all students is a relatively new idea (McGuire et al., 2006). However, its potential in supporting all students' access to the general education curriculum is intuitive, and as such, it has received increasing attention in the field of special education as a potential strategy to support the development of inclusive educational programs for students with developmental disabilities (Renzaglia, Karvonen, Drasgow, & Stoxen, 2003; Wehmeyer, 2006).

Focus Question 3	How does the application of universal design principles to curriculum and instruction support the participation of students in the general education curriculum?

Universally designed curriculum and instruction provide alternative means to represent and interact with curriculum content so that it is equally accessible to students with different abilities and needs (Rose, Meyer, & Hitchcock, 2005). Dymond and colleagues (2006) describe a study focused on the application of universal design principles to a high school science course. A team comprising the general education teacher, a special education teacher who also taught the science course to students with mild disabilities, and the special education teacher for students with developmental disabilities worked collaboratively to restructure each science lesson using universal design principles. The restructuring process was guided by a rubric that laid out specific questions about curriculum content, instructional delivery, promoting students' participation, materials, and assessment. The team met weekly throughout the semester to restructure the traditional lesson plans so that they were accessible to all students in the class, including those with developmental disabilities. The results suggested that while the process of redesigning the class was time-consuming, structuring the course to meet the needs of all students had a number of benefits for both students with disabilities and those without them. For example, the researchers found that for students with disabilities, the process led to improved social interactions with their peers without disabilities and improved their participation in instructional routines and activities. The researchers noted positive outcomes for students without disabilities, including improved class participation, personal responsibility, completion of work, grades, and end-of-year test scores.

Cooperative Learning. Cooperative learning has been defined as "the instructional use of small groups so that students work together to maximize their own and each other's learning" (Johnson, Johnson, & Holubec, 1993, p. 6). There are a number of cooperative learning approaches, and although they vary in structure, research has consistently shown that they produce improved academic and social outcomes for students, including those with disabilities (Slavin, 1995). Cooperative learning approaches share the following characteristics: (a) Small groups of students (i.e., fewer than five) are given a group assignment that they must complete together, (b) the students are directly taught the skills necessary to cooperate with each other, (c) teachers encourage the development of "positive interdependence" among members of the group in order to support each other's learning, and (d) each individual in the group must be able to account for what he or she learns.

Cooperative learning has been examined extensively as a way to improve the quality of instruction provided to students with developmental disabilities in general education classes (Cushing, Kennedy, Shukla, Davis, & Meyer, 1997; Dugan et al., 1995; Hunt, Staub, Alwell, & Goetz, 1994; Jacques, Wilton, & Townsend, 1998; Kamps, Leonard, Potucek, & Garrison-Harrell, 1995; Putnam, 1993). Cushing and colleagues (1997) examined the effects of two cooperative learning arrangements on two students with developmental disabilities and their peers without disabilities enrolled in an eighth-grade English class. In the first condition, all students were assigned to collaborative groups based on class performance. Each group included two to three students with average performance, one student with above-average performance, and one student with below-average performance. In this condition, each group received 10 min of group lecture, 18 min of reciprocal peer tutoring from a group member, 5 min of group activities, and 5 min of group wrap-up directed by the teacher. In the second condition, the sequence of instructional activities was the same, but the mixed grouping procedure was eliminated. Instead, students were assigned to specific peers to work in two-member teams. The authors found that both cooperative learning approaches were effective for both students with disabilities and those without them. There were no differences in the two conditions in terms of the number of social interactions that occurred between students with and without disabilities. However, the posttest scores on the content covered during the lessons were slightly higher for students in the condition in which two students were paired together for instruction.

Peer-Mediated Instruction. Peer-mediated instruction is designed to allow students to serve as instructional agents for one another (Harper, Maheady, & Mallette, 1994). Research has clearly documented the effectiveness of peer-mediated instruction for students in general education classes (Kamps, Barbetta, Leonard, & Delquardri, 1994; McDonnell, Thorson, Allen, & Mathot-Buckner, 2000; McDonnell et al., 2001; Moortweet et al., 1999; Weiner, 2005). For example, McDonnell and colleagues (2001) examined the impact of a class-wide peer tutoring program on the academic responding and rates of inappropriate behaviors of three junior high school students with intellectual and developmental disabilities. The researchers also examined the impact of the program on three peers without disabilities who participated in the peer tutoring arrangement with the students with disabilities. The peer tutoring program was implemented in a pre-algebra class, a physical education class, and a history class. All students in these classes were organized in tutoring teams comprising three students of varying ability. Each member of the team was asked to serve as a tutor, a tutee, and an observer. The students' roles shifted following each tutoring trial. Content for the class-wide tutoring sessions focused on the material in the units being presented by the general education teacher. The results showed that the class-wide peer tutoring program resulted in increased rates of academic responding and lower rates of inappropriate behaviors by both students with disabilities and those without them. In addition, the program resulted in improved weekly posttest scores for the students without disabilities on the content presented by the general education teacher. The general education teachers participating in the study reported that the class-wide peer tutoring program was an effective strategy for both students with disabilities and those without them.

Effective Social Support Strategies

In addition to providing adequate instructional support to students, successfully including them in general education classes requires that they have access to ongoing social supports. The main purpose of these strategies is to promote social interaction between students with disabilities and their peers without disabilities (Carter & Kennedy, 2006). Typically, these strategies are designed not only to foster relationships between students and specific peers but also to connect them to the natural social networks of the classroom and the school. These support strategies include informal peer-to-peer interventions and structured strategies, such as peer buddies.

Peer-to-Peer Strategies

Peer-to-peer support strategies can be organized easily within content-area classes by pairing a single peer or group of peers without disabilities with a student with disabilities to help him or her participate in class routines and activities. Although establishing peer-to-peer supports is critical to successful inclusion at any age level (Hunt & McDonnell, 2007), it is especially important in high schools because of greater class rotation and the need for students to participate in multiple social groups throughout the day (Cutts & Sigafoos, 2001). Additionally, the nature of instruction in content-area classes can often limit students' opportunities to interact with their peers and therefore inhibit the natural development of supportive social relationships (Carter & Kennedy, 2006). Consequently, teachers will need to establish peer-to-peer support strategies to help students meet the academic and social demands of content-area classes.

In a study by Kennedy, Cushing, and Itkonen (1997), peers without disabilities were trained to provide support to a middle school student and a high school student participating in four different general education classes. One peer was recruited to provide support to the student in each class. Initially, class seating arrangements were changed to allow the peer to sit next to the student. Peers were taught how to communicate and interact with the students appropriately during class time. The peers were also taught how to adapt classroom assignments and activities to allow the student to participate. The researchers examined the impact of the peer support strategy on social contacts between the student and peers in the class and the number of peers with whom students had social contact outside of class periods. The results showed that the number of peers with whom students interacted during and outside of class periods increased significantly over the course of the study.

While strategies that pair one student with one peer have been quite successful, recently it has been recommended that teachers begin to use multiple peers to support students in content-area classes. These multiple-peer strategies are commonly known as social groups (Cushing & Kennedy, 2004). For example, Carter, Cushing, Clark, and Kennedy (2005) examined the impact of the number of peers without disabilities providing support to three middle or high school students with developmental disabilities enrolled in general education classes. The primary dependent variables used in the study included the extent to which students were participating in instructional activities that were aligned with the general education curriculum, engagement in typical class activities, and social interactions with peers. The results showed that all three students were more likely to participate in instructional activities that aligned with the general education curriculum, were more engaged in typical class activities, and had higher levels of social interactions with peers when receiving support from two peers without disabilities rather than one.

Multiple-peer support strategies have a number of potential advantages over pairing students with a single peer. First, they allow students to develop relationships with several different individuals who can, in turn, create increased opportunities for them to access a variety of social groups within the school (Ryan, 2000). Second, multiple-peer strategies provide students with several different sources of support when one peer is absent. The use of multiple peers to support students in classes ensures that assistance will be continuously available to students in content-area classes. Finally, the use of multiple peers to support students fosters a sense of classroom community that may not otherwise be established (Carter, Cushing, et al., 2005; Kennedy, Shukla, & Fryxell, 1997).

Peer Buddies. In addition to informal peer-to-peer supports, a number of authors have argued for the development of organized peer support systems within secondary schools. One strategy that has received a significant amount of attention in the last several years is a program called peer buddies (Hughes & Carter, 2006). Peer buddy programs are typically offered through classes in the general education curriculum, and peers receive credit for their participation. The focus is on establishing a broader level of support to help students participate in the routines and activities of the school, such as getting to and from classes successfully, having lunch, and participating in extracurricular activities. This is encouraged by educating the general education students on how to engage their buddy in noninstructional activities, social interactions, and even leisure activities. The peer buddy classes are designed to provide peers with information about the support needs of students with disabilities and strategies for interacting appropriately with their buddy. However, the classes also emphasize that peers are not their buddy's "teacher" and are not in charge of students. Peer buddies are meant to be an effective source of social supports rather than additional authority figures in the lives of students with disabilities. Finally, peer buddy programs are most effective when staff members fade their support to the peer buddy. This allows students and their peers to develop a relationship in which they rely on each other for interaction and support, and it increases the opportunities for spontaneous interaction between the peers.

Carter, Hughes, Guth, and Copeland (2005) examined the impact of peer buddies on the social interactions that high school students with intellectual and developmental disabilities had with their peers throughout the school day. The peer buddies interacted with students during instructional and noninstructional activities during one 50-min period each day and were encouraged to interact outside of the class during the school day. They were provided with information on how to communicate and interact with the students. The results showed that social interactions between students with disabilities and their peers without disabilities increased and that the affect of the peers during social interaction improved when the peer buddy was in close physical proximity to students with disabilities.

In another study, Carter, Hughes, Copeland, and Breen (2001) compared the perceptions of and attitudes toward students with disabilities of peers without disabilities who participated in a peer buddy program and those who did not. The students who volunteered to participate in a peer buddy program reported a more positive perception of people with disabilities and a higher level of willingness to interact with students with disabilities than their peers who did not volunteer. After one semester of participating in a peer buddy program, the volunteers' perceptions of people with disabilities and willingness to interact with them increased significantly, while there were no changes in perceptions of those peers who did not participate in the program. This study suggests that structured programs like peer buddies that promote increased contact and interaction between students with disabilities and their peers are critical to promoting successful inclusive education.

Designing Effective Inclusive Education Programs

Most successful approaches to developing inclusive education programs are based on school-wide efforts to improve the quality of education for all students (Fisher et al., 1999; Jorgensen, 1998; Wehmeyer & Sailor, 2004). These system change efforts have been driven by a number of general principles (Berry, 2006; Burnstein, Sears, Wilcoxen, Cbello, & Spagna, 2004; Sailor & Roger, 2005; Stockall & Gartin, 2002):

- The administration and faculty have established a clear vision for the school that embraces high standards and expectations for all students.
- Significant efforts are made to create a cohesive learning community in which all students are valued and diversity is celebrated.
- Faculty members collaborate to develop a universally designed curriculum.
- Faculty members engage in ongoing professional development activities designed to increase their capacity to meet the educational needs of all students.
- The school institutes a system of technical supports that can help teachers meet the instructional, behavioral, and social needs of challenging students.
- Evaluation of system change efforts are based on measures of student academic achievement, school connectedness (e.g., attendance, dropout rate), and safety. Administrators and faculty use evaluation data to guide ongoing system change efforts.

At the individual level, teachers can complete a number of steps that will increase a student's access to the general education curriculum and successful participation in general education classes. These steps include (a) implementing a team-based support process, (b) developing student- and class-specific adaptations and accommodations, (c) fostering peer-based instructional and social supports for the student, (d) developing individualized teaching plans, and (e) scheduling instruction on student-specific goals and objectives.

Window 8-1

Including Robert in Science Class

Robert is a 10th grader at East Lake High School. He is very interested in science because his mother is a science professor at the local community college and his father works as a research scientist at the medical school. During his IEP/transition planning meeting, Robert indicated that after school he'd like to be able to work in a lab like his dad. The IEP/transition planning team discussed Robert's goal extensively and decided that working as a lab tech in a customized job placement might be a realistic employment outcome for him. In order to achieve his goal, Robert would need to have more experience working in laboratory settings and become familiar with the equipment typically found in science labs. Consequently, the team decided that participating in the 10th-grade science sequence would be a good way for him to get these kinds of opportunities.

Ms. Hill, Robert's special education teacher, met with Mr. Blake, who taught the 10th-grade science sequence, to identify possible skills that Robert would learn during the first trimester. They agreed that Robert should learn to read and define several key vocabulary words in the first unit on ecosystems. In addition, they agreed that Robert would also work on initiating conversations with peers and using a class schedule to initiate moving from one activity to another.

Mr. Blake, Ms. Hill, and Mrs. Dalton (Ms. Hill's paraprofessional) met to develop a comprehensive support plan for Robert in the science class. Mrs. Dalton committed to creating audiotapes of each of the assigned readings so that Robert could access the information. In addition, Mrs. Dalton would also assist Mr. Blake with developing modified worksheets and materials that highlight the target vocabulary words for Robert. He would be provided with embedded instruction on learning to read and define the targeted vocabulary words from two peers (Jacob and Lizzie) under the supervision of Ms. Hill and Mrs. Dalton. Jacob and Lizzie would also provide Robert with other supports necessary for him to participate in class routines and activities.

Mr. Blake, Ms. Hill, and Mrs. Dalton agreed to meeting weekly to review the support plan and track Robert's progress in the class.

Implement a Team-Based Support Process

Following the development of a student's IEP/transition plan, it is necessary to establish a process to ensure that special educators, general educators, paraprofessionals, and related service personnel continue to work together to meet the needs of the student in general education classes. The importance of professional teaming to successful inclusive education has prompted a number of researchers to examine ways to formally support these activities within schools (Giangreco, Edelman, & Nelson, 1998; Hunt, Doering, Hirose-Hatae, Maier, & Goetz, 2001; Hunt, Soto, Maier, & Doering, 2003; Hunt, Soto, Maier, Muller, & Goetz, 2002). While the specific steps of these professional teaming approaches vary, they all have a number of common components, including (a) regularly scheduled meetings to address the changing needs of students, (b) collaborative development of students' social and academic supports by team members, and (c) a specific accountability system to evaluate the effectiveness of students' education programs.

Hunt and colleagues (2003) describe a process for developing Unified Plans of Support (UPS) to support the inclusion of students in general education classes. The focus of this process is to ensure that the educational plans for students identify meaningful learning outcomes that are consistent with the general education curriculum and the routines and activities of the general education class. However, the UPS process is designed to go beyond simply identifying meaningful learning outcomes to include the development of the specific supports necessary to ensure that the IEP/transition plan is implemented successfully. The UPS process is based on four key steps:

1. Each student's learning and social profile is identified.

2. Based on the profile, the team brainstorms curricular, instructional, and social support strategies that will allow the student to successfully participate in each domain of the general education curriculum.

3. Once each support strategy is identified, a team member is assigned responsibility for ensuring that the strategy is put into place and for coordinating the activities of other team members in implementing the strategy.

4. A system of accountability that allows the team to evaluate the effectiveness of the UPS in meeting the student's needs is developed and implemented. This step involves regular team meetings that allow the team members to evaluate the impact of each strategy and refine the UPS.

Figure 8.1 presents an example of a UPS for a student enrolled in a science class. The plan specifies the adaptations and modifications, social supports, and student-specific instructional plans to be implemented for the student in the general education class.

Develop Student- and Class-Specific Adaptations and Modifications

An essential element of supporting students in content-area classes is to develop adaptations and modifications that will maximize their ability to participate in all routines and activities. Janney and Snell (2000) have argued that adaptations may be necessary in three areas, including the curriculum, instruction, and the environment.

Curriculum adaptations are changes to what is being taught to a student and include supplemental, simplified, or alternative curricula. Supplemental curricula are designed to expose a student to additional knowledge or skills that will help him or her meet the standards of the class. For example, a student might be taught various learning strategies to allow him or her to develop a deeper understanding of the content being presented or to learn the content more quickly (Schumaker & Deshler, 2006). This would include such strategies as self-questioning to help a student generate questions about a passage that he or she is reading in order to identify key information later in the text or teaching a student a mnemonic strategy that can assist him or her with remembering lists of key concepts or ideas. Simplified curriculum entails the identification of modified standards that are directly referenced to the core curriculum. For example, in Robert's case, Mr. Blake and Ms. Hill decided that he would learn to read and provide a verbal definition of key vocabulary words (e.g., *ecosystem, food chain,* and *biosphere*) rather than predict how changes in abiotic or biotic factors might affect specific ecosystems. Finally, alternative curricula are focused on teaching knowledge and skills that are not directly referenced to the core curricula in the class but are nonetheless important to a student's successful transition to community life. For Robert, these skills included initiating conversations with peers and using a class schedule. However, they could also include such skills as using an electronic communication device to communicate with peers or transferring from a wheelchair to a regular chair.

Instructional adaptations are focused on changing either the input (i.e., the stimulus materials) or the output (i.e., the behavior that the student completes) during instructional activities. Adaptations to the input that a student receives could include such things as having him or her listen to a passage recorded on a CD or an audiotape rather than read it or using an advanced organizer that provides a list of the key concepts on which he or she should take notes when listening to a lecture by the teacher. Adaptations to a student's output focus on changes in the expected response—for example, pointing to a flashcard of a word rather than writing its definition during a vocabulary test or completing every other item on a worksheet rather than completing them all.

Figure 8.1   Example of a Unified Plan of Support (UPS)

Unified Plan of Support (UPS)

Student: Robert

Team Members Present: Mr. Blake, Ms. Hill, Mrs. Dalton

Class: Earth Science

Date: September 15, 2007

EDUCATIONAL SUPPORT
(Adaptations, curriculum modifications, alternate instructional formats)

Supports	Person Responsible	Level of Implementation
Embedded instruction on reading vocabulary words.	Ms. Hill Mrs. Dalton	• (Full) • Partial • Pending
Assigned chapter reading recorded on audiotape.	Ms. Hill Mrs. Dalton	• (Full) • Partial • Pending
Modified worksheets highlighting selected vocabulary words.	Ms. Hill Mrs. Dalton	• Full • (Partial) • Pending
		• Full • Partial • Pending

SOCIAL SUPPORT
(Circles of support, buddy systems, social facilitation)

Peer support from Jacob and Lizzie.	Mr. Blake Mrs. Dalton	• Full • (Partial) • Pending
		• Full • Partial • Pending
		• Full • Partial • Pending
		• Full • Partial • Pending

Other issues or concerns:
Robert's desk should be located next to Jacob's and Lizzie's at the front of the classroom.

Note. From "Across-Program Collaboration to Support Students with and without Disabilities in General Education Classrooms," by P. Hunt, K. Doering, A. Hirose-Hatae, J. Maier, & L. Goetz, 2001, *Journal of the Association for Persons with Severe Handicaps, 26,* pp. 240–256. Adapted with permission.

Finally, ecological adaptations may include changes to where a student is located in the classroom, changes to his or her schedule, or changes to whom he or she works with. Changing the location in the class might include moving to a quieter area of the classroom so that the student has fewer distractions in completing a task or moving his or her desk closer to the front of the room to improve his or her ability to see PowerPoint slides. Changing a student's schedule might include allowing him or her to complete a task during study hall rather than during class to give him or her more time or allowing him or her to have regular breaks during a task to prevent fatigue or behavior problems. Similarly, the supports could be changed so that a student is provided with one-on-one instruction rather than group instruction, or instruction could be provided by peers rather than paraprofessionals.

It is important to note that the team may need to use a number of curricular, instructional, and ecological adaptations in order to promote students' success in classes. Further, as discussed above, it is critical that the accommodations be designed specifically to meet students' needs in the typical routines and activities of the class (Fisher & Frey, 2001). Each individual who is supporting a student in a class should be made aware of the adaptations and modifications he or she uses and be given the training necessary to ensure they are implemented correctly.

Focus Question 4	Why are peer supports preferable to paraprofessional supports in general education classes?

Foster Peer-Based Instructional and Social Supports

One of the most common approaches to providing instructional and social support to students in general education classes is to assign a paraprofessional to work with them in completing class routines and activities (French, 2003b; Giangreco, Broer, & Edelman, 2002). While initially the role of paraprofessionals was limited, the available evidence suggests that in a number of schools across the country, paraprofessionals are assuming increasing responsibility for planning and designing instruction for students, even though they do not have the knowledge and skills necessary to do so (Giangreco & Broer, 2005). This raises questions about the overall quality of the educational programs that students may be receiving in general education classes, especially in secondary content-area classes that require that teachers have specialized knowledge in specific disciplines (e.g., math, science, history). Further, research suggests that the presence of paraprofessionals in a general education class can actually have unintended negative impacts, ranging from reducing general educators' engagement with students to lowering the rates of social interactions between disabled students and their peers without disabilities (Downing, Ryndak, & Clark, 2000; Giangreco, Edelman, Luiselli, & MacFarland, 1997; Marks, Schrader, & Levine, 1999; Shukla, Kennedy, & Cushing, 1998; Young, Simpson, Smith-Myles, & Kamps, 1997). Researchers are recognizing that paraprofessional supports should be used sparingly and only in situations in which peer support strategies cannot be used to meet the student's needs (Giangreco & Broer, 2007). This might include situations in which there are concerns about a student's safety, in which he or she might need personal support to care for daily needs, or in which he or she needs intensive assistance or support to communicate with others.

While paraprofessional support should be used judiciously, paraprofessionals can be a critical source of support for students in content-area classes when their roles are well defined and they are provided with the necessary training and ongoing assistance necessary to complete their assignments (Broer, Doyle, & Giangreco, 2005; Carter, Cushing, et al., 2005; Causton-Theoharis & Malmgren, 2005; Devlin, 2005). Although a detailed description of the procedures necessary to prepare paraprofessionals for their roles in general education classes is beyond the scope of this chapter, there are a number field-test programs that can provide valuable resources to teachers and schools in addressing this need (e.g., Doyle, 2002; French, 2003a).

The most appropriate and readily available sources of instructional and social support in general education classes are peers (Carter & Kennedy, 2006; Hunt & McDonnell, 2007). This support can be used when teachers employ cooperative learning or peer-mediated instructional strategies but also when IEP/transition planning teams develop both informal and formal peer support strategies in classes and the school. Peers can play a number of roles in supporting students with intellectual and developmental disabilities in general education classes, including (a) implementing curricular, instructional, or ecological adaptations; (b) providing assistance and feedback in completing assigned tasks; (c) modeling appropriate communication and social skills; (d) facilitating social interactions between students and other peers; and (e) providing embedded instruction on specific skills drawn from the general education curriculum or IEP/transition plan. A number of steps have been recommended for developing and implementing successful peer support programs:

- Identify one or more peers in the same class who can provide support to the student (Carter & Kennedy, 2006). A number of factors should be considered in selecting peers for a support role, including the kinds of supports they will be expected to provide to the student, who will be training and monitoring the peers, and the individual needs of the student.

- Provide training on the specific support roles that peers will play (Carter & Kennedy, 2006). The training should focus on the procedures that they will be implementing with a student. These procedures should be modeled for each peer by a teacher or a paraprofessional, and the peer should be provided with guided practice in implementing them with the student. It is important to structure the training to emphasize to the peer that he or she is not the student's "teacher" but is helping the student participate in class routines and activities.
- Systematically fade support from the peer as the student becomes more competent and confident (Carter & Kennedy, 2006).
- Regularly monitor the supports provided by the peer to ensure that the student is getting what he or she needs. An important part of the monitoring process is to talk with the peer about how things are going and whether he or she is encountering any problems in providing support to the student. Research suggests that peers often have important insights into how to improve the supports provided to students (Fisher & Frey, 2001).

Develop Individualized Teaching Plans

Students will often require explicit, systematic instruction to learn content drawn from the general education curriculum or achieve goals included in their IEPs/transition plans. Research over the last several decades has led to the development of robust technology of instruction for students with intellectual and developmental disabilities (Snell & Brown, 2006; Westling & Fox, 2009). Instruction focused on the individual needs of students with disabilities in general education classes should be designed and implemented following the same principles that guide instruction in separate educational settings. These principles include the following:

- Instruction should be based on a clear and specific statement of the intended learning outcomes for the student.
- A sufficient number of instructional trials should be provided to promote efficient learning.
- Careful selection and sequencing of instructional examples should be practiced to promote generalization and maintenance of targeted skills.
- Response prompting and fading procedures designed to minimize errors during instruction should be used.
- Student errors should be systematically corrected when they do occur.

- Natural reinforcers should be used to support student learning, as should fading schedules of reinforcement to levels found in typical performance environments.
- Student performance data should be collected regularly, and that information should be used to modify instructional procedures as necessary to maximize student learning.

Figure 8.2 provides an illustration of a teaching plan format for implementing embedded instruction in general education classes (McDonnell et al., 2008). The form contains the essential elements of any effective teaching plan and could be easily adapted for use in any individualized instructional format for students in general education classes. The example shows the instructional procedures for teaching Robert to read key vocabulary words drawn from the general education science curriculum. Figure 8.3 presents an illustrative data collection form that could be used to track his performance during the week.

Figure 8.2   Example of an Embedded Instruction Teaching Plan

Student: Robert

Instructional Objective: When presented in different print forms, Robert will read five sight words from the unit on ecosystems with 80% accuracy on two consecutive probes.

Supplemental Instruction Opportunities	*Natural Instruction Opportunities*
Activity transitions.	Textbook.
Breaks during lab.	Worksheets.
Independent seatwork.	Lab summaries.

Presentation Sequence (Vary print forms.)

1. system
2. ecosystem
3. system or ecosystem
4. biodiversity
5. system, ecosystem, or biodiversity

6. atmosphere
7. system, ecosystem, biodiversity, or atmosphere
8. biomass
9. extinction
10. All six words

Assistance Strategy

I. Present word. "Read this word." 0-s delay and model word.
II. Present word. "Read this word." 3-s delay and model.

Reinforcement Procedures

Descriptive social praise. "That's right; it is (word)."

Error Correction Procedures

1. "No, this says (word)."
2. Represent word. "Read this word."
3. Model word.
4. Descriptive feedback. "Yes, that says (word)."

Figure 8.3   Example of an Embedded Instruction Data Collection Form

		Embedded Instruction Data Sheet											
	Assistance/ Sequence Step		Distributed Trial										
Date		1	2	3	4	5	6	7	8	9	10	%
9/20	I	1	+	+	+	+	+	+					100
9/21	I	1	+	+	+	+	+						100
9/22	II	1	0	+	0	+	+	+	+	+	+	+	80
9/23	II	1	+	+	+	+	+						100
9/24	I	2	+	+	+	+	+						100
9/27	I	2	+	+	+	+	+						100
9/28	II	2	0	+	+	+	+	+	+	+	+	+	90

Note. From *A Data Based Classroom for the Moderately and Severely Handicapped,* by H. D. Fredericks, V. L. Baldwin, D. N. Grove, C. Riggs, V. Furey, W. Moore, et al., 1975, Monmouth, OR: Instructional Development Corporation. Adapted with permission.

Schedule Instruction on Individualized Teaching Plans

Once students' individualized teaching plans have been developed, the teacher will need to develop a schedule that will ensure these plans are implemented consistently. One of the most widely used approaches to accomplish this is the scheduling matrix, originally developed as a strategy to schedule embedded instruction on academic and developmental skills into the typical routines and activities of special education classrooms (Guess & Helmstetter, 1986). More recently, it has been suggested as a strategy for planning instruction for students on supplemental, simplified, or alternative curricular goals in general education classes (Downing, 1996; Giangreco, Cloninger, et al., 1998; Ryndak & Alper, 2003).

The development of the scheduling matrix begins with an analysis of the typical routines and activities completed by the teacher and the student each day. Although the content covered by teachers will vary daily, teachers usually have an established pattern for organizing their lessons. For example, they may begin class by reviewing the homework assignment, then present new information in a large group lecture, then have students break into small groups for a collaborative instructional activity, and so on. These routines and activities are analyzed to identify opportunities for providing embedded instruction to students or parallel one-on-one or small-group instruction to students.

Following the analysis, the special education teacher develops a matrix that includes a list of the typical routines and activities and the specific goals that will be addressed with the student throughout the class (Figure 8.4). The teacher then checks the routines or activities in which instruction on each goal should occur. The matrix can serve as a guide for any individual who will provide instruction to a student on these specific goals.

Figure 8.4   Example of a Scheduling Matrix

Student: Robert

Class: Earth Science

	Routines/Activities				
Goals	*Opening*	*Homework Review*	*Lecture/ Demonstration*	*Lab Groups*	*Lab Group Summary*
Initiates conversations with peers.	✓			✓	✓
Reads vocabulary words.	✓	✓		✓	
Uses class schedule.	✓	✓	✓	✓	✓

Summary

The available evidence suggests that secondary-age students benefit from participating in the general education curriculum and in general education classes. Ideally, efforts to support inclusive educational opportunities for students are nested within larger reform efforts within the school to improve the quality of education provided to all students. However, teachers can make students' inclusion in general education classes more successful by collaborating with general educators in developing plans of support that fit within the typical routines and activities of the general education class, developing student- and class-specific adaptations and modifications, creating peer support systems, carefully scheduling instruction on core content and IEP goals, and providing systematic instruction as necessary to ensure student achievement. The potential benefits of participating in the general education curriculum and general education classes are enhanced if the content of the courses in which students are enrolled is directly aligned with their desired postschool goals.

Focus Question Review

Focus Question 1: What factors improve educational benefits for students enrolled in content-area classes?

- The content in the class aligns with students' expected postschool outcomes.
- Students receive instructional supports that allow them to interact with course content and receive individualized instruction tailored to their unique needs.
- Students receive support from peers to participate in the routines and activities of the class.

Focus Question 2: Why are self-directed learning strategies important to improving students' participation in content-area classes?

- They increase students' autonomy in participating in class routines and activities.
- They allow support from special and general education teachers to be reduced.

Focus Question 3: How does the application of universal design principles to curriculum and instruction support the participation of students in the general education curriculum?

- It allows all students to access content covered in the classes.
- It provides alternative ways for students to demonstrate knowledge and skills.

Focus Question 4: Why are peer supports preferable to paraprofessional supports in general education classes?

- Peer supports provide a more natural and age-appropriate source of support to students.
- Research has documented that paraprofessional support often has a number of unintended negative outcomes, including student dependence on the paraprofessional and inhibiting social interactions with peers.

CHAPTER 9

Instruction in
Community Settings

JOHN MCDONNELL

R esearchers have recognized for a number of years that instruction for students without disabilities should be anchored to real-life situations and the applied problems that they will face as employees and citizens (Darling-Hammond, Rustique-Forrester, & Pecheone, 2005; DiMartino & Castaneda, 2007; Herman, 1997). They argue that anchoring instruction to real-life contexts and settings serves two important purposes. First, it increases the relevance of the school's curriculum because students can link what they learn in school with what they will do after graduation. Second, anchoring instruction to the demands of the community also helps students generalize skills learned in school to actual performance settings.

These two ideas are equally applicable to students with intellectual and developmental disabilities. Research has confirmed that these students will frequently need to be provided with direct instruction in actual performance settings to become independent (Horner, McDonnell, & Bellamy, 1986; Rosenthal-Malek & Bloom, 1998). Consequently, community-based instruction is essential to effectively preparing students for their transition from school to adulthood (McDonnell, Mathot-Buckner, & Ferguson, 1996; Wehman, 2006). This chapter addresses the issues related to supporting student learning in community settings. In addition, guidelines for the design of instruction programs are outlined. Finally, we address some of the key logistical issues that teachers face in carrying out community-based instruction.

Importance of Community-Based Instruction

Community-based instruction (CBI) has become a key element of effective secondary programs for students with intellectual and developmental disabilities. The adoption of community-based instruction in secondary programs was driven primarily by a shift in curriculum for this group of students during the 1980s and 1990s from instruction on isolated academic and developmental skills to routines and activities that students would be expected to complete on a day-to-day basis. This shift in curriculum focus was intended to improve the adjustment of students during their transition from school to community life and enhance postschool outcomes. The importance of CBI is also recognized in the Individuals with Disabilities Education Act of 2004, which identifies it as one of the key transition services that school districts must provide to students. CBI has a number of documented benefits for students, including

- Improved generalization of skills learned in school to home, work, and community settings (Horner, McDonnell, et al., 1986; Rosenthal-Malek & Bloom, 1998).
- Increased scores on standardized tests of adaptive behavior (McDonnell, Hardman, Hightower, & Drew, 1993).
- Improved adjustment to employment following school (Bambara, Wilson, & McKenzie, 2007; Phelps & Hanley-Maxwell, 1997).
- Improved social relationships with peers without disabilities following school (Chadsey, 2007).

Students' participation in community-based instruction is enhanced when it is based on several principles (McDonnell et al., 1996; McDonnell & McGuire, 2007). First, the expected outcomes of CBI should reflect the values, preferences, and expectations of students and their families. The overall goal is to use CBI in ways that will improve students' immediate and future quality of life in the community. This can be accomplished only if the routines and activities selected for CBI have a direct impact on students' ability to function more independently in home and community settings. Second, CBI is most effective when it is done in the neighborhoods and communities where students live rather than where their schools are located. This approach increases the likelihood that students will have regular opportunities to complete the routines and activities targeted for CBI and that they will be able to maintain reliable performance across time. Further, focusing on students' neighborhoods and communities makes it more realistic for parents and families to support their participation in routines and activities. Third, the effectiveness of CBI is increased if students are supported by same-age peers as tutors or mentors. Peers can serve as role models who can set an example of appropriate communication and social behaviors in community settings, and they can facilitate students' involvement in typical social networks. CBI provided by peers may also be more motivating to students because it creates opportunities for age-appropriate social interactions and the development of friendships. Fourth, the complexity and logistical demands of CBI require that instructional time and staff resources be focused on establishing reliable performance of a small number of routines and activities that are critical to students' home and community life. Finally, CBI must be designed to build on the natural supports offered by peers, family members, coworkers, or community members. The remaining sections of this chapter will describe some of the steps that teachers can use to design and implement CBI based on these principles.

POINT/COUNTERPOINT 9.1

Inclusive Education Versus Community-Based Instruction

Community-based instruction is a widely accepted strategy for improving the postschool outcomes for students with intellectual and developmental disabilities. However, some have argued that community-based instruction also conflicts with the goals of inclusive education. This Point/Counterpoint explores the various perspectives concerning community-based instruction for secondary students.

POINT

"This practice [community-based instruction] erects barriers to full academic and social inclusion, and gives mixed messages to students and communities alike. While many schools involved in the restructuring movements are embracing educational experiences in the community for all students (for example, community-service requirements, internships, and apprenticeships), most schools have not yet implemented this practice. Therefore, the practice of separate community-based instruction during the school day only for students with disabilities continues to be exclusive" (Tashie, Jorgensen, Shapiro-Barnard, Martin, & Schuh, 1996, p. 20).

COUNTERPOINT

"It would be very difficult to provide the context for instruction in some skills within the walls of many schools; take street crossing, for instance, or selecting and purchasing age and culturally appropriate clothing, or working in a commercial laundry or as a greeter at a discount department store. Certainly, situations can be developed in school settings for teaching the components of such skills, but only in nonschool environments can all of the required components be practiced and addressed under the conditions in which they will actually be required.... To effectively teach and promote the generalization of functional skills, some degree of community based instruction is necessary" (Billingsley & Albertson, 1999, p. 300).

Designing Community-Based Instruction

Figure 9.1 presents the recommended steps for developing community-based instructional programs.

Figure 9.1   Program Development Steps

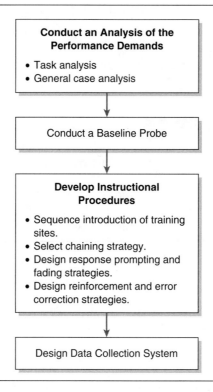

Focus Question 1   When should the teacher conduct a general case analysis of a routine or an activity?

Conduct an Analysis of Performance Demands

Routines and activities are complex chains of behaviors that occur in a consistent sequence. The first challenge to teaching a student to complete a routine or an activity is to identify (a) the specific responses that make up the chain and (b) how these responses may change across various contexts and settings. For example, shopping for groceries requires a student to complete a number of steps in a prescribed sequence. The student demonstrates competence on this activity when he or she can complete these steps reliably across different items, stores, and conditions (e.g., the number of people in the store, time of day). The scope of the analysis is controlled by the number of settings in which a student will ultimately be expected to perform the routine or activity. In some cases, the Individualized Education Program/transition planning team may determine that the student will only need to complete routines or activities in a single site. For example, he or she may only need to shop in the grocery store that is located near his or her home. In other cases, the team may decide that the student needs to learn to shop in a number of different stores in his or her neighborhood or community.

It is recommended that a task analysis be conducted when a student's performance is going to be limited to a single setting (Cooper, Heron, & Heward, 2007; McDonnell et al., 1996). However, if a student is expected to perform across multiple settings, it is recommended that a general case analysis of the activity be conducted (Albin & Horner, 1988; Albin, McDonnell, & Wilcox, 1987).

Task Analysis. The purpose of a task analysis is to (a) break down the routine or activity into a sequence of teachable units of behavior called steps and (b) identify the stimuli that should control when and how a student should complete each step. Figure 9.2 illustrates a task analysis for the activity of shopping for groceries.

There are no empirically validated rules for conducting a task analysis. The aim is to identify the smallest number of steps that functionally describe what a student is expected to do and that allow the teacher to reliably track the student's progress in learning the activity. One way to identify the steps of a task analysis is to think about how you might use short phrases to describe to someone else how to complete an activity. For example, you could describe shopping for groceries by saying "enter the store foyer," "enter the cart storage area," "pull the cart to the foyer," "enter the store," "push the cart to the first aisle," and so on. While each of these steps could be broken down even further (e.g., "enter the store" could be broken down into "place right hand on door handle," "pull door open," "walk through door," "release handle"), initially this level of detail is probably unnecessary to guide instruction or to monitor a student's performance. In addition, it is important that each step in the task analysis be observable and measurable. In other words, anyone watching a student complete an activity would be able to see him or her do the behavior described in the step and be able to determine whether it was done correctly or incorrectly.

Figure 9.2 Illustration of a Task Analysis

Student: Brad

Activity: Shopping at Reams

Performance Conditions:

 When: Afternoons

 What: One-step meals

 How: Picture cards of each item and use a $20 bill to pay

Stimuli	Response
1. Door on west side of the building.	1. Walk through "in" door.
2. Cart lineup. Cart at back of line.	2. Pull cart from back.
3. Produce section.	3. Push cart through produce section.
4. Canned food aisle. Item picture.	4. Push cart to canned food aisle.
5. Item picture. Item section.	5. Push cart to item section.
6. Item picture. Item on shelf.	6. Pick up item.
7. Item. Cart.	7. Place item in cart.
8. Frozen food aisle.	8. Push cart to frozen food aisle.
9. Item picture. Item section.	9. Push cart to item section.
10. Item. Cart.	10. Place item in cart.
11. Express checkout.	11. Push cart to express checkout kiosk.
12. Monitor. Start button.	12. Press "start" button.
13. Monitor. Prompt—scan your item.	13. Scan first item.
14. Bag holder. Bag.	14. Place item in bag.
15. Monitor. Promptly scan your item.	15. Scan second item.
16. Bag holder. Bag.	16. Place item in bag.
17. Monitor. Pay button.	17. Press pay button.
18. Monitor. Cash button. Bill slot.	18. Insert $20 bill.
19. Bill change dispenser. Coin change dispenser.	19. Get change.
20. Receipt printer. Receipt.	20. Get receipt.
21. Bag.	21. Pick up bag.
22. Door on east side of building.	22. Walk through "out" door.

Teachers also need to identify the stimuli that tell a student when and how to complete each step. For example, in the grocery store, the stimuli for giving money to the cashier include the total price appearing on the register display and the cashier requesting the amount. Stimuli can include objects that are present in the setting (e.g., the door, the checkout counter, one's grocery list, the cash register) or events or actions that consistently precede the step (e.g., the door opening automatically, the manager stating "cereal is on Aisle 6," a person moving forward in line). This information is used to design instructional procedures that minimize the number of errors that a student makes in learning the activity.

Finally, the task analysis should be validated. This can be done either by observing others complete the routine or activity in the same setting or by simply doing the routine or activity. Redundant or unnecessary steps should be eliminated from the task analysis. In some cases, an alternative performance strategy will need to be identified to allow a student to meet the functional demands of a step. For example, a student could pay for items using a $20 bill rather than counting out a specific amount.

General Case Analysis. A general case analysis expands traditional task analysis procedures to identify the variation in the steps and stimuli that occur across performance settings (Horner, Sprague, & Wilcox, 1982). For example, it is likely that the location of items or the cash register displays will be different across grocery stores. In fact, depending on the number of stores, the variation in the steps and stimuli may be very large. From a practical standpoint, helping a student learn to deal with this variation would be much easier if the teacher could carry out instruction in two or three stores rather than in every store in the neighborhood. This is precisely the logic underlying general case analysis procedures. These procedures have been used successfully to teach students with intellectual and developmental disabilities to generalize their performance of a number of routines and activities, including bussing tables in a restaurant (Horner, Eberhardt, & Sheehan, 1986), crossing streets (Horner, Jones, & Williams, 1985), using telephones (Horner, Williams, & Stevely, 1987), and using vending machines (Sprague & Horner, 1984).

Figure 9.3 presents an example of a general case analysis for the activity of shopping for groceries. There are six steps in conducting a general case analysis:

1. *Identify the settings in which a student will be expected to complete the activity.* In this step, the teacher should identify all of the settings in which a student will be expected to complete the activity. Typically, the number of settings identified will be based on the neighborhood and community

Figure 9.3   Illustration of a General Case Analysis

Student: Brad

Activity: Grocery shopping

Performance Conditions:

    Where: Reams, Smith's, Dan's, Safeway, Albertsons

    When: Afternoons

    What: One-step meals

    How: Picture cards of target items and use $20 bill to pay

Stimuli	Stimuli Variation	Response	Response Variation
1. Door.	a. Automatic—Swing. b. Automatic—Slide. c. Double—Push.	1. Enter store.	a. Walk through. b. Push door and walk through.
2. Cart storage. Carts.	a. Storage in foyer. b. Front wall. c. Both sides of checkout.	2. Get cart.	a. Pull from back of line. b. Pull from front of line.
3. Aisle. Picture card.	a. Canned food. b. Frozen food.	3. Scan aisle for target item.	a. Front aisle. b. Middle aisle.
4. Picture card. Item section.	a. Top shelf location—open shelf, closed freezer case. b. Middle shelf location—open shelf, closed freezer case. c. Bottom shelf location—open shelf, closed freezer case, open freezer case.	4. Get item.	a. Remove from top shelf. b. Hold door open and remove from top shelf. c. Remove from middle shelf. d. Hold door open and remove from middle shelf. e. Remove from bottom shelf. f. Hold door open and remove from bottom shelf.
5. Express checkout.	a. Kiosks side-by-side. b. Push through kiosks.	5. Go to open kiosk.	a. Push cart to open kiosk. b. Push cart through line.
6. Monitor. Scan plate.	a. Monitor at eye level. b. Monitor at counter level.	6. Scan items.	a. Bar code on side. b. Bar code on bottom.
7. Bag holder. Bags.	a. Right of scan plate. b. Left of scan plate. c. Paper. d. Plastic.	7. Place items in bag.	a. Pull bag open in holder. b. Pull bag from holder and open.
8. Touch screen. Bill slot.	a. Pay. Cash. b. Finish. Cash. c. Beside monitor. d. Beside receipt printer.	8. Pay.	a. Touch pay and touch cash. b. Touch finish and cash. c. Move to slot and insert.

Stimuli	Stimuli Variation	Response	Response Variation
9. Bill change dispenser. Coin change dispenser.	a. Beside monitor. b. Below monitor. c. Beside receipt printer.	9. Get change.	a. Move to dispenser. b. Reach down.
10. Bag holder. Bag.	a. Right of scan plate. b. Left of scan plate. c. Paper. d. Plastic.	10. Get bag.	a. Pull bag from holder by handles. b. Lift bag from bottom.
11. Door.	a. Automatic—Swing. b. Automatic—Slide. c. Double—Push.	11. Exit store.	a. Walk through. b. Push door and walk through.

where a student lives and that student's specific needs. The student would not need to shop in every grocery store located in a large urban area. It would be more functional to focus instruction on the stores located in his or her immediate neighborhood. In the example presented above, the IEP/transition planning team decided that Brad should learn to shop in five stores near his home. The information gathered in these settings will be used by his teacher to select a subset of training sites for instruction.

2. *Define the scope of a student's performance in the activity.* What students are expected to do in completing an activity can vary significantly based on their specific needs. For example, a student could be taught to purchase snacks (e.g., a can of soda, a piece of fruit) or shop for all food, household, and hygiene items needed to maintain a home. In our example, Brad's IEP/transition planning team decided that he should learn to purchase one-step meals (e.g., a can of soup, frozen entrees) that he can prepare for lunch or dinner when he is home alone. In addition, it is useful to identify how students will be expected to complete the activity. Essentially, the question is whether they will do the activity the way that it is typically done by peers or whether they will use alternative performance strategies to complete one or more of the activity steps. Since Brad cannot read or count money, his IEP/transition planning team decided that he can use a picture list to remember the things that he wants to buy at the store and a $20 bill to pay for the items in order to avoid having to count out specific amounts.

3. *Identify "generic" activity steps.* The teachers should identify a set of steps that are common to *all* of the expected performance settings. For example, instead of describing the specific steps that a student would complete to get a cart in each store, a generic step like "get the cart" that

accommodates the differences in where the carts are located and how customers get them out across stores is included in the analysis. These generic activity steps are used to guide instruction and track a student's progress across all of the training sites.

4. *Identify the "generic" stimuli that set the occasion for each activity step.* The teacher should identify the generic stimuli that control when and how a student completes each activity step. For example, the generic stimuli for the step "get the cart" would include the storage area and the cart.

5. *Survey expected performance settings.* It is recommended that the teacher go to each of the expected performance settings and record the variation observed in the generic activity steps and stimuli. For the generic stimuli, the teacher should record the differences in the objects or events that set the occasion for each activity step found in each setting. For example, the cart storage area at Dan's is in front of the entrance, carts at Smith's are stored in an area adjacent to the foyer, and so on. Next, the way the student's behaviors need to change in response to the differences in stimuli variation across the sites should be listed on the form. At Dan's, Brad will need to pull the cart from the front of the lineup, and at Smith's, he will need to pull it from the back of the lineup and back up into the store foyer. The list of variations in the generic stimuli and activity steps is used to select the subset of training sites used during instruction.

6. *Select training sites.* The goal of this step is to identify the smallest number of sites for instruction that will expose a student to the range of variation in the stimuli and steps found across all of the expected performance settings. In our example, Brad's teacher found that she could account for all of the variation in the stimuli and steps found across the five grocery stores targeted for performance by using Reams, Smith's, and Dan's as training sites. A simple process can be used to ensure that the training sites account for the full range of variation:

- Begin by selecting the nearest site to where instruction will be carried out, and check off the variation in the stimuli and steps that it presents to students. Selecting the site closest to where instruction will be carried out cuts down on travel time and maximizes the time available for instruction. In the example, the teacher selected Reams as the first training site because it was only one block away from the school. She went through the general case analysis form and simply checked off the variation in the stimuli and steps found at Reams.

- Select the site that is the most different from the first site, and check off the variation it presents to a student. The training sites selected for instruction should expose a student to the widest possible variation in the stimuli and activity steps. By selecting the site that is the most different from the first site, the teacher increases the likelihood that the subset of training sites will include the full range of variation. In our example, Brad's teacher selected Smith's as the second training site because it was significantly different from Reams in the areas of cart location, layout of items within the store, and range of check-out counter configurations.
- Finally, select the least number of sites necessary to account for the remaining variation in the stimuli and steps. Brad's teacher found that she could accommodate the remaining variation by including Dan's in the training set.

Focus Question 2	What information should be obtained from a baseline probe?

Conduct a Baseline Probe

Conducting a baseline probe of a student's performance helps a teacher tailor instructional procedures to the student's specific needs. A baseline probe should focus on assessing a student's expected level of performance once instruction is completed. For example, the goal for Brad was for him to purchase two one-step meals using pictures of the items and a $20 bill to pay. Consequently, his baseline probe was structured to reflect these demands. The baseline probe should be focused on (a) identifying whether a student completes the steps of the task or general case analysis correctly or incorrectly and (b) identifying the level of assistance that he or she will need to complete the steps that he or she cannot do correctly. Figure 9.4 illustrates a baseline probe summary form.

In our example, Brad was able to correctly enter the store at Reams, Smith's, and Dan's. However, he required assistance to complete the remaining steps across the training sites. Brad's teacher recorded the amount of assistance that he needed to complete each of the steps. On Step 2, he needed both a verbal direction to get the cart and a model to demonstrate how to pull it from the lineup in all three stores. The types of prompts required by students to complete a step can be determined by providing increasing levels of assistance following an error. For example, when Brad did not immediately go to get a cart, his teacher asked, "What do you

Figure 9.4 Illustration of a CBI Baseline Probe Summary Form

Student: Brad	I-Indirect Verbal	G-Gesture	+-Step
Activity: Grocery shopping	D-Direct Verbal	P-Physical Prime	completed
	M-Model	F-Full Physical	without assistance

		Date/Site/Task		
		9/15	9/16	9/17
		Reams	Smith's	Dan's
Stimuli	Response	Stew Meat Pie	Soup Macaroni	Chili Pizza
1. Door.	1. Enter store.	+	+	+
2. Cart storage. Carts.	2. Get cart.	D/M	D/M	D/M
3. Aisle. Picture card.	3. Scan aisle for target item.	D	D	D
4. Picture card. Item section.	4. Get item.	D/P	D/G	D/G
5. Express checkout.	5. Go to open kiosk.	D/G	D/G	D/G
6. Monitor. Scan plate.	6. Scan items.	D/G	D/G	D/G
7. Bag holder. Bag.	7. Place item in bag.	D	D	D
8. Touch screen. Bill slot.	8. Pay.	D/G	D/G	D/G
9. Bill change dispenser. Coin change dispenser.	9. Get change.	D/G	D/G	D
10. Bag holder. Bag.	10. Get bag.	D	+	D
11. Door.	11. Exit store.	+	+	+

need to do?" When he did not get the cart, she provided a verbal direction: "Go get a cart." When he still did not pull out a cart, she repeated her verbal direction and showed him how to pull the cart from the lineup. After he got the cart with this level of assistance, she recorded that he required a verbal direction and a model on Step 2 on the Baseline Probe Summary Form. This process continues with each step in the task or general case analysis. When students are expected to complete an activity across settings, a baseline probe should be conducted in all of the training sites.

Develop Instructional Procedures

Effective instructional procedures for students with intellectual and developmental disabilities have been discussed extensively elsewhere and are beyond the scope of this chapter (Cooper et al., 2007; Snell & Brown, 2006; Westling & Fox, 2004; Wolery, Ault, & Doyle, 1992). However, McDonnell and colleagues (1996) outlined several specific recommendations for teachers in designing the components of CBI programs. These include the sequence in which training sites should be introduced, the chaining strategy used to teach the steps of the activity, response prompting and fading procedures, reinforcement procedures, and error correction (Table 9.1).

Introducing the Training Sites. The difficulty of a CBI program for a student can be controlled by number and order of training sites introduced for instruction. Three strategies have been discussed in the literature, including serial introduction, concurrent introduction, and cumulative introduction (McDonnell et al., 1996). Research has generally supported the use of the concurrent or cumulative introduction strategies with students with intellectual and developmental disabilities (Albin & Horner, 1988; Carnine & Becker, 1982; Ferguson & McDonnell, 1991; Panyan & Hall, 1978; Waldo, Guess, & Flanagan, 1982).

In the concurrent introduction strategy, all of the training sites are introduced simultaneously to a student. The sites are presented randomly throughout the instructional program. Training continues until the student is able to complete the activity reliably across all of the training sites. Using this strategy, Brad's teacher would randomly select Reams, Smith's, or Dan's for instruction on any given day. This strategy requires students to demonstrate that they can generalize their performance of the activity across the training sites. However, introducing all of the training sites at the same point in time might be too difficult for some students and ultimately increase the time necessary for them to learn the activity.

The cumulative introduction strategy introduces one site to a student at a time but requires him or her to regularly demonstrate the ability to perform across previously introduced sites. Training begins with a single site. When a student is able to complete the activity reliably in that site, a new site is introduced for instruction. Training continues in the second site until he or she can complete the steps of the activity correctly. At this point, the student is required to complete the activity across the two sites when they are selected randomly for instruction. This step in the introduction sequence ensures the development of a generalized response by requiring the student to adjust his or her performance of the activity to the variation found in the stimuli and steps in the two sites. The introduction of subsequent training sites follows the same pattern until a student can complete the activity reliably across all of the sites. In our

Table 9.1 Recommended Procedures for CBI Programs

Sequence Instructional Sites for Introduction

1. Use concurrent introduction if all training sites and tasks can be presented to the student during a typical school week (e.g., Monday–Friday), and use cumulative introduction if they cannot.

2. Shift to a cumulative introduction sequence if students do not make adequate progress through concurrent introduction.

Select a Chaining Strategy

1. Begin instruction with whole task instruction for most students and activities.

2. If the student does not make adequate progress, implement a backward chaining strategy and increase the intensity of the reinforcement provided at the end of the activity.

Design an Assistance Strategy

1. Use either the system of most prompts or time delay during the acquisition phase of instruction.

2. Use a time delay procedure if the student has a history of prompt dependency.

Design Reinforcement Procedures

1. During initial acquisition, provide praise to the student following each correct response in the activity, and provide the student with a power reinforcer at the end of the activity.

2. Provide intermittent praise to students throughout the chain after the student's performance begins to improve, and fade out all praise as soon as possible.

3. Begin to delay the end-of-activity reinforcement as soon as the student can independently complete the activity.

4. Use reinforcers that are naturally available in the performance settings and logically related to the activity being taught.

Design Error Correction Procedures

Ensure that the error correction procedure is designed to

1. Interrupt errors immediately.

2. Require the student to perform the correct response before moving on in the chain.

3. Provide the level of assistance necessary to ensure a correct response.

4. Provide low-intensity feedback on the correct response.

example, Brad's teacher began instruction at Reams. Instruction shifted to Smith's when he completed all of the steps correctly at Reams. When he met criteria at Smith's, his teacher randomly asked him to shop at Reams or Smith's until he could correctly complete the steps of the activity across both sites. Finally, Brad was provided with instruction at Dan's. When he met criteria there, he was asked to shop at Reams, Smith's, or Dan's when these were selected at random. Instruction continued until he completed the activity correctly across all three sites.

Select a Chaining Strategy. Chaining strategies are also used to control the difficulty of the activity for a student during the initial stages of instruction. Two different chaining strategies have been discussed in the literature, including forward and backward chaining (Snell & Brown, 2006; Westling & Fox, 2004). In addition, whole task presentation has been suggested as an alternative to the use of forward or backward chaining in CBI (McDonnell et al., 1996).

In forward chaining, the steps of the activity are cumulatively introduced to a student for instruction in their natural order of performance. For example, in teaching grocery shopping, instruction is provided on the first step of the activity ("enter the store"), and assistance is provided to the student to complete the remaining steps. The focus is on teaching students to complete the first step of the activity without assistance. During initial stages of instruction, the teacher provides assistance to the student to complete the first step in the activity and then fades his or her assistance as quickly as possible. When the student is able to do the first step without assistance, the second step of the activity ("get the cart") is introduced, and instruction is provided on these two steps ("enter the store," "get the cart") until the student completes them correctly without assistance. Each subsequent step would be introduced for instruction in a similar manner until the student is able to complete all of the steps in the activity without assistance. Backward chaining employs essentially the same approach, but steps are introduced for instruction beginning with the last step in the activity and added cumulatively for instruction from the end of the activity to the beginning. Instruction continues until a student can do all of the steps without assistance.

An alternative to forward and backward chaining is to teach a student to complete all of the steps of an activity at the same time. This strategy is generally referred to as whole task instruction. In this approach, a teacher provides assistance to a student on each step of the activity as necessary and then systematically fades his or her assistance on each step as the student becomes more independent. Research comparing the relative efficacy of forward and backward chaining and whole task instruction within CBI has generally favored whole task instruction (Kayser, Billingsley, & Neel, 1986; McDonnell & Laughlin, 1989; McDonnell & McFarland, 1988; Spooner, Weber, & Spooner, 1983).

Focus Question 3	What does the available research suggest are the most effective ways to fade response prompts during CBI?

Design Response Prompting and Fading Strategies. Teachers will typically need to provide students with assistance to complete the steps of an activity during the initial stages of instruction. This assistance is typically provided in the form of response prompts, such as verbal directions, models, or hand-over-hand assistance (Table 9.2). However, these response prompts will need to be faded so students can learn to perform the activity independently. A number of response prompting and fading procedures have been described in the research literature (Wolery et al., 1992). The three strategies that have received the most examination in CBI include the system of least prompts, the system of most prompts, and time delay.

The system of least prompts is structured to provide increasing levels of assistance to a student following an error until he or she correctly completes the step. For example, Brad would be given an opportunity to enter the express checkout lane independently during instruction. If he didn't initiate this step himself, the teacher would provide an indirect verbal prompt like "What do you need to do now?" If he still didn't go to a checkout lane, the teacher would provide a direct verbal prompt, such as "Go to the express checkout lane." If this prompt did not lead to the correct response, the teacher would physically guide Brad to the correct checkout lane. The logic of the system of least prompts is that students will require less and less assistance across instructional sessions as they learn the steps of the task or general case analysis.

The system of most prompts is designed to provide assistance to a student before he or she makes an error. Initially, a student is provided with a prompt that will automatically lead to a correct response. This prompt is identified during the baseline probe. The teacher begins the fading procedure with this prompt, and then the amount of assistance provided to the student is systematically reduced across training trials or sessions. Using the example from above, when it was time for Brad to go to the express checkout lane, his teacher would provide a direct verbal prompt ("Go to the express checkout lane") and point at the correct location (see Figure 9.4). When he was able to go to the correct lane with these two prompts, she "faded" the amount of assistance that she provided to him by giving him only a direct verbal prompt ("Go to the express checkout lane"). When Brad reliably went to the checkout lane with a direct verbal prompt, his teacher faded her level of assistance to an indirect verbal prompt ("Where do you go?"). Finally, Brad would be expected to find the correct checkout lane without any assistance from his teacher.

Table 9.2   Types of Prompts

Prompt	Description
Indirect Verbal Prompt	A statement that tells the student a response is expected.
	Examples: "What do you do now?"; "What is next?"
Direct Verbal Prompt	A verbal statement that explicitly describes the expected response.
	Examples: "Open the door"; Go to the express checkout lane."
Gestural Prompt	Nonverbal behavior by the teacher that indicates the expected response.
	Examples: Motioning with your hand to indicate the student should enter the store; pointing to an item on the shelf.
Model	Demonstrating the expected response for the student.
	Examples: Showing the student how to pull the cart from the lineup; showing the student how to pull a plastic bag from the roll in the produce section.
Physical Prime	Brief physical contact with the student to indicate the expected response.
	Examples: Pushing the student's hand to correct the path of the cart; touching the student lightly on the back to get him or her to move forward in the line.
Physical Assistance	Sustained physical contact to assist the student to complete the expected response.
	Examples: Placing your hand on the student's when he or she pulls open the door; placing your hand on the student's forearm to assist him or her with pushing the cart in a straight line.
Pictures or Symbols	Pictures, symbols, or words that tell the student the expected response.
	Examples: A written self-management checklist that helps the student remember what to take to the store; pictures of items to be located in the store.

The third strategy that has been used successfully in CBI is time delay. Like the system of most prompts, time delay is structured to prevent student errors during instruction. However, instead of changing the type of prompt provided to students across instructional sessions, the prompts are "faded" by systematically increasing the time between the natural presentation of the stimuli and teachers' prompts.

There are two types of time delay: progressive time delay and constant time delay (Wolery et al., 1992). In progressive time delay, training begins by pairing the prompt that leads to a student's correct response (identified during the baseline probe) with the presentation of the natural stimulus for a step. This is commonly referred to as the 0-s-delay step. When the student completes the step correctly with the prompt being presented immediately, the time period between the presentation of the natural stimulus and the teacher's prompt is gradually increased. Typically, the delay period is increased in 1-s intervals until the student completes the step without a prompt. In our example, Brad's teacher would begin instruction by giving her prompts ("Go to the express checkout lane" and pointing) as soon as the express checkout sign was in view. When he could go to the correct lane with her prompts being presented immediately, she would change the procedure by delaying her prompts by 1 s. So, when the checkout sign came into view, she would count to herself ("1, one-thousand, 2, one-thousand," and so on). If Brad started to go to the correct lane during the 1-s interval, she would praise him ("Good job! You are going to the right lane"). If he did not start to go to the correct lane or if he began going to the wrong lane, she would provide her prompts ("Go to the express checkout lane" and pointing). The period across which Brad's teacher delayed her prompts was systematically increased by 1 sec (1 s, 2 s, 3 s) as his performance improves.

In constant time delay, the length of time that the prompt is delayed remains the same across instructional trials and sessions. Instruction begins with a 0-s delay period in which the prompt is presented immediately with the presentation of the natural stimulus. When a student reliably completes the step with a 0-s delay, the prompt is delayed by a prespecified time interval (i.e., 3 s). The delay interval would remain the same across instructional sessions.

In general, research has shown the systems of most prompts and time delay to be more effective for students during the initial stages of instruction (Bennett, Gast, Wolery, & Schuster, 1986; McDonnell, 1987; Zane, Walls, & Thvedt, 1981). Research comparing the overall efficacy of the systems of most prompts and time delay has generally favored time delay (Schuster et al., 1998). Some researchers have suggested that time delay procedures are more appropriate for students who have a history of prompt dependency because time delay encourages them to initiate the target response without assistance. Finally, constant time delay has been recommended for CBI because it requires the individual carrying out instruction to remember only whether the prompt is to be presented immediately with the natural stimulus or whether it is to be delayed by a consistent period of time.

Reinforcement and Error Correction Procedures. The importance of differential reinforcement in establishing the reliable performance of new behaviors has been well established (Cooper et al., 2007). Differential reinforcement is structured to provide students with positive feedback when they make a correct response and no feedback when they make an incorrect response. Although differential reinforcement is an essential component of CBI, it is critical that reinforcement be faded to natural levels in order to promote the maintenance of students' performance across time.

In the initial stages of instruction, reinforcement is provided on all steps of the activity that the student completes correctly. However, as his or her performance improves, reinforcement during the activity is faded. When the student can regularly complete all steps without assistance, reinforcement should be provided only at the end of the activity. Next, the reinforcement should be delayed for longer and longer periods of time (when the student gets back to school or every other instructional session). The goal is to reduce reinforcement to the lowest levels that will maintain the student's performance. Finally, reinforcement systems used during CBI should rely to the greatest extent possible on the natural reinforcers that are available within an activity.

Although research suggests that teachers should use response prompting and fading procedures in CBI that minimize errors during instruction, no instructional program is foolproof, and student errors are a common part of teaching in community settings. The critical components of error correction in CBI include (a) immediately interrupting an incorrect response and providing students with feedback ("No, that's not the correct checkout lane"), (b) requiring students to complete the correct response before moving on in the activity, (c) providing the level of assistance necessary to ensure that students will make the correct response on the next attempt ("Go to the express checkout lane" and pointing to the correct lane), and (d) providing low-key descriptive feedback after students have corrected their response ("This is the express checkout lane").

Develop a Data Collection System

Collecting regular student performance data is essential to ensure the effectiveness of CBI. Data collection provides the mechanisms necessary to document student learning and to modify instructional procedures to meet a student's needs. Figure 9.5 presents a format that can be used to gather data on a student's performance during instruction. The form is designed to include the key components of the instructional program, including the training site, the tasks students are asked to complete, the response prompting and fading procedures, and reinforcement and error correction

Figure 9.5 Illustration of a CBI Data Collection Form

Student: Brad

Activity: Shopping at Reams

Stimuli	*Response*	*Prompt*	*Date/Site/Task* 10/1 Reams Stew Macaroni
1. Door.	1. Enter store.	None.	+
2. Cart lineup. Carts.	2. Get cart.	1. 0 s delay—"Get a cart." Plus a model. 2. 3 s delay—"Get a cart." Plus a model.	1 ✓
3. Aisle. Picture cards.	3. Scan aisle for target item.	1. 0 s delay—"Look for _____." 2. 3 s delay—"Look for _____."	1 ✓
4. Item picture. Item section.	4. Get item.	1. 0 s delay—"Put it in." Plus a point. 2. 3 s delay—"Put it in." Plus a point.	2 +
5. Express checkout.	5. Go to open kiosk.	1. 0 s delay—"That one is open." Plus a point. 2. 3 s delay—"That one is open." Plus a point.	2 +
6. Monitor. Scan plate.	6. Scan items.	1. 0 s delay—"Scan it." Plus move hand over plate. 2. 3 s delay—"Scan it." Plus move hand over plate.	2 0
7. Bag holder. Bag.	7. Place item in bag.	1. 0 s delay—"Put it in the bag." 2. 3 s delay—"Put it in the bag."	2 ✓
8. Touch screen. Bill slot.	8. Pay.	1. 0 s delay—"Put it in here." Plus a point. 2. 3 s delay—"Put it in here." Plus a point.	2 ✓
9. Bill change dispenser. Coin change dispenser.	9. Get change.	1. 0 s delay—"Get your change." 2. 3 s delay—"Get your change."	2 +
10. Bag holder. Bag.	10. Get bag.	1. 0 s delay—"Get the bag." 2. 3 s delay—"Get the bag."	2 +
11. Door.	11. Exit store.	None.	+

Reinforcement	*Error Correction*
1. Social praise throughout chain.	1. Say, "No," and interrupt response.
	2. Say, "Try again."
	3. Provide immediate assistance.
	4. "That's right, you _____."

procedures. The level of prompts or time delay intervals to be provided to a student is indicated in the top right-hand corner of the data box for each step of the activity. This system allows the teacher to designate the prompts to be provided to a student prior to each instructional session and helps ensure that he or she will receive the correct prompt no matter who is carrying out the training. During instruction, a student's performance is recorded on each step of the activity using a three-code system. A "+" indicates that the student completed the step of the activity correctly and independently. A "✓" indicates that the student completed the step of the activity correctly but with the designated prompt or time delay interval. Finally, a "0" indicates that the student made an error on the step.

Raw data collected during instruction are transferred to a summary sheet that allows teachers to track changes in prompt levels across sessions and to identify the steps of the activity that are difficult for students (Figure 9.6). In summarizing the raw data, a teacher would "color in" the appropriate box for each step of the activity that a student completed correctly and independently. If a student completed the step correctly with the designated prompt, the appropriate prompt number would be entered in the box. If a student made an error, the box would be left blank. This format quickly highlights the difficult steps that are preventing students from successfully completing the activity. A teacher can use this information to modify the instruction procedures on difficult steps of the task and general case analysis as necessary to promote student learning.

Implementing CBI

Carrying out CBI is often made more difficult by several logistical challenges. These include providing a sufficient amount of instruction to maximize student learning, staffing, transportation, and staff liability. There are no universal solutions to these challenges, but several strategies may assist teachers in ensuring that the benefits of CBI are maximized for students.

Enhancing the Effectiveness of CBI

Early research on strategies promoting the performance of routines and activities by students often focused on the use of classroom- or school-based "simulations" (Bates, 1980; Coon, Vogelsberg, & Williams, 1981; McDonnell, Horner, & Williams, 1984; Page, Iwata, & Neef, 1976; van den Pol et al., 1981). Simulations are training formats in which the natural stimuli found in the performance environment are represented through some alternative form or medium during instruction (Horner, McDonnell, et al., 1986). For example,

Figure 9.6 Illustration of a CBI Data Summary Form

	Date/Site/Task					
	9/26	9/27	9/28	9/29	9/30	10/1
	Reams	Reams	Reams	Reams	Reams	Reams
Response	Stew Meat Pie	Soup Mac	Chili Pizza	Soup Pizza	Soup Meat Pie	Stew Mac
1. Enter store.						
2. Get cart.				1	1	1
3. Scan aisle for item.					1	1
4. Get item.	1	1	2	2		
5. Go to open kiosk.			1	1	2	
6. Scan items.	1	1	2	2	2	
7. Place items in bag.			1	1	2	2
8. Pay.		1	1	2	2	2
9. Get change.	1	1	2	2		
10. Get bag.	1	1	2	2		
11. Exit store.						

McDonnell and colleagues taught students to use the next-dollar strategy (counting out one more dollar than the amount presented on the cash register display—e.g., if the display reads $2.45, the student will count out three $1 bills) using paper flashcards and photographic slides of cash registers to represent amounts. The flashcard condition utilized a typical one-to-one instructional format in which a student and a teacher were seated at a table across from one another. In the slide condition, the amounts presented to the student were displayed on an image on the wall that approximated the size of the displays of cash registers found in the local community. In addition, the student and the teacher role-played the typical interactions that customers and cashiers would have to pay for items in stores.

The logic underlying classroom simulations is that they allow teachers to increase the amount of instruction provided to students because simulation eliminates the time required to travel to community sites; decreases the costs associated with carrying out instruction in community settings; and, perhaps most important, promotes generalization of skills learned in school to community settings. Unfortunately, the early research suggested that the level of generalization achieved by students from classroom simulations to community settings was extremely low and often inconsistent across students (Horner, McDonnell, et al., 1986; Rosenthal-Malek & Bloom, 1998). Further, students typically did not develop reliable performance of routines and activities in actual settings until they were provided with CBI.

This prompted researchers to examine the utility of combining classroom simulations and community-based instruction to improve students' generalized performance (Branham, Collins, Schuster, & Klienert, 1999; Coon et al., 1981; Gaylord-Ross, Haring, Breen, & Pitts-Conway, 1984; Marchetti, McCartney, Drain, Hopper, & Dix, 1983; Marholin, O'Toole, Touchette, Berger, & Doyle, 1979; McDonnell & Horner, 1985; Morrow & Bates, 1987; Sarber & Cuvo, 1983; Sarber, Halasz, Messmer, Bickett, & Lutzker, 1983). In general, these studies found that this approach substantially improved students' levels of generalization of routines and activities to nontrained community sites. This was especially true when the classroom simulations were designed to approximate as closely as possible the stimulus conditions found in actual performance sites. The implications of these studies for practitioners are that students' performance in community settings can be improved by systematically using classroom- or school-based instruction to supplement CBI.

Advancements in computer and video technology have spurred renewed interest in how classroom- or school-based instruction can be used to enhance student performance in actual performance settings and the effectiveness of CBI. For example, Mechling and Cronin (2006) used computer-based video instruction to teach three students with intellectual and developmental disabilities to generalize the use of their augmentative and alternative communication devices to order food and drink items in fast food restaurants. Other studies have shown that computer-based video simulations improved students' performance in locating items in grocery stores (Hutcherson, Langone, Ayres, & Clees, 2004; Mechling, 2004), using an automated teller machine (Mechling, Gast, & Barthold, 2003), using the next-dollar strategy to make purchases (Ayres, Langone, Boon, & Norman, 2006), and completing job tasks (Mechling & Ortega-Hurndon, 2007).

Although advancements in computer and video technologies have increased the potential utility of simulations in teaching community-based routines and activities to students, we have little information about the design principles that should drive the development of simulations (Wissick, Gardner, & Langone, 1999). However, previous research suggests that several guidelines may assist teachers in using these technologies more effectively (Horner, McDonnell, et al., 1986; Wissick et al., 1999):

1. *Use general case analysis to select instructional examples.* One of the most powerful advantages of computer-based simulations is their capacity to present a student with the full range of variation in the stimuli and steps of the routine or activity across settings. General case analysis of the routine and activity can assist teachers with identifying that range of variation and selecting examples for instruction.

2. *Require students to approximate the response completed in the actual environment as closely as possible.* Although computer-based technologies allow for a variety of potential response topographies (e.g., touch screen, voice activation), research suggests that a student's responses should be as similar as possible to those required in actual performance settings (e.g., actually counting out money, touching numbers on the screen in sequence to enter an ATM personal identification number).

3. *Sequence instructional examples to require students to demonstrate a generalized response across simulation examples.* The capacity of computer-based simulations to present an extremely large number of instructional examples to a student suggests the need to systematically sequence instructional examples for introduction. Previous research suggests that cumulative introduction of examples is most appropriate when the number of potential examples is extremely large (McDonnell et al., 1996).

4. *Pair computer-based simulations with CBI.* Although computer- and video-based simulations improve generalization to community settings, the available research suggests that it is most effective when it is paired with CBI (Branham et al., 1999). Although we do not know the best approach to pairing simulations and CBI, the few studies that have been completed to date suggest that pairing simulation with CBI on the same day produces better generalization than other strategies, such as alternating simulation and CBI across successive days (Cihak, Alberto, Kessler, & Taber, 2004; Nietupski, Clancy, Wehrmacher, & Parmer, 1985; Nietupski, Hamre-Nietupski, Clancy, & Veerhusen, 1986).

5. *Use peers to support instruction in computer-based multimedia simulations.* One of the potential dangers of this technology is that students could become more isolated within the classroom and the school. Teachers can address this problem by using peers to support students' interaction with computer simulations. Given the tech savvy of most adolescents and young adults today, computer-based multimedia simulations could provide a potentially powerful bridge for building and supporting the development of friendships.

Staffing

It is recommended that the student-to-staff ratios in CBI should be kept as low as possible (Baumgart & Van Walleghem, 1986; McDonnell et al., 1996; Sailor et al., 1989). Ideally, CBI would have a one-to-one student-to-staff ratio. This can often be achieved by using same-age peers as tutors in carrying out instruction in community settings. Peer tutors are most appropriately used to carry out CBI on leisure/recreation or personal management routines and activities. It is recommended that peers not be used to provide support to students in community-based employment sites. Our experience suggests that employers may have concerns about whether same-age peers will have the maturity necessary to support students.

Small groups can be used if a one-to-one staff ratio is not possible. However, we suggest that groups not exceed three students. Otherwise, the number of instructional trials that students can be provided with will be significantly reduced. In addition, students who need significant physical or behavioral support should not be grouped together for CBI. In this situation, the teacher is likely to spend more of his or her time supporting the students' unique needs than providing instruction on the target routine or activity.

Transportation

Getting to and from training sites may present a significant challenge in carrying out CBI. Unfortunately, there is no single solution to this problem. Most secondary programs will need to rely on a variety of transportation options to meet students' needs. These alternatives include walking, riding a bike, using public transportation, using specialized transportation services, using school vehicles, or having staff transport students to CBI sites. Teachers should rely primarily on transportation strategies that will be available to students after graduation. Staff should transport students only if no other means of transportation is available *and* other alternatives will be available after leaving school to replace these supports.

Focus Question 4	How can teachers minimize the potential liability of staff and peer tutors in carrying out CBI?

Staff Liability

A final issue of concern to teachers and administrators in carrying out CBI is liability protection for peer tutors and paid staff. Most school districts have insurance policies in place that cover field trips and off-campus job training programs for students and staff. Generally, staff members are covered under existing insurance policies *if* the student's IEP/transition plan includes specific goals and objectives that require CBI. Peer tutors are also usually covered *if* they are enrolled in a credit-based peer tutoring class. However, teachers and administrators should review the district's existing policies and make sure that CBI is covered in both cases. The risk of liability is reduced if the teacher can document that paid staff and peer tutors have been trained to implement CBI, their performance in implementing CBI is regularly monitored, data on student progress are gathered, and the district has developed programs and staff are trained to meet students' needs in emergency situations.

Summary

CBI can be used to promote students' generalization of skills learned in school to actual performance settings, improve their quality of life, and promote their postschool adjustment to adulthood. Achieving these outcomes will require that target routines and activities be selected to meet students' immediate and future needs in the neighborhoods and communities in which they live. In addition, CBI needs to be systematically designed and implemented. Finally, individuals providing CBI will need to be trained and closely monitored to ensure program effectiveness.

Focus Question Review

Focus Question 1: When should the teacher conduct a general case analysis of a routine or an activity?

- A general case analysis should be done when students will be expected to complete a routine or an activity in three or more settings.

Focus Question 2: What information should be obtained from a baseline probe?

- The steps of the task or general case analysis that the student can complete correctly.
- The level of assistance that the student requires to complete error steps correctly.

Focus Question 3: What does the available research suggest are the most effective ways to fade response prompts during CBI?

- The systems of most prompts or time delay are more effective than the system of least prompts.
- Research has generally favored the use of constant time delay over the system of most prompts.

Focus Question 4: How can teachers minimize the potential liability of staff and peer tutors in carrying out CBI?

- Time delay may be more effective for students who have a history of prompt dependency.
- Provide staff and peer tutors with direct training on carrying out CBI with students.
- Regularly monitor staff members' and peer tutors' implementation of CBI.
- Collect data on student performance.
- Establish emergency procedures.

Section IV

CRITICAL PROGRAM COMPONENTS

CHAPTER 10

Home and Community Living

J. MATT JAMESON

JOHN MCDONNELL

T he transition from school to community living has long been recognized as one of the most exciting and one of the most difficult periods in the lives of young adults and their families. It is the point at which many of the supports that we enjoy through childhood and adolescence are faded and we are required to assume responsibility for taking care of ourselves and our own homes. Our ability to cope with these demands has a significant impact on our sense of competence and on the overall quality of our lives. Further, our ability to meet our own daily living needs often influences how we are perceived by parents, teachers, peers, and other community members. For students with intellectual and developmental disabilities, the lack of competence in these areas can also negatively affect the quality of their lives by restricting opportunities to be fully included in the community (Nisbet, Clark, & Covert, 1991).

This chapter will address several issues faced by students and their Individualized Education Program/transition planning teams in preparing for home and community living. These include (a) the importance of family involvement and participation in developing student competence in home and community living, (b) considerations in selecting home and com-munity living goals for students' IEPs/transition plans, (c) instructional approaches available to teachers to develop student competence in

home and community settings, and (d) the importance of alternative performance strategies in supporting student independence and autonomy.

Home and Community Living Curriculum

Successful home and community living requires students to care for themselves, care for their belongings and home, meet their nutritional needs, meet
their own safety and health needs, manage their personal finances, get to places
in the community, and use the resources of the community. It is important to
stress that there is no single set of home and community routines, activities, and
skills that will meet every student's needs or preferences. The goals included in
a student's IEP/transition plan must be selected by the team to achieve the student's postschool goals and meet his or her immediate needs (Browder, 2001;
McDonnell, Mathot-Buckner, & Ferguson, 1996; Wehman, 2006).

Window 10-1

Connecting Postschool Goals and IEP/Transition Plan Goals

Marsha is a 20-year-old with significant intellectual and developmental disabilities enrolled in
a post-high school program at Canyon Community College. Marsha has significant articulation
problems due to a cleft palate and communicates most effectively using an augmentative communication device. With support from school transition staff, Marsha has been working at a
hotel as a housekeeper. During the person-centered and ecological assessment process lead-
ing up to her IEP/transition planning meeting, Marsha, her family, and her employer indicated
a mutual desire for her to keep her job after school. In addition, she would like to move into
a supported living apartment near her parents' home during the following summer.

   During the IEP/transition planning meeting, Marsha and her IEP/transition planning
team identified several community living management routines, activities, and skills that
would be necessary for her to stay in her job and live in her own apartment (see list).
Specifically, they thought that Marsha needed to learn to use the public transportation
system to get to and from work independently and develop the ability to use a savings
account and an ATM card. These priorities provided the basis for the development of
several goals and objectives included in Marsha's IEP.

Routines	Riding Public Transportation (Bus/Light Rail)	Personal Banking Skills
Activities	• Riding bus/light rail to work • Riding bus/light rail to family members' and friends' houses • Riding bus/light rail to access leisure activities	• Make savings deposits of work checks • Use ATM/debit card to make withdrawals and purchases • Track savings balance using ATM and retail receipts

Routines	Riding Public Transportation (Bus/Light Rail)	Personal Banking Skills
Skills	• Locate appropriate bus/train stop • If appropriate, make transfer • Identify and notify needed stop • Complete trip to location	• Fill out savings deposit slip • Use ATM/debit card to make withdrawals and purchases • Keep receipts and enter into computer budgeting program weekly

Students and the other members of the planning team often face a number of problems in making the connection between the student's postschool goals and the goals and objectives included in the IEP/transition plan (Steere & Cavaiuolo, 2002). These include the development of vague or unrealistic postschool goals and the lack of specificity in goals and objectives that are included in the student's IEP (Table 10.1). Most, if not all, of these issues can be addressed by engaging in formal person-centered planning with the

Table 10.1   Challenges and Strategies in Connecting Goals, Objectives, and Transition Outcomes

Challenge	Strategies
Outcomes are too vague.	Outcomes must be objectively defined and observable. Students need prior experiences to clarify outcomes. Use person-centered planning to identify specific outcomes.
Outcomes are perceived as unrealistic.	Thoroughly explore actual demands of outcome. Provide experience in community settings.
Goals and objectives are too vague.	Consider alternative performance strategies. Objectively define the target behavior, conditions, and criteria for completion of the IEP.
Connection among objectives, goals, and outcomes is unclear.	Use person-centered and ecological assessments to identify meaningful outcomes.
Outcomes are not refined and revised.	Collect instructional data and review regularly to make adaptations to instructional programming.
Limited expectations for student performance.	Teach with high expectations to avoid learned helplessness and self-fulfilling prophecies.
Lack of action planning with adult service agencies.	Define specific steps and necessary agency linkages to achieve transition outcomes.

Note. From "Connecting Outcomes, Goals, and Objectives in Transition Planning," by D. E. Steere & D. Cavaiuolo, 2002, *Teaching Exceptional Children, 34*(6), pp. 54–59. Adapted with permission.

student, his or her parents, his or her family members, and others who have a vested interest in the student's life prior to the development of the IEP/transition plan. The remaining concerns can be addressed by carefully considering several key factors in selecting the specific goals and objectives included in the student's IEP/transition plan. The remaining sections of this chapter will discuss these considerations.

Importance of Family Involvement and Participation

Research suggests that a student's family plays an important role in preparing him or her for community living (Schalock et al., 1986; Schalock & Lilley, 1986; Turnbull & Turnbull, 2001; Turnbull, Beegle, & Stowe, 2001). In addition, parents who are actively involved in the transition planning process report that they are more satisfied with the outcomes of their child's educational program than parents who do not play an active role (Miner & Bates, 1997). Some researchers have suggested that family participation in transition planning is so important that parents and other family members should begin preparing for the process as soon as their child enters elementary school (Dunst, 2002; Wehman, 2006). Viewing transition planning as a longitudinal process, rather than a one-time event, gives families the time necessary to gather the information to make informed decisions about their children's future and to be effective participants in the transition planning process (Turnbull & Turnbull, 2001).

Focus Question 1	Describe five steps that would help professionals assist families with identifying appropriate home and community living goals during transition planning.

Researchers and advocates are currently suggesting that professionals adopt a Person-Family Interdependent Planning perspective in developing students' educational programs (Kim & Turnbull, 2004). The view of the family in this approach has three common threads. First, a student and members of his or her family are the ones who make choices related to the student's current and future needs. Second, all families have strengths but will also require support to successfully promote a student's transition to community living. And finally, the family is a "functioning social support unit" (Kim & Turnbull, 2004, p. 55) for most students during and following school and will need to be continuously involved in the student's life. Turnbull and Turnbull (2001) suggest that professionals can use five strategies to assist families to become more effective in the transition planning process. These include helping families

- Identify what is important to the individual with disabilities.
- Identify the supports already in place that meet the individual's values, preferences, and needs.
- Determine what needs to change to create a better match among individual and family values, preferences, and strengths and what currently exists.
- Develop action plans to implement supports and services that have been identified as impacting individual and family quality-of-life criteria.
- Actualize the supports with resources so that the quality-of-life criteria can be achieved.

Focus Question 2	Describe how conceptualizations of "successful transition to adulthood" may vary according to the beliefs and values of families and communities.

It must also be emphasized that successful transition to adulthood is influenced by culture-specific beliefs and values of the student's family (Geenen, Powers, & Lopez-Vasquez, 2001). For example, there is increasing awareness that most definitions of transition and self-determination are rooted in an Anglo-European value of individuality (Turnbull & Turnbull, 2001). In contrast, many other cultures place a greater emphasis on collectivism and choices rooted in the best interest of the family or community. Schools and professionals need to be sensitive and aware of these differences and understand how they will affect the process and outcomes of transition planning and instruction. Professionals will be more effective helping families identify postschool goals and needed transition services if they are responsive to their cultural and linguistic differences (Geenen et al., 2001).

Focus Question 3	What are four important considerations in selecting home and community living goals for students?

Selecting Goals and Objectives

Students and the members of their IEP/transition planning teams must take into account a number of factors in selecting appropriate home and community living goals (Browder & Snell, 1993; McDonnell et al., 1996; Spooner & Test, 1994; Wilcox, 1988). These include the extent to which routines and activities (a) are age appropriate, (b) cumulatively build the student's competence, (c) support the student's choice and preferences, and (d) promote interactions with peers without disabilities.

Age-Appropriate Routines and Activities

Research has shown that individuals with intellectual and developmental disabilities who engage in behaviors that are not age appropriate are perceived less favorably by peers and others in the community (Calhoun & Calhoun, 1993). Behavioral expectations change across time for all adolescents and young adults. Consequently, it is essential that the routines, activities, and skills that are taught to students are consistent with their chronological age. This can be accomplished by ensuring that the goals and objectives selected for students reflect what their same-age peers would be expected to do (McDonnell et al., 1996). For example, it would not be appropriate to expect a middle school student to complete all the routines, activities, and skills necessary to independently manage his or her finances. However, it would be appropriate to expect him or her to be able to use a calculator to perform simple mathematical computations related to balancing a savings account.

Cumulatively Build Competence in Home and Community Settings

Adolescents and young adults are expected to become more independent and exert more control over their lives as they get older. For example, the first household chore that many students have is cleaning their room. As students grow older, they are often given increased responsibility for taking care of themselves, their belongings, and the family home. A student's IEP/transition plan can provide an important vehicle to assist him or her with cumulatively developing the capacity to live more independently. A critical step in the planning process is to continuously evaluate the student's needs during and after school and target more complex outcomes for the student across each successive IEP/transition plan. For example, during middle or junior high school, the goals for a student's home economics class might focus on preparing simple meals that do not require him or her to cook (e.g., making a sandwich or a salad). As the student enters high school, the goals included in the IEP/transition plan might shift to using picture recipes to prepare meals that require the student to use a microwave or heat food on the stove. Finally, as the student approaches graduation, the focus might shift to planning and preparing nutritious meals across a week. This approach allows the team to select goals and objectives that are age appropriate for the student but that build his or her capacity to achieve his or her postschool goals.

Choice and Preference

Research suggests that adults with intellectual and developmental disabilities—especially adults with severe disabilities—living in community residential programs often have significantly fewer opportunities to make choices about their lives than same-age peers without disabilities (Smith, Morgan, & Davidson, 2005). This occurs in spite of clear evidence that demonstrates that this group of individuals can learn to make choices and express preference (Browder, Cooper, & Lim, 1998; Hughes, Pitkin, & Lorden, 1998; Lancioni, 1996; Schwartzman, Martin, Yu, & Whiteley, 2004). Further, mastery of choice making is strongly correlated to the levels of independence experienced by individuals in home and community environments (Heal, Rubin, & Rusch, 1998; Wehmeyer & Palmer, 2003). This emphasizes the need for students, families, and professionals to select routines and activities that will promote and support choice. Finally, it is strongly recommended that opportunities to make choices and express preferences be embedded into all routines and activities that a student completes each day (Wehmeyer, Palmer, Agran, Mithaug, & Martin, 2000).

Interactions With Peers

Meaningful social relationships are valued by everyone and are one of the desired outcomes of transition planning. Unfortunately, the development of friendships between students with disabilities and peers without disabilities has been hindered by numerous factors and often results in limited social interactions between the two groups of students. This is particularly troubling given the findings that students with intellectual and developmental disabilities indicate higher levels of happiness when engaged with peers without intellectual and developmental disabilities than when engaged with peers with disabilities (Logan et al., 1998).

Unfortunately, the goals and objectives included in students' IEPs/transition plans are too often focused on simply learning how to accurately complete the steps of a routine or an activity. The social aspects of participating in these routines and activities are ignored in the planning process. Many home and community living routines and activities require social interaction, and the quality of the experience is often enhanced by interaction with peers. For example, eating dinner in a restaurant requires that we interact with the server. However, the enjoyment of going out to dinner is enhanced when we have the opportunity to talk with friends. The IEP/transition planning team should structure goals and objectives to encourage and support opportunities to interact with peers without disabilities whenever possible.

Focus Question 4	List three instructional approaches used to support students with intellectual and developmental disabilities in the acquisition of personal management routines, activities, and skills.

Instructional Approaches

One of the challenges facing teachers in carrying out instruction on home and community living goals is determining where instruction should be conducted. Research suggests that there are three options for teachers, including community-based instruction, inclusion in general education classes, and embedded instruction in typical school, home, and community routines (Horner, McDonnell, & Bellamy, 1986; McDonnell et al., 1996; McDonnell, Johnson, & McQuivey, 2008).

Community-Based Instruction

As discussed, the curriculum for secondary students with intellectual and developmental disabilities should be concerned with the performance of routines and activities in actual situations. In order to achieve this, instruction for students often requires that much of the instruction on home and community living routines and activities be delivered in natural settings and that students use the materials that peers without disabilities would typically use to complete the routine or activity (Horner et al., 1986; Rosenthal-Malek & Bloom, 1998). The considerations in designing, implementing, and evaluating the effectiveness of community-based instruction were discussed in Chapter 9.

General Education Classes

Research suggests that students with intellectual and developmental disabilities can succeed in general education classes when provided with proper supports and adaptations (Hunt & McDonnell, 2007; Turnbull, Turnbull, Shank, & Smith, 2004). The general education curriculum typically offers a variety of classes that provide opportunities to teach important home and community living routines, activities, and skills to students. These include classes on healthy lifestyles, personal finance, and adult roles and responsibilities. As such, the IEP/transition planning team should use the general education curriculum to the maximum extent possible to achieve the student's desired postschool home and community living goals.

While students with intellectual and developmental disabilities often have difficulty generalizing skills learned in school to actual performance settings (Horner et al., 1986; Rosenthal-Malek & Bloom, 1998), teachers can overcome these limitations by anchoring curriculum material presented in the general education classes in routines and activities that students will complete in home and community settings. This includes the following:

- Using common stimuli for instruction and actual performance. For example, a student could be taught to prepare assigned dishes in a food preparation class using a picture recipe that he or she could also use at home.
- Require the student to complete the same responses at school that will be used at home or in community settings. For instance, a student learning to balance his or her checkbook in a personal finance class would be taught a prescribed sequence of steps focused on reconciling entries in his or her checkbook with the bank statement (deposits, checks, automatic teller transactions, and so on). The student would then use the same sequence of steps when balancing his or her checkbook at home.
- Provide supplemental instruction in actual performance settings. Instruction in school settings is more effective if it is paired with instruction in real settings. For example, if a student was learning to use an electronic scheduling program in his or her educational technology class at school, the teacher would also provide direct instruction on using this program at his or her work experience site using the actual scheduling tasks presented by the employer.

Embedded Instruction

Embedded instruction can be used to teach students with intellectual and developmental disabilities to demonstrate home and community living skills within typically occurring routines and activities. For example, teaching the self-help skill of zipping and unzipping a coat could be done during the naturally occurring routines of the school day, including arriving and leaving school, going to lunch off-campus with friends, or going off-campus for work experiences or other community-based instruction. Similarly, students could be taught purchasing skills in such activities as buying lunch in the cafeteria, purchasing snacks or supplies at the school store, or using vending machines during the lunch period, breaks, or study halls. The effectiveness of embedded instruction hinges upon the student being directly taught the skill when and where it occurs in home, school, and community environments.

Another option is to work with parents and other family members to provide embedded instruction to students on routines, activities, and skills at home and in the community (Algozzine, O'Shea, & Algozzine, 2001; Berry & Hardman, 1998). The ability of parents and family members to provide instruction will be based on a number of factors, including the structure of the family, school and work schedules, and resources (see Chapter 7). The most effective approaches tailor instructional programs to the unique needs of the parents and other family members. Beakley and Yoder (1998) suggested that teachers can support the involvement of parents in instruction on home and community living routines, activities, and skills by

- Promoting parents' and families' ownership over the program by ensuring that they are active participants in the selection of goals and objectives during the IEP/transition planning process.
- Working with parents to identify natural opportunities for carrying out instruction that fit within the family's typical schedule.
- Tailoring instructional and data collection procedures to the abilities and capacity of the parents and family members.
- Integrating information provided by parents and family members in assessing student progress toward goals and objectives.

Developing Alternative Performance Strategies

Students with intellectual and developmental disabilities may not always have the academic, communication, social, or motor skills necessary to successfully complete all home and community living routines and activities. However, it is essential that students not be prevented from participating in these routines and activities because they do not have these skills.

| Focus Question 5 | Describe five considerations in designing and implementing alternative performance strategies for students with intellectual and developmental disabilities. |

Table 10.2   List of Potential Alternative Performance Strategies

Skill	Alternatives
Counting Coins	An envelope that has the specific coins necessary to complete an activity (vending machine).
	Using a coin card that has pictures of coins for specific amounts.
Counting Bills	An envelope with specific bills necessary to complete an activity.
	Using a large bill ($20) to pay for items.
	Next-dollar strategy.
	Use a check/credit card.
Requesting/Ordering	Communication card/page with specific request printed on it ("I would like a small Coke").
	Communication board.
	Electronic communication device.
Listing Items for Purchase	Use labels from desired products.
	Pictures of desired products.
	A checklist of desired products that is completed prior to shopping.
Scheduling Daily Activities	A picture schedule developed by teachers or parents.
	A picture scheduling template that identifies specific times and has a variety of activity pictures placed in order by the student.
	Computer scheduling program.

In order to avoid this pitfall, professionals can develop and teach students alternative performance strategies. These strategies provide students with different ways of meeting the academic and developmental skill demands of completing routines and activities in home, school, and community settings. Table 10.2 presents an illustrative list of alternative performance strategies that students can use in completing home and community living routines and activities. McDonnell, Wilcox, and Hardman (1991) suggest that professionals focus on five primary considerations when designing or selecting alternative performance strategies:

- Does the alternative performance strategy utilize the person's current strengths and skills?
- Is the alternative performance strategy acceptable to the individual, his or her family members, and other community members?

- Is the strategy the least restrictive alternative?
- What are the maintenance costs and requirements of the alternative performance strategy?
- Is the alternative performance strategy applicable to other activities, routines, and environments?

With careful consideration of these five issues, professionals can identify alternative performance strategies that will help students enjoy greater levels of independence and autonomy in their homes and communities.

Summary

Secondary students with intellectual and developmental disabilities will require instruction on home and community living routines and activities to achieve their postschool goals. The impact of this instruction is maximized when the routines and activities selected for instruction are tailored to a student's immediate and future needs. This is most easily accomplished when the student and his or her family are actively involved in the planning and instructional process. Parents can assist students with articulating their needs and preferences, support opportunities for students to learn and participate in routines and activities at home, and provide the ongoing support necessary for successful adjustment to community life. A student's IEP/transition plan should be designed to cumulatively build his or her competence. The plan should also ensure that the student's home and community living goals are age appropriate, increase the student's opportunity to make choices, and promote his or her interactions with peers without disabilities.

In order to achieve these outcomes, teachers and other professionals may utilize community-based instruction, include students in general education classes, and embed instruction in home, school, and community settings. In addition, students may require alternative performance strategies to meet the skill demands of many home and community living routines. The focus of students' educational programs should be to maximize their participation in home and community life prior to and following graduation.

Focus Question Review

Focus Question 1: Describe five steps that would help professionals assist families with identifying appropriate home and community living goals during transition planning.

- Identify what is important to the individual with disabilities.
- Identify the supports already in place that meet his or her values, preferences, strengths, and needs.
- Determine what needs to change to create a better match among individual and family values, preferences, strengths, and what currently exists.
- Develop action plans to implement supports and services that have been identified as affecting individual and family quality-of-life criteria.
- Actualize the supports with resources so that the quality-of-life criteria can be achieved.

Focus Question 2: Describe how conceptualizations of "successful transition to adulthood" may vary according to the beliefs and values of families and communities.

- The goals and outcomes of transition planning are determined by culture-specific beliefs and values about issues ranging from employment to community and social participation to family and gender roles and expectations to social functioning.

Focus Question 3: What are four important considerations in selecting home and community living goals for students?

- The age-appropriateness of the routine or activity.
- The extent to which the routine or activity cumulatively builds the student's competence toward achieving his or her postschool goals.
- The extent to which the goal is designed to support the student's choice and preferences.
- The extent to which the routine or activity promotes the student's interactions with peers without disabilities.

Focus Question 4: List three instructional approaches used to support students with intellectual and developmental disabilities in the acquisition of personal management routines, activities, and skills.

- Community-based instruction.
- Inclusion in general education classes.
- Embedded instruction in home, school, and community routines.

Focus Question 5: Describe five considerations in designing and implementing alternative performance strategies for students with intellectual and developmental disabilities.

- Does the alternative performance strategy utilize the person's current strengths and skills?
- Is the alternative performance strategy acceptable to the individual, his or her family members, and other community members?
- Is the strategy the least restrictive alternative?
- What are the maintenance costs and requirements of the alternative performance strategy?
- Is the alternative performance strategy applicable to other activities, routines, and environments?

CHAPTER 11

Leisure and Recreation

TESSIE ROSE

Involvement in leisure and recreation activities is widely recognized as essential for quality of life for people with and without disabilities (Hawkins, 1997; U.S. Department of Health and Human Services, 1999, 2000). Most people are aware of the health benefits of regular physical activity through leisure and recreation. Beginning in the 1980s, the federal government—and most likely your high school gym teacher—stressed the importance of engaging in a minimum of 30 min of physical activity each day to combat obesity, heart disease, and other chronic diseases (U.S. Department of Health and Human Services, 2005). Regular participation can also increase eye-hand coordination, fine and gross motor skills, agility, and muscular strength (Dunn, 1997), which can be essential for independence in home and work activities. For example, Walter and Harris (2003) found that higher levels of health-related fitness components had significant influence on employee-perceived work enjoyment and habits. Beyond increasing general physical fitness and cardiovascular endurance, many depend on their leisure for social engagement, stress release, relief from boredom, and overall mental wellness (Dattilo, 1999; Russell, 2002).

Leisure and recreation education is an essential but often overlooked element of comprehensive secondary transition services (Bedini, Bullock, & Driscoll, 1993; Dattilo & St. Peter, 1991; Rose, McDonnell, & Ellis, 2007). Transition programs void of comprehensive leisure and recreation programming can lead to negative postschool outcomes and decreased quality of life. Adults with intellectual and developmental disabilities are particularly at risk for obesity, declining health, and early onset of physical old age associated with lack of leisure time, physical activity, and access to preventative health care (Draheim, Williams, & McCubbin, 2002; Graham & Reid, 2000; Lennox, Green, Diggens, & Ugoni, 2001; Rimmer, Braddock, & Fujiura, 1993). They are also more likely to be isolated from peers without disabilities and engage in very little meaningful activity during their free time (Halpern, 1993; Yu et al., 2002). Roth, Pyfer, and Huettig (2007) found that some young adults with intellectual and developmental disabilities were unable to independently choose and engage in postschool leisure activities, leaving them dependent on their parents or paid support. While most parents stated that their child had been exposed to a variety of leisure and recreation activities during high school, students did not receive the formal training in the skills needed to pursue these activities beyond the high school setting.

Comprehensive leisure and recreation transition programs allow educators to provide students with the knowledge and skills necessary to engage in healthy living, proper nutrition, and regular exercise. Effective leisure programs also provide students with opportunities to gain awareness of a variety of leisure activities, develop leisure and social skills, increase self-determination, and improve mental and physical health (Dattilo & Hoge, 1999; Dattilo & St. Peter, 1991). In addition, secondary transition leisure programs provide educators with natural opportunities to teach other essential postschool living skills, such as self-determination, social skills, and purchasing. This chapter will explore the role of secondary education programs in developing leisure and recreation curriculum and routines for students with intellectual and developmental disabilities. The chapter begins with an overview of current service delivery models used in training programs and follows with a discussion of the considerations that the Individualized Education Program/transition planning teams must take into account when developing appropriate leisure and recreation IEP goals and objectives. The chapter concludes with a discussion of research-based instructional approaches and alternative performance strategies that educators should consider when developing individualized programs.

Approaches to Leisure and Recreation Training

What are leisure and recreation? *Leisure* can be defined as the "activities which people participate in during their free time, because they want to, for their own sake, for fun, entertainment, self-improvement, or for goals of their choosing" (Argyle, 1996, p. 17). The term *recreation* is often used to describe more active leisure pursuits. In essence, leisure and recreation involve making choices about personal free-time activities. The term *free time* describes time not obligated for self-maintenance or sustaining life (Dattilo, 1999). A common misconception among educators is that free time is leisure time. However, unstructured free time can be considered by some as a negative experience that leads to boredom or loneliness or, in some cases, adverse behaviors (Weissinger, Caldwell, & Bandolos, 1992). The important distinction is that leisure and recreation are self-selected for personal benefit. This explains why some people view rock climbing as a recreation activity while others find it terrifying or why some individuals enjoy collecting stamps and others find it boring.

Leisure and recreation education typically begins at home and continues throughout the life span. Most will remember playing board or video games with friends or family, going to the movies or amusement parks, or participating in family vacations. Although not part of formal instructional programs, experiences such as these increased our awareness of leisure and recreational opportunities. Through repeated observations and experiences with friends, family, and school activities, we gained the leisure skills needed to independently seek and choose these desired activities. We discovered what types of activities we prefer. Some choose more passive leisure activities—such as reading, watching television, hanging out with friends, or playing on the computer—while others choose more active leisure activities—such as club sports, dance lessons, or outdoor activities. In most states, school-age children receive additional formalized instruction through school-based physical education programs. These programs teach us about physical fitness, nutrition, and the skills for lifelong leisure and recreation activities, such as tennis, golf, or running.

Unfortunately, many individuals with intellectual and developmental disabilities lack access to the same leisure and recreation opportunities as their peers without disabilities. Participation in after-school and noncurricular programs by students with disabilities is often ignored (Heyne & Schleien, 1996). In some cases, instruction in leisure and recreation is viewed as unnecessary or less important than that in other curricular domains (Rose et al., 2007). Lack of access to skill education and personal choice in leisure activities is common for people with intellectual and developmental disabilities and leads to unhappiness in their leisure pursuits (Green & Reid, 1996, 1999; Yu et al., 2002). Braun, Yeargin-Allsopp, and Lollar (2006) found that young adults with intellectual disabilities participated in significantly fewer leisure activities than their peers without disabilities and thus did not have the same opportunities to gain skills and engage in various leisure experiences. Furthermore, many individuals with intellectual and developmental disabilities transition into settings that are segregated from the general population, such as group homes or assisted living centers (Yu et al., 2002). Their leisure and recreation activities are often chosen by service delivery coordinators and tend to involve large group sedentary activities (e.g., watching TV or movies, eating dinner, drinking coffee). Prolonged absence of meaningful free-time activities and social engagement grounded in leisure experiences can significantly decrease quality of life (Sands & Kozleski, 1994).

Educators have the opportunity to improve postschool outcomes by providing intensive, high-quality leisure programming and education during transition. Although Bullock and Mahon (2001) noted that segregated group-based recreation programming remains prevalent today, the field is moving toward a more person-centered service delivery approach. Recent advances in recreation equipment and adaptive technology have dramatically changed how students access and participate in leisure and recreation activities. Many parks and recreation departments offer a variety of accessible programs and adapted sports and activities. The shift among many local recreation programs from segregated special programs to a continuum of leisure and recreation services has led to increased participation in inclusive recreation activities. Through new technology, individuals with intellectual and developmental disabilities can independently access books and the Internet, travel with friends and family, and participate in general community leisure activities. Advances in adaptive equipment have also increased participation and access to both traditional and adventure sports. Over the last several decades, the country witnessed an explosion of adaptive outdoor recreation programs that offer opportunities for individuals of all ability levels. Traditionally, many programs focused on providing access and exposure to large groups of people with disabilities with a limited focus on teaching skills. Today, many sports and outdoor recreation programs focus on specific skill development to encourage independent participation in desired leisure activities. Once considered unlikely, people with intellectual and developmental disabilities can participate and gain skills in alpine and cross-country skiing, horseback riding, rock climbing, white-water rafting, and mountaineering.

Focus Question 1	What four service delivery models are commonly used in leisure and recreation programming?

Service Delivery Models

All people have a right to inclusive leisure and recreation activities that require varying skill levels and diverse leisure settings. This section presents four general service delivery models used in recreation and leisure programming for people with disabilities. Regardless of the service delivery model chosen, the goal of the program is to increase community inclusion and quality of life. IEP/transition planning teams must take into account the student's individual needs and preferences. A discussion of the benefits and concerns of each service delivery model is provided to assist educators in selecting the most appropriate approach. In most cases, a combination of service delivery models provides the greatest benefit for students.

Special Programs. Special, or adaptive, recreation programs are common service delivery options for people with intellectual and developmental disabilities. Special recreation programs are designed to meet the unique needs of a particular group of individuals with disabilities. The Special Olympics is considered one of the most popular—and controversial—examples of this delivery model. The Special Olympics began as a small track and field program in the 1960s and evolved into an internationally renowned event that serves nearly 2.5 million people with intellectual and developmental disabilities each year (Special Olympics, 2008). The program provides year-round sports training in 30 Olympic-type summer and winter events. Other examples of special programs include community recreation programs designed specifically for individuals with specific disabilities (e.g., autism, mental retardation) or segregated school-based programs provided by adaptive physical educators, special educators, or recreation therapists.

Special programs are desirable for many service providers and parents. Resources and staff are typically centralized at a few specific locations. For example, a local parks and recreation adaptive program might provide services to people with disabilities at two of a city's five community centers. Costs can be lower since specialized equipment is needed at fewer locations. The centralization of services also allows specialized staff, whose availability is often limited, to serve more individuals with involved disabilities. Special programs typically have more staff trained in adaptive leisure and recreation, which can lead to a wider range of specialized opportunities. Special programs also appeal to parents because of a perceived element of safety. Roth and colleagues (2007) found that some parents felt more comfortable when their child participated in segregated, supervised activities because they believed their child needed constant supervision and support during these activities.

POINT/COUNTERPOINT 11.1

Participation in Special Olympics

POINT

"Children and adults with intellectual disabilities who participate in Special Olympics develop improved physical fitness and motor skills, greater self-confidence and a more positive self-image. They grow mentally, socially and spiritually and, through their activities, exhibit boundless courage and enthusiasm, enjoy the rewards of friendship and ultimately discover not only new abilities and talents but 'their voices' as well" (Special Olympics, 2008).

COUNTERPOINT

"Social interactions that do occur between people with and without disabilities at the Special Olympics are likely to be short term and unlikely to develop into friendships or social networks . . . there is a lack of skill acquisition, and much precious teaching time of functional activities is lost. . . . The adult participants in the Special Olympics are often perceived as children because both children and adults participate in the same activities, which often leads to infantilization of adults with disabilities" (Storey, 2004, pp. 35–36).

Many believe that there are inherent problems with this approach (Johnson, 2003; Storey, 2004). One of the major concerns about special programs is that they fail to provide meaningful interactions with peers without disabilities. In fact, these types of models may actually reinforce negative stereotypes about people with intellectual and developmental disabilities and demonstrate that segregation is acceptable and necessary (Smart, 2001). Some programs include volunteers and staff without disabilities whose role is to help the individuals participate and to simulate peer interaction and friendships. However, these interactions rarely lead to long-term relationships and natural supports for future community activities (Storey, 2004). Another major concern is the group format commonly used in special programs. Instead of teaching students the skills necessary for independent postschool leisure participation, special programs often focus on providing students with fun activities or activities meant to increase present physical functioning ability (Krebs & Block, 1992). Many recreation therapists and adaptive physical educators in special school-based programs spend the majority of their time providing disability-based group leisure instruction and very little time working on students' IEP goals (Ashton-Schaeffer, Johnson, & Bullock, 2000; Dunn, 1997; Krueger, DiRocco, & Felix, 2000). In addition, Ashton-Schaeffer and colleagues (2000) found that the majority of special leisure and recreation programs are geared toward elementary and junior high school students (63.3%), not high school (27.7%) and post-high school students (3.9%).

Reliance on special leisure and recreation programs may also lead to additional negative postschool outcomes. Roth and colleagues (2007) noted that parents and students who only participated in special programs, like the Special Olympics, during high school transition had difficulty independently making leisure and recreation choices and accessing new activities 2 to 3 years postschool. Despite being exposed to a variety of leisure activities, the group nature of the special programs made it more difficult to provide the individualized instruction in skills necessary for independent leisure participation.

Partnering Programs. Several programs have adopted a partnering approach to service delivery. These types of programs, also known as reverse mainstreaming or peer tutoring, are designed to provide people with disabilities with opportunities to recreate with individuals without disabilities. One such program is the Unified Sports division of the Special Olympics. Special Olympics Unified Sports involves an equal number of individuals with and without disabilities during training and competition (Special Olympics, 2008). Individuals without disabilities are viewed as partners in the activities, not as volunteers or assistants as they are in special programs. In school programs, special educators might use this model to provide students with access to leisure interactions with their same-age peers. For example, each Friday the special education teacher might have "game day" where students without disabilities come to the special education classroom and play board games with their peers with disabilities. To be effective, both partners should benefit from participating in the partnered leisure activity. This type of programming is viewed as desirable by some because it is able to meet the needs of people with disabilities while facilitating more normal interactions with peers without disabilities. The program staff is typically trained to work with individuals with disabilities, and adaptive equipment is readily accessible. In addition, peers without disabilities who participate in such programs often receive some training prior to the activity in order to effectively communicate with and include students with intellectual and developmental disabilities (Houston-Wilson, Lieberman, & Horton, 1997).

Partnering approaches evolved from the desire to allow people with and without disabilities to recreate together. Although they lack the same attention and research given to other leisure service delivery approaches, partnering programs are gaining popularity. There are several things educators should be aware of when considering a partnering approach. First, equal numbers of people with and without disabilities do not represent the natural proportions of people with disabilities in the general population. Thus, the focus of these programs remains on people with disabilities. This may stigmatize individuals and could result in further segregation from the community. Second, partnering programs tend to pair one individual with a disability with a peer without a disability, which may lead to fewer social interactions than would occur in more natural social configurations. Carter, Cushing, Clark, and Kennedy (2005) found increased social interactions when secondary students worked with two peers instead of one peer without disabilities. Interestingly, though, interactions with peers without disabilities in structured partnered situations did not extend beyond the peer partnering activities. Secondary transition providers must consider not only the immediate access to peers but also whether the current access will lead to an increase in desired postschool outcomes.

General Participation With Accommodations and Modifications. Opportunities for leisure and recreation participation exist in nearly every community, including rural and urban settings. General recreation and leisure programs are developed with the general community in mind and are not specifically for people with disabilities. However, this does not limit individuals with disabilities from participating in these activities. The Americans with Disabilities Act of 1990 (ADA) ensures "no qualified individual with a disability shall, by reason of such disability, be excluded from participation in or be denied the benefits of services, programs, or activities of a public entity, or be subjected to discrimination by any such entity" (ADA, 1990, Sec. 12132). In other words, leisure and recreation facilities and services available for the general public—such as ice rinks, sporting venues, and recreation centers—must be accessible. Such entities cannot deny participation in offered activities solely because an individual has a disability. In this inclusive model, individuals participate in general programs with adequate support to enjoy and gain skills in their desired leisure and recreation activities. Secondary transition providers have access to numerous inclusive school- and community-based teaching environments in which to provide skill instruction. General school-based leisure programming includes civic clubs, school sports, drama activities, and school dances. School leisure and recreation activities provide educators with easily accessible opportunities to teach leisure skills in inclusive environments. Participation in general school-based programs may also assist students in transitioning to community-based leisure activities. General community-based programs may include health clubs, libraries, continuing education classes, and parks and recreation programs. Educators considering participation in general recreation programming with accommodations and modifications may initially need to work with the recreation service provider to ensure that the student will have meaningful participation in the activity, not just physical presence. In Window 11.1, staff from the city adaptive parks and recreation department in collaboration with Marianne's IEP/transition planning team agreed to meet with and prepare the instructor prior to her participation. Adequate support is critical to the success of an inclusive service delivery model (Werts, Wolery, Snyder, & Caldwell, 1996; Wolery, Werts, Caldwell, Snyder, &

Lisowski, 1995). Sparrow, Shrinkfield, and Karnilowicz (1993) noted that without adequate support, individuals with intellectual disabilities are less likely to gain acceptance and feel included in general recreation and leisure programming. Marianne is more likely to experience success and enjoyment from her leisure activities because the team ensured staff training prior to her participation, provided support during the activities, and pretaught skills required for the activity. Other supports that could be made available are specialized equipment, accommodations, and leisure coaching (Dattilo & Hoge, 1999).

Window 11-1

Selecting Appropriate Programs and Supports

Marianne is a 19-year-old student with a severe intellectual disability attending a postsecondary training program in a large urban school district. Through the program, she works part-time at a local grocery store and works on independent living skills several times a week. While she is doing well in the program, her parents and teacher are concerned that she spends the majority of her free time alone watching TV. Parent interviews and a non-formal leisure assessment indicate that Marianne enjoys arts and crafts, music, and small quiet activities. She does not like sports, outside activities, or large group situations. With Marianne, the IEP/transition planning team meets to brainstorm possible opportunities that may be of interest to her. The team presents all possible options and discusses the benefits and concerns of each. For example, the team considers a special craft program for people with disabilities at the local nonprofit organization but believes the long-term impact of the program is undesirable. The program focuses primarily on completing simple activities with volunteers without disabilities. Marianne and her parents are looking for something more engaging, where she can meet diverse people and learn a new skill. The city adaptive parks and recreation programs do offer activities that focus on skill development, but none is of interest to Marianne. The team decides that Marianne will enjoy and benefit from 10-week-long arts and crafts classes (e.g., beading, painting, and pottery) offered through the local community recreation center. She will have access to different activities with a variety of people. The team consults with the local adaptive parks and recreation staff to determine the best way to support Marianne in the classes. Through this collaboration, each member of the team will have a role in ensuring Marianne's success in the program. The city adaptive parks and recreation staff will ensure that the environment is accessible and that the instructor is prepared to work with Marianne. Her parents will assist Marianne in signing up for the class and paying the required fees. Since the classes are offered midmornings, the school will provide community-based instruction to increase Marianne's independence in the art classes and work to develop natural supports within the class. This will also be supplemented with in-class instruction to preteach essential skills needed to be successful in the course. By working together with her IEP/transition planning team, Marianne can participate in desired leisure activities with peers without disabilities while learning leisure routines and skills for participation in post-school activities.

With the proper supports, participation in general programming with accommodations is preferred over more segregated programming. General school- and community-based leisure programs offer a wider array of choices than those typically available through special programs. Since the programs are geared toward the general public, the activity choices are more likely to include age-appropriate and functional activities popular among same-age peers without disabilities. Research has shown that individuals with similar leisure interests are more likely to become friends (Terman, Larner, Stevenson, & Behrman, 1996). These interactions can lead to even greater postschool success by creating opportunities to facilitate the development of friendships and natural supports (Cimera, 2007). Natural supports include those that already exist in the community and could take the place of paid supports, such as individuals or staff already participating in the activity. With Marianne, the long-term goal will be to develop more natural supports so that she can participate independently. This might include working with the registrar so that she can help Marianne register in the future or with the instructors so that they can more easily accommodate her needs.

Unfortunately, using general programming can be difficult and may not lead to the desired outcomes. ADA regulations require that leisure and recreation programs provide reasonable accommodations to ensure access for people with disabilities. Small private programs, because of the unreasonable financial burden, may be unable to provide the adapted equipment required for some individuals to participate. Under ADA, the service provider is not obligated to provide expensive adaptive equipment. It is only required to ensure accessibility of its services to eligible participants. Barriers related to lack of program equipment and resources may be overcome by collaborating with special program service providers. The City of Las Vegas Adaptive Recreation Division collaborates with the Department of Parks and Recreation to provide support and equipment to individuals with disabilities participating in general recreation program offerings. For example, they will provide adaptive golf carts for wheelchair users interested in playing at any of the city's public golf courses. In some cases, advanced notice, such as that for the latter, and significant preplanning are required to access some accommodations and special equipment. Such "extra" requests may direct undesired attention to the participant, which may make him or her feel uncomfortable or isolated from the rest of the participants. Unlike special or partnering programs, many general recreation service providers may be unprepared to effectively include individuals with intellectual disabilities. In addition, other program participants may also feel uncomfortable around people with intellectual and developmental disabilities and unintentionally avoid interacting with them (Siperstein, Parker, Bardon, & Widaman, 2007). Thus, creating a positive inclusive experience may require significant supplemental support.

Universal Design. Universal design in recreation programming is considered best practice since it enables all users to participate in the activities regardless of their ability level. The concept of universal design in the recreation and leisure field became more prevalent after the passage of ADA (Kermeen, 1992). The U.S. Forest Service, which typically manages rugged terrain across the United States, incorporated universal design to increase access to national parks and recreation areas. When applied, universal design principles are subtle, and most people do not realize that they even exist. One of the most common universal design features in recreation areas is the use of boardwalks for nature trails. The design is viewed as optimal because it increases access for all people, including those with physical disabilities, parents with baby strollers, and the elderly, while protecting the area from overuse. Universally designed programs provide services that employ a framework, philosophy, and concept that support the widest range of abilities, to the maximum extent possible, without the need for specialized programs or services (Odem, Brantlinger, Gersten, Thompson, & Harris, 2005). They provide all participants, not just those with special needs, with various ways to access, engage in, or enjoy an activity.

Educators are traditionally taught to develop the lesson plan first and then consider individual modifications (Lieberman, Lytle, & Clarcq, 2008). This approach can lead to increased planning time and alienation of students receiving accommodations or modifications during the lesson (Tripp, Rizzo, & Webbert, 2007). Teachers using universal design in lesson and program development can increase learning opportunities for all students and reduce the need for individualizing each lesson. The needs and abilities of all participants, including those with and without disabilities, are considered prior to implementation as opposed to afterward. Lieberman and colleagues (2008) noted that the following variables must be addressed when developing universally designed leisure and recreation programs: outcomes or objectives, student characteristics, and universal modifications. The first step in universal design is to identify the key outcomes or objectives of the program. For example, is the outcome to engage in an enjoyable experience or develop specific leisure skills? Without clear outcomes, educators will have difficulty determining appropriate program modifications to meet the diverse needs of the group. Differences in student preference, motivation, previous experiences, and cognitive and physical ability exist in every group and will inevitably affect how participants perceive the benefit or value of a leisure activity. Effective teachers consider these differences when developing programs. Understanding student differences also assists the instructor in determining which program or lesson modifications meet the widest range of ability levels. The instructor may find that more than one variation or modification is needed to meet the needs of the target population.

Although universal design is considered best practice in including individuals with disabilities, its application to leisure programming for transition is relatively new. One of the biggest barriers in implementation may be lack of experience and training in how to create universally designed programs. Collaborating with other leisure service providers and special educators can provide support and feedback during and after the program implementation. Educators must know that part of this process is ongoing assessment of the effectiveness of the lesson. Newer educators will quickly discover that this is a dynamic learning process that will only improve with experience. Other barriers may also exist. Initial startup costs can be high in programs where universally designed practices were not previously used. In addition, some worry about decreased quality of services or a perceived "dumbing down" of the content, especially among inexperienced educators. Clearly defining the desired outcomes prior to considering program modifications may help prevent service providers from unintentionally doing this. Despite these barriers, many programs are successfully implementing universally designed leisure programming. It is becoming increasingly popular in local parks and recreation programs and nonprofit organizations across the country.

Age-Level Differences

The service delivery models discussed above are used across the life span. However, the outcome and the focus of the program will vary based on the age level of the participants. It makes sense that elementary-age students would receive different services than young adults. They have different leisure needs and desire different outcomes of the program. Below are age-level considerations for the development of instructional leisure programs for middle and junior high school students, high school students, and students in post-high school programs.

Although IDEA does not require formal transition planning until age 16, leisure and recreation transition programming should begin in middle or junior high school. Middle schools and even elementary schools provide educators with an excellent opportunity to help students develop leisure awareness and acquire foundational skills needed for independent postschool leisure participation. Poor communication and social skills can be significant barriers to leisure participation. Early leisure education programs should focus on developing social skills necessary for interactions with peers with and without disabilities. Specific skills include turn taking, following directions, initiating, self-regulation, and choice making. An important outcome of middle school programs should be to identify and begin to develop natural supports that the students can maintain throughout high school and then extend into postschool living. Students at this age should be included in general school- and community-based leisure and recreation with peers without disabilities to the maximum extent possible. Educators should also educate families about their role in developing leisure awareness and skills (Witman & Munson, 1992). Ideally, middle school students should be able to independently participate in several desired leisure activities that are similar to those participated in by their peers without disabilities.

As students enter high school, leisure and recreation training and instruction should build on previously learned skills and increase awareness of both school- and community-based leisure options. Participation in school-based activities should remain an important component of the leisure and recreation training program. However, students should be introduced to more community-based leisure opportunities in order to expose them to potential postschool leisure activities and environments. Educators and parents must encourage peer or natural supports, as opposed to paid staff or adults, during both school and community activities in order to facilitate independence and peer interactions. Whether at school or in the community, instruction should focus on the development of leisure routines as opposed to activity skill development. In other words, instruction should include not only how to play a card game but also how to select and initiate the card game with peers with and without disabilities.

By the time students enroll in post-high school programs, they will have been exposed to a wide variety of leisure activities. Post-high school programs should use the results of comprehensive leisure assessments, including an ecological assessment, to identify postschool leisure opportunities and interests, as well as which supports and resources are needed for independent participation. Assessment results and previous leisure experiences can be helpful in developing and implementing individualized leisure education programs. Instructional leisure routines should be embedded within the instructional routines from other transition domains, such as employment, independent living, or postsecondary education routines. For example, post-high school programs can embed instruction in playing a board game—a desired leisure routine—into free time found between vocational instruction and instruction in cooking dinner.

Selecting IEP Goals and Objectives

Bullock and Mahon (2001) define leisure education as "an individualized and contextualized educational process through which a person develops understanding of self and leisure and identifies and learns the cluster of skills necessary to participate in freely chosen activities which lead to an optimally satisfying life" (p. 332). The concept of a contextualized process supports the purpose of transition planning by looking at where the student is now, where the student is going, and what types of supports exist or will be necessary. Leisure and recreation program components and objectives should be based on individual needs and abilities. Person- or student-centered planning activities should serve as the framework from which educators can develop and provide recreation and leisure instruction. Leisure and recreation transition programs should involve family members, peers, and community- and school-based service providers in developing and delivering a comprehensive leisure and recreation transition education.

Focus Question 2	What five areas should educators consider when developing appropriate IEP goals and objectives?

Window 11–2

Identifying Age-Appropriate Leisure Activities

Michael, a 14-year-old with cerebral palsy, recently began high school. In elementary and junior high school, Michael had many friends with and without disabilities. However, his teachers have noticed that since arriving at high school, he has become more isolated during his free time. Observations conducted by his teachers indicate that his leisure activities may be negatively impacting his interactions with peers without disabilities. Michael regularly asks other students to play with his matchbox cars or look at one of his favorite picture books. The IEP/transition planning team determines that Michael would benefit from more age-appropriate leisure activities. Mrs. Black, Michael's special education teacher, conducts a survey of peers his age to identify the activities in which they participate during their free time at school. The results show that most students participate in one of five popular activities: talking to friends, reading books or magazines, playing cards, playing handheld video games, and playing handball. Mrs. Black shares the findings with Michael and conducts a preference assessment to determine which of the activities would be most desirable. Michael selects magazines—specifically car magazines—and card games as being preferred activities. Mrs. Black determines that these two activities would be age-appropriate, functional leisure activities. The IEP/transition planning team meets and adds a leisure goal to his IEP. The goal is for Michael to independently initiate and participate in age-appropriate leisure activities with peers without disabilities. Mrs. Black enlists the assistance of peer tutors to teach Michael two popular card games and the appropriate social skills to engage with his peers. The peer tutors also help Michael participate in one of these activities with peers without disabilities two or three times a week. The program will continue until Michael can independently initiate his new leisure routines.

Age-Appropriateness

As with all transition areas, secondary leisure and recreation activities must be appropriate for the student's chronological age. Choosing age-appropriate activities can be quite challenging in cases where students consistently choose age-inappropriate activities. One could argue that all individuals have personal choice in selecting their free-time activities. However, like Michael in Window 11.2, engagement in activities associated with younger children can lead to further exclusion and increase negative perceptions of people with disabilities. Some students and adults may treat the individual like a child, despite his or her chronological age, and others may choose to ignore him or her. Secondary training programs can assist students in accessing and selecting activities that are more age appropriate yet still desirable. In Michael's case, the IEP/transition planning team was unsure of what types of activities were desired by same-age peers. By conducting a simple survey, Michael's teacher was able to identify what types of activities were not only age appropriate but also preferred by his peers without disabilities. Selecting age-appropriate activities is essential for increasing opportunities for interactions with peers without disabilities and community inclusion.

Choice and Preferences

Choice making and personal preference are essential components of leisure education for students in transition (Browder & Cooper, 1994; Lieberman & Stuart, 2002). Without these two components, leisure, by its very definition, does not exist. The nature of leisure and recreation instruction requires that student choice and preferences guide the development of related goals and objectives. Educators can use a variety of formal and informal assessments to identify specific activities and general interest areas of a student. Parent and peer interviews, observations during free-time activities, ecological assessments, and interest surveys are common informal assessment tools used by educators. The easiest approach to assessing leisure preferences is to simply ask the individual or his or her family about preferred activities. Observations during a variety of leisure choices can also provide valuable information about leisure preferences. In some cases, the IEP/transition planning team may consider that a comprehensive leisure and recreation needs and preference assessment is necessary. Licensed adapted physical educators or school- or community-based therapeutic recreation specialists can provide the team with valuable information concerning the student. IDEA (2004) considers physical education and recreation services as key elements of special education (Sec. 1401 [29][B]) and related services (Sec. 1401 [26][A]), respectively.

Educators will encounter instances where the student's leisure and recreation preferences are unclear. Difficulty with using traditional modes of communication, particularly when it exists with significant physical impairments, may inhibit some students from sharing their preferences and interests. Students' ability to accurately and independently select desired leisure activities can be affected by the method selected by educators (Conyers et al., 2002). For example, in investigating leisure preferences of adults with disabilities, Parsons, Harper, Jensen, and Reid (1997) found that some individuals were able to independently select a desired activity when the activity was presented as objects but not as pictures. Failing to take into consideration a student's choice-making skills could lead to instruction in undesired activities—and thus not leisure activities—for the student. Another common problem for many students is lack of experience and exposure to a variety of leisure and recreation pursuits. The IEP/transition planning team should consider IEP goals and instructional programming targeted at increasing the student's awareness of potential leisure and recreation activities to facilitate accurate choice making.

Functionality and the Impact on Quality of Life

Modell and Valdez (2002) noted that participation in sports, recreation, and leisure can make a difference in the quality of life of individuals with disabilities. However, educators must remember that it is not the activity itself but how the student perceives the function of the activity (e.g., enjoyment, relaxation) that leads to pleasurable leisure experiences. How do you know if an activity is appropriate? Given the vast array of leisure and recreational pursuits available, activity selection may seem like a daunting task. As in Michael's case, the team first considered the age-appropriateness of the activity and students' preferences. Then, the IEP/transition planning team considered the functionality of the activity and the long-term impact on quality of life. Storey (2004) expressed concern about the functionality of many of the events found in the Special Olympics. For example, the program offers a number of individual skill competitions—such as the softball throw, target pass, and run and kick—that are viewed as necessary skills for future team participation (Special Olympics, 2008). However, instruction in these individual skills has little functionality outside of the Special Olympics. While the program may provide opportunities for structured events through the year, the individual nature of the sports does not encourage interactions with peers without disabilities; nor does it help individuals develop personal leisure and recreation skills that can be utilized during their free time. The following questions may assist educators in determining the functionality of potential activities:

- Do these activities match other preferences indicated by the student (e.g., enjoys outdoors, quiet activities, tactile or sensory preferences)?
- Is long-term participation realistic for the individual?
- Are appropriate supports available to encourage independent participation?
- Will the activities increase or allow for social interaction with peers without disabilities?
- Can the leisure and recreation skills generalize to other settings (e.g., home, school, community)?
- Are the activities acceptable to same-age peers?
- Are the participation costs reasonable?

Comprehensive leisure and recreation training programs should focus on instruction in developing functional leisure routines. Functional leisure routines include all of the skills needed to complete a leisure activity, not just specific leisure skills. Imagine what it takes to see a movie at the local theater. First, an individual must determine that seeing a movie is desirable and then initiate the steps needed to go to the movies. This may involve calling to see if friends want to go, checking movie times, and choosing a movie. Next, an individual must access transportation to the theater and then, once there, purchase the movie tickets. Finally, the individual can enjoy the leisure activity of watching the movie. This requires its own set of skills, including finding a seat, staying quiet during the movie, and remaining seated. By focusing on functional leisure routines as opposed to specific leisure skills, students are better able to independently participate in desired leisure activities. Leisure routines offer educators opportunities to teach other functional independent living and communication skills. Several studies have shown that independent living skills, such as decision making (Mahon & Bullock, 1992), money management (Bullock & Luken, 1994), and public transportation use (Ashton-Schaeffer, Shelton, & Johnson, 1995), can be learned when presented as part of leisure routines.

Interactions With Peers

While many leisure and recreation activities can be enjoyed individually, most people find that peer interactions enhance leisure experiences. Individuals with disabilities who share experiences and interests in leisure activities with others around them are more likely to be integrated in the community (Terman et al., 1996). Thus, IEP/transition teams should consider the extent to which the proposed recreation and leisure education program promotes social interaction with peers without disabilities. Social skill development should be integrated into the recreation and leisure training program when students lack appropriate social skills to engage with same-age peers. In Michael's case, the social norms were different from those of his previous environment, and the IEP/transition planning team determined that social skill instruction was necessary for him to achieve his leisure goal. Social skills taught through leisure education (e.g., greeting, asking for help, listening, sharing experiences) are essential for positive postschool outcomes and increased quality of life (Heyne, Schleien, & McAvoy, 1993; Patton et al., 1996). Michael's teacher incorporated peers without disabilities in his leisure education program to model and teach age-appropriate peer interactions. These skills are vital for developing reciprocal relationships and friendships while decreasing feelings of isolation, boredom, and depression.

Mastery Versus Variety

IEP/transition planning teams must also consider whether the focus of the training program is mastery or variety. For some students, the purpose of the leisure and recreation instruction is to expose them to a wide *variety* of age-appropriate leisure activities that they, based on personal preferences, may enjoy. Selection of leisure activities should not be limited to those only available in the teacher's classroom or those provided by the district. Just like people without disabilities, people with disabilities have diverse interests. Secondary programs should provide students with an array of age-appropriate activities that are available across settings, vary in activity level, and provide opportunities for social and individual participation. Table 11.1 provides a sample of common leisure and recreation activities.

Table 11.1   Passive and Active Leisure Activities

	Passive Leisure Activities	*Active Leisure Activities*
Home	Watching TV or movies	Exercising
	Reading	Yoga
	Cooking	Gardening
	Listening to music	Running/walking
	Knitting or sewing	Walking dogs
	Tanning	Basketball
	Pet care	Playing catch or Frisbee
	Fashion/make-up	
	Collecting (stamps, cards, etc.)	
	Internet/video games	

	Passive Leisure Activities	*Active Leisure Activities*
	Home decorating	
	Card and board games	
	Hanging out with friends	
	Parties	
School	Art/drawing classes	Baseball
	Reading	Football
	Listening to music	Soccer
	Elective courses	Tennis/ping-pong
	Music and instruments	School dances
	Drama/theater clubs	Golf team
	Social committees	Weight lifting
	Service clubs	Track and field
	Hanging out with friends	
Community	Parks	Club sports
	Libraries	Special Olympics
	Movies/theater	Wheelchair sports
	Golf	Roller skating
	Scouts	Weight lifting/aerobics
	Church activities	Swimming/diving
	Bars or social clubs	Bowling
	Shopping	Community dances
	Dining	
	Traveling/sightseeing	
	Recreation classes	
	Sporting events	
Outdoor	Bird-watching	Hiking
	Trail running/hiking	Canoeing/kayaking
	Fishing	Rock climbing
	Camping	Snow and water skiing
	Collecting (e.g., seashells, rocks)	White-water rafting
	Photography	Horseback riding
		Sledding

A student's IEP/transition planning team may determine that mastery is the focus of the training program. In this case, the goal of the program is on the *mastery* of a few important instructional routines and skills so that the student can independently participate in a preferred activity. For example, a student may receive targeted instruction in how to play a common board game, including how to set up the game and play the game by the rules.

How do IEP/transition planning teams choose between a focus on mastery and a focus on variety? In most cases, both are recommended for comprehensive leisure and recreation programs. Few adults engage in the same activities they mastered as adolescents or young adults. As we move away from home and meet new people, we are exposed to new leisure and recreation activities. Some choose to master the new activities while others try them out and move on. Through regular exposure to new activities, we become better able to make choices about how we spend our free time.

Focus Question 3	What instructional approaches are available for leisure and recreation instruction?

Instructional Approaches

Do students with intellectual and developmental disabilities really need instruction in how to play or engage in meaningful free-time activities? Many people, including parents of individuals with disabilities and special education teachers, are under the assumption that systematic instruction is not necessary (Dattilo, 1999; Rose et al., 2007). They may believe that, like individuals without disabilities, students with intellectual and developmental disabilities will naturally acquire these skills over time. However, current research demonstrates that students need explicit instruction to develop the critical skills needed to independently participate in school and community recreation activities (Collins, Hall, & Branson, 1997; Modell & Valdez, 2002).

Critical leisure and recreation skills go beyond just specific activity skills and include skills that fall under three broad domains: leisure and recreation awareness, skill learning, and self-determination. In the first critical domain, individuals must become aware of the differences between work and recreation and leisure time. This is especially true for individuals with disabilities whose activities have traditionally been chosen for them. Leisure awareness also involves being introduced to a wide variety of leisure activities, as well as the resources needed to participate in those activities. Skill learning, the second critical domain, is an essential component of leisure participation. Other than specific activity skills, it includes instruction in all of the skills needed to engage in a leisure activity, including social and communication skills and related independent living skills (e.g., using public transportation, money management). The last domain, which Bullock and Mahon (2001) deemed as crucial, is self-determination. During leisure training, students must learn to make choices about activities, plan for leisure time, and independently initiate leisure and recreation activities. Comprehensive leisure and recreation transition programs include instruction in all three critical domains in order to achieve positive postschool leisure outcomes.

Community-based instruction is optimal for teaching desired functional leisure routines and is more likely than segregated programs to lead to positive leisure benefits and generalization for students with intellectual and developmental disabilities (Ashton-Schaeffer et al., 1995; Lanagan & Dattilo, 1989). The procedures for developing CBI programs were discussed in Chapter 9. It is also recommended that leisure instruction continue over an extended period of time to ensure the maximum benefit (Bedini et al., 1993). Significant positive results are less likely to result from short-duration leisure education programs (fewer than 12 hr), especially for individuals with disabilities (Zoerink, 1988; Zoerink & Lauener, 1991).

Developing Alternative Performance Strategies

Participation in leisure and recreation activities requires varying levels of communication, social, cognitive, and motor skills. People with intellectual and developmental disabilities are more likely to possess skill deficits in one or more of these areas. However, these difficulties should not prevent students from learning functional leisure routines or independently participating in preferred leisure activities. Secondary programs can teach students alternative performance strategies to help them achieve their leisure goals. When considering alternative strategies, educators need to remember that it is not the activity that is the desired outcome. The outcome of leisure and recreation education is for the individual to be actively involved in a preferred leisure activity. A person-centered approach should be used in selecting alternative performance strategies.

Alternative performance strategies are useful when students have not mastered all of the tasks or skills of a leisure routine or, due to their disability, will be unable to complete a component of the leisure routine. Educators should select strategies that meet the demands of the task and lead to increased independence and inclusion. The best strategies are those that can be used across settings and instructional domains. An alternate augmentative communication (AAC) device is an example of an alternative performance strategy that can be used across settings and activities. Educators can incorporate this previously learned strategy into a student's functional leisure routine to help initiate activities and conversations with peers. For many students with disabilities, strategies must be taught within the context of the routine in order to encourage skill acquisition and generalization, even if the strategy is used in other settings. Educators should avoid alternative performance strategies that alter the desired outcomes. For example, being the score keeper in the class baseball game is not the same as participating in the game. Recreation specialists, adaptive physical educators, and other specialists can assist educators in developing appropriate alternative performance strategies. Table 11.2 provides a sampling of leisure and recreation alternative performance strategies commonly used for students with disabilities.

Table 11.2 Sample of Alternative Performance Strategies for Leisure and Recreation

Component Altered	Strategy
Performance	**Simplify Rules**—Focus on a few important rules of the activity or game.
	Picture Schedule—Use pictures to show the sequence of steps in the activity.
	Peer Assistance—Use peers or partners to complete the steps in the activity.
	Prompting Cues—Incorporate verbal, auditory, or visual indicators to assist the students in completing the activity.
	Rule Changes—Alter the rules to improve participation but still receive the same outcome (e.g., wheelchair basketball, beeper ball).
	Duration of Activity—Shorten or lengthen the amount of time typically required to complete the activity.
	Location of Activity—Change where the activity is completed.
	Partial Participation—Complete only parts of the activity versus the entire routine.
Equipment and Materials Used	**Specialized Wheelchairs**—Use specially designed wheelchairs for sports, community, and wilderness activities.
	Large Print—Increase the font of reading material to allow access by those with visual impairments.
	Input Devices and Switches—Utilize alternative modes of access to leisure activities using computers.
	Enlarged Cards/Game Pieces—Alter game pieces or components to allow for access by the individual.
	Adapted Balls—Incorporate specially designed balls, including balls of all sizes, weights, and textures and balls that beep.
	Adaptive Outdoor Equipment—Choose from a variety of specialized equipment to help people with cognitive and physical impairments access outdoor activities.

Summary

Leisure and recreation training is essential not only for transitioning from school to community but also for quality of life. Individuals with intellectual and developmental disabilities rely on their parents and educators to provide them with the knowledge and skills to select desired activities. Unfortunately, without systematic instruction, some individuals with intellectual and developmental disabilities will be denied the right to leisure enjoyment. Numerous service delivery models exist to assist secondary educators in leisure programming. However, inclusive models more effectively prepare students to transition into community environments with peers with and without disabilities. Students participating in general programming with accommodations or universally designed programs have the greatest access to peers without disabilities and diverse leisure opportunities. The needs and preferences of the student should guide the development of a person-centered approach to leisure programming. A comprehensive evaluation of needs and preferences can be conducted in collaboration with local community- or school-based recreation therapists and adaptive physical educators. The leisure and recreation evaluation can also assist educators in identifying the most appropriate instructional approaches for teaching leisure skills and routines. Educators have access to numerous supports to facilitate inclusive leisure programming. Parents and school and community service providers can assist not only in the development of the program but also in its implementation. Including more natural and community supports has the added advantage of decreasing the need for long-term paid supports and increasing independence. Many students will need direct instruction in specific leisure skills that should be taught through community-based instruction to facilitate generalization. Either way, students should participate in programs that enhance leisure awareness, develop leisure and social skills, and encourage self-determination.

Focus Question Review

Focus Question 1: What four service delivery models are commonly used in leisure and recreation programming?

- Special, or adaptive, programs
- Partnering programming approach
- General programs with accommodations or modifications
- Universally designed programs

Focus Question 2: What five areas should educators consider when developing appropriate IEP goals and objectives?

- Age-appropriateness
- Choice and preferences
- Functionality and impact on quality of life
- Interaction with peers
- Mastery versus variety

Focus Question 3: What instructional approaches are available for leisure and recreation instruction?

- Observational learning
- Task analytic instruction with prompting strategies
- Community-based instruction

CHAPTER 12

Employment Training

JOHN MCDONNELL

I t is well documented that employment plays an important role in shaping our economic and psychological well-being as adults (Szymanski, Ryan, Merz, Trevino, & Johnston-Rodriquez, 1996). Consequently, it is not surprising that a significant portion of the general secondary curriculum centers on teaching students the skills necessary to succeed in the workplace, exposing them to career alternatives, and developing a work ethic (Berryman, 1993). Employment training options in secondary schools range from participation in vocational education classes, such as metal and wood shop, to community-based work experience programs. The opportunity to develop the skills and dispositions necessary to have a productive and satisfying job is no less important for secondary students with intellectual and developmental disabilities than it is for their peers without disabilities.

Research in the last decade has clearly shown that if they are provided with adequate training and support, adults with intellectual and developmental disabilities can be productively employed (Wehman, Inge, Revell, & Brooke, 2007). Most researchers and advocates have argued that secondary programs should be designed to place students in paid employment settings before they exit school (Hasazi et al., 2005; McDonnell, Mathot-Buckner, & Ferguson, 1996; Rusch & Braddock, 2004; Wehman, 2006). This recommendation is based on research that shows that students who have had a paid job before graduation are more likely to adjust successfully to employment than students who have not (Benz, Lindstrom, & Yovanoff, 2000; Blackorby & Wagner, 1996; Phelps & Hanley-Maxwell, 1997).

As recommended in Chapter 3, post-high school programs should assume primary responsibility for obtaining paid employment for students. However, middle school and high school programs play an important role in preparing students for work. This chapter focuses on the strategies that middle school and high school programs can use to help students achieve this outcome.

Focus Question I	What is the purpose of employment training for middle or junior high school and high school students?

Focus of Employment Training

Employment training in middle school and high school programs should be focused on three activities (McDonnell et al., 1996; Simmons & Flexer, 2008; Wehman, 2006): (a) teaching work and work-related skills, (b) identifying a student's work interests and preferences, and (c) determining the supports necessary to ensure a student's success in the workplace.

Teach Work and Work-Related Skills

An important function of employment training is to provide students with a solid foundation of work and work-related skills that will support their success in whatever job they choose to do. In 1990, the Carl D. Perkins Vocational and Applied Technology Education Act established the Secretary's Commission on Achieving Necessary Skills (SCANS) to develop standards that would help schools prepare students for high-skill and high-wage employment. The commission determined that students need preparation in three areas, including basic literacy and computation skills, thinking skills, and development of personal qualities that contribute to successful employment (Table 12.1). The commission placed emphasis on teaching students skills that will enhance their productivity in any job and their ability to work cooperatively with others. The general knowledge and skills identified in the SCANS report are equally applicable to students with intellectual and developmental disabilities and can provide a framework for developing goals and objectives within the Individualized Education Program/transition plan.

In addition to the skills in the SCANS report, students will require instruction on a number of work-related activities and skills that are necessary to support successful employment (McDonnell et al., 1996; Sitlington, 2003). These may range from using assistive technology in the workplace to using public transportation to get to and from work. Instruction on work-related skills

Table 12.1   SCANS Foundation Skills and Competencies

Foundation Skills	
Basic Skills	Reading, writing, arithmetic, mathematics, listening, and speaking.
Thinking Skills	Creative thinking, decision making, problem solving, mental visualization, knowing how to learn, and reasoning.
Personal Qualities	Responsibility, self-esteem, sociability, self-management, and integrity/honesty.
Workplace Competencies	
Resources	Manages time, money, material and facility resources, and human resources.
Interpersonal	Participates as a member of a team, teaches others, exercises leadership, negotiates to arrive at a decision, and works with cultural diversity.
Information	Acquires and evaluates information, organizes and maintains information, interprets and communicates information, serves clients/customers, and uses computers to process information.
Systems	Understands systems, monitors and corrects performance, and improves and designs systems.
Technology	Selects technology, applies technology to tasks, and maintains and troubleshoots technology.

Note. From *Learning a Living: A Blueprint for High Performance,* by The Secretary's Commission on Achieving Necessary Skills, April 1992, Washington, DC: U.S. Department of Labor. Adapted with permission.

should be focused on increasing students' independence in the workplace and reducing the supports they require to be successful.

Identify Students' Interests and Preferences

Another critical role for middle school and high school programs in employment training is to help a student and his or her IEP/transition planning team determine the student's career interests and preferences. For most people, the selection of a career path is based on several factors, including their strengths and weaknesses, the type of work they like to do, the kind of work environment they like, whether they like to work alone or with other people, and so on. It is accepted that adolescents come to understand what they want from work through their courses, part-time jobs, and talking with people that they respect about their jobs (Mortimer, 2003).

The practical implication of this for middle schools and high schools is that employment training must be structured to expose students to a wide range of employment options through participation in vocational education classes and job sampling experiences (McDonnell et al., 1996; Steere, Rose, & Cavaiuolo, 2007; Wehman, 2006). This is especially true for students with more severe disabilities who may lack the communication and academic skills necessary to gather information about career alternatives through traditional avenues. The primary purpose of these experiences is to provide a student and his or her planning team with the information necessary to identify a paid job that will match his or her long-term employment goals and expected outcomes.

Identify Necessary Supports

Students will require different amounts and types of support to be successfully employed. Consequently, a critical outcome of employment training during middle or junior high school and high school is identifying the formal supports that will be necessary from service agencies for students to succeed in their jobs, how natural supports in the workplace can be best structured to meet their needs, and what alternative performance strategies are needed to allow them to complete their job duties. This information is used to identify the mix of supports that will be necessary to allow students to learn their job duties and maintain their performance across time.

Instructional Approaches

While there is broad agreement that middle or junior high school and high school students should be provided with comprehensive employment training, there is much less agreement on how this is best accomplished. Advances in our ability to support the inclusion of students in the general education curriculum and general education classes has led some to suggest that employment training for students with intellectual and developmental disabilities should be restricted to the vocational education classes available to students without disabilities (Fisher, Sax, & Pumpian, 1999; Jorgensen, 1998). Others have argued that students must also be provided with individualized community-based employment training experiences (McDonnell et al., 1996; Rusch & Braddock, 2004; Steere et al., 2007; Wehman, 2006).

The research indicates that inclusion in both vocational classes and community-based experiences promotes students' adjustment to employment after school (Blackorby & Wagner, 1996; Phelps & Hanley-Maxwell, 1997). However, much more research is needed to determine the unique contributions of each approach to improving students' postschool outcomes. Without these data, the decision about the best combination of general vocational education classes and community-based work experiences for students must be made by the IEP/transition planning teams based on students' specific needs.

Focus Question 2	What instructional approaches should be used with middle or junior high school and high school students?

It has been recommended that middle school programs emphasize students' participation in vocational education classes and other in-school work experiences (Inge & Moon, 2006; McDonnell et al., 1996). In addition to developing the work and work-related skills discussed above, the focus of employment training in middle school should be on helping students develop an understanding of the importance of work in our lives and exploring different types of careers. These experiences should also be structured to maximize students' participation in the natural social networks of the school so that they can develop the communication and social skills necessary to be socially competent and develop positive relationships with peers without disabilities.

Window 12–1

A Job Sampling Placement for Dave

Dave is a junior at Canyon View High School. He is enrolled in general education classes in the morning, including Furniture Design and Manufacturing I. He took a woodworking class during his sophomore year and really enjoyed it. His grandfather has a shop at his house and has taught Dave how to use many of his hand and power tools. Dave has expressed an interest several times about working in the cabinetry or carpentry business. During Dave's IEP/transition planning meeting last spring, the team decided that he should enroll in the furniture design class and have a job sampling placement in a cabinet shop to see if he'd really like it. Dave's special education teacher knew very little about cabinetry, so she talked with Dave's shop teacher about businesses in the community that might be interested in working with her to develop a job sampling placement for Dave. She was able to establish a partnership with Rowley's Custom Cabinets. She and Gene Rowley, the shop owner, worked out a schedule that allowed Dave to work 2 hours a day on Monday, Wednesday, and Friday as an assistant to Mike, one of Gene's best employees. Dave has only been on the job for about 3 weeks, but he is making progress in learning his assigned duties. Gene and Mike really like him and think he is a hard worker.

(Continued)

(Continued)

He's been working in the shop, helping assemble the cabinet frames, finishing sanding, cleaning up, and helping Mike load the cabinets in the truck for delivery. Dave works under Mike's direction but gets assistance from a paraprofessional to do the more routine jobs like cleaning up. Not only is Dave learning a lot about working in a shop; his teacher and paraprofessional are getting information that will help them select other job sampling placements for Dave in the future. Gene has agreed to allow Rowley's Custom Cabinets to serve as a job sampling site in the future for other students who might be interested in woodworking.

Once students enter high school, employment training needs to be expanded beyond participation in general vocational education classes to include community-based work experiences. In some high schools, these work experiences can be provided through courses in the general education curriculum. For example, many high schools have apprenticeship programs in construction in which students enrolled in the class build a house from the foundation up. Whenever possible, students with intellectual and developmental disabilities should be included in these classes. However, in most cases students will also need to be provided with job sampling programs that will expose them to the range of employment options available within the local community.

In-School Employment Training

The technology necessary to support students with intellectual and developmental disabilities in general education classes has improved dramatically over the last 10 years (Hunt & McDonnell, 2007). The challenges in supporting students in vocational education classes are identical to those found when students are included in other content-area classes. The successful inclusion of students in content-area classes requires teachers to develop personal supports for students in completing activities and assignments, adapt curriculum and instruction as necessary to meet their unique needs, and provide embedded instruction on specific skills that are important to their educational progress. Recommendations for implementing these strategies were discussed in Chapter 8.

Another employment training strategy is the use of in-school jobs (Inge & Moon, 2006; Sowers & Powers, 1991). In most middle schools and high schools, students perform a number of tasks necessary for the day-to-day operation of the school. For example, students may gather attendance slips,

Table 12.2 Examples of In-School Jobs

Site	Possible Work Activities
Main Office	Typing Data entry Filing Collating the school newsletter Photocopying
Attendance Office	Collecting attendance sheets Data entry Message running
Library	Delivering audiovisual equipment Reshelving books Affixing scan codes to new books
School Store	Stocking Inventory Cashier

reshelve books in the library, deliver audiovisual equipment to classrooms, or work in the school store (Table 12.2). These types of jobs can provide an effective and efficient method for teaching important work and work-related skills to students. These jobs also approximate many of the same conditions that students face in community-based work experience programs. Consequently, they can serve an important role in preparing students for these experiences.

The first step in developing in-school work experiences is to inventory the school to identify potential placement options. The best way to accomplish this is to identify the locations in the school where students without disabilities already work. Teachers should avoid developing jobs that are not done by peers. For example, it is quite common to see students working in the office, but it is not common to see students as custodians during school hours. Placing students in these types of jobs highlights the differences rather than the similarities between students with and without disabilities and may negatively affect the acceptance of students by their peers.

The next step is to develop an instructional program to teach the specific tasks of the job. This requires that the teacher analyze performance demands, conduct a baseline probe of student performance on the job, develop instructional procedures that meet the needs of students, and develop a data collection system. The considerations in carrying out these steps were discussed in detail in Chapter 9.

Community-Based Job Sampling

Job sampling involves placing students in a variety of unpaid work experiences in community businesses (Inge & Moon, 2006; McDonnell et al., 1996; Wehman, 2006). Job sampling provides teachers with a mechanism for exposing students to a range of employment options available in the community, teaching students work and work-related skills, identifying career interests of students, and identifying the level of support necessary to ensure success in community work settings. Job sampling is perhaps best thought of as a series of situational assessments. The information gathered during job sampling will ultimately help students and their planning teams select a job that matches students' interests and needs.

Job sampling requires teachers to move instruction beyond the school and into the community. Thus the scope of teachers' instructional activities increases substantially and more closely matches that of employment specialists in the adult service system (Izzo, Johnson, Levitz, & Aaron, 1998). The steps necessary to design and implement a job sampling program include developing sampling sites, selecting a site for training, job analysis, and instruction and follow-along.

Focus Question 3	What are the considerations in developing job sampling sites?

Site Development. An effective job sampling program requires students to be exposed to the range of jobs that will likely be available to them after graduation. This can be accomplished by conducting a labor market analysis of the local community. This information can often be found at the Web sites of the state departments of labor or workforce services. These sites typically have search engines that will sort jobs currently available by city or ZIP code. In addition, they frequently have projections on the employment areas that are expected to grow over the next several years. Additional information can also be obtained from such sources as local chambers of commerce or by surveying the help-wanted ads of local newspapers. The number of employment areas available to students will vary based on the size and economic base of the community.

The labor market analysis is used by school staff to establish ongoing partnerships with local businesses that are willing to serve as job sampling sites. The focus is on developing a list of sites that represents the range of potential jobs in each identified employment area. For example, in an area like domestic services, school staff would attempt to identify sites that sample typical jobs (janitor and hotel maid), businesses (manufacturing and service), and the size of the businesses commonly found in the community. The development of job sampling sites is a time-consuming process. Consequently, it is important for school staff to concentrate on businesses that are willing to develop an ongoing relationship with the job sampling program.

Initially, staff members should contact businesses by telephone to determine their interest in participating in the job sampling program. The purpose of the call is to establish a time for an introductory meeting with the employer to describe the program in more detail. During the meeting, school staff should outline advantages of the program for the student as well as the business. In addition, the specific roles and responsibilities of the school and the business in supporting the student should be described. Once the employer has agreed to participate as a site, a written agreement should be developed that specifies the work activities to be completed by the student(s), the times when work will be completed, the training and follow-along to be provided by the school, and the level of training and supervision to be provided by the business.

Selecting a Job Sampling Site. The primary factor in selecting a job sampling site is whether the type of work and the environment are consistent with the student's preferences. For students who cannot express their job preferences, the team will need to rely on "behavioral" indicators of their interests. For example, if a student has been reluctant to complete specific jobs in the past either at school or at home, a job sampling site that would require him or her to do similar tasks would not be an appropriate placement. A student should never be placed in a site that would require him or her to do a job that he or she dislikes or to perform under conditions that he or she would find uncomfortable.

A second consideration is whether the site exposes the student to a new employment area and job. The number of job sampling sites in which a student is placed each school year must be based on his or her specific needs. However, McDonnell and colleagues (1996) recommended that students have at least two job sampling placements each school year. This increases the likelihood that students will be exposed to the employment areas, business types, and business sizes commonly found in most communities.

A final consideration is whether the job sampling site will provide students with opportunities to learn or maintain important work-related skills, such as riding the bus, using a self-management system, or interacting with peers without disabilities. Job sampling sites should provide students with opportunities to learn new skills that will enhance their future success in the workplace.

Job Analysis. Before a student can be trained to perform a job, the teacher must be thoroughly acquainted with the demands of the job. The process of conducting a job analysis is similar to conducting a task analysis of community activities. The job analysis should focus on four aspects of the work activities assigned to the student.

1. *Student responses.* The analysis should identify the specific responses that will be required to complete each work activity assigned to the student. These responses should be stated in a way that is both observable and measurable.

2. *Stimuli.* The analysis should also identify the natural stimuli that should set the occasion for each response. As in other community activities, there may be multiple cues that control when and how the student completes a response.

3. *Speed requirements.* Fluent performance is critical to success in employment settings. Consequently, the analysis should identify the speed requirements for each work activity or a "production" rate (the number of tasks completed by an individual within a prespecified period of time). Speed requirements or production rates may be established by the business. In other situations, the teacher may need to develop his or her own standards. This can be done by calculating the average performance time or production rate of other workers doing the same job.

4. *Quality requirements.* The job analysis should also specify the quality requirements for each response. The quality requirements identify the employer's expectations. The teacher should have the employer or manager identify the quality requirements for each task to be completed by the student. It is also good practice to determine the accuracy of the supervisor's expectations by discussing them with other workers who complete the same job.

Job Training. The instructional procedures needed to carry out effective employment training are identical to those described in Chapter 9. The teacher should conduct a baseline probe of the student's performance on all job tasks before training begins. This information should be used to select instructional procedures that will allow the student's performance to come under control of the natural stimuli and consequences found in the job sampling site. Teachers should regularly track student progress toward independent performance of job tasks and modify instructional procedures to meet the individual needs of the student.

In addition to the assigned work activities, students may need to learn various work-related activities and skills that are necessary for success on the job site. Instruction of these activities and skills should be included as part of ongoing training at the job site rather than as separate, or prerequisite, training activities.

Follow-Along. After students have learned to complete assigned work activities, teachers should follow their performance in the job for several weeks. This phase of job sampling has several purposes. First is to identify the amount, frequency, and type of support that will be necessary for students to maintain their job performance. This information will help students and their planning teams anticipate the formal and informal supports that will be needed to promote their success in paid employment.

A second and equally important purpose is to identify the factors that influence students' maintenance of job performance. These factors may include variation in work demands, difficulties in maintaining appropriate relationships with coworkers or supervisors, and motivation. This information can help identify instructional approaches or alternative performance strategies that can be used to address these issues in students' future job sampling placements or in paid employment.

Finally, follow-along is necessary to ensure that the needs of the employer are being met by both the student and school staff. An employer will continue to participate in the job sampling program only if the placement of students does not interfere with operation of the business. During follow-along, the teacher needs to frequently assess the employer's satisfaction with both the student's performance and the staff's support of the student.

Teachers should follow three general guidelines in carrying out job follow-along:

1. *Establish a regular schedule of contact with the student and employer.* The frequency of contact should be based on the needs of the student and employer.

2. *During each follow-up visit, the teacher should probe the student's performance on assigned work activities.* The probe should be structured to assess the student's performance of his or her duties. The teacher should observe the student and record discrepancies in his or her accuracy or speed in completing the job. If there are consistent errors, the teacher must be prepared to provide additional training and supervision until the problem is corrected.

3. *Regularly assess the employer's satisfaction with the training program.* The teacher should meet and discuss student performance

with the immediate supervisor during each follow-along visit. These informal contacts can highlight problems that have recently occurred or that may arise in the future (for example, if new equipment or tasks are introduced in the job site). It is also advisable to discuss the student's performance with coworkers.

Evaluate the Job Sampling Placement. The teacher should summarize the student's performance at the conclusion of each job sampling experience and place this information in the student's file. The summary should identify any problems in completing assigned job tasks (for example, accuracy of task completion, speed or quality, or maintenance), in completing work-related skills (traveling to and from the work site, interacting with coworkers, and so forth), and with the level of support provided to the student. Figure 12.1 presents an example of a job sampling placement summary. The purpose of the summary is to provide a cumulative record of the job sampling process over a student's high school career. This information should guide the selection of subsequent job sampling sites and, ultimately, the job into which the student is placed before graduation.

Figure 12.1 Job Sampling Placement Summary

Student: Mark

Date: 3/22/06

Site: Eve's Buffet

Period: 1/10/06–3/15/06

Work Activities: Bus tables, wash dishes

Supervisor: Judith Wright

1. Level of independent task completion: Mark completed all job activities with 100% accuracy. He maintained work performance at 100% accuracy on four consecutive weekly probes.

2. Quality of work: Judith consistently rated Mark's quality of work as good to excellent.

3. Productivity/rate: Mark's work rate ranged from 80% to 85% of the established time standard.

4. Work-related skills:
   a. Self-management: Mark used a picture checklist to prompt him to initiate work activities at the correct time. He learned to use the checklist within 3 weeks and continued to use it successfully without prompting.
   b. Transportation: Mark walked independently to and from the site. He was shown the route by the employment specialist and was shadowed for 1 week.
   c. Social skills: Overall, Mark's social skills are good. He sometimes repeats topics of conversations.

5. Other observations: Mark's work rate slowed when he bussed tables because he tried to avoid getting food, grease, or sauces on his hands.

Job Sampling and Fair Labor Standards. Congress has enacted a number of laws to ensure that employers do not take advantage of the nation's workforce. Many of these laws are designed to protect children and youth from exploitation. The authority for the prevention of such abuses is in the Fair Labor Standards Act (FLSA; 1990). It is important for school personnel to understand that the FLSA does affect the community-based work experiences that may be provided to students (National Center on Secondary Education and Transition, 2005). In an effort to help schools comply with the FLSA, the U.S. Department of Labor and the U.S. Department of Education have developed guidelines for designing and implementing community-based work experiences. These guidelines are presented in Table 12.3. They are designed to ensure that the relationships that secondary programs develop with employers are focused on providing students with employment training rather than a paid job.

Table 12.3   Fair Labor Standards Act Guidelines

---

1. The participants in the program will be youth with physical and/or mental disabilities for whom competitive employment at or above the minimum wage is not immediately attainable and who, because of their disability, will require intensive ongoing support to perform in a work setting.

2. Participation in the program will be for vocational exploration, assessment, or training in community-based placement work sites under the general supervision of public school personnel.

3. Community-based placements will be clearly defined components of individual education programs developed and designed for the benefit of each student. The statement of needed transition services established for the exploration, assessment, training, or cooperative vocational education components will be included in the student's Individualized Education Program.

4. The student and the parent or guardian of the student will have been fully informed of the IEP and the community-based placement component and will have indicated voluntary participation with the understanding that participation in such a component does not entitle the student-participant to wages.

5. The activities of the students at the community-based placement site should not result in an immediate advantage to the business.

6. While the existence of an employment relationship will not be determined exclusively on the basis of the number of hours, as a general rule each component will not exceed the following limitation during any one school year:
   - Vocational exploration: 5 hours per job experience.
   - Vocational assessment: 90 hours per job experience.
   - Vocational training: 120 hours per job experience.

(Continued)

Table 12.3 (Continued)

7. Students are not entitled to employment at the business at the conclusion of the IEP. However, once a student has become an employee, the student cannot be considered a trainee at the particular community-based placement unless in a clearly distinguishable occupation.

Note. From "OSEP Memorandum 90-20: Guidelines for Implementing Community-Based Educational Programs for Students with Disabilities," by the U.S. Department of Education, Office of Special Education, 1992, Washington, DC: Author. Reprinted with permission.

Focus Question 4	What are the primary factors in determining whether a job sampling placement complies with the Fair Labor Standards Act?

These guidelines are based on two assumptions. First, the partnership between the business and the school program exists solely to provide employment assessment and training. There can be no significant financial benefit to the employer for agreeing to participate in the job sampling program. In order to avoid potential problems, job sampling placements should be structured to ensure that the following conditions obtain:

- The student is not completing another employee's duties while the employee is assigned to complete other work that is typically not part of his or her job responsibilities. For example, a bagger in a grocery store could not be replaced by a student so that he or she could restock shelves. However, the student could work as a bagger as long as the employee also continued to work as a bagger.
- The student cannot complete work that is not regularly done by employees. An example would be having a student wash the employer's car if other employees in the business are not assigned this duty.

The second guideline is that the student's job sampling experiences be based on explicit goals and objectives included in his or her IEP/transition plan. The goals and objectives should describe specific learning outcomes for the student in the job sampling placement and the criteria that will be used to determine when these outcomes are achieved. In addition, the student and his or her parents must clearly understand that the student will not be paid for his or her work in the placement and that there is no promise of employment upon completion of the experience.

Summary

Preparation for employment is a critical element of secondary programs. In this chapter, we have argued that the focus of employment training for middle school- and high school-age students should be on teaching the work and work-related skills that are common to most jobs. In addition, employment preparation for this group of students should be structured to gather information that will be necessary to allow the IEP/transition planning team to make a wise decision about the kind of paid job that will meet the student's employment goals and expected outcomes. This will require documentation of the student's strengths and weaknesses, the student's interests and preferences, and the level of support necessary to ensure his or her success in community employment settings. Teachers can achieve these aims thorough in-school and community-based training strategies. Focus of employment training for middle school students should be on their participation in vocational education classes and in-school jobs typically done by peers without disabilities. Once students move into high school, the focus should shift to community-based experiences. Whenever possible, these experiences should be delivered through the student's participation in general education classes.

Obtaining meaningful employment is crucial to the successful transition of students from school to community life. As with other areas of community life, this outcome is achieved most effectively when students' educational programs are designed to cumulatively develop necessary routines, activities, and skills across their secondary program. This requires educators to develop and implement a longitudinal training program for students.

Focus Question Review

Focus Question 1: What is the purpose of employment training for middle or junior high school and high school students?

- Teach work and work-related skills.
- Determine the student's preferences and needs.
- Identify the level of support necessary to ensure the student's success in the workplace.

Focus Question 2: What instructional approaches should be used with middle or junior high school and high school students?

- Middle or junior high school students:
  o Participation in general vocational education classes.
  o In-school jobs commonly done by peers without disabilities.

- High school students:
  o Participation in general vocational education classes.
  o Community-based job sampling placements.

Focus Question 3: **What are the considerations in developing job sampling sites?**

- Identifying job sampling sites that represent the range of employment options available within the local community.
- Establishing long-term partnerships with businesses that are open to providing placements for students.

Focus Question 4: **What are the primary factors in determining whether a job sampling placement complies with the Fair Labor Standards Act?**

- The placement is solely for vocational exploration, assessment, and training.
- The business receives no financial benefit for participating in the program.
- The job sampling placement is guided by explicit goals and objectives in the student's IEP.
- The student and his or her parents understand that the student will receive no wages and the placement will not result in employment within the business.

CHAPTER 13

Job Placement

JOHN MCDONNELL

O ne of the best predictors of whether students with intellectual and developmental disabilities will successfully adjust to employment following graduation is whether they have had a paid job before they leave school (Benz, Lindstrom, & Yovanoff, 2000; Blackorby & Wagner, 1996; Phelps & Hanley-Maxwell, 1997). This research has led a number of researchers to argue that secondary programs—and especially post-high school programs—should be structured to provide job development, training, and support services to students (Hasazi et al., 2005; McDonnell, Mathot-Buckner, & Ferguson, 1996; Rusch & Braddock, 2004; Wehman, 2006). It is generally accepted that the shift from employment training, which emphasizes the acquisition of general work and work-related skills (see Chapter 12), to job placement, which emphasizes obtaining paid employment, should occur for students with intellectual and developmental disabilities at age 19 or when they enter the post-high school program. In most states, this provides staff in the post-high school program with several years to establish stable employment for students before they leave school.

The focus on paid employment for students affects virtually every aspect of program operation from how programs are staffed to where they are located. The change in emphasis also has a dramatic impact on the day-to-day roles and responsibilities of program staff (Izzo, Johnson, Levitz, & Aaron, 1998). Fortunately, research in the last 2 decades has produced a comprehensive technology for supporting adults with intellectual and developmental disabilities in paid community employment that can be adopted by post-high school programs (Griffin, Hammis, & Geary, 2007;

Wehman, Inge, Revell, & Brooke, 2007). This technology focuses on three broad program activities, including job development, job analysis, and job training and follow-along. The following sections will describe strategies for carrying out each of these activities.

Job Development

Job development is the process of creating and securing employment opportunities for students. In the past, many employment programs adopted an approach to job development that was designed to "sell" the individual with disabilities to a potential employer (Brooke, Wehman, Inge, & Parent, 1995; Riehle & Datson, 2006; Unger, 2007). This approach was often structured to appeal to employers' philanthropic and altruistic values rather than to adopt marketing approaches that emphasized the advantages to employers of hiring qualified individuals with disabilities. A number of researchers and advocates have argued that programs conducting job development, training, and support abandon these "deficit marketing" approaches and adopt market-driven or demand-side models (Brooke et al., 1995; Riehle & Datson, 2006; Unger, 2007; Wehman et al., 2007). These models to job development emphasize the added value that employees with disabilities provide to businesses and the important services that employment programs can provide to employers to help them diversify their workforces.

By necessity, job development is an ongoing process because students may lose their jobs, choose new career paths, or be laid off during depressed economic times. Adopting an effective and efficient job development process is critical to the success of post-high school programs in promoting the transition of students from school to work. Job development requires a unique set of skills and personal characteristics. Consequently, many post-high school programs have opted to assign to specific individuals the responsibilities for conducting job development for all students in the program rather than dispersing these responsibilities across all staff. Employment training specialists then assume responsibility for carrying out the remaining job placement process.

Regardless of the staffing pattern adopted by post-high school programs, the activities required to carry out effective job development are (a) conducting outreach to the business community; (b) developing student employment goals, an employment profile, and a résumé/portfolio; (c) conducting a labor market appraisal; (d) contacting employers; and (e) job matching.

Outreach to the Business Community

The success of post-high school programs in securing paid employment for students depends on developing strong relationships with the business community. The focus of these efforts is to promote the program as a valuable resource to businesses in meeting their needs for high-quality employees. This can be accomplished by joining and becoming an active participant in business and trade associations, such local business clubs as Rotary or the U.S. Junior Chamber of Commerce (Jaycees), and the chamber of commerce. Emphasis should be placed on networking with businesses that may have immediate personnel needs or that can refer you to other businesses that do. In addition, effective outreach programs are designed to educate local businesses about the program as a source for qualified employees with disabilities and the services that the program can provide.

Owens-Johnson and Hanley-Maxwell (1999) conducted a survey of more than 900 manufacturing, commerce, and food service businesses in Wisconsin that examined employers' preferences on outreach strategies that could be used by employment programs. They found that this group of employers preferred to receive information about employment programs through advertisements in trade association magazines and newsletters, booths at local trade and business shows, and such general mailings as brochures, flyers, or personal letters sent to local businesses. They also found that these simple and less expensive strategies were more highly rated by employers than such media-based marketing strategies as radio, television, and Internet ads.

Establish Student Employment Goals, a Student Employment Profile, and a Résumé/Portfolio

It is recommended practice that job placement activities be driven by a clear employment goal that reflects the student's preferences and needs (Callahan & Condon, 2007; Flexer, Baer, Luft, & Simmons, 2008; Inge, Targett, & Armstrong, 2007). In post-high school programs, identifying student employment goals is best accomplished through the comprehensive person-centered planning conducted as part of the IEP/transition plan development process (see Chapter 5). The focus of this process should be to identify an area of employment that best matches students' interests and that will allow them to achieve their expected postschool outcomes.

| **Focus Question 1** | What is the best source of data for establishing a student's employment goal and employment profile? |

Once an employment goal has been established, a student employment profile should be developed that summarizes the student's work strengths and weaknesses, the types of work settings that best accommodate these strengths and weaknesses, and the accommodations and supports that the student will need to succeed in a job (Figure 13.1). This information is readily available to the student and his or her IEP/transition planning team if the student has had opportunities for systematic job sampling experiences during high school and if his or her performance in these experiences has been evaluated and summarized (Chapter 12). These evaluations can be used to inform the development of an employment goal and a profile for the student. If the student has not had these experiences, it is recommended that post-high school programs provide him or her with several job sampling experiences before an employment goal and profile is developed.

Finally, the information gathered through a student's job sampling experiences can be consolidated into a résumé or portfolio that can be used during the job application process. While traditional résumés can be a useful tool in assisting students with representing their skills and experiences to a potential employer, it is often difficult to clearly convey the capabilities of individuals with the most significant support needs on paper. Mast, Sweeny, and West (2001) have suggested that employment programs can address the limitations of résumés by developing presentation portfolios for students. Portfolios can be easily developed using binders that include photographs and associated text. Mast and colleagues suggest that the portfolio include two sections. The first provides a general description of customized or supported employment programs and illustrations of many different people with disabilities in different jobs. This section highlights the process that is used to train and support the individual in becoming an effective employee. This section is also used to highlight the services provided to the employer in meeting its workforce needs.

The second—and the most important—section is tailored to the individual and is designed to illustrate his or her abilities and preferences in completing various work-related tasks, how he or she interacts with coworkers, and what he or she does outside of work. Like any résumé, the portfolio is structured to present the individual in the most positive light and allows the employer to see how the individual's skills and abilities can contribute to the business. With the advances in computer technology, some employment programs are developing digital video portfolios on compact discs for students that can be shown to employers during job development activities and be left with the employers to allow them to review a student's qualifications and abilities for a specific job.

Figure 13.1 Illustration of a Student Employment Profile

Student: Mark

High School: Riverview

Job Sampling Placements

Dates	Business/Supervisor	Duties
1/10/06– 3/15/06	Eve's Buffet Judith Wright	Bussing tables. Washing dishes.
9/15/06– 11/10/06	Davis Nursery Bob Richards	Filling planting pots. Moving flats from greenhouse to sales floor. Sweeping.
1/30/07– 5/15/07	County Library—Riverview Rachel Dawes	Collecting books from return bins. Collecting books in the shelves. Removing scan code stickers.

Performance Summary

1. Work strengths:
   a. Accuracy: Mark learns work activities quickly and is able to maintain his performance.
   b. Quality: Quality of work is rarely a problem for Mark except when he does not like the job he is doing.
   c. Productivity: Mark's work rate is extremely good and generally matches that of his coworkers. His work rate slows significantly when he does not like the job that he is doing.

2. Work preferences:
   a. Days and times: Daytime shift, Monday through Friday.
   b. Work activities: Mark likes variety. He does not like work activities that require him to get dirty.
   c. Work environment: Mark likes working indoors.
   d. Social context: Mark likes working with other people around.

3. Needed supports:
   a. Alternative performance strategies: Mark benefits from the use of a picture schedule to help him remember the sequence of his work activities.
   b. Specialist supports: Mark requires direct training to learn most work activities. However, the intensity of support can be faded quickly because he learns work activities quickly. He is able to maintain his performance with daily checks.
   c. Workplace supports: Mark benefits from having a workplace mentor who can provide occasional directions and feedback. He prefers having one individual to whom he can go if he needs help with a work activity.

4. Logistical considerations:
   a. Travel: Mark uses mass transit independently and is able to cross streets without assistance.
   b. Physical/health/medical factors: Not applicable.
   c. Family restrictions: None. Mark's family is extremely supportive of him, and they want him to get a paid job.

Recommended Workplace Characteristics

Work Activities: Mark would do well working in an office or another professional environment. He prefers having a lot of different tasks to do. He is flexible and would be open to doing most clerical or office-related tasks.

Physical Environment: Mark prefers working indoors. However, he likes to be able to move from area to area within the business.

Social Characteristics: Mark is a very social person and enjoys interacting with other people. He takes directions well and is always responsive to his mentor and/or supervisor.
Ideally, Mark would prefer working in a business that has people who are approximately his age.

Appraise the Labor Market

It is recommended that employment programs conduct an analysis of the local labor market to identify business hiring trends before contacting specific employers (Green, Wehman, Luna, & Merkle, 2007). The focus of this analysis is to identify the jobs that are available within the community and the types of businesses that are doing most of the hiring (e.g., large vs. small businesses). In addition, this information is used to help job developers formulate a demand-side approach to outreach and marketing that is responsive to the local business environment. Specifically, the job developer needs to become familiar with the key businesses or business groups in the area and develop marketing strategies that emphasize how the employment program can help them meet their work-force needs. This can be accomplished by reviewing information from state departments of labor or workforce services. These agencies typically have accessible Web sites that include information about the jobs that are currently available within specific cities or regions and career areas that are expected to grow over the next several years. These sites also typically include information about the kinds of skills or experiences that job seekers need for these jobs, the nature of the work that individuals are expected to complete in these jobs, and the prevailing wages and benefits for specific classes of jobs.

Once this information is compiled, it is used to guide the business outreach activities described above. The businesses identified during the appraisal should be sent information that describes the employment program and the services that it can provide. In addition, this information can be used to help students and IEP/transition planning teams develop realistic employment goals and identify potential employers that match each student's employment profile.

Contacting Businesses

Identifying and securing a job for a student requires that the job developer establish a mutually beneficial relationship with a business. This relationship cannot be established in a single contact or meeting but is developed over time. For that reason, it is useful to think about interactions with potential employers occurring in three phases, including the initial contact, the introductory meeting, and negotiation.

Initial Contacts With Employers. The first direct contact with employers by a job developer should occur after the business has received information about the program through the business outreach activities. The focus of the contact is to determine if the business (a) has a job or can develop a customized job that matches the student's employment goal and profile and (b) is interested in working with the program to hire a student with disabilities.

One strategy for contacting a potential employer is by telephone. A telephone call should be used primarily to establish a date for an introductory meeting on the program and the student. Such a meeting will allow the job developer to give more details about the program and more effectively address the employer's questions. The second strategy is to conduct a drop-in visit to the business. As with a telephone contact, the primary purpose of a drop-in visit is to establish a time to make a more in-depth presentation about the program. However, the job developer should be prepared to make the presentation on the spot if the employer shows interest in learning more about the program. Before phoning or conducting a drop-in visit, the job developer should research the business. In particular, he or she should become familiar with the business's products or services, learn the range of jobs that are done within the local business site, and identify the individual who typically makes hiring decisions. The job developer should directly contact the individual who is in charge of hiring and be prepared to offer several times that he or she could meet with the individual to discuss the program.

Conducting an Introductory Meeting. The introductory meeting with a prospective employer is the first real opportunity to describe the services the program has to offer. During the meeting, the job developer should succinctly describe the procedures the program uses to match a student to the job, how training is carried out, and how the support for the student is faded across time. While the job developer should highlight the support the program can provide to the student, it is equally important to stress that the student will be an employee of the business and that the employer has the same responsibilities to the student that he or she has to all of his or her employees. A significant part of the discussion should focus on the services that the program can provide to the employer to help him or her become more effective in supporting the student to be a successful employee in his or her business.

In business, as in other areas of life, honesty is the best policy. Employers will ask difficult and pointed questions about students and the program. The job developer should be straightforward about the strengths and weaknesses of the students he or she serves. The long-term success of the students in a job will hinge on the employer having a full understanding of the challenges he or she may face in hiring a student with significant support needs. As suggested above, a presentation portfolio may facilitate this discussion and help the employer understand the skills and capabilities of the student in meeting his or her personnel needs.

In addition to sharing information about the program, the job developer should attempt to gather as much information as possible about the business. Ask the employer about the specific responsibilities of the job and, if possible, tour the facility. The object is to gain an understanding of the demands of the job, the employer's expectations for his or her workers, the social "culture" of the workplace, and the layout of the physical plant. An employer interview form can help the job developer summarize this information (Figure 13.2). The form is designed to allow the job developer to gather information on the typical work schedules of employees, wages and benefits, the number of coworkers, the labor-management environment, and special requirements of the job (for example, academic skills or uniforms). The form also allows the job developer to give a subjective impression of the atmosphere of the workplace. During the interview and tour, the job developer should ask the employer probe questions about potential flexibility in restructuring the available position and current unmet personnel needs of the business. These probe questions become the focal point of the negotiation process and provide ways to a customized job through job carving, job restructuring, job sharing, or job creation (Table 13.1).

Figure 13.2   Illustration of an Introductory Meeting Form

Business Information

Name: _____

Address: _____

_____

Telephone: _____

Contact: _____ Title: _____

Position Profile

Position Title: _____ Work Schedule: _____ Days: _____

Hours: _____

Qualifications/Experience: _____

_____

Wage/Salary: _____ Benefits: _____

Dress/Uniform Requirements: _____

Work Activities/Requirements

1.   6.
2.   7.
3.   8.
4.   9.
5.   10.

Ability/Skill	Requirements
Mobility within work setting.	
Physical strength and endurance.	
Communication.	
Academic skills.	
Time- and self-management skills.	
Work rate.	
Work independence.	
Personal management skills.	

Work Environment

Characteristic	Observations/Comments
Indoor ___ Outdoor ___	
Loud ___ Noisy ___	
Light ___ Dark ___	
Busy ___ Slow ___ Variable ___	
Crowded ___ Isolated ___	
Repetitive ___ Variable___	
One Location ___ Multiple Locations ___	
Confined ___ Open ___	

Social Context

Characteristic	Observations/Comments
Clear lines of communication.	
Peer-to-peer interactions on work activities.	
Social interactions with coworkers.	
Social interactions with supervisors.	
Nonwork social interactions (breaks, lunch).	

Logistics

Issue/Concern	Observations/Comments
Transportation.	
Physical/heath/medical needs.	
Family support.	

Customized Job Opportunities

Option	Observations/Comments
Job carving.	
Job restructuring.	
Job creation.	
Job sharing.	

Table 13.1 Types of Negotiation

	Customized Job Options
Job Carving	A job description is created by modifying an existing job description. The carved job description contains one or more but not all of the tasks from the original job description.
Restructuring a Position	A job is developed by consolidating work activities from one or more jobs in the business to create a new, individualized job description for the student.
Job Creation	A newly created description is negotiated based on unmet work needs.
Job Sharing	Two or more people share the tasks and responsibilities of a job based on each other's strengths.

Note. Adapted from *Customized Employment: Practical Solutions for Employment Success*, by Office of Disability Employment Policy, U.S. Department of Labor, 2005.

At the conclusion of the meeting with the employer, the job developer should leave a business card; a brochure describing the program; and, if possible, a student's portfolio on a compact disc. In addition, the job developer should offer to provide the employer with a list of other businesses that have developed partnerships with the program and are willing to serve as references.

Following the introductory meeting, the job developer should do as much as possible to keep the program in the forefront of the employer's mind. For example, send the employer a note following the first meeting to thank him or her for his or her time and consideration of the program. Include with this letter any information that was promised to the employer during the initial meeting. If another meeting time was not established during the initial contact, follow up with a telephone call after sending the thank-you letter. Continue following up with phone contacts as long as it appears that the employer is still interested.

Focus Question 2	How can a job developer help the employer customize a job for a student who cannot complete the typical job duties?

Negotiating a Job. A key component of effective job development is negotiating job duties and expectations with employers (Griffin et al., 2007; Inge & Targett, 2006). Ideally, a student would be able to complete a job as described in an employer's position announcement. However, in some cases students may be unable to complete all of the expected work activities. In these cases, the employment specialist should attempt to develop a customized work option for the student in the business. This can be accomplished through job carving, job restructuring, job creation, or job sharing. The ultimate goal of negotiation is to determine employment options that mutually benefit the student and the employer. There is no single negotiation strategy that will be effective in every circumstance. However, several principles can increase the likelihood that a job can be negotiated that meets the needs of both employer and student:

- Know the student's bottom line. The job developer is primarily representing the student's interest. He or she should be intimately familiar with the student's employment goal and profile and should stay focused on negotiating job responsibilities, working conditions, and supports that will help the student achieve his or her expected employment outcomes.

- Know the employer's bottom line. While the job developer represents the student, he or she also needs to be in tune with the employer's needs and demonstrate that the negotiated job responsibilities will be a benefit for the employer. The job developer needs to show the employer how the student's negotiated job responsibilities can contribute to increased productivity and cost-effectiveness.

- Stress the added value of the partnership between the program and the business. The job developer needs to emphasize the additional benefits that can come from entering into a partnership with the program. These include reducing employee turnover through the ongoing support provided to the student, increasing the capacity of the business to hire and train other individuals with disabilities, and helping the business address day-to-day issues related to accommodating individuals with disabilities in the workplace.

Window 13-1

Customizing a Job for Sara

Sara has always dreamed of working in a hair salon. The job developer from her post-high school program was visiting a salon owner who expressed interest in working with the program. During the meeting, the specialist observed that each stylist spent a significant amount of time washing, folding, and restocking towels in each station; sterilizing combs; and sweeping up hair. Frequently, the stylists were required to do these tasks while customers waited for their appointments. The specialist proposed the idea to the owner of creating a job position to specifically complete these activities, thus freeing the stylists to serve additional customers. By restructuring existing jobs in the salon, the owner could increase her income each day and was also able to diversify her workforce. The other stylists also liked the idea because it provided an opportunity for them to earn more tips. Sara benefited because she got a job doing what she liked and that matched her specific needs.

Job Matching

Research has shown that systematically matching the strengths and weaknesses of an individual to the demands of a job before placement is strongly associated with the individual's long-term success (McDonnell, Nofs, Hardman, & Chambless, 1989; Smith, Webber, Graffam, & Wilson, 2004). In the previous chapter, we suggested that job sampling during a student's high school years is perhaps the best source of data about his or her ability to complete a particular job. Figure 13.3 illustrates a format for

Figure 13.3 Illustration of a Job Matching Form

Student: _____   Business: _____

Position: _____   Job Developer: _____

Position aligns with student's employment goal and expected outcomes?   Yes   No

Work Activities/Requirements

| | | Student can complete activity with: | | |
Activity/ Requirement	Currently Has Skill	Training	An Alternative Performance Strategy	Work Site Accommodations
1.				
2.				
3.				
4.				
5.				
6. Mobility within work setting.				
7. Physical strength/ endurance.				
8. Communication.				
9. Academic skills.				
10. Work rate.				
11. Work independence.				
12. Personal management skills.				

Work Environment

Characteristic	Meets Student Preferences/Needs?		
Indoor/Outdoor	Yes	No	NA
Loud/Noisy	Yes	No	NA
Light/Dark	Yes	No	NA
Busy/Slow/Variable	Yes	No	NA
Crowded/Isolated	Yes	No	NA
Repetitive/Variable	Yes	No	NA
One/Multiple Locations	Yes	No	NA
Confined/Open	Yes	No	NA

Social Context

Characteristic	Meets Student Preferences/Needs?		
Lines of communication	Yes	No	NA
Peer-to-peer support on work activities	Yes	No	NA
Social interactions with coworkers	Yes	No	NA
Social interactions with supervisor	Yes	No	NA
Nonwork social interactions (breaks, lunch)	Yes	No	NA

Logistical Issues

Issue	Meets Student Preferences/Needs?		
Transportation	Yes	No	NA
Physical/health/medical factors	Yes	No	NA
Family support	Yes	No	NA

carrying out the job matching process. In the matching process, the job developer needs to consider whether the student can meet the performance demands of the job. In some cases, the student may already have the skills necessary to complete the job, but more frequently the job developer will need to determine whether the student can learn to do the job with training, alternative performance strategies, or workplace accommodations. In addition, the job developer needs to consider whether the workplace accommodates the student's preferences and logistical needs.

While a post-high school program can provide support for students in obtaining a job that matches their strengths and preferences, ultimately the employment relationship is between the student and the business owner. Consequently, the student should be involved in all decisions regarding job placement. The job developer should discuss the job opportunity with the student and key members of his or her IEP/transition planning team during the job matching process. The student's feelings about the job and the ability of his or her IEP/transition team to support him or her in the placement should be the *primary* factors in deciding whether the job is appropriate. Once a decision has been made to pursue a job in a specific business, the student should be involved as much as possible in applying for the job and negotiating his or her job duties.

Job Analysis

Once an employer has agreed to hire a student, the employment training specialist will need to develop an instructional program to teach the student how to complete his or her assigned duties. At the heart of this process is the job analysis. This analysis is used by the specialist for three purposes. First, it is a mechanism to identify the expectations of the employer. The job analysis should identify the steps of each work activity and the criteria by which the student's performance will be evaluated by his or her supervisor and coworkers. This information aids in determining the level of support that the student will need to complete job duties and when support can be reduced. Second, a job analysis provides the information necessary to maximize the efficacy of instruction by tailoring the instructional program to the needs of the student. Third, a job analysis allows the specialist to identify potential supports that could be made available to the student. Effective job analysis procedures include three steps: developing a task analysis, analyzing the social context, and identifying alternative performance strategies.

Develop a Task Analysis

The first step in training a student to complete a job is to develop a task analysis that clearly defines the steps of the work activities the student will complete. The procedures for analyzing work tasks are similar to those described in Chapter 9. However, the employment specialist should also identify the criteria that will be used to evaluate a worker's productivity. In some cases, this may focus on the amount of time that it takes the student to complete a specific work activity or specific steps within an activity. For example, if a student is learning to work as a housekeeper in a hotel, the amount of time required to clean a room might be a critical factor in evaluating his or her effectiveness as an employee. In other cases, productivity may be assessed by the number of tasks that an employee completes. For instance, the effectiveness of a cashier in a grocery store might be evaluated in terms of how fast he or she can scan items or enter product codes. Finally, the criteria for evaluating the student's performance may be linked to the quality of his or her work. Figure 13.4 presents an illustration of a task analysis form for part of the work activity of washing dishes.

Figure 13.4   Illustration of a Task Analysis Form

Student: Mark

Business: Eve's

Position: Kitchen Assistant

Employment Specialist: Lucy

Work Activity: Wash Dishes

Stimulus	*Response*	*Performance Criteria*
1. Cart. Back kitchen door.	1. Push bus cart to back kitchen door.	Liquid, food, and dinnerware stay in cart.
2. Back kitchen door. Cart handle.	2. Pull cart through door.	
3. Sink.	3. Push cart to sink.	Cart touches sink wall.
4. Glasses. Sink.	4. Empty glasses in sink.	Ice and liquid in sink. Debris or food placed in can.
5. Glasses. Rack.	5. Place glasses in rack.	Glasses sit flat in rack.
6. Rack. Belt.	6. Slide rack onto washer belt.	Rack centered on belt.
7. Bowls. Sink.	7. Empty soup bowls in sink.	Liquid in sink. Solid food placed in can.
8. Bowls. Rack.	8. Place soup bowls in rack.	Bowls equally spaced in rack.
9. Bowls. Food and debris. Can.	9. Scrape solid food bowls into can.	Bowls free of food and debris.
10. Bowls. Rack.	10. Place solid food bowls into rack.	Bowls equally spaced in rack.
11. Plates. Food and debris. Can.	11. Scrape plates into can.	Plates free of food and debris.
12. Plates. Rack.	12. Place plates into rack.	Plates equally spaced in rack.
13. Rack. Belt.	13. Slide rack onto washer belt.	Rack centered on belt.

Carrying out a comprehensive job analysis generally requires that the employment specialist observe a coworker do the job and complete the student's job duties for 1 or 2 days. This approach ensures that the specialist will identify all of the possible discriminations and responses that the student must complete in each activity. The amount of time required to complete a job analysis will vary based on the complexity of the job and the accessibility of the work environment. Time to carry out a job analysis should be negotiated with the employer during job development.

Focus Question 3	Why is analyzing the social context important for promoting the long-term success of a student in a job?

Analyzing the Social Context

The social aspects of employment are often as critical to a student's success as the mastery of specific work skills (Chadsey, 2007). It is important for the student's social behavior to be consistent with the expectations and norms of workers in the business. "Fitting in" with the peer group promotes the development of supported relationships that can help the student be successful in the job. For example, coworkers can provide an important source of assistance and support to help the student complete his or her job duties.

Research has shown that numerous environmental and situational variables affect the social acceptance of individuals with disabilities in the workplace (Butterworth, Hagner, Helm, & Whelley, 2000; Chadsey, 2007). Social demands and requirements vary significantly from one workplace to another. For example, the types and frequency of social interaction that occurs between workers at a fast food restaurant are significantly different from those of social interaction that occurs between workers at a day care center. The specialist can learn much about the social conventions of a work site by observing the workers. The purpose of these observations is to determine the types and frequency of interactions that occur between workers and supervisors. For example, during work periods, do workers talk only about job-related topics, or is personal conversation allowed? How are questions or requests for assistance addressed? What are the general topics of conversation? Do workers joke with one another? Similarly, during break periods, do workers converse, read, play games, or engage in other leisure activities? If conversations are the most typical social interaction during breaks, what do workers talk about? The specialist then uses this information to create opportunities for the student and coworkers to interact with one another. By focusing on the types of social interaction necessary to be accepted in the workplace and by promoting interactions between the student and coworkers, the specialist can assist the student with assimilating more quickly into the work environment and increase the likelihood that friendships and relationships with coworkers will develop.

Identify Alternative Performance Strategies

Students may often require alternative performance strategies in order to meet the expectations of their job. For example, a student may need to use a small picture schedule to remind him or her of the order in which work activities should be completed. Another example is to have a student carry a card to help him or her remember the access codes for different accounts for a copy machine. Sowers and Powers (1991) suggest that three factors be considered in designing these strategies for employment settings: effectiveness, impact on the site, and cost. Effectiveness is the extent to which the adaptations reduce the difficulty of the step for the student. Any adaptation should maximize the student's current skills and abilities and be applicable in as many settings or contexts as possible. Impact on the site refers to the degree to which the adaptation affects coworkers, the physical environment of the site, or the general operations of the business. Cost may be an issue because some adaptive devices are quite expensive (for example, large-print computer screens). However, financial support may be available through vocational rehabilitation or another outside agency. Consult the related service providers (such as communication specialists or occupational or physical therapists) within the school district for specific suggestions and recommendations for developing adaptations to meet students' needs.

Job Training and Follow-Along

The purpose of training and follow-along is to establish the student as a valued employee of the business. This occurs when the student's work enhances the business's ability to provide high-quality products and services to its customers and when the student becomes an accepted member of the work group. The procedures required to develop community-based instructional programs were discussed in detail in Chapter 9. However, employment specialists must address several additional instructional issues to ensure students' long-term success in a job. These include enhancing production rate, ensuring the maintenance of job performance, fading assistance, and establishing natural supports.

Enhancing Production Rate

Following a student's acquisition of basic job tasks, the focus of job training should be to ensure that the student's production rate matches the expectations of the employer. To the extent possible, the student's production rate should match that of his or her coworkers. However, alternative production rates that accommodate the abilities of the student can be negotiated with the employer prior to the initiation of job training.

The general approach for improving the production rate of workers with disabilities is to reinforce the person for working faster (Bellamy, Horner, & Inman, 1979; Rusch & Mithaug, 1981; Sowers & Powers, 1991; Wehman & Moon, 1988). These authors have suggested several guidelines for enhancing the production rates of workers with disabilities.

1. *Clearly state the expected levels of production for the individual.* Specialists should establish specific expectations for production for each training session. Communicating the expected production levels to students can be accomplished by a variety of strategies. These include but are not limited to direct verbal instructions (for example, "You need to finish cleaning this room by 10:30"), visual prompts (for example, check marks on a student's task worksheet), or auditory prompts (such as an alarm on a digital wristband). These prompts can be faded as the student's production begins to match expected performance levels.

2. *Gradually change the criteria for reinforcement.* Ratio schedules of reinforcement should be used to gradually increase the amount of work expected from the student. The rate at which the criteria for reinforcement are increased must be based on the complexity of the task and the student's level of performance. The primary mistake made by specialists is to increase the criteria too quickly. When this occurs, the student's performance will deteriorate rapidly. Consequently, initial changes in the schedule should be small until the amount of additional work the student can do is well established.

3. *Require quality and quantity.* It is critical for the specialist to maintain high standards for the student's job performance. It is not uncommon to see the quality of a student's job performance begin to slip as the demands for additional work are placed on the individual. When this occurs, the specialist should review the criteria that have been established for reinforcement and adjust as necessary to ensure that the student maintains an acceptable quality of work.

4. *Collect productivity data.* Assessing the impact of the strategies being used to enhance a student's production rate will require that the specialist regularly collect productivity data. This information will be used to

determine the effectiveness of the reinforcement strategies being used with the student, as well as to evaluate whether the production criteria established for the student are acceptable.

Maintaining Work Performance

Employment specialists face significant challenges in creating conditions on the job site that will support the maintenance of the student's work performance. Despite the importance of maintenance as an outcome of educational programs, there has been surprisingly little research on how best to achieve it with students with intellectual and developmental disabilities (Horner, Dunlap, & Koegel, 1988). However, several strategies may help promote the student's maintenance of his or her work performance (Cooper, Heron, & Heward, 2007):

1. *Use intermittent schedules of reinforcement.* Intermittent schedules of reinforcement have two advantages for specialists. First, they allow specialists to reduce the frequency of reinforcement provided to the student. Second, intermittent schedules of reinforcement are more resistant to extinction because they reduce the "predictability" of reinforcement for the student. This feature of intermittent reinforcement schedules increases the likelihood that the student will continue to work when reinforcement is not continuously available.

2. *Use natural reinforcers.* A student's continued access to reinforcement is more likely when his or her instructional program relies on reinforcers that are present in the work site. The use of reinforcers that are not typically available in the work site increases the student's dependence on staff from transition or community service agencies.

3. *Delay reinforcement for work performance.* Another intervention strategy known to promote maintenance is to delay reinforcement for appropriate behavior. During initial training, reinforcers are delivered immediately after the student has performed the correct response. This process enhances the rate of learning by the student. However, in most work settings, there is often a significant delay between the completion of assigned tasks and reinforcement. For example, most people are not paid immediately after completing a job task but receive their paycheck on a weekly or monthly basis.

4. *Establish self-management procedures.* Another approach in facilitating the maintenance of work performance is to teach students to "self-manage" their work performance (Storey, 2007). Self-management strategies

include antecedent prompting procedures, such as visual or auditory cues that tell the student whether his or her work performance matches expectations (e.g., using pictures to prompt changes in work activities or setting a watch alarm to prompt the student to go to another area). These strategies can also include strategies that the student implements after his or her work activities to assess his or her performance, including self-monitoring and self-recording, self-evaluation, self-recruited feedback, and self-reinforcement. Frequently, antecedent and consequence strategies can be used concurrently to assist the student with maintaining his or her performance across time.

For example, Grossi and Heward (1998) used a self-management package to teach four adults with developmental disabilities how to improve their performance as restaurant workers. Their work activities included scrubbing pots, racking dishes for the dishwasher, bussing and setting tables, and sweeping and mopping. The self-management package included goal setting, self-monitoring, and self-evaluation of their work performance. The results demonstrated that the self-management package led to improved performance by all of the study participants. In addition, the participants learned to accurately self-monitor and self-evaluate their performance.

Fading Employment Specialist Support

The process of fading trainer support begins the first day of employment and takes several weeks to several months to accomplish (McDonnell et al., 1996; Moon, Inge, Wehman, Brooke, & Barcus, 1990). Instructional programs must be designed with a specific plan to decrease the level of assistance provided by the employment specialist and to transfer control of the student's performance to coworkers and supervisors. The plan should specifically state how and when the specialist will fade from assigned work tasks and from the job site.

Determining when to begin the process of fading the specialist's presence in the job site is based on three data sources: task acquisition data, production rate data, and employer evaluation data. Employer evaluation data assess the employer's satisfaction with the student's work performance. When the available data sources show that the student is ready for the specialist to gradually fade from the work site, the specialist must inform the student, the employer, and coworkers. Just as in the initial phases of instruction, the specialist should develop a written plan for fading his or her presence in the job site. The plan should articulate the steps of the fading procedure and the criteria to be used to decide when to reduce the specialist's presence in the job site.

The exact procedures for fading the specialist's presence should be based on the student's past work history, the complexity of the student's job, and the employer's perceptions of the need for support during the transition period. Although fading procedures must be individualized, several guidelines for reducing specialist support in community work sites are recommended:

1. *Fade proximity.* Once the student has mastered assigned job tasks and is working near expected production rates, the specialist should begin to gradually increase his or her distance from the student. For example, the specialist may begin instruction by standing directly beside the student. As the student's performance improves, the specialist may move 3 feet away from the student, then 5 feet away, and so on until the student is able to complete his or her work activities when the specialist is no longer in the immediate area.

2. *Develop a schedule of unpredictable supervision.* Having faded the physical proximity to the student, the specialist can use "unpredictable" observations to monitor the maintenance of the student's performance. In this procedure, the specialist schedules brief supervisory interactions with the student throughout the work period. For example, he or she might "drop by" every 30 min to check on the student. During these observations, the specialist would provide feedback to the student about performance and would correct any errors or problems. These drop-by observations can be scheduled randomly so that the student cannot predict when he or she will be observed. The average time period between observations should be systematically increased as the student's performance improves.

3. *Leave the job site.* When the employee is consistently completing all work activities with unpredictable supervision, the specialist should leave for an entire shift. Following the shift, the specialist should check with the employer and coworkers to determine the student's success for the day. Gradually, the specialist will reduce the daily checks to every other day and then perhaps weekly. The objective during this step of the procedure is to reduce support provided to the minimum level. It is important to note that the level of support required by the student may vary across time. Specialists must be prepared to adjust the schedule of observations to meet the needs of the student and the employer.

4. *Establish a schedule for ongoing follow-along.* Job follow-along refers to the ongoing evaluation of the student's performance of job duties and how well the student is satisfying the employer's expectations. During each follow-along visit, the specialist should probe the student's performance to ensure that all tasks are being done correctly. In addition, the specialist should continue to regularly discuss the student's performance with his or her employer, supervisor, and coworkers. Any concerns should be addressed immediately, and the specialist should be prepared to provide additional training and support as necessary to ensure that the student's performance is matching expectations.

The ongoing data collected by the specialist during the follow-along phase should not replace or eliminate normal employee evaluation procedures. For example, if all employees are hired for a 30-day trial period and then evaluated to determine retention or salary adjustment, the student should also be evaluated on this schedule. Follow-along data collected by staff from the transition program may be used to supplement the evaluation tools used by the employer.

Developing Natural Supports

By definition, supported employment is designed to provide an individual with the assistance necessary to ensure success in the job (Wehman et al., 2007). Typically, such support is provided by the employment specialist. While this support is necessary to help the student learn to complete his or her job, research also suggests that the interactions between the employment specialist and the individual with disabilities may impede the student's social inclusion in the workplace (Chadsey & Sheldon, 1998). This has led to the recommendation that the support provided by employment specialists be structured to supplement rather than supplant the natural supports available to the student from coworkers and supervisors (Griffin et al., 2007; Wehman et al., 2007).

Hagner (1992) defines natural supports as all the assistance typically available from an employer and other employees that can be used to learn job skills and maintain reliable work performance. Utilization of natural supports must occur from the first day of employment. Fostering natural supports for students in work settings can be accomplished through three strategies:

1. *Establish a collaborative working relationship with coworkers and supervisors.* It is critical for the specialist to establish a collaborative relationship with the student's coworkers and supervisor from the first day of training. The student's long-term success in his or her job will require that

the specialist, coworkers, and the supervisor be able to communicate openly and honestly with each other about the student's performance.

2. *Identify and support the student's participation in typical orientation and employee training activities.* Most businesses have standardized procedures for training a new employee. The specialist should identify how training is typically done and support the student's participation in these activities. The student's acceptance as part of the peer group will be enhanced if he or she is treated the same as his or her coworkers.

3. *Train coworkers and supervisors to support the student.* Most adults without disabilities have had few, if any, opportunities to interact with people with disabilities. Consequently, coworkers are often anxious about how to interact with a student. The concerns of coworkers can often be overcome as a result of direct training on how to interact with the student and of receiving opportunities to interact positively with the student (Mautz, Storey, & Certo, 2001; Weiner & Zivolich, 2003). Training should be structured so that the specialist works directly with the coworkers and the supervisor to provide appropriate cues, corrections procedures, and reinforcement to the student. In addition, the specialist should encourage coworkers and the supervisor to communicate directly with the student. For example, if a coworker tells the specialist what the student should do next, the specialist should encourage the coworker to talk directly with the student. Similarly, if the student is having difficulty or encounters a problem on the job, the specialist should have the student seek assistance directly from his or her coworkers or supervisor.

Summary

Secondary programs must be structured to place students in paid employment before graduation. This requires that staff in post-high school programs develop employment opportunities for students, train students to complete job assignments, and provide ongoing support to students to ensure long-term success. To attain these outcomes, professionals working in post-high school programs must significantly expand their traditional teaching roles. They must not only design and implement effective instructional programs; they must also work successfully with business owners, supervisors, and other employees. The focus of instruction shifts from providing educational services to ensuring that students are productive employees who are part of the social culture of the workplace. Fortunately, research over the last decade has led to the development of a comprehensive technology for achieving these outcomes.

Focus Question Review

Focus Question 1: What is the best source of data for establishing a student's employment goal and employment profile?

- Job sampling experiences during high school provide information about the types of jobs that students like to do, the kinds of work environments that match their preferences, and the level of support that they will need to be successful in the workplace.
- It is recommended that employment programs provide students with job sampling experiences before an employment goal and profile is established.

Focus Question 2: How can a job developer help the employer customize a job for a student who cannot complete the typical job duties?

- Job carving: A job is created by consolidating one or more but not all of the work activities from the original job description.
- Restructure a position: A job is created by consolidating work activities from two or more job descriptions to create an individualized job description for the student.
- Job creation: A new job description is created based on unmet work needs.
- Job sharing: Two or more people share the tasks and responsibilities of a job based on each other's strengths.

Focus Question 3: Why is analyzing the social context important for promoting the long-term success of a student in a job?

- It helps the employment specialist develop strategies that will help the student become part of the peer group.
- It helps the employment specialist identify individuals within the workplace who could provide assistance and support to the student in completing his or her job duties.

Focus Question 4: What strategies can employment specialists use to fade their assistance to students in the job site?

- Fade physical proximity to the student.
- Implement a schedule of unpredictable supervision.
- Intermittently leave the job site.
- Develop a long-term plan of job site follow-up with the student.

Section V

POSTSCHOOL OPTIONS

CHAPTER 14

Postschool Residential Alternatives

TIM RIESEN

The provision of transition services as outlined in the Individuals with Disabilities Education Act requires that secondary programs develop a coordinated set of transition services designed to improve students' postschool outcomes in employment, postsecondary education, adult living, and community participation. One area of planning that is often underemphasized is preparation for adult independent living. The importance of systematic planning for adult living options is reinforced by the fact that the National Longitudinal Transition Study-2 reports that 48.8% of youth with mental retardation, 45.8% of youth with autism, and 40.8% of youth with multiple disabilities expect to live away from home without supervision when they exit school (Wagner, Newman, Cameto, Levine, & Marder, 2007). Addressing this expectation requires parents, students, and teachers to conduct in-depth planning to determine what types of living opportunities are realistic for the student, what types of supports are needed to make adult living possible, and what personal management and leisure routines and activities students need to learn to have a high quality of life.

The purpose of this chapter is to examine some of the critical issues facing students as they prepare to make the transition from school to adult living. First, the chapter will describe the historical structure of residential programs for adults with intellectual and developmental disabilities. Second, the chapter will explore residential alternatives that promote increased residential independence for adults with disabilities. Finally, the chapter will review federal programs that support more typical residential alternatives for this group of individuals.

Historical Structure of Residential Programs

As large institutional programs began to reduce their populations during the 1970s and 1980s, the number and types of community-based residential alternatives for adults with intellectual and developmental disabilities expanded dramatically. Nationally, for example, the number of individuals living in public or private institutional settings declined from 207,356 in 1977 to 67,066 in 2005 (Lakin & Stancliffe, 2007). During the same time, individuals receiving residential services in smaller homes (six or fewer residents) increased from 20,400 to 291,000, and those in homes with three or fewer residents increased from 8,700 to 184,000 (Lakin, Prouty, & Coucouvanis, 2006).

The deinstitutionalization movement was driven in large part by the concept of a continuum of services (Figure 14.1). The continuum was seen as a way to provide residential support to people with disabilities by offering a variety of living arrangements. The underlying assumption of the continuum was that people with disabilities would be placed in a residential setting based on their perceived functioning level and support needs. When individuals demonstrated a capacity to function more independently in community settings, they transitioned to more inclusive (less restrictive) placements. The continuum of placements included public institutions, private institutions, intermediate care facilities for the mentally retarded (ICF/MR), group homes, semi-independent living, and independent living. Public institutions were viewed as the most restrictive placement and were characterized as providing the least integrated and normalized services, and independent living was the least restrictive placement with the most integrated and normalized services.

Focus Question 1	What is the continuum of residential services for people with disabilities?

Although the continuum of service has allowed may people with disabilities to move out of institutional settings and other congregate care facilities, many researchers and advocates view the continuum as an antiquated service delivery model that has a number of fundamental problems (Wieck & Strully, 1991). Taylor (2001) contends that there are four primary conceptual flaws associated with the continuum of residential support. First, he believes that the continuum erroneously confuses intensity of services with the most restrictive placements, and people who are placed in the least restrictive placements will not receive the same level of support. Second,

Figure 14.1   Illustration of the Continuum of Residential Services

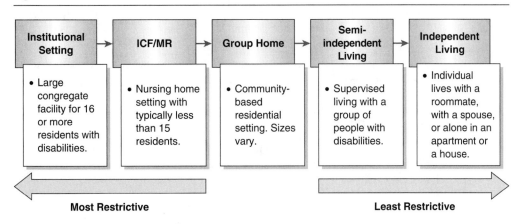

the continuum infringes on basic human rights, and placement in restrictive residential environments denies people with disabilities the fundamental right of community living. Third, the continuum of residential services uses a "readiness" model that does not prepare people with significant support needs for the demands of community living. Finally, the continuum aligns people with disabilities with the physical setting and ignores the services and supports that are necessary to live in the community.

In spite of the fact that research has repeatedly shown that smaller, less restrictive living options result in improved adaptive, social, and daily living skills for adults with intellectual and developmental disabilities (Kim, Larson, & Lakin, 2001; Stancliffe & Lakin, 2007), a significant portion of individuals continue to live in facilities that serve six or more people (Prouty, Alba, Scott, & Lakin, 2008). The fact that most individuals with disabilities still do not live in homes that are comparable to those of their peers without disabilities has prompted advocates and researchers to call for development of alternatives to the continuum of residential services (Lakin, Gardner, Larson, & Wheeler, 2005).

Alternatives to the Residential Continuum

Over the last 2 decades, a number of alternative residential program models have been discussed in the literature (Boles, Horner, & Bellamy, 1988; Klien, 1992; Nisbet, Clark, & Covert, 1991; O'Brien, 1994; Stancliffe & Lakin, 2007; Walker, 1999). These alternatives range from individuals living in their own homes with support to individuals living in apartments or houses with roommates without disabilities. Although the settings in which people live are quite diverse, these alternatives are based on a philosophical assumption that the setting is the person's home rather than a service program. This assumption undergirds the two most common approaches to providing residential alternatives to the continuum of services: supported living and personal assistance services. Each of these alternatives is described in more detail below.

Supported Living

Focus Question 2	What are the important characteristics of supported living programs?

Many advocates and researchers have embraced the concept of supported living as the primary alternative to the "continuum" of residential services. Supported living focuses on placing people in their own homes and building supports around each individual. Supported living emphasizes the need to separate residences from support services by giving individuals with disabilities the opportunity to live in their own homes and exercise more control over their day-to-day functions. People with disabilities can live in a variety of supported living arrangements, such as apartments, shared housing, homes they own with agency supervision, collectives, and cooperatives (Nisbet et al., 1991). The expectation of supported living is that individuals with disabilities need to be self-determined and actively participate in determining where they want to live. Stancliffe and Lakin (2007) elaborated on the idea of individualizing the supported living process and described six principles of supported community living for people with disabilities (Table 14.1).

Table 14.1 Six Principles of Supported Community Living

Principle	Definition
Separation of housing from supports.	Decisions about housing options are made on an individual basis. The individual with a disability chooses his or her home and community independent of service and support systems.
Living in one's own home.	Individuals with disabilities gain autonomy and independence from owning or renting their own homes.
Supported living manifests differently for each individual.	Supported living encourages an individualized approach to supporting the individual with a disability. Supports are developed based on the individual needs and preferences of the individual with a disability.

Principle	Definition
Supported living requires choice making among competing desires.	Individuals with disabilities must take an active role in finding affordable housing options. They must balance the cost of housing with other factors of independent living.
Supported living involves more participation in instrumental activities.	Individuals with disabilities must be allowed to fully participate in all activities associated with independent living. Support is provided as needed or requested by the person with a disability.
Supported living integrates informal supports.	In order to maximize independence and reduce dependence on paid supports, individuals with disabilities need to develop natural supports that are commonly available in community settings.

Note. Adapted from "Independent Living," by R. J. Stancliffe and C. K. Lakin, 2007, in *Handbook of Developmental Disabilities,* by S. L. Odom, R. H. Horner, M. E. Snell, and J. Blacher (Eds.), New York: Guilford. Adapted with permission.

Research suggests that supported living improves the quality of life of individuals with intellectual and developmental disabilities (Gardern & Carran, 2005; Howe, Horner, & Newton, 1998). For example, Howe and colleagues conducted a study that compared supported living with traditional residential programs in Oregon. The authors found that people living in supported communities participate in a variety of community and social activities, are more self-determined and have more control over decisions, and participate in preferred activities, compared with people with disabilities living in "traditional" residential settings.

The number of people with disabilities living in homes they own or rent has substantially increased; in 1995 there were 40,881 people with disabilities receiving residential supports in their own homes, and in 2005 there were 101,143 people with disabilities receiving support in their own homes (Lakin & Stancliffe, 2007).

Window 14-1

Example of Supported Living

Jerry is a 47-year-old with Down syndrome who has been living in his current supported living apartment for the past 6 years. Jerry has a Medicaid waiver that pays his rent and for the supported living services he receives. He independently works part-time at Sears doing janitorial and maintenance work weekdays from 8 A.M. to 11 A.M. After he finishes work, he takes public transportation to his apartment and is met by a staff member from

(Continued)

(Continued)

a local community service provider. The staff member subsequently assists Jerry with such independent living skills as laundry, cooking, administering medication, and any other types of support Jerry requests. After the staff member assists Jerry with these independent skills, he or she leaves the apartment for the evening, and Jerry has what he calls his "free time." Jerry explains that during "free time" he gets to do whatever he likes, such as watching movies, going for walks, or just "hanging out."

Personal Assistance Services

States have had the option of providing personal assistance services (PAS) under the umbrella of Medicaid since the 1970s. The earlier PAS followed a medical model of service delivery in that these services typically had to be prescribed by a physician and be supervised by a nurse. PAS have evolved over the past 3 decades, and services are moving from the medical model to a more integrated model of support. PAS offer support to many people with disabilities who need additional support to successfully live and participate in integrated community environments. Personal assistance services provide a person with a disability with supplemental supports to maintain well-being, personal appearance, safety, and interaction in community environments (Litvak, Zukas, & Heumann, 1987). Personal assistance services, therefore, provide people with disabilities with assistance on a variety of tasks, including (a) grooming, dressing, and feeding; (b) transportation and mobility in the community; (c) home maintenance, including cooking, cleaning, and laundry; and (d) financial management.

Agency-Directed PAS. Traditionally, funding for long-term support programs, such as PAS, has been fragmented and lacked a coordinated federal policy framework. The fragmented policy resulted in a strong institutional bias because Medicaid funding mechanisms favored placement of individuals in segregated residential facilities (Dautel & Frieden, 1999). In fact, approximately 68% of Medicaid long-term service spending goes to institutional-based programs, whereas 32% of Medicaid dollars goes to such community-based services as personal assistance programs (Kaiser Commission on Medicaid and the Uninsured, 2004). The issue is further compounded because each state is given a great deal of latitude in decisions about how to allocate Medicaid dollars to people with disabilities, which has resulted in varying reimbursement rates for personal assistant programs.

To date, most people with disabilities receive PAS through home care agencies that contract with Medicaid. This agency-directed model of service delivery is often criticized because of the lack of consumer control in selecting the types of services performed and the people who will provide support (Hagglund, Clark, Farmer, & Sherman, 2004). These agency-directed programs are often limited in scope because of structural and financial oversight of related PAS activities resulting in limited authorized providers.

| **Focus Question 3** | What is a consumer-directed PAS? |

Window 14-2

Perspectives on Personal Assistance

"What I would like to see happen, for people with all types of disabilities, would be for us to sit down with the people who provide services, tell them what are the goals and expectations we have for our lives, and really work together on making them happen. I'd like to see this done without so much paperwork and red tape and with respect for our privacy. If we could get out from under the disability blanket, the world would look different for us. We'd still get services but they wouldn't be programs. We'd have our privacy because all the details of our lives wouldn't be written down for everyone to see. Professionals would treat us like they would want to be treated. They would appreciate our strengths. They'd consult us about what we want and need and how they could help us to live as independently as we can. We might have goals for our lives, but they wouldn't have to be written down and reviewed and updated regularly in team meetings. We would be asked to evaluate the services we receive instead of always being evaluated" (Kennedy, 2004, p. 231).

Consumer-Directed Models for PAS. A consumer-directed model for PAS allows individuals with disabilities to select the types of services they need and to select and manage their own assistants. Hagglund and colleagues (2004) report that individuals who receive consumer-directed PAS have a greater sense of empowerment and satisfaction because these services and tasks are performed in the community. According to the World Institute on Disability, personal assistance services are an essential element of independent living, and without consumer control of these services many people with disabilities would not be able to live in integrated community environments. As such, the World Institute believes "people with disabilities are entitled to be enabled to achieve the highest possible level of personal functioning and independence through appropriateeducation, health care, social services and assistive technology, including, as necessary, the assistance of other people" (World Institute on Disability, 1991, ¶ 5). The World Institute issued a resolution that contains 14 principles that ensure equitable access to PAS (Table 14.2). These principles reflect the need to develop a comprehensive system of consumer-controlled supports for people with disabilities that is based on integration in all aspects of community living.

Table 14.2 World Institute on Disability: Resolution on Personal Assistant Services

We call on governments and policy makers to assure greater and more equitable access to personal assistance services based on the following principles:

1. Personal assistance services are a human and civil right. These services shall serve people of all ages, from infancy throughout a person's lifetime, when the person's functional limitation(s) shall necessitate the services. This right is irrespective of disability, personal health, income, marital and family status and without discrimination on the basis of race, national origin, cultural background, religion, gender, sexual preference, or geography.

2. All people with disabilities (and their self-designated or legal representatives if applicable) shall be informed about their rights and opinions related to personal assistance services in accessible formats and appropriate languages. All levels of personal assistance services should respect the privacy and confidentiality of the user.

3. Personal assistance users shall be able to choose from a variety of personal assistance services models which together offer the choice of various degrees of user control. User control, in our view, can be exercised by all people regardless of their ability to give legally informed consent or their need for support in decision making or communication.

4. Services shall enable the users to exercise their rights and to participate in every aspect of sociocultural life including, but not limited to, home, school, work, cultural and spiritual activities, leisure, travel and political life. These services shall enable disabled people, without penalty, if they so choose, to establish a personal, family and community life and fulfill all the responsibilities associated with those aspects of life.

5. No individual shall be forced into or kept in an institutionalized setting because of lack of resources, high costs, sub-standard or non-existent services or the refusal and/or denial of any or all services.

6. These services must be available for up to seven days a week for as many hours as needed during the 24-hour period of the day, on long-term, short-term and emergency bases. These services shall include, but are not limited to, assistance with personal bodily functions; communicative, household, mobility, work, emotional, cognitive, personal and financial affairs; community participation; parenting; leisure; and other related needs. The user's point of view must be paramount in the design and delivery of services. Users must be able to choose or refuse services.

7. Government funding shall be an individual entitlement independent of marital status and shall not be a disincentive to employment.

8. Government funding must include competitive wages (based on consumer cost experience within the private sector) and employment benefits for assistants and related administrative and management expenses.

9. Payments to the user shall not be treated as disposable, taxable income and shall not make the user ineligible for other statutory benefits or services.

10. Sufficient governmental funding shall be made available to ensure adequate support, outreach, recruitment, counseling, and training for the user and the assistant. Government efforts shall ensure that a pool of qualified, competent assistance shall be available for users to access through a variety of personal assistance services models, including, but not limited to, individual providers and full service agencies.

11. The user should be free to select and/or hire as personal assistants whomever s/he chooses, including family members.

12. Children needing personal assistance services shall be offered such services as part of their right to inclusive education as well. Such education and personal assistance services shall include age appropriate opportunities to learn to use and control personal assistance services effectively.

13. There shall be a uniform appeals procedure which is independent of funders, providers and assessors that is effected in an expeditious manner and allows the applicant/user to receive advocacy services and legal counsel at the expense of the statutory authority.

14. In furtherance of all of the above, users must be formally and decisively involved and represented at all levels of policy making through ongoing communication and outreach in planning, implementation, design and development of personal assistance services.

Note. From Resolution on Personal Assistance Services, by World Institute on Disability, 1991. Available at http://www.wid.org/publications/personal-assistance-services-a-new-millennium/resolution-on-personal-assistance-services

Programs for Supporting Alternative Residential Programs

Although the number of people living in more typical residential arrangements has increased dramatically in the last several years, funding for these programs continues to be a significant barrier to their expansion. Further, the number of individuals who can access these programs is hindered by the fact that there is no mandate to states to provide these supports to people with intellectual and developmental disabilities. In fact, there is significant variation in the types of residential options that states choose to develop and fund (Prouty et al., 2008). Even though individuals may desire these supports and be eligible for them under federal statute, traditional residential service programs, such as group homes, may be the only options available to a person based on the priorities that have been established by the state in which he or she lives. Alternatives to the residential continuum are currently being supported through the Home and Community-Based Waiver program, the Attendant Care program, and several programs through the U.S. Department of Housing and Urban Development (HUD).

Home and Community-Based Waivers

In 1981, Congress authorized the Medicaid Home and Community-Based Waiver program under Section 1915(c) of the Social Security Act to provide funding to states for certain community-based supports to individuals with disabilities. Waivers are designed to give people who would otherwise be placed in institutional settings more options regarding adult service support in residential and employment settings. The waiver program is one of the fastest growing long-term support programs for people with disabilities, and national spending for home- and community-based services (HCBS) has grown exponentially in the past 20 years, increasing from $1.2 million in 1982 to $7.2 billion in 2002 (Braddock, Rizzolo, Hemp, & Parish, 2005). The expansion in HCBS spending has led to more community-based residential placements for people with disabilities and a decrease in people with disabilities who are served in more restrictive settings, such as ICF/MR. In 1992, 142,260 individuals with mental retardation were served in ICF/MR, compared with 62,462 receiving HCBS waivers who live independently or with parents. By 2006, the number served in ICF/MR had dropped to 98,554, while the number participating in HCBS waiver programs had increased to almost 479,196 (Lakin, Braddock, & Smith, 2007).

Federal Support for Attendant Care

The Medicaid Community Attendant Services and Supports Act (MiCASSA, Senate Bill 1935) was first introduced in 1999 to address the lack of access to PAS for people with disabilities. The legislation was aimed at amending Title XIX of the Social Security Act (Medicaid provisions) to allow individuals who are eligible for nursing home and ICF/MR services to choose to receive community attendant services and supports in lieu of institutional care. MiCASSA was not considered during the 106th Congress and has been reintroduced numerous times, and in 2007, the Community Choice Act (Senate Bill 799) was introduced in place of MiCASSA. The act is an attempt to reform the Medicaid program by providing "services in the most integrated setting appropriate to the individual's needs, and to provide equal access to community-based attendant services and supports in order to assist individuals in achieving equal opportunity, full participation, independent living, and economic self-sufficiency" (Sec. 2[b(1)]). In a statement before the Senate Finance Committee in 2007, Senator Tom Harkin (D-Iowa) articulated the need to pass this legislation:

> It is time to end the institutional bias in Medicaid. We need to move beyond today's unfortunate, discriminatory status quo, with two-thirds of Medicaid long-care dollars spent on institutional services, and only one-third going to community-based care.

The goal of the act is to provide individuals with disabilities with the meaningful choice of receiving long-term services and supports in the most integrated setting and to allow individuals to have greater latitude and control over the services they receive. The Community Choice Act outlines services and supports that should be made available to people with disabilities. The supports and services include (a) tasks necessary to assist an individual in accomplishing activities of daily living; (b) the acquisition, maintenance, and enhancement of skills necessary to accomplish daily living; and (c) back-up systems or mechanisms to ensure continuity of services and supports. At its core, the act will allow support dollars to follow the person with a disability and allow eligible individuals to select and manage the services and supports they receive.

Funding Sources for Homeownership

The evolution of personal assistance has allowed people with disabilities to participate more fully in community settings. Because of the independent living movement, supported living, and PAS, people with disabilities are beginning to realize that homeownership is a reality. More people with disabilities are recognizing that homeownership is possible and that it gives a person with a disability a great sense of control, autonomy, and economic participation (Feinstien et al., 2006).

According to the American Association on Intellectual and Developmental Disabilities (n.d.), there are various options for homeownership for people with disabilities: (a) Individuals with disabilities may own their own home (tenant owned); (b) parents may purchase the home for the individual (parent owned); (c) parents and others may set up a corporation to purchase, own, and maintain housing (corporation owned); (d) parents may combine resources with other parents to buy a house (partnership); (e) an individual may make a purchase with another and eventually buy him or her out (shared equity); and (f) ownership may be assigned to a living trust that is established by the parents (trust owned).

There are a number of funding sources that can be used to help people with disabilities and their families purchase a home, such as HomeChoice, Federal Home Loan Banks, the HOME Investment Partnerships Program, and housing finance agencies (Klien, 2000).

- HomeChoice—HomeChoice is a single-family mortgage loan designed to meet the needs of low- to moderate-income borrowers with disabilities or those who have a family member with a disability.
- Federal Home Loan Banks—The program provides grants to member banks that partner with community agencies to build or renovate housing for low-income buyers.
- HOME Investment Partnerships Program—The program provides formula grants through HUD to states and localities to fund activities that build, buy, or rehabilitate affordable housing for rent or home-ownership or that provide direct rental assistance to people with low incomes.
- Housing finance agencies—These were created to meet the needs of people with low incomes by financing the development of affordable housing.

Each of these funding sources does not guarantee homeownership for people with disabilities but does, however, serve as a resource for individuals who wish to purchase a home. Table 14.3 provides a list of Internet resources for each of the programs listed above.

Table 14.3 Web Resources for Funding Sources for Homeownership

Program	URL
FannieMae HomeChoice	http://www.fanniemae.com/index.jhtml
Federal Home Loan Banks	http://www.fhlbanks.com/
HOME Investment Partnerships Program	http://www.hud.gov/offices/cpd/affordablehousing/programs/home/
Housing Financing Agencies	http://www.ncsha.org/

Summary

Residential options for people with disabilities are continually evolving. Traditional models of residential support provided services in the most restrictive environments. Because of efforts of specific advocacy groups, litigation, and advances in funding structures, people with disabilities are receiving residential services in the least restrictive settings. Because residential options for people with disabilities are a complicated web of state and federal policy, it is important that students with disabilities and their families begin the process of planning for the transition to postschool residential living. Comprehensive residential planning will help students access the appropriate adult service programs.

Focus Question Review

Focus Question 1: What is the continuum of residential services for people with disabilities?

- The continuum comprises different residential options for people with disabilities ranging from institutionalized settings to independent living.
- The continuum uses a "readiness" approach where individuals must demonstrate certain competencies before they can live in the least restrictive environment.

Focus Question 2: What are the important characteristics of supported living programs?

- The individual with a disability chooses his or her home and community independent of services and support systems.
- Individuals gain autonomy and independence from owning or renting their own homes.
- Supports are developed based on individuals' needs and preferences.
- Individuals must balance the costs of housing with other factors of independent living.
- Individuals must participate in all activities associated with independent living.
- Individuals need to develop natural supports that are commonly available in community settings.

Focus Question 3: What is a consumer-directed PAS?

- A consumer-directed personal assistance service allows individuals to select the supports needed to allow them to live independently based on their needs and preferences.

CHAPTER 15

Postschool Employment Alternatives

TIM RIESEN

C hronic unemployment or underemployment of people with disabilities continues to be a concern of advocates for people with disabilities. In fact, only 35% of working-age adults with disabilities are employed (National Organization on Disability, 2004). In addition, young adults with severe disabilities have low rates of community-based employment after exiting school (Wagner, Newman, Cameto, Garza, & Levine, 2005). In order to improve postschool outcomes, transition programs must emphasize comprehensive career planning, vocational education, and employment training for students with disabilities. The importance of comprehensive employment preparation is highlighted by the fact that paid employment during a student's last 2 years of school is highly predictive of postschool success for students with disabilities (Benz, Lindstrom, & Yovanoff, 2000). While a number of variables contribute to postschool success of students with disabilities, teachers must also understand the nature and scope of postschool adult employment services provided by vocational rehabilitation and local mental retardation and developmental disabilities (MR/DD) agencies. Many parents lack knowledge about these agencies and believe that postschool options are limited to segregated employment programs (Chambers, Hughes, & Carter, 2004). To alleviate this concern, secondary teachers need to articulate what postschool employment options are available to people with disabilities and help facilitate the transition from school to the appropriate employment program.

A number of employment programs have been developed to assist individuals with disabilities in entering the workforce. Each of these employment programs reflects the evolution of different support philosophies that have emerged over the years. Because of the unique nature of these programs, secondary teachers need to understand the critical components and underlying values of each employment alternative. This chapter will review the structure and defining characteristics of employment programs for people with disabilities, including the flow-through model of employment, supported employment, and customized employment. In addition, the chapter will review the structure of federal work incentive programs that are designed to assist individuals in obtaining meaningful employment.

Structure of Adult Employment Programs

Since the early 1980s, we have learned a great deal about how to support an individual with disabilities in competitive employment. Adult employment programs offer a wide array of employment supports for people with disabilities, and each program or model has unique features and defining characteristics. Such specific factors as legislation and consumer advocacy have created an increased emphasis on inclusive, competitive employment for individuals with significant support needs. The following section will review how employment services have evolved from a segregated service delivery philosophy to one that reflects consumer-driven, inclusive employment.

Focus Question 1	Describe some of the problems associated with the flow-through model of employment.

The Flow-Through Model of Employment

The flow-through model was conceptualized as a way to teach people with disabilities the requisite prevocational skills that lead to employment. In the flow-through model, individuals are placed in a variety of congregate, facilities-based settings that include sheltered workshops, work activity centers, and day treatment centers. Individuals perform a variety of prevocational and vocational tasks in these settings, such as assembly and packaging, and are typically paid a subminimum or piece rate that falls well below minimum wage (Migliore, Mank, Grossi, & Rogan, 2007). Facilities-based employment programs are typically operated by community service providers who contract with local vocational rehabilitation and MR/DD agencies to provide services.

While the flow-through model was conceptualized as a way to increase vocational outcomes for individuals with disabilities, it has not produced quality inclusive employment placements for many individuals with disabilities. The underlying structure of the flow-through model is based on a continuum of services that assumes that individuals with disabilities need to possess certain prevocational skills and competencies before they can work in inclusive, community-based settings. Movement in the continuum is based on the ability of the person with a disability to perform prevocational skills. Once an individual demonstrates that he or she possesses these prevocational skills, he or she can transition to more inclusive employment settings. As illustrated in Figure 15.1, individuals with severe disabilities are typically placed in more restrictive settings, such as day treatment, work activity centers, and sheltered workshops, while individuals with moderate disabilities are placed in least restrictive settings, such as transitional employment training. The basic assumption of this model is that more intensive services and supports can be provided to a person in a more restrictive placement.

Unfortunately, the skills that are taught in this setting are often based on simulated work and do not resemble actual community-based jobs. Consequently, the individual may be learning a prevocational skill that he or she will not be able to generalize to an actual performance setting. This training approach does not necessarily prepare people with disabilities for

Figure 15.1   Illustration of the Continuum of Employment Supports

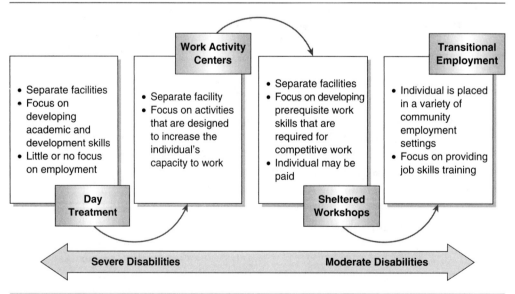

the demands of community-based employment because these individuals need to be provided with instruction and support in the actual performance environments (Horner, McDonnell, & Bellamy, 1986; Westling & Fox, 2000). In addition, development of social skills is impeded when individuals with disabilities are placed in sheltered programs because they have less exposure to real-life social interactions.

One of the greatest shortcomings of facilities-based programs is that few people move from these settings to inclusive employment. In fact, research has shown that once an individual with a disability is placed in a sheltered setting, the chance of transitioning to inclusive employment is near zero (Zivolich, 1991). Research also indicates that placement of individuals with disabilities in segregated workshop settings outpaces placement in inclusive programs, such as supported employment (Braddock, Rizzolo, & Hemp, 2004), and MR/DD funding for segregated programs is nearly four times higher than funding for supported employment (Rusch & Braddock, 2004). In an attempt to explain why conversion from segregated facilities to supported employment was slow, West, Revell, and Wehman (1998) conducted a survey of community service providers to determine what barriers they face during the conversion process. The authors found that a number of variables obstruct the process of community-based employment, such as family reluctance, resistance from agency staff, limited program funds, and attitudes of the community members and employers.

The growth in sheltered programs, barriers, and the funding disparities between segregated and supported employment programs is particularly discouraging because when individuals with intellectual and developmental disabilities are provided with proper supports, they can successfully obtain employment in inclusive employment settings (Mank, Cioffi, & Yovanoff, 1997, 2000, 2003). Moreover, research has also demonstrated that individuals who work in community-based employment have increased social interactions with peers without disabilities (Wehman, 2003; Storey, 2002), have increased wages as compared with sheltered employment participants (Kregel & Dean, 2002; Kregel, Wehman, Revell, Hill, & Cimera, 2000), and have increased self-determination and choice (West & Parent, 1992).

Supported Employment

Supported employment emerged in the 1980s as an alternative to sheltered employment placements, and the movement to develop alternative employment supports was influenced by the fact that the segregated employment programs did not produce quality outcomes. As a result, advocates, researchers, and policymakers wanted to abandon the "train-place" model for vocational preparation and began to develop innovative methods to support an individual with significant support needs in the competitive labor market. By the mid-1980s, the Office of Special Education and Rehabilitative Services provided funding to 27 states to develop and implement systems change initiatives in supported employment. In 1986, the Rehabilitation Act (PL 99–506) was amended, and the federal government made formula grants available to states to develop supported employment programs for people with disabilities. By 1992, federal legislation embraced the view that supported employment is a viable option for people with significant support needs. The 1992 amendments define supported employment as

> competitive work in integrated work settings, or employment in integrated work settings in which individuals are working toward competitive work, consistent with the strengths, resources, priorities, concerns, abilities, capabilities, interests, and informed choice of the individuals, for individuals with the most significant disabilities—for whom competitive employment has not traditionally occurred. (U.S.C. § 705)

As evidenced by the Rehabilitation Act amendments, supported employment was specifically designed to assist individuals with the most severe disabilities in finding competitive employment. One of the underlying principles of supported employment is its focus on paid, competitive employment and not prevocational training. That is, individuals who wish to work need not demonstrate specific vocational competencies through prevocational or work readiness programs before they can enter the competitive workforce. Rather, individuals need only demonstrate a desire to work.

When an individual with a disability receives supported employment services, he or she is placed in a competitive job, is paid commensurate wages and benefits, and is entitled to other ancillary benefits of working, such as vacation time, sick pay, lunch breaks, and the opportunity to interact with other employees without disabilities. To achieve this outcome, supported employment providers must make a concerted effort to incorporate several core values into comprehensive supported employment service delivery. Wehman, Revell, and Brooke (2003) developed nine core supported employment values that are the foundations of quality supported employment programs (Table 15.1). These values reflect the philosophy that all people, regardless of disability, have the ability to work in competitive working environments given proper support and autonomy. These values also emphasize a need to implement systems change that recognizes the capabilities of people with disabilities to work in inclusive environments.

Table 15.1   Supported Employment Values

Values	Values Clarification
Presumption of employment	Everyone, regardless of the level or the type of disability, has the capability to do a job and the right to have a job.
Competitive employment	Employment occurs within the local labor market in regular community businesses.
Self-determination and control	When people with disabilities choose and regulate their own employment supports and services, career satisfaction will result.
Commensurate wages and benefits	People with disabilities should earn wages and benefits equal to that of co-workers performing the same or similar jobs.
Focus on capacity and capabilities	People with disabilities should be viewed in terms of their abilities, strengths, and interests rather than their disabilities.
Importance of relationships	Community relationships both at and away from work lead to mutual respect and acceptance.
Power of support	People with disabilities need to determine their personal goals and receive assistance in assembling the supports for achieving their ambitions.
Systems change	Traditional systems must be changed to ensure customer control, which is vital to the integrity of supported employment.
Importance of community	People need to be connected to formal and informal networks of a community for acceptance, growth, and development.

Note. Reprinted from "Competitive Employment: Has It Become the 'First Choice' Yet?" by P. Wehman, W. G. Revell, and V. Brooke, 2003, *Journal of Disability Policy Studies, 14*(3), pp. 163–167. Reprinted with permission.

Supported Employment Models. Different supported employment models have emerged over the years, including the individual placement model, the enclave model, and the mobile work crew model (Rusch & Hughes, 1989). Each of these models provides individuals with disabilities with various levels of support, and they each produce a valued employment outcome. However, vocational rehabilitation prefers the individual model because it is the most inclusive service delivery strategy (Wehman, Revell, & Kregel, 1998). The individual placement model is designed to provide support to a single individual who works in a local business. The supported employee receives 1:1 support by an employment specialist; once the supported employee gains more confidence and independence, the support is gradually faded to natural levels. The enclave model consists of a small-group placement of individuals (fewer than eight) who work in a host business. These businesses often include manufacturing plants, hotels, and large businesses. Direct training and supervision is provided by an on-site supervisor and does not fade from the individual. The mobile work crew comprises a group of six or fewer individuals who are trained and supervised by a paid crew leader. The mobile work crew contracts with a local business to provide such services as janitorial services and landscaping. The business typically pays the community service provider for the service, and wages are dispersed to the supported employee.

| **Focus Question 2** | Describe the defining characteristics of supported employment. |

Characteristics of Supported Employment Service Delivery. Supported employment is designed to maximize inclusion and community participation by providing an individual with consumer-driven, ongoing, and flexible support (Wehman et al., 2003; Wehman & Bricout, 2001; Brooke, Wehman, Inge, & Parent, 1995). To achieve this outcome, the employee is supported by a community employment specialist or job coach who is responsible for assisting the individual with finding meaningful inclusive employment. Job coaches are typically employed by community rehabilitation service providers who contract with either vocational rehabilitation or long-term MR/DD support agencies. The employment specialist assists the supported employee with assessment, including developing a vocational profile, job development, job training, and extended support and follow-along.

Assessment and Developing Individual Vocational Profiles. A critical component of the supported employment process is identifying the career interests and preferences of the supported employee and then developing a comprehensive vocational profile. It is important to note that employment assessments are not used to determine whether an individual can or cannot work but rather to determine where an individual would like to work and to determine the necessary supports to make the job placement successful. The assessments should be consumer driven and should use a person-centered planning approach that reflects the needs of the supported employee (Brooke et al., 1995; Kregel, 1998). In addition, such community-based assessments as situational assessments, job tours, and informational interviews are used to gather firsthand knowledge about the local labor market and the individual's ability to perform the essential functions of a job.

The information compiled during the consumer-driven assessment process is incorporated into a comprehensive vocational profile. The profile lists the individual's strengths and career interests, the types and level of natural and paid support needed to work in inclusive settings, methods of transportation, and Social Security benefit information. This information serves as a planning document so the supported employee and job coach can target potential employers based on the unique strengths and interests of the individual with a disability.

Job Development. The job development process requires that the employment specialist and the supported employee conduct a targeted job search based on the information gathered during the assessment. This targeted job search allows the employment specialist and the supported employee to identify existing job openings that match the skills and abilities of the supported employee. Because many people with severe disabilities cannot perform all of the essential functions of market-driven jobs, many employment specialists rely on job carving and modification as a way to maximize employment opportunities during the job development process. Job carving requires the employment specialist, supported employee, and potential employer to examine existing jobs to determine if there are job components that can be redistributed and reassigned to meet the needs of the supported employee (Nietupski & Hamre-Nietupski, 2000; Griffin, 1996). Once the needs of the employer are matched to the strengths and capabilities of the supported employee, the employment specialist develops a hiring proposal that is presented to prospective employers. The hiring proposal outlines the benefits of hiring the supported employee, the proposed job duties, a description of the proposed supported employee, the proposed hours and wages, and the proposed implementation timeline (Nietupski & Hamre-Nietupski, 2001).

Job-Site Support. Supported employment uses a "place-train" model of service delivery where an individual is placed in a job and is subsequently taught the necessary skill to perform the essential elements of that job. The role of the employment specialist, therefore, is to support the supported employee and teach specific job skills in the actual performance setting. Research suggests that the more typical an employment experience is for individuals with disabilities, the more success that individual has on the job (Mank et al., 1997). Therefore, individuals with disabilities should be encouraged to participate in regular training and employment activities, and attempts should be made to facilitate natural supports in the workplace. However, there may be times when the supported employee needs systematic instruction in order to perform the demands of a job. When this occurs, the employment specialist should conduct a thorough job analysis to identify areas that need systematic training and support. Once these areas are identified, the employment specialist should use the appropriate training approach to teach the supported employee the employment skill.

POINT/COUNTERPOINT 15.1

Shelter Workshops and Supported Employment

POINT

"Supportive employment takes workers out of the full time work environment of the workshop and places them in fifteen hours per week part time employment. What do they do the rest of the time? Who watches over them? Do they get to socialize with their buddies? What is even worse now that many have been moved into the community with inadequate support, they are 'home alone' to be used and abused when they should be in a structured environment. This is not acceptable. This defeats the purpose of the workshop programs in the first place. . . . Parents are tired of bureaucrats and professionals designing programs that are 'easy' to administer i.e. 'pass the money around.' It's time they go back to work and design programs for the mentally retarded. That's what they supposedly are paid to do! It's time for professionals in the field of mental retardation to wake up! Place common sense back into your repertoire. Persons with mental retardation are not normal and they never will be. Quit trying to make them something they are not! Let's give the mentally retarded the help to attain their constitutional right of the pursuit of happiness instead of placing them in environments without adequate supports" (Mentally Retarded Citizens of Missouri, Inc., n.d., ¶ 3).

COUNTERPOINT

"I want to tell you about my past experience at the sheltered workshop. To me it looked like an institution or a warehouse. There were no non-disabled people employed there except for the supervisors, and they only interacted with other staff and not any of the people with disabilities. The people with disabilities only interacted with each other. The staff didn't look beyond the workers' disabilities and recognize that they were people. This was unacceptable because the staff was being paid to support and train people with disabilities in skills for their independence. What I would like to see happen is for government officials to pull the funding out of sheltered workshops and to put the money into supported work instead. The reason why I would like for this to happen is so people will feel like they are doing something good and worthwhile in their life out in the community. If people work out in the community, they develop a wider range of contacts, unlike going to a segregated building every day" (Kennedy, 1988, ¶ 3).

Extended Support. A fundamental characteristic of supported employment is ongoing support. When a supported employee first starts a job, the employment specialist provides frequent support. As the supported employee becomes more confident on the job and begins to master the essential functions of the job, the employment specialist fades his or her support. During the fading process, the employment specialist periodically conducts maintenance probes to ensure that the supported employee is executing the requirements of the job. The employment specialist also provides ongoing support by serving as a liaison between the supported employee and the employer to ensure the employer's needs are being met.

Focus Question 3	Describe the defining characteristics of customized employment.

Customized Employment

Customized employment is a set of strategies and interventions that are designed to help an individual with significant support needs obtain paid employment. The term *customized employment* was first used in 2001 when the U.S. Department of Labor's Office of Disability Employment Policy (ODEP) was developing ways for One-Stop Career Centers to better serve individuals with disabilities. The ODEP defines customized employment as follows:

> Customized employment means individualizing the employment relationship between employees and employers in ways that meet the needs of both. It is based on an individualized determination of the strengths, needs, and interests of the person with a disability, and is also designed to meet the specific needs of the employer. It may include employment developed through job carving, self-employment or entrepreneurial initiatives, or other job development or restructuring strategies that result in job responsibilities being customized and individually negotiated to fit the needs of individuals with a disability. (Federal Register, 2002, p. 43156)

Customized employment embodies the core principles of supported employment and represents a logical extension of the supported employment service delivery model. Customized employment builds on the strengths of supported employment in that it requires that the employment process be individualized and tailored to the unique strengths and capabilities of the individual. The process, however, is not based on the demands of the local job market. Rather, it seeks to establish a mutual relationship between the job seeker and an employer by carving, modifying, restructuring, or negotiating a specific job. The ODEP (2005) established a set of customized employment principles that illustrate the customized employment process. First, the employer voluntarily negotiates specific job duties or principles. Second, the negotiated employment relationship meets both the unique needs, strengths, and interests of the employee and the discrete needs of the employer. Third, the job seeker is the primary source of information and decides the direction in which to explore the job market, as well as controls the planning process that captures his or her preferences, interests, and connections in the community. Finally, exploratory time is essential to uncover the job seeker's unique needs, abilities, and interests.

The ODEP has funded customized employment demonstration projects around the country and found that a customized process is particularly effective in helping individuals with significant support needs find jobs. An independent review of the ODEP customized demonstration projects found significant improvements in quality-of-life and employment outcomes as a result of customized employment, including pay at or above minimum wage, an increase in fringe benefits, and a decrease in the amount of time spent in segregated day services (Elinson & Frey, 2005). Similarly, Luecking, Gumpman, Saeker, and Cihak (2006) conducted a survey of 30 individuals with severe disabilities who were seeking employment using the customized employment process. Twenty of the participants found employment with a mean wage of $6.35, working an average of 16.45 hours per week. The participants also reported that their perceived quality of life had changed as a result of the customized employment process. In another study, Luecking and Luecking (2006) surveyed 135 individuals who received services through a customized employment model demonstration project. Seventy-one individuals acquired customized jobs in an average of 128 days from intake to placement. The mean hourly wage was $6.65, and participants worked an average of 19 hours per week. These data support the utility of customized employment for individuals with severe disabilities.

Customized employment can be conceptualized as a series of interrelated interventions that lead to paid employment. Like supported employment, customized employment uses a blend of strategies to increase employment options for individuals with significant support needs, including self-determination training, discovery, negotiation, job training, and follow-along (Callahan & Condon, 2007). Each of these strategies is used to support an individual in securing paid, inclusive employment.

Self-Determination Instruction. Customized employment is an individualized process that encourages job seekers to make career choices based on personal preferences and informed choice. Therefore, individuals with disabilities need to be provided with opportunities to make choices and develop self-determination skills. Research has shown that individuals with disabilities who exhibit self-determined behaviors are more successful in employment settings (Wehmeyer & Schwartz, 1998; McGlashing-Johnson, Agran, Sitlington, Cavin, & Wehmeyer, 2003; Martin, Marshal, & De Pry, 2005). The first step in the customized employment process, therefore, is to infuse self-determination training into the career planning process and to teach individuals with disabilities such self-determination skills as (a) the ability to set goals and solve problems, (b) the ability to make appropriate choices based on personal preferences, (c) the ability to advocate for themselves by choosing a personalized career path, and (d) the ability to self-regulate and manage their day-to-day behavior so that they can perform the essential function of the job with minimal support.

The Discovery Process. The second step of the customized employment process is "discovery." Discovery focuses on gathering comprehensive information about an individual to support the development of a customized job (Callahan & Condon, 2007). Unlike traditional vocational profiles that are based on labor market demands, discovery uses an individualized approach to obtain a comprehensive picture of an individual's life, including the individual's strengths, needs, interests, and available supports. Discovery relies on the perspective not only of the individual with a disability but also of people who know the individual best, including, parents, friends, community members, teachers, and service providers. The steps of the discovery process include person-centered planning, conducting discovery meetings, identifying support strategies, identifying transportation, observing the individual in multiple environments, and developing an employment summary and plan that includes an employment proposal and individual portfolio. The information gathered during the discovery process serves as a blueprint from which the individual and his or her support staff begin to develop a customized employment plan.

Negotiation. A key component of customized employment is negotiating job duties and expectations with potential employers. The ultimate goal of negotiation is to determine employment options that mutually benefit the job seeker and the employer. Job negotiations are implemented after the comprehensive discovery process wherein the individual's strengths, contributions, and supports are identified. Once an individual career plan is developed, the individual and the employment specialist begin the negotiation process. The process begins by conducting a workplace analysis via informational interviews and job tours. Informational interviews allow the individual and the job coach to gather detailed information and personal perspectives about a specific job (Simmons, Flexer, & Bauder, 2005; Griffin, Hammis, & Geary, 2007). During these interviews, the individual with a disability and his or her job coach begin to probe the employer about unmet needs of the business. These probes become the focal point of the negotiation process, and the individual and his or her job coach look for ways to negotiate a customized job through job carving, job restructuring, and job negotiations, job sharing, or job creation.

Job Training. To be successful in inclusive employment environments, individuals with severe disabilities need to be provided with systematic instruction that is grounded in empirically validated techniques. Research has shown that individuals with severe disabilities must be taught new skills in the natural settings where they are expected to perform (Horner et al., 1986; Rosenthal-Malek & Bloom, 1998). Therefore, customized employment requires support staff to conduct an analysis of the performance demands of the job and implement systematic instruction to teach the employee the essential functions of the customized job. These instructional procedures must be designed to meet the unique needs of the individual with a disability.

Follow-Along. Follow-along provides a customized employee with sufficient levels of support to ensure ongoing success in the customized job. A primary focus of the follow-along process is for the individual with a disability, his or her employment specialist, and his or her employer to identify and establish the natural supports necessary to maintain employment (Nisbet & Hagner, 1988). This process is critical because it ensures that the needs of both the individual with a disability and the employer are being met. It is also critical that employment specialists implement a systematic approach to ensuring the individual's continued success on the job, including making regular contact with the student and the employer to identify potential problems, probing the student's job performance, and regularly assessing the employer's satisfaction with the student's performance (McDonnell, Mathot-Buckner, & Ferguson, 1996).

To that end, customized employment represents a natural evolution in the way employment support services are developed for people with disabilities. Customized employment expands on the original intent of supported employment and recognizes that individuals with more severe disabilities can work in inclusive settings given the proper supports. Customized employment also recognizes the value of a demand-side approach to employment support and seeks to establish a mutual benefit between the employer and the job seeker by negotiating and carving jobs for people with disabilities that help employers increase their productivity. This mutual benefit provides inclusive employment opportunities for people with disabilities who traditionally have not been employed.

Federal Work Incentives

The Social Security Administration has two major programs from which individuals with disabilities receive financial support: Supplemental Security Income (SSI) and Social Security Disability Insurance (SSDI). Each of these programs functions differently and has different eligibility requirements (see Table 15.2). Social Security annually adjusts various dollar figures that affect the monthly benefits of Social Security beneficiaries. Therefore, individuals with disabilities and professionals need to obtain up-to-date information from the Social Security Administration regarding any changes in benefits. Table 15.3 provides information on resources for obtaining information regarding Social Security programs and benefits.

As illustrated in Table 15.2, the Social Security Administration examines a variety of factors when determining eligibility for both SSI and SSDI beneficiaries. An important component of the determination process is an individual's work activity and earned wages. Social Security uses an earnings guideline to evaluate the work activity to determine whether the individual is engaging in Substantial Gainful Activity (SGA). Therefore, a person whose

Table 15.2   Eligibility Requirements for SSI and SSDI

SSI Eligibility Requirements	*SSDI Eligibility Requirements*
To be eligible for SSI, an individual must:	To be eligible for SSDI, an individual must:
1. Have limited income and resources. 2. Be a U.S. citizen or meet the requirements for noncitizens. 3. Meet the Social Security Administration's definition of medically disabled. 4. Be a resident of the 50 states, the District of Columbia, or the Northern Mariana Islands. 5. File an application. 6. File for all other benefits for which the individual is eligible. 7. Not be working or be working but not performing SGA when applying for benefits.	1. Have worked and paid Social Security taxes for enough years to be covered under Social Security insurance; some of the taxes must have been paid in recent years. 2. Be the worker, the worker's widow(er), the surviving divorced spouse, or the worker's child with disabilities (requirements for a childhood disability beneficiary include the facts that the individual must be unmarried and age 18 or over and that his or her disability must have begun before age 22). 3. File an application. 4. Meet the Social Security Administration's definition of medically disabled. 5. Not be working or be working but not performing SGA.

Note. Adapted from the *2007 Red Book: A Summary Guide to Employment Support for Individuals With Disabilities Under the Social Security Disability Insurance and Supplemental Security Income Programs,* SSA Pub. No. 64-030, by the Social Security Administration, 2007, Washington, DC: Author. Adapted with permission.

Table 15.3 Online Resources for SSI and SSDI

Resource	URL
2007 Red Book: A Summary Guide to Employment Support for Individuals With Disabilities Under the Social Security Disability Insurance and Supplemental Security Income Programs	www.socialsecurity.gov/disabilityresearch/redbook.htm
WorkWORLD.org	http://www.workworld.org/
BEST (Benefits Eligibility Screening Tool)	https://secure.ssa.gov/apps7/best/benefits/
Work Incentives Planning and Assistance (WIPA)	https://secure.ssa.gov/apps10/oesp/providers.nsf/bystate

earnings exceed the established SGA limits will not be eligible for a cash benefit. It is important to note that SGA functions differently for SSI and SSDI beneficiaries.

Social Security examines the work activity of individuals who apply for SSI benefits. If the individual is employed and his or her income exceeds SGA, his or her claim for benefits will be denied. If, however, the individual begins working after he or she is determined eligible for SSI benefits, the individual becomes eligible for the 1619(a) work incentive.

Social Security examines SGA levels at two different points for SSDI beneficiaries. First, Social Security will examine the onset of the disability to determine if the individual engaged in SGA. If an individual engages in SGA within 12 months of the onset date, he or she will be determined ineligible. The onset date is the date on which an individual meets the definition of a disability. Second, Social Security examines SGA after the Trial Work Period (TWP). If an individual engages in SGA after the TWP, the benefit will stop during each month income exceeds SGA.

Both SSI and SSDI share some common concepts and terms but function differently. SSI is strictly a needs-based program that pays beneficiaries a cash benefit that is prorated based on income or resources. SSDI, on the other hand, is based on the individual's prior work history and how many quarters the individual has paid into the Social Security Trust Fund. Because each program has differences, Social Security has created different employment supports or work incentives for each program. These work incentive programs were created because the Social Security Administration was often criticized for financially penalizing people who wanted to work. Individuals with disabilities who want to return to work—and who receive SSI or SSDI benefits—must understand how employment can affect their cash benefit.

Supplemental Security Income Work Incentives

A variety of work incentives for SSI beneficiaries have been created by the Social Security Administration to help an individual work and still receive a cash benefit. These incentives can be used by students with disabilities to help them obtain an employment goal. Table 15.4 describes specific work incentives for SSI recipients.

General and Earned Income Exclusions. The Social Security Administration examines a beneficiary's earned and unearned income to determine the amount of the monthly cash benefit the individual receives. Earned income

Table 15.4   SSI Work Incentives

SSI Work Incentives	
General Income Exclusion and Earned Income Exclusion	Social Security deducts the first $65 (earned income exclusion), $20 (general exclusion), and half of all earnings (1 for 2).
1619(a)	An individual with a disability can receive a cash benefit when his or her earned income is at the SGA level.
1619(b)	An individual's Medicaid coverage can continue even if his or her earnings become too high for an SSI benefit.
Student-Earned Income Exclusion (SEIE)	The SEIE is a work incentive that was created to allow a student under age 22 to deduct up to $1,510 a month with a yearly cap of $6,100.
Plan for Achieving Self-Support (PASS)	A PASS allows an individual with a disability to set aside cash and resources for a specified work goal.
Impairment-Related Work Expense (IRWE)	An IRWE allows an individual to deduct expenses that he or she has as a result of his or her disability that are necessary to work.

Note. Adapted from the *2007 Red Book: A Summary Guide to Employment Support for Individuals With Disabilities Under the Social Security Disability Insurance and Supplemental Security Income Programs,* SSA Pub. No. 64-030, by the Social Security Administration, 2007, Washington, DC: Author. Adapted with permission.

is defined as money received from wages earned during employment, and unearned income is money received from all other sources (Social Security Administration, 2007). While the administration requires that an individual account for all earned and unearned income, not all of the income counts when calculating a benefit. Social Security allows an individual to exclude $20 (general exclusion), $65 (earned income exclusion), and half of all the remaining income when calculating an adjusted benefit. After these exclusions are calculated, the remaining dollar amount is subtracted from the established federal benefit rate (FBR) to determine the adjusted SSI monthly payment. The FBR is the maximum monthly cash benefit an SSI beneficiary can receive, and it is adjusted annually.

1619(a) and 1619(b). The Social Security Administration created 1619(a) and 1619(b) to protect the monthly benefits an individual receives. 1619(a) is a provision that allows an individual to still receive a monthly cash benefit even when his or her income exceeds the SGA limits. The Social Security Administration will continue to determine the SSI payment amount in the same way that it does earnings that are below the SGA levels until the individual exceeds the break-even point or the point at which the earnings decrease a monthly benefit to zero. 1619(b) is a provision that provides continued Medicaid benefits to SSI beneficiaries whose income exceeds the limits for an SSI cash payment. Under this provision, an individual maintains his or her eligibility for Medicaid as long as his or her income does not exceed the threshold amount established by each state and the individual still meets the eligibility criteria established by the Social Security Administration. The threshold amounts are established by each state and range from $23,432 (Oklahoma) to $50,685 (Alaska) (Social Security Administration, 2007).

Student-Earned Income Exclusion. The Student-Earned Income Exclusion (SEIE) is a work incentive that allows eligible individuals, under age 22, to deduct earned income as long as they are regularly attending school. Under this provision, an eligible student can deduct up to $1,510 of earned income each month to a maximum yearly limit of $6,100. These deductions are applied before the general and earned income exclusions, and the amounts are adjusted annually based on the cost-of-living allowances. In order to be eligible for the SEIE work incentive, an individual must be regularly attending school or classes in (a) a college or university for at least 8 hours a week, (b) Grades 7 to 12 for at least 12 hours a week, or (c) a training course to prepare for employment for at least 12 hours a week (15 hours if the course involves shop practices). Students who attend school or classes for less time than indicated above for reasons beyond their control, such as illness, are still eligible for the SEIE work incentive (Social Security Administration, 2007).

Window 15-1

Using an SEIE

Steven is a 20-year-old student with intellectual and developmental disabilities. As part of his transition plan, he has participated in a variety of unpaid community-based job sampling programs. During his last transition planning meeting, he stated that he would like to begin working for wages and expressed interest in working for a pet store. However, both his mother and his father had strong reservations about Steven working because they were told that Steven would lose his monthly SSI benefit if Steven worked.

To alleviate the parents' concerns, the transition coordinator and special educator explained that because Steven is a student and has an IEP/transition plan, he can use the Student-Earned Income Exclusion. This exclusion allows Steven to earn wages from employment and still receive his $624 benefit from Social Security. To use this exclusion, Social Security needs to verify that Steven is a student, and he needs to maintain detailed records of his monthly wages.

Plan to Achieve Self-Support. The Plan to Achieve Self-Support (PASS) was created to allow an individual to set aside and save income and resources to achieve a specific work-related goal. The income that an individual uses for a PASS must be either earned or unearned income and cannot be SSI income. That is, income must be from earned wages, in-kind income, or deemed income. The income and resources that are set aside during a PASS are excluded when determining an SSI benefit. As a result, a PASS helps an individual maintain his or her SSI eligibility while he or she is preparing for a realistic work goal.

A PASS can be used to help an individual obtain a realistic occupational goal, and expenditures can be used to fund such specific goods and services as equipment or supplies to establish a business, attendant care, uniforms and special clothing, the least costly alternatives for transportation, licenses and certifications, and supported employment. The Social Security Administration requires that specific expenses be reasonable, and the individual must demonstrate how cost calculations for the goods or services were determined. These goods or services expenses must be paid for by the individual for whom the PASS is written and cannot be reimbursed by any other source.

The Social Security Administration requires that each plan be individualized and be specifically designed for the individual for whom the plan was written. The plan must be in writing and must follow specific guidelines in the administration's PASS application form (SSA-545-BK). In addition, the plan must meet the basic requirements outlined in Table 15.5. Individuals must submit a completed PASS to their local Social Security Administration office, and the representative will forward the completed PASS to one of eight regional PASS cadres for final approval. Once the PASS application is received, a benefits specialist will be assigned to the individual to assist with oversight and implementation of the PASS.

Window 15–2

Using a PASS

Steven has been successfully employed at Tropical Fish and Pet Supply and is using the SEIE to exclude his earnings. His primary job responsibilities include cleaning the fish tanks, feeding the fish, sweeping, and mopping the floor. He is working 15 hours a week and is currently supported by a school paraprofessional during working hours. His transition team determined that he would need ongoing support to be successful on the job after transitioning from school. Steven and his parents applied to his local MR/DD agency for long-term support; unfortunately, Steven was placed on a wait list for services with no guarantee that he would receive long-term employment support. The transition team recommended that he develop a PASS in order to set aside funds to help him pay for an employment specialist when he exits school.

The transition coordinator assisted Steven and his parents with writing the PASS. The plan was designed so that Steven sets aside $300 a month for his remaining 2 years of school. By developing a PASS, Steven can save money in excess of the $2,000 resource limit established by the Social Security Administration as long as the money will be used for an approved PASS goal.

Once his PASS was approved by the local PASS cadre, Steven opened a PASS savings account and deposited $300 a month into the account. Because Steven has 2 years remaining in school, he will save approximately $3,600 to pay for ongoing support.

Table 15.5 Requirements for a PASS

PASS Requirements

Each PASS must:

1. Be individualized.
2. Be in writing.
3. Have a specific work goal that the individual is capable of performing.
4. Have a specific timeline for reaching the work goal.

5. Show what money and any other contributions will be used to reach the goal.

6. Show how the money will be saved and spent.

7. Show how the money will be kept separate from any other funds.

8. Be approved by a PASS cadre.

9. Be reviewed periodically to ensure compliance.

Note. Adapted from the *2007 Red Book: A Summary Guide to Employment Support for Individuals With Disabilities Under the Social Security Disability Insurance and Supplemental Security Income Programs,* SSA Pub. No. 64-030, by the Social Security Administration, 2007, Washington, DC: Author. Adapted with permission.

Impairment-Related Work Expense. An Impairment-Related Work Expense (IRWE) is another work incentive that allows an individual to deduct the cost of certain impairment-related items and services that he or she needs in order to work. An IRWE provides individuals with an opportunity to recover some of the cost of the expense related to work by deducting the expense of the item from the individual's earned income. As a result, an individual's SSI benefit will increase during the month in which an IRWE is deducted.

In order to use an IRWE, an individual must demonstrate that the item or service is needed to obtain employment and that the item or service is needed because of a disabling impairment. The expense must be reasonable, and the individual has to pay for the expense in the month in which he or she is working. In addition, the individual has to pay the cost for items or services, and he or she cannot be reimbursed by any other source, such as Medicaid or private insurance (Social Security Administration, 2007). Social Security has an extensive list of allowable and nonallowable expenses under the IRWE work incentive; examples of these allowable expenses include attendant care, transportation costs, medical devices, work-related equipment and assistants, prosthesis, residential modification, routine drugs and medical services, diagnostic procedures, and nonmedical appliances and devices. It is highly recommended that if the individual has questions about whether an IRWE expense is allowable, he or she should contact the local Social Security office to consult with a claims representative or an area work incentives coordinator about the expense.

Focus Question 4	What is the primary difference between SSI and SSDI?

Social Security Disability Insurance Work Incentives

SSDI is a program that provides a benefit to people with disabilities who are insured by the Social Security Administration because of contributions they made to the Social Security Trust Fund. While SSI and SSDI have some similar features, the two programs have unique work incentives that are designed to help a person with a disability return to work. The specific work incentives for SSDI are listed in Table 15.6.

Trial Work Period. When a person with a disability is determined eligible for SSDI benefits, he or she is entitled to participate in a Trial Work Period. The TWP is designed to provide the SSDI beneficiary with an opportunity to test his or her ability to work without reducing the monthly cash benefit. That is, during the TWP, an SSDI beneficiary can earn wages that exceed the SGA limits and still receive a full SSDI cash benefit. The TWP begins the first month that the individual is determined eligible for SSDI benefits or in the month that the individual files for benefits. The Social Security Administration established that the duration of the TWP is 9 months in which an individual performs work or "services." These months do not need to be consecutive; however, the individual must earn more than the amount established by the administration. This monthly amount is adjusted annually based on the national average wage. The TWP stops after the individual has engaged in 9 months of work performed during a 60-consecutive-month period.

Table 15.6 SSDI Work Incentives

	SSDI Work Incentives
Trial Work Period (TWP)	The TWP allows an individual with disabilities to test his or her ability to work for at least 9 months and still receive full SSDI benefits regardless of earned wages.
Extended Period of Eligibility (EPE)	A 36-month time period after the TWP where an individual with a disability can receive a benefit when his or her income is below SGA without filing a new application.
Unsuccessful Work Attempt (UWA)	A UWA is an effort to perform substantial work that was stopped or reduced below SGA after a short period (6 months or less) because of the individual's disability.
Impairment-Related Work Expense (IRWE)	An IRWE allows an individual to deduct certain work-related expenses that he or she has as a result of his or her disability that are necessary to work.

Note. Adapted from the *2007 Red Book: A Summary Guide to Employment Support for Individuals With Disabilities Under the Social Security Disability Insurance and Supplemental Security Income Programs,* SSA Pub. No. 64-030, by the Social Security Administration, 2007, Washington, DC: Author. Adapted with permission.

Extended Period of Eligibility. Once an SSDI beneficiary has completed his or her TWP, the Extended Period of Eligibility (EPE) begins. During this 36-month period, the Social Security Administration examines whether the beneficiary can maintain employment at SGA. If the administration determines that an individual can work at SGA, his or her benefits will stop. However, there is a 2-month grace period in which the SSDI beneficiary will receive a cash benefit regardless of his or her earnings. Following the 2-month grace period, the individual will not receive a cash benefit for any month he or she earns wages at SGA. During the 36-month EPE, an individual is entitled to an SSDI benefit anytime his or her earnings are below SGA. After the EPE, in the 37th month, an SSDI beneficiary's case is closed when he or she earns more than SGA. During this time, the individual has to reapply for SSDI benefits or request an expedited reinstatement of benefits.

Unsuccessful Work Attempt. The Social Security Administration created an unsuccessful work attempt for individuals who engaged in employment for 6 months or less but had to stop working or earned below SGA levels because of their disability. If the individual demonstrates that he or she stopped working because of his or her disability, the administration may consider that the individual had an unsuccessful work attempt and will not count earnings during this time period. For example, if an individual's earnings exceed SGA levels for a 3-month period, he or she will not receive an SSDI benefit for those months. If, however, the individual stops working because of his or her disability, the administration may consider the work attempt unsuccessful, and the individual is entitled to SSDI benefits for the months he or she earned wages at SGA levels.

Impairment-Related Work Expense. The IRWE for SSDI beneficiaries functions in the same way as it does for SSI beneficiaries in that it allows individuals to deduct the cost of certain impairment-related items and services that they need in order to work. The primary difference, however, is that an SSDI beneficiary deducts IRWE expenses from his or her monthly gross wages. This deduction, therefore, may decrease the earnings for an individual to a level that does not exceed SGA levels.

Summary

Students with disabilities face a number of challenges as they prepare to transition from school to employment. In order to address the unique employment challenges individuals with disabilities face, different employment alternatives have emerged. The flow-through model was created to teach individuals with disabilities prevocational skills in facilities-based settings. Research has consistently demonstrated, however, that individuals with severe disabilities can be successful in inclusive jobs. As a result, supported employment and customized employment have emerged as a viable strategy to support individuals with disabilities in obtaining meaningful, paid employment.

There are a number of federal work incentives that are designed to help an individual work without substantially reducing the amount of his or her monthly cash benefit. The Social Security Administration administers both the Supplemental Security Income and the Social Security Disability Insurance programs for people with disabilities. Each of these programs provides eligible beneficiaries with a monthly cash benefit. Paid employment can decrease the amount the individual receives. Since many people with disabilities rely on this income, the administration created specific work incentives that allow an individual to obtain valuable work experiences without substantially reducing his or her cash benefit.

Focus Question Review

Focus Question 1: Describe some of the problems associated with the flow-through model of employment.

- Prevocational training does not accurately predict inclusive employment success.
- Individuals do not generalize skills learned in segregated settings to inclusive settings.
- Individuals do not learn appropriate social skills.

Focus Question 2: Describe the defining characteristics of supported employment.

- Supported employment is paid, competitive work in inclusive environments for individuals with significant support needs.
- Supported employment uses consumer-driven, person-centered planning to determine an individual's career preferences.
- A job coach assists the supported employee with job development, job training, and extended support.

Focus Question 3:   Describe the defining characteristics of customized employment.

- Customized employment seeks to establish a mutual relationship between the job seeker and an employer by carving, modifying, restructuring, or negotiating a specific job.
- Customized employment is used in self-determination training, discovery, negotiation, job training, and follow-along to support an individual with a disability in finding customized jobs.

Focus Question 4: What is the primary difference between SSI and SSDI?

- SSI is an entitlement program administered by the Social Security Administration. It provides a monthly cash benefit to eligible beneficiaries with disabilities, and it is not based on the individual's prior work history. SSDI is a program that provides a monthly cash benefit to eligible beneficiaries with disabilities for individuals who have a prior work history.

CHAPTER 16

Transition to Postsecondary Education

JOHN MCDONNELL

SHARLENE A. KIUHARA

MARGARET COLLIER

In a study examining the benefits of postsecondary education, Baum and Payea (2005) concluded that "higher education does pay. It yields a high rate of return for students from all racial/ethnic groups, for men and for women, for those from all family backgrounds. It also delivers a high rate of return for society. We all benefit from both the public and the private investment in higher education" (p. 8). Research has consistently shown that *any* college experience produces meaningful improvements in quality of life for individuals in terms of annual income, the amount earned over a lifetime, access to health care, access to pensions and retirement accounts, and perception of well-being (Baum & Ma, 2007).

Window 16-1

College Is a Reality for Rachel

Rachel attends a 2-year college located in a rural community. Her life is pretty much like that of any other college student. She goes to classes, has a part-time job, and hangs out with her friends. Although she is living at home now, she is planning on moving into the

---

dorm next year and sharing a room with her friend April. Rachel loves to cook and work in the kitchen, so she is hoping to be able to get a full-time job working in a restaurant after she graduates.

This semester, Rachel is enrolled in a ceramics class and a culinary arts class. Her ceramics class meets in the afternoon on Tuesday and Thursday, and her culinary arts class meets in the morning 4 days a week. She goes to the student recreation center twice a week to work out. She also enjoys going to the football and basketball games with her friends. She works part-time at a restaurant in town preparing the salad bar during dinner. Her parents' home is close to the campus, so she is able to walk back and forth from school, and she rides to work with a friend.

During the summer, Rachel's mom helped her enroll as a nonmatriculated student at the college. Prior to the beginning of the fall semester, Rachel and her special education teacher met with an advisor from the disabilities support services office at the college to establish her eligibility for accommodations under the Americans with Disabilities Act and to identify the accommodations that she would request from her professors. The special education teacher worked with the service learning office on campus to identify an educational coach who could help her with getting around campus and provide support to help her complete course assignments. The coach meets with Rachel and her special education teacher once a week to identify additional supports that she might need during the upcoming week. In addition, the disability support services staff worked with Rachel's professors to identify another student in her classes to take notes and provide other supports as necessary to help her complete class activities.

Staff members from the high school program trained Rachel to do her job at the restaurant, and they provide ongoing support and monitoring to make sure that she is successful. The staff members also meet with Rachel daily at the library to help her learn a budgeting system and to use her checking account so she can manage her own money when she moves into the dorm.

Like most young adults in college, Rachel loves her independence and is excited about her future.

Beyond the benefits to individuals and society as a whole, it is becoming increasingly clear that postsecondary education is no longer a luxury but a necessity in obtaining productive employment. For example, in 1959 only 20% of workers needed at least some college for their jobs, and by 2000 that number had increased to 56% (Carnevale & Fry, 2000). More recently, the Bureau of Labor Statistics projected that by 2016 the number of jobs that require only short-term on-the-job training will decline and the proportion of jobs requiring at least some level of postsecondary training will grow (Dohm & Shniper, 2007). Further, it has been estimated that 80% of new careers in the 21st century will require some postsecondary education (Macabe, 2000). Clearly, access to postsecondary education must become a viable alternative for individuals with intellectual and developmental disabilities if they are going to successfully transition from school to adulthood.

Unfortunately, the available data suggest that the majority of students with disabilities do not access postsecondary education, and the proportion of students with intellectual and developmental disabilities who are enrolled in postsecondary courses or programs is even more dismal (Newman, 2005). Data from the National Longitudinal Transition Study-2 indicate that only about 15% of students with intellectual disabilities and 16% of students with multiple disabilities enrolled in any postsecondary education classes following graduation (Newman). These rates of attendance are significantly lower than those of their peers without disabilities. Further, it appears that neither students with intellectual and developmental disabilities nor their parents identify postsecondary education as a realistic option following graduation. Nearly 83% of parents of students participating in NLTS2 indicated that their child would probably or definitely not attend postsecondary education following school. Only about 27% of the students participating in the study listed attending a postsecondary school or program as a postschool transition goal in their Individualized Education Program.

The discrepancy between the critical need for postsecondary education for successful transition to adulthood and the postschool experiences of young adults with disabilities has prompted a number of researchers and school districts to begin to create programs that provide these opportunities to students (Grigal, Neubert, & Moon, 2001). This chapter will discuss the current state of postsecondary education (subsequently referred to as college) for students with intellectual and developmental disabilities. It will also summarize the research to date on the factors that influence the effectiveness of college programs for students. Finally, the chapter will outline key considerations in preparing students for transition to college programs.

Postsecondary Programs

It is not uncommon for young adults with intellectual and developmental disabilities to continue to attend comprehensive high schools past their 18th birthday. Unfortunately, the structure and organization of many high school programs are frequently incompatible with the educational needs of older students. For example, it is widely accepted that young adults should receive regular instruction in community-based employment settings to prepare for their transition to work (Benz, Yovanoff, & Doren, 1997; McDonnell, Mathot-Buckner, & Ferguson, 1996; Phelps & Hanley-Maxwell, 1997; Wehman, 2006). Yet the typical schedule used in comprehensive high schools does not allow students or staff the flexibility necessary to effectively provide this instruction. Similarly, it is recommended that students develop friendships and other social relationships that will allow them to be fully included in adult social networks (Chadsey & Shelden, 1998; McDonnell et al., 1996; Wehman, 2006). However, the limited access that these young adults have to same-age peers in the high school often makes it difficult, if not impossible, to foster the development of age-appropriate relationships.

The growing concern over the inability of typical high schools to meet the unique needs of this group of students has led a number of advocates, researchers, and professional organizations to call for the development of programs that will promote these students' access to technical/vocational schools, colleges, and universities (Doyle, 2003; Fisher, Sax, & Pumpian, 1999; Grigal et al., 2001; Halpern, 1994; McDonnell et al., 1996; Patton et al., 1996; Smith & Puccini, 1995; Tashie, Malloy, & Lichtenstein, 1998; Wehman, 2006). As for other young adults, having access to these settings would create opportunities for students to acquire the knowledge and skills necessary for productive employment, establish their independence and autonomy from their parents and families, and develop the social relationships that are required to support their full participation in community life. Consequently, these settings are ideal for meeting the transition needs of 19- to 22-year-old students.

Focus Question 1	What are the potential advantages of dual enrollment college programs for students with intellectual and developmental disabilities?

The primary approach used by school districts to support the access to and participation in college of students with intellectual and developmental disabilities is dual enrollment programs (Hoffman, 2005; Grigal et al., 2001; Hart, Zimbrich, & Parker, 2005; Jordan, Cavalluzzo, & Corallo, 2006). In these programs, students are simultaneously enrolled in secondary programs provided by their school district and in courses offered by the college. While the original intent of dual enrollment programs was to provide challenging educational opportunities to advanced high school students, such programs are now also being used to meet the needs of students who are at risk for dropping out of high school and to help ease the transition to college for students who have disabilities (Barnett, Gardner, & Bragg, 2004; Hoffman, 2005). These types of programs exist in 18 states, but eligibility, tuition requirements, funding streams, and program features vary widely from state to state (Weiss, 2005). Typically, the school district bears the primary costs for providing services to the students with disabilities under IDEA. However, in many programs this support is supplemented by the state department of vocational rehabilitation, the mental retardation/developmental disabilities agency, and the college's disability support service program.

Stodden and Whelley (2004) describe three different dual enrollment models that have been used to support students' participation in postsecondary education: substantially separate models; mixed models; and inclusive, individualized support models. Substantially separate models are located on college campuses, but the programs are often housed separately and students do not matriculate into recognized certificate, licensure, or degree programs. The curriculum used by these programs focuses on providing community-based instruction on personal management, leisure, and employment skills. In essence, students are physically present on the college campus, but their interactions with students without disabilities are limited, and they are typically not included in the natural social networks of the campus. Mixed program models provide separate community-based programming for students but make attempts to increase students' presence on the campus by including students in campus activities and supporting students' participation in selected courses that are compatible with their postschool goals. Finally, the inclusive, individualized support model is designed to maximize students' access and participation in recognized certificate, license, or degree programs. Community-based instruction is provided to students, but it is delivered around their course schedule and campus activities. Hart, Mele-McCarthy, Pasternack, Zimbrich, and Parker (2004) conducted a national survey of 25 dual enrollment programs and found that 13 (52%) used the mixed model; 8 (32%) used the inclusive, individualized model; and 4 (16%) used the separate model.

The available research suggests that participation in college programs has a number of positive outcomes for students with intellectual and developmental disabilities (Dolyniuk et al., 2002; Grigal et al., 2001; Hall, Kleinert, & Kearns, 2000; McDonnell, Ferguson, & Mathot-Buckner, 1992; Page & Chadsey-Rusch, 1995; Park, Hoffman, Whaley, & Gonsier-Gerdin, 2001; Tashie et al., 1998; Zafft, Hart, & Zimbrich, 2004). For example, Zafft and colleagues (2004) reported the results of a comprehensive evaluation of a mixed model dual enrollment program called the College Career Connection (CCC) Program. The CCC Program included student-centered planning to identify goals and the establishment of an interagency Student Support Team to develop individualized support services for each student. Twenty students participating in the CCC Program were compared with

20 students in a traditional high school program. The two groups of students were matched on age, gender, ethnicity, school/district, and disability. The researchers found that the CCC Program had a number of positive impacts on employment outcomes for students. For example, all of the students in the CCC Program were in paid employment, compared with 43% of the students attending traditional secondary programs. Students in the CCC Program also worked more hours and received higher wages than the employed students in the traditional secondary program.

Legislative Foundations for Postsecondary Education

The federal laws that affect a student's participation in postsecondary education are the Individuals with Disabilities Education Act (PL 108–446); the Rehabilitation Act of 1973, Section 504 (PL 93–112); the Americans with Disabilities Act (PL 101–336); and the Family Educational Rights and Privacy Act (FERPA; PL 93–380). IDEA remains the controlling statute for a student's educational program as long as he or she is receiving special education services under IDEA from a local education agency (LEA). In most states, students with intellectual and developmental disabilities are eligible for services under IDEA through their 21st or 22nd birthday. The majority of college programs for 19- to 22-year-old students are provided through dual enrollment programs by the LEAs. Consequently, students have the same rights and access to services that they would have if they were attending a comprehensive high school.

It is important to note, however, that postsecondary education institutions are not bound by IDEA; instead, their services to students with disabilities are governed by Section 504 of the Rehabilitation Act, ADA, and FERPA. These laws are designed to ensure equal access and treatment to students with disabilities but do not require postsecondary education institutions to provide the kind of educational services mandated under IDEA. Students, parents, and school professionals must understand that if a student graduates or exits the school system, he or she loses the protections and services offered through IDEA. At that point, the primary protections for equal access and treatment in postsecondary institutions are embedded within Section 504 of the Rehabilitation Act, ADA, and FERPA.

Students are not automatically eligible for accommodations under Section 504 or ADA. A key principle underlying these bills is that it is the individual's responsibility to disclose his or her disability and to self-advocate for the accommodations he or she needs to participate in courses or certification, license, or degree programs. Further, colleges are not required to provide all accommodations or supports requested by the student but only "reasonable" accommodations and supports necessary for the student to meet the essential functions of the course or program of study in which he or she is enrolled. The following sections provide a brief description of the protections provided to students according to these laws.

The Rehabilitation Act of 1973, Section 504

Section 504 and the regulations that govern its implementation essentially require that individuals with disabilities be provided with an equal opportunity to achieve the same result, earn the same benefit, or attain the same level of achievement as their peers without disabilities in the most integrated setting that meets their needs. Section 504 mandates that no program or activity that receives federal funding may discriminate against or deny benefits to any individual based on his or her disability. Subpart E of the regulations requires that colleges adapt academic methods or procedures that do not discriminate against individuals with disabilities. However, colleges are not required to modify the requirements that are essential to the integrity of a course or program of study or the essential elements of licensing or accreditation programs. Further, colleges are not required to change the processes that they use to evaluate a student's performance in a course or a certificate, license, or degree program. What colleges are required to do is provide the accommodations necessary to ensure students' equal access to and opportunities to benefit from the course or program of study.

Focus Question 2	With what general protections and rights are vocational/technical schools, colleges, or universities required to provide students with disabilities under ADA?

Americans with Disabilities Act

The Americans with Disabilities Act extends the protections under Section 504 of the Rehabilitation Act. It is organized into five separate titles, each dealing with different arenas of public life ranging from employment to telecommunications. Titles II and III are the most relevant to the participation of individuals with disabilities in college. Title II prohibits state and local government entities from discriminating against individuals with disabilities. Title II explicitly states that no qualified individual with a disability can be denied the benefits of services, programs, or activities of a public entity.

Consequently, this title applies to state-funded technical/vocational schools, colleges, and universities. Title III mandates that privately owned businesses that serve the public may not discriminate on the basis of disability. The title ensures that individuals with disabilities have full and equal access to goods, services, and facilities of private business that serve the public. Consequently, this title would apply to private colleges and universities.

Window 16-2

Accommodations Under ADA

The Office for Civil Rights identifies accommodations as "academic adjustments":

> Academic adjustments may include auxiliary aids and modifications to academic requirements as are necessary to ensure equal educational opportunity. Examples of such adjustments are arranging for priority registration; reducing a course load; substituting one course for another; providing note takers, recording devices, sign language interpreters, extended time for testing and, if telephones are provided in dorm rooms, a TTY in your dorm room; and equipping school computers with screen-reading, voice recognition or other adaptive software or hardware. (U.S. Department of Education, Office for Civil Rights, 2005, pp. 2–3)

It is important to understand that the definition of disabilities is different under ADA than under IDEA. So it is possible that a student who was eligible for special education services under IDEA during high school might not be eligible for accommodations under ADA. The opposite is also true. A student who was not eligible for special education services during high school could be eligible for accommodations under ADA in college. The ADA requires postsecondary educational institutions to allow students with disabilities to meet the requirements of certificate, license, or degree programs with "reasonable accommodations." As indicated above, institutions are not required to change the integrity of the program or the criteria used to evaluate a student's performance in the program. ADA and its related regulations provide a detailed definition of what constitutes a "reasonable accommodation." Consequently, it is important that students work closely with the college's disabilities support services office to establish their eligibility for accommodations under ADA and to identify the specific accommodations that they can use to complete the requirements of specific courses or programs.

Family Educational Rights and Privacy Act

FERPA mandates that a student's disclosure of a disability to a postsecondary education institution and his or her educational records remain confidential. The law outlines the conditions and circumstances under which information included in a student's educational record may be released. It is important for students and parents to understand that under FERPA, control of the information in the educational record transfers to the student at the age of majority (i.e., 18 years) or when he or she attends a postsecondary education institution beyond high school. This requirement is also part of IDEA, and it highlights the need for students with intellectual and developmental disabilities and their parents to address the issue of guardianship prior to the student's 18th birthday. Parents must understand that once the rights to information transfer to the student, they can no longer have access to the student's records unless the student gives his or her permission to the institution. In most cases, the institution will require written permission from the student or his or her parents to release information in the educational record. However, the law does allow for the release of some information in the student's educational records to school officials, accrediting bodies, and state and local officials under specific conditions.

Characteristics of Successful Postsecondary Programs

A number of innovative approaches to transition programs at the college level for students with intellectual and developmental disabilities have been described in the literature over the last decade (Doyle, 2003; Hall et al., 2000; McDonnell et al., 1992; Page & Chadsey-Rusch, 1995; Park et al., 2001; Pearman, Elliott, & Aborn, 2004; Zafft et al., 2004). For example, Pearman and colleagues discuss a partnership between the Southwest Special Education Local Plan Area (SELPA) and El Camino College in Torrance, California. The program was designed to serve students with disabilities between the ages of 18 and 22 years. The 12 school districts within the Southwest SELPA pooled their resources to develop and support a postsecondary program at El Camino College. One of the school districts assumed responsibility for operating the program on behalf of the Southwest SELPA and the other cooperating school districts. Students enroll in classes based on their postschool goals, and specific support plans are developed to help them succeed. In addition, the program supports students' participation in the recreational and social activities of the campus, employment training and placement, and training on key community living and life skills.

Doyle (2003) describes a program located at Trinity College, a private 4-year college in Vermont. Trinity College partnered with local high schools to create a program for college-age students with intellectual and developmental disabilities. The program initially began as a self-contained class located on the campus but, over the years, evolved into an inclusive, individualized support program designed to promote students' participation in all aspects of college life. The program adopted many of the curriculum and instructional strategies used to support students in general education classes in typical high schools to support their participation in college courses. The program also implemented strategies to promote the students' involvement in the social activities and networks of the college. The supports that students received were based on an individualized plan developed cooperatively between the high school and the college.

These two programs illustrate the kind of innovative thinking that is happening in many school districts across the country. The number of postsecondary programs for students with intellectual and developmental disabilities continues to grow as students and their parents seek out more age-appropriate alternatives to the traditional high schools. Although these programs vary based on the needs of students, school districts, and colleges, they share a number of critical organizational features, including individualized, student-centered planning; interagency collaboration; and preparing faculty and staff to meet the needs of students with disabilities.

Individualized, Student-Centered Planning

At the heart of all successful postsecondary programs is the implementation of a student-centered approach to educational planning. The steps for developing student-centered IEPs and transition plans were discussed in Chapter 5, and the strategies for promoting self-directed planning were outlined in Chapter 6. The key for successful planning for college is that the student and members of his or her IEP/transition planning team establish a clear vision of the purpose of the college experience for the student. This vision should be directly anchored to the student's postschool goals, and the services and resources of the secondary program, the college, and other agencies should be coordinated to ensure that these goals are achieved. Although IDEA only requires that the IEP and transition plan be reviewed annually, successful college programs regularly review the IEP and transition plan in order to adjust the services provided to students. The list of activities needed for students to obtain the supports, accommodations, and services embedded in the transition plan will frequently need to be modified as students progress through their program. Finally, as students near graduation, their IEP and transition plan should be aligned with the planning documents developed by other adult service agencies that may provide services to students after they leave school. For example, Kochhar-Bryant and Izzo (2006) recommended linking secondary students' IEP/transition plan and their Individual Plan for Employment (IPE) to improve service coordination between school and vocational rehabilitation agencies.

Focus Question 3	How can interagency collaboration among secondary programs, colleges, and adult service agencies enhance the effectiveness of postsecondary programs?

Interagency Collaboration

Better alignment of supports and services within and across secondary and postsecondary environments can strengthen the transition process experienced by students with disabilities to college and community living (Stodden, Conway, & Chang, 2003). College programs require that special education, college, and community service agency staff work closely together to meet the needs of individual students and to sustain the program as a whole (Kochhar-Bryant, 2002). A common feature of successful college programs is the establishment of a local interagency team comprising representatives from the school district, the college, the vocational rehabilitation agency, and the MR/DD agency. The purpose of the team is to (a) establish policies and procedures that allow students to efficiently transition to the college campus for their educational services, (b) develop ways to pool available resources that allow students to enroll in appropriate courses and programs, (c) coordinate community-based employment and residential services provided to students, and (d) promote uninterrupted supports for employment and community life as students leave the public school system and enter the adult service system.

Preparing the College Faculty and Staff

Direct responsibility for the operation of dual enrollment programs typically falls to the special education teacher assigned to the college program and disability support service staff from the college. These individuals provide the supplemental supports and services necessary for students to succeed in specific courses and programs of study. However, it is faculty members who most significantly affect the academic success of students. In addition, college and departmental staff also play an important role in helping students navigate the demands of going to college. Getzel and Finn (2005) have argued that the long-term success of postsecondary programs hinges on developing the capacity of faculty and staff members to meet the needs of students with disabilities. This requires that the postsecondary and disability support services staff (a) seek input from faculty and staff on the most critical areas of training and technical assistance (e.g., universal design, technology); (b) create multiple opportunities for faculty and staff to gain the knowledge and skills necessary to meet the needs of students (e.g., face-to-face training, online resources); (c) establish technical assistance resources that can assist faculty and staff with putting new strategies and approaches in place; and (d) regularly evaluate the impact of the training and technical assistance activities on the acceptance by faculty and staff of students with disabilities.

Implementing College Programs

Students with intellectual and developmental disabilities are an extremely heterogeneous group with a wide range of abilities and educational needs. The dual enrollment programs discussed above have sufficient flexibility to accommodate the needs of most students. However, a key decision facing every student and his or her IEP/transition planning team is whether the student's college experience will focus on seeking admission to a recognized certificate, license, or degree program or on enrolling in selected courses that can help the student achieve his or her postschool goals in combination with other community-based instructional activities. This decision should be made as part of the transition planning process done during the development of students' IEPs/transition plans (see Chapter 5). Whatever decision is made by the IEP/transition planning team, the student must be prepared for the demands of attending college and college life. Obviously, students seeking a standard high school diploma and enrolling in a recognized certificate, license, or degree program will need to complete the preparatory classes recommended by the institution and meet the state performance standards for graduation. For students who are not seeking a standard high school diploma and are only interested in taking selected courses at the college or university, the IEP/transition planning team should carefully match the general education courses taken during high school to the demands of the courses that students will take once they are in college and that match their postschool employment and community living goals.

While taking courses in the general education curriculum is critical to successfully transitioning to college for students with intellectual and developmental disabilities, researchers are recognizing that preparatory classes alone are not sufficient to allow students to meet all of the demands of going to college (Adreon & Duroscher, 2007; Basset & Smith, 1996; Blalock & Patton, 1996; Bouck, 2004; Brinckerhoff, McGuire, & Shaw, 2002; Dunn, 1996; Sitlington, 2003; Wasburn-Moses, 2006; Zafft, Kallenbach, & Spohn,

2006). Effectively preparing students for college also requires that secondary programs address several key issues. These are (a) assessing students' readiness for postsecondary education, (b) developing survival knowledge and skills, and (c) developing an individualized support plan to maximize the benefit realized by the student from his or her participation in the program.

Assess Readiness for Postsecondary Education Programs

A critical component of preparing students for postsecondary education programs is to help them understand that there are significant differences between high school and college with regard to class time, class size, independent study time, frequency of exams, approach to grading, teaching styles, and amount of free time (Brinckerhoff et al., 2002). The student must have a clear understanding of his or her ability to meet these demands and use this information to design his or her IEP/transition plan and support plans to actively prepare for college during high school. Babbitt and White (2002) present a student questionnaire that assesses the student's readiness for postsecondary education (Figure 16.1). The topics addressed in the questionnaire include social skills, self-awareness and self-advocacy, daily functional skills, knowledge of academic modifications and accommodations, preparedness, and support considerations. The results of the questionnaire can help the IEP/transition planning team shape the student's IEP and transition plan to focus on developing needed skills and strategies for coping with college.

Figure 16.1   Student Questionnaire: Assessing Postsecondary Readiness

Name: _____ Grade: _____ Date: _____

Directions: Please put a check ✓ in the correct box: Y = Yes; N – No; NS = Not Sure; NA= Not Applicable

	Y	N	NS	NA
1. I want to continue my education after high school.				
2. I have taken the classes needed in high school to prepare me for postsecondary education.				
3. I know what type of employment I want after postsecondary education.				
4. I have reviewed information from different postsecondary institutions.				
5. I know how to use the phone book.				
6. I have met with or spoken to a representative from the postsecondary institution that I would like to attend.				
7. I know how to budget money.				
8. I have access to regular transportation.				
9. My family is helping me make plans for postsecondary education.				

	Y	N	NS	NA

10. I know how to use a course catalog.
11. I will be helping pay for postsecondary education.
12. I know how to use an ATM.
13. I need help making plans for postsecondary education.
14. I will seek assistance at the disability center at the institution I attend, if needed.
15. I will be living at home while attending a postsecondary institution.
16. I plan to have a job while attaining my postsecondary education.
17. I have health/dental/vision insurance.
18. I know where I will be living during postsecondary education.
19. I can manage a bank account.
20. I know the resources/adaptations that will help me be successful in postsecondary education.
21. I am aware that I, not my parents, need to initiate a request for services at the institution I attend.
22. I know how to apply for financial aid to continue my education.
23. I know how to obtain public assistance.
24. I will need help filling out all necessary paperwork that is required to go to a postsecondary institution.
25. I will be paying rent during my postsecondary education experience.
26. I know all the differences between high school and postsecondary education.
27. I know how to schedule an appointment.
28. I am aware of how my disability will affect me during postsecondary education.
29. I can identify the areas that I need to improve on to be successful in postsecondary education.
30. I know how to use public transportation.
31. I have a backup plan in place if I find that postsecondary education is not for me.
32. I have the skills to make new friends.
33. I have the skills to live on my own.
34. I will ask for help when I need it.
35. I know how to advocate for myself.
36. I know how to access the disability center.
37. My IEP is written to help me prepare for postsecondary education.
38. I know how to keep my personal information private.
39. I know how to obtain medical assistance.
40. I know where the post office is located.
41. I am comfortable in groups.
42. Being around new people will interfere with my learning.
43. I have the skills to use a computer or word processor.
44. I need specific tools for writing and reading. Write down your preferences:
45. My computer requires technological modifications. Write down what these are:
46. My academic assignments are modified. Write down what modifications you have:
47. Instructional methods have been modified to assist my learning. Write down what these modifications are:
48. I know my academic strengths. Write down your strengths:

(Continued)

Figure 16.1 (Continued)

	Y	N	NS	NA
49. I know my academic weaknesses. Write down your weaknesses:				
50. I need help in the following areas to be successful in postsecondary education. Write down these areas:				

Identified Areas of Concern

Social skills	32, 41, 42
Self-awareness, self-advocacy	1, 3, 18, 28, 29, 35, 48, 49
Daily functional skills	5, 8, 10, 12, 19, 23, 27, 30, 33, 39, 40
Academic modifications, accommodations, and needs	20, 36, 37, 44, 45, 46, 47
Preparedness	2, 4, 6, 26, 31, 43
Support considerations	9, 13, 15, 17, 24, 50
Employment and financial concerns	7, 11, 16, 22, 25
Responsibility	14, 21, 34, 38

Source: Adapted from "R U Reading? Helping Students Assess Their Readiness for Postsecondary Education," by B. C. Babbitt and C. M. White, 2002, *Teaching Exceptional Children, 35,* pp. 62–66. Adapted with permission.

Depending on the student's postschool goals and the accessibility of postsecondary education in his or her community or state, the IEP/transition planning team may need to help the student select a college or university that will meet his or her needs. This decision must take into account a number of factors, including the size of the school, its location and accessibility within the community, the types of support services provided to students with disabilities by the institution, and so on. Adreon and Durocher (2007) outlined areas that students and their IEP/transition planning teams should consider when selecting a college (Figure 16.2).

Window 16–3

Preparing for College

Critical skills in academic areas require students to (a) develop a repertoire of learning strategies to counterbalance their disability for reading and synthesizing college-level texts, computing algebraic problems, and writing essays and reports; (b) take notes during a lecture and apply a variety of study skills strategies; and (c) learn how to use assistive technology (Brinckerhoff et al., 2002; Crist, Jacquart, & Shupe, 2002; Mull & Sitlington, 2003; Zafft et al., 2006).

Critical skills in nonacademic areas require students to (a) develop an awareness of their academic and social strengths and weaknesses, (b) increase their ability to self-advocate to faculty and staff, (c) understand their service needs and appropriate accommodations, (d) prioritize multiple-task completion, and (e) develop problem solving, organizational, self-monitoring, and time management skills (Black & Ornelles, 2001; Brinckerhoff et al., 2002; Durlak, Rose, & Bursuck, 1994; Siperstein, 1988).

Figure 16.2   Areas to Address When Selecting a College

Issue	Considerations
1. Decide what type and size of college to attend	• Community college • 4-year university
2. Decide where the student is going to live	• Dormitory (on-campus) • Apartment (off-campus) • Do I have roommates? • Do I live alone?
3. Assess the student's independent living skills	• Budgeting • Transportation needs
4. Understand contexts in which to disclose one's disability	• Whom do I tell? • When do I tell?
5. Identify appropriate academic supports and accommodations	• Do I need a note taker? • Do I need extended time on tests? • Do I need and know how to use assistive technology?
6. Identify necessary social supports	• Do I know whom to contact in case of an emergency? • Can I introduce myself and maintain friendships? • Can I form study groups with peers in class? • Do I have a peer mentor?
7. Identify strategies to help adjust to the college environment	• Do I know where the disability center is, and have I accessed it? • Do I understand the differences between IDEA and ADA? • Do I understand the institution's policies for paying tuition, financial aid, etc.? • Do I know how to plan and cook meals?

Note. Adapted from "Evaluating the College Transition Needs of Individuals With High-Functioning Autism Spectrum Disorders," by D. Adreon and J. S. Durocher, 2007, *Intervention in School and Clinic, 42,* pp. 271–279. Adapted with permission.

Develop Related Survival Skills

While students need to acquire content knowledge and academic skills to succeed in college, they also need to develop knowledge and skills that will allow them to successfully navigate the college environment and manage the other aspects of their daily lives. Research suggests that five areas are particularly important to being a successful college student: (a) developing self-advocacy skills, (b) developing time management and study skills, (c) increasing proficiency in using technology, (d) orienting students to the campus and support services, and (e) establishing the skills necessary to cope with the demands of independent living (Brinckerhoff et al., 2002; Gajar, 1998; Getzel, Stodden, & Briel, 2001; Sitlington, 2003).

Focus Question 4   Why is teaching self-advocacy and self-determination skills so important for college-bound students with disabilities?

Develop Self-Advocacy and Self-Determination Skills. Studies of successful adults with disabilities suggest they have a clear understanding of their strengths and weaknesses and how their disabilities will affect their response to the demands of adulthood (Durlak, Rose, & Bursuck, 1994; Speckman, Goldberg, & Herman, 1992). Further, these individuals can develop specific plans to achieve their goals and are effective in advocating for themselves (Hitchings et al., 2001; Janiga & Costenbader, 2002; Sitlington, 2003). Secondary and college programs need to provide students with opportunities to develop a specific understanding of the accommodations that will be necessary for them to succeed in classes and their selected program of study. Students must also be provided with instruction on how to explain to professors the accommodations they will need to complete course and program requirements (Durlak et al., 1994; Hitchings et al., 2001; Janiga & Costenbader, 2002).

Although the ability to identify and explain their needs is critical, students must be provided with the support necessary to develop the confidence to advocate for themselves. Many students have relied on their parents or special educators to meet these functions (Janiga & Costenbader, 2002). Strategies that can be used to help students become more effective in communicating their needs and developing the self-confidence necessary to approach professors and advisors include fostering their active participation in educational planning, supporting positive interactions with general educators about their needs, and providing counseling services to assist young adults with developing realistic perceptions of their strengths and weaknesses.

Develop Time Management and Study Skills. The significant differences in the structure of classes in secondary and postsecondary education require that students develop the skills necessary to manage their time and assume more responsibility for their learning (Brinckerhoff, 1996; Gajar, 1998). This means that students must develop the ability to organize schoolwork, prioritize tasks, master study strategies that accommodate a wide range of academic tasks from memorization to synthesis and integration of knowledge, and self-monitor their academic performance. In addition, students must be prepared to cope with the pressures associated with increased levels of competition among students and reduced levels of student-teacher contact. Secondary programs should attempt to replicate these demands as students move toward graduation, providing direct instruction and support to students to develop these skills when participating in general education classes (Sitlington, 2003).

Reis, McGuire, and Neu (2000) recommend that students be taught a variety of compensatory strategies to prepare them for college. Reis and colleagues define compensatory strategies to include study strategies (note taking, test preparation, such memory strategies as flashcards or mnemonic devices, having students form study groups as a way to compare notes and clarify understanding of class content); self-regulating learning strategies (strategies that promote how to learn rather than what is to be learned); compensatory supports (tape recorders, word processing programs, books on tape or CD, spelling machines, voice-activated software programs); and testing accommodations (extended time, quiet environment, reference sheet, having directions read aloud, having a scribe). The authors also emphasize that students need to be taught how to choose a specific strategy according to the demands of a task and based on their personal preference or style.

Oliver, Hecker, Klucken, and Westby (2000) suggest that when identifying and teaching relevant learning strategies, educators should identify the following specific factors that will increase academic demands: (a) the rate of presentation (how quickly the material is presented); (b) the volume of material to be learned (how much material needs to be read per week); (c) the organization of the materials (can the information be broken down into smaller units?); (d) the complexity of the vocabulary, syntax, and ideas; (e) simultaneous processing demands (what other tasks does the student need to complete?); and (f) availability of support in terms of concepts presented in a variety of ways or materials offered in alternative formats.

Proficiency in Using Technology. Technical/vocational schools, colleges, and universities are technology-rich environments. Students must use technology to meet academic demands and navigate the administrative processes of the college. Consequently, the ability of students to use computer and other assistive technologies is recognized as a critical prerequisite skill for their transition to these settings (Anderson-Inman, Knox-Quinn, & Szymanski, 1999; Mull & Sitlington, 2003). Improving a student's ability to use technology should be based on an assessment of the demands that will be placed on him or her by the postsecondary program and the current abilities of the student (Mull & Sitlington). Once appropriate options have been identified, the student must be provided with direct instruction on the use of the technology that is designed to promote generalized application to a variety of tasks and activities (Anderson-Inman et al.).

Orientation to the Campus and Student Services. Another activity recommended to prepare students for college is to provide orientation programs for students (Durlak et al., 1994; Gajar, 1998; Hitchings et al., 2001; Sitlington, 2003). These programs are designed to assist students with becoming familiar with the campus, inform them about the programs that can provide academic and social supports, assist them with developing a program of study and enrolling in classes, and make connections with student self-help groups. School districts and colleges have used several approaches to help students learn to navigate the campus ranging from formal orientation programs that are implemented by staff from the college and other students with disabilities to summer transition programs that are designed to allow students to acclimate to the campus before the academic year begins.

Independent Living Skills. It is often assumed that students who go to college do not require instruction or support in learning to cope with the demands of home and community living (Patton, Cronin, & Jarriels, 1997; Sitlington, 2003). Not unlike their peers, many students with intellectual and developmental disabilities may struggle with the demands of increased independence and responsibility for their daily lives. Students may need instruction and support on a wide variety of skills ranging from money management and budgeting to using public transportation. This highlights the need for comprehensive transition planning that systematically addresses all of the areas in which students will need to be successful in college (Bouck, 2004; Patton et al., 1997; Sitlington, 2003).

Develop an Individualized Plan of Support

One of the advantages of dual enrollment programs is that students can receive supports from both the secondary program and the college. The plan of support should be tailored to the student and should build on his or her specific strengths and needs. There is no single mix of supports that will be appropriate for all students, but the support plans for all students should be based on several important principles:

- Students should assume as much responsibility for meeting the requirements of their program as possible.
- Students should take advantage of the academic and social supports that are typically provided to students with disabilities by the postsecondary institution. Students should be encouraged to seek out these supports on their own whenever possible.
- Secondary program staff should help students establish informal and formal peer-to-peer support strategies to assist them in meeting the demands of specific courses.
- Secondary program staff should provide direct instruction and monitoring to help students address other employment and personal management needs.

One of the first issues that should be addressed in the support plan is how the student will gain access to college and obtain the supports he or she will require to be successful. This includes applying for admission as either a matriculated or a nonmatriculated student, obtaining financial assistance, obtaining appropriate housing if necessary, obtaining a student identification card, establishing eligibility for accommodations under ADA, enrolling in courses, and paying tuition. For students with disabilities, as for their peers without disabilities, getting into college requires several months of planning and work. Most colleges and universities provide students with planning guides that can help them through the application process and assist them in getting started on campus. The IEP/transition planning team should obtain these materials and use them to help guide the development of the student's transition plan.

In addition to the requirements established by the college, the support plan should identify other areas of support that will be needed by the student and lay out the activities necessary to ensure that these supports are in place when the student begins. Establishing peer-to-peer supports is often a critical area of need for students if they are to participate successfully in courses and use the resources of the campus. The kinds of peer-to-peer supports discussed in Chapter 8 to support high school students in general education classes are appropriate for support of students in college courses. Some colleges have established formal peer support programs that identify "educational coaches" who can assist the students with completing course requirements and using campus resources. These programs are often operated through the college's service learning office. Additional support can be provided by friends and family members. Finally, secondary program staff may also provide support to students in courses and in such other activities as employment training, using public transportation, using the services at the student union, or developing a self-management and scheduling system.

Summary

Postsecondary education significantly improves the quality of life of adults. Unfortunately, students with intellectual and developmental disabilities have not had the opportunity to attend college and benefit from the academic and social experiences it provides. The need for more age-appropriate educational programs for students between the ages of 18 and 22 years has prompted a number of school districts and colleges around the country to begin to develop innovative dual enrollment programs to meet this need. One of the primary assets of college is the ability to tailor educational programs to meet students' specific needs. Dual enrollment programs need to embrace this key feature of colleges and avoid the temptation to develop a "one size fits all" approach to providing postsecondary programs to students with intellectual and developmental disabilities. College programs will need to develop individualized plans of support to maximize the benefits to each student. In addition, high schools will need to prepare students for the academic and social demands of going to college.

Focus Question Review

Focus Question 1: What are the potential advantages of dual enrollment college programs for students with intellectual and developmental disabilities?

- The age-appropriate education setting of dual enrollment college programs has the flexibility to meet the postschool goals of young adults.
- Dual enrollment college programs allow students to continue to receive services under IDEA through their 22nd birthday.
- Dual enrollment college programs provide a mechanism to pool resources of the public schools, colleges, and adult service agencies to meet the transition needs of young adults.

Focus Question 2: With what general protections and rights are vocational/technical schools, colleges, or universities required to provide students with disabilities under ADA?

- They must ensure equal access to the benefits of the services, programs, and activities provided by the college.
- They must provide reasonable accommodations to allow the student to meet the essential functions of the course or program of study.

Focus Question 3: How can interagency collaboration among secondary programs, colleges, and adult service agencies enhance the effectiveness of postsecondary programs?

- Interagency collaboration promotes a smooth transition from high school into college.
- Interagency collaboration allows for the pooling of resources to maximize the educational outcomes of college programs for students.
- Interagency collaboration promotes uninterrupted employment and residential services when students transition into community life.

Focus Question 4: Why is teaching self-advocacy and self-determination skills so important for college-bound students with disabilities?

- Research supports the idea that students who acquire self-determination skills in high school will be more likely to succeed in attaining postsecondary education.
- Self-determination fosters autonomy and independence, which are essential skills for college-level students.

References

Chapter 1

Bambara, L. M., Wilson, B. A., & McKenzie, M. (2007). Transition and quality of life. In S. L. Odom, R. D. Horner, M. E. Snell, & J. Blacher (Eds.), *Handbook of developmental disabilities* (pp. 371–389). New York: Guilford.

Centers for Medicare & Medicaid Services. (2008). *Ticket to Work and Work Incentives Improvement Act* (TWWIIA). Retrieved February 12, 2008, from http://www.cms.hhs.gov/twwiia/

Education for All Handicapped Children Act, 20 U.S.C. § 1400 *et seq.* (1975).

Elementary and Secondary Education Act, 20 U.S.C. § 6301 *et seq.* (1965).

Goals 2000: Educate America Act. 20 U.S.C. § 5801 *et seq.* (2000).

Halpern, A. (1985). Transition: A look at the foundations. *Exceptional Children, 57,* 479–486.

Hardman, M. L., & Mulder, M. (2003, November). *Federal education reform: Critical issues in public education and the impact on students with disabilities.* Paper presented at the Texas Eagle Summit on Personnel Preparation for Students with Emotional and Behavioral Disorders, Dallas, TX.

Hasazi, S. B., Furney, K. S., & Destefano, L. (1999). Implementing the IDEA transition initiatives. *Exceptional Children, 65*(4), 555–566.

Houtenville, A. (2002). *Estimates of employment rates for persons with disabilities in the U.S.* Ithaca, NY: Rehabilitation Research and Training Center for Economic Research on Employment Policy for Persons with Disabilities, Cornell University.

Hunt, P., & McDonnell, J. (2007). Inclusive education. In S. L. Odom, R. H. Horner, M. E. Snell, & J. Blacher (Eds.), *Handbook of developmental disabilities* (pp. 269–291). New York: Guilford.

Improving America's Schools Act, 20 U.S.C. § 6301 *et seq.* (1994).

Individuals with Disabilities Education Act of 2004, 20 U.S.C. § 1400 *et seq.* (2004).

Kohler, P. D. (1996). *A taxonomy for transition programming: Linking research and practice.* Champaign: Transition Research Institute, University of Illinois.

Kohler, P. D., Field, S., Izzo, M., & Johnson, J. (1999). *Transition from school to life: A workshop series for educators and transition service providers.* Washington, DC: Office of Special Education Programs, Office of Special Education and Rehabilitative Services, U.S. Department of Education.

Larkin, K. C., & Turnbull, A. (Eds.). (2005). *National goals and research.* Washington, DC: American Association on Mental Retardation.

Mank, D. (2007). Employment. In S. L. Odom, R. H. Horner, M. E. Snell, & J. Blacher (Eds.), *Handbook of developmental disabilities* (pp. 390–409). New York: Guilford.

McDonnell, J., Wilcox, B., & Boles, S. M. (1986). Do we know enough to plan for transition? A national survey of state agencies responsible for service to persons with severe handicaps. *Journal of the Association for Persons With Severe Handicaps, 11*(1), 53–60.

McLaughlin, M. J., & Tilstone, M. (2000). Standards and curriculum: The core of educational reform. In M. Rouse & M. J. McLaughlin (Eds.), *Special education and school reform in the United States and Britain* (pp. 38–65). London: Routledge.

National Commission on Excellence in Education. (1983). *A nation at risk.* Washington, DC: U.S. Department of Education.

National Council on Disability. (2000). *Back to school on civil rights.* Washington, DC: Author.

National Organization on Disability, Harris, L., & Associates. (2004). *National Organization on Disability/Harris survey of Americans with disabilities.* New York: National Organization on Disability.

No Child Left Behind Act of 2001, 20 U.S.C. § 6301 *et seq.* (2001).

President's Commission on Excellence in Special Education. (2002). *A new era: Revitalizing special education for children and their families.* Washington, DC: Education Publications Center, U.S. Department of Education.

School-to-Work Opportunities Act of 1994. Public Law 103–239, 20 U.S.C. § 6703 *et seq.* (2001).

Sebba, J., Thurlow, M. L., & Goertz, M. (2000). Educational accountability and students with disabilities in the United States and England and Wales. In M. J. McLaughlin & M. Rouse (Eds.), *Special education and school reform in the United States and Britain* (pp. 98–125). New York: Routledge.

Steere, D. E., Rose, E., & Cavaiuolo, D. (2007). *Growing up: Transition to adult life for students with disabilities.* Boston: Pearson Education.

Ticket to Work and Work Incentives Improvement Act of 1999. 20 U.S.C. § 1320b-19 *et seq.* (1999).

U.S. Department of Education. (2008). *Introduction to No Child Left Behind.* Retrieved September 25, 2008, from http://www.nclb.gov/next/overview/index.html

U.S. Department of Education, National Center for Education Statistics. (2008). *Projections of education statistics to 2016.* Retrieved February 4, 2008, from http://nces.ed.gov/programs/projections/projections2016/sec3b.asp

Vinovskis, M. A. (1999). *The road to Charlottesville: The 1989 education summit.* Washington, DC: National Education Goals Panel.

Vocational Rehabilitation Act of 1973 and its amendments, 29 U.S.C. § 794. Retrieved March 3, 2004, from http://www.ed.gov/policy/speced/reg/narrative.html?exp=0

Wagner, M., & Blackorby, J. (1996). Transition from high school to work or college: How special education students fare. *Special Education for Students With Disabilities, 6*(1), 103–120.

Wagner, M., Newman, L., Cameto, R., & Levine, P. (2005). *Changes over time in the early postschool outcomes of youth with disabilities: A report from the National Longitudinal Study (NLTS) and the National Longitudinal Transition Study-2 (NLTS2).* Menlo Park, CA: SRI International.

Will, M. (1985). OSERS programming for the transition of youth with disabilities: Bridges from school to working life. *Rehabilitation World, 9*(1), 4–7.

Workforce Investment Act of 1998. Public Law 105–220. 20 U.S.C. § 112 *et seq.* (1998).

Chapter 2

Baer, R. M., Flexer, R. W., & Dennis, L. (2007). Examining the career paths and transition services of students with disabilities exiting high school. *Education and Training in Developmental Disabilities, 42*(3), 317–329.

Bellamy, G. T., Rhodes, L. E., Borbeau, P., & Mank, D. M. (1986). Mental retardation services in sheltered workshops and day activity programs: Consumer outcomes and policy alternatives. In F. R. Rusch (Ed.), *Competitive employment: Issues and strategies* (pp. 257–272). Baltimore: Paul H. Brookes.

Berndt, T. J. (2002). Friendship quality and social development. *Current Directions in Psychological Science, 11*(1), 7–10.

Berndt, T. J. (2004). Children's friendships: Shifts over a half-century in perspectives on their development and their effects. *Merrill-Palmer Quarterly, 50*(3), 206–223.

Causton-Theoharis, J., & Malmgren, K. (2005). Building bridges: Strategies to help paraprofessionals promote peer interactions. *Teaching Exceptional Children, 37,* 18–24.

Downing, J. E., & Peckham-Hardin, K. D. (2007). Inclusive education: What makes it a good education for students with intellectual and developmental disabilities? *Research and Practice for Persons With Severe Disabilities, 32*(1), 16–30.

Field, S., & Hoffman, A. (2002). Preparing youth to exercise self-determination: Quality indicators for school environments that promote the acquisition of knowledge, skills, and beliefs related to self-determination. *Journal of Disability Policy Studies, 13,* 113–118.

Field, S., Martin, J., Miller, R., Ward, M., & Wehmeyer, M. (1998). *A practical guide for teaching self-determination.* Reston, VA: Council for Exceptional Children.

Garner, H., & Dietz, L. (1996). Person-centered planning: Maps and paths to the future. *Four Runner, 11*(2), 1–2.

Giangreco, M. F., & Broer, S. M. (2005). Questionable utilization of paraprofessionals in inclusive schools: Are we addressing symptoms or causes? *Focus on Autism and Other Developmental Disabilities, 20*(1), 10–26.

Hardman, M. L., Drew, C. J., & Egan, M. W. (2007). *Human exceptionality: School, family, and community* (9th ed.). Boston: Houghton-Mifflin.

Holburn, S., Jacobson, J. W., Vietze, P. M., Schwartz, A. A., & Sersen, E. (2000). Quantifying the process and outcomes of person-centered planning. *American Journal on Mental Retardation, 105*(5), 402–416.

Hughes, C., & Carter, E. W. (2000). *The transition handbook: Strategies high school teachers use that work!* Baltimore: Paul H. Brookes.

Kim, K., & Turnbull, A. (2004). Transition to adulthood for students with severe intellectual disabilities: Shifting toward person-family interdependent planning. *Research and Practice for Persons With Severe Disabilities, 29*(1), 53–57.

Kohler, P. D., & Field, S. (2003). Transition-focused education: Foundation for the future. *The Journal of Special Education, 37*(3), 174–183.

Kraemer, B. R., McIntyre, L. L., & Blacher, J. (2003). Quality of life for young adults with mental retardation during transition. *Mental Retardation, 41*(4), 250–262.

Martin, J., Woods, L., Sylvester, L., & Gardner, J. (2005). Inching toward self-determination: Vocational choice agreement between caregivers and individuals with severe disabilities. *Research and Practice for Persons With Severe Disabilities, 30*(3), 147–153.

Mautz, D., Storey, K., & Certo, N. (2001). Increasing integrated workplace social interactions: The effects of job modification, natural supports, adaptive communication instruction, and job coach training. *JASH, 26*(4), 257–269.

McDonnell, J., Hardman, M., & McDonnell, A. (2003). *An introduction to persons with intellectual and developmental disabilities.* Boston: Allyn & Bacon.

McDonnell, J., Mathot-Buckner, C., Thorson, N., & Fister, S. (2001). Supporting the inclusion of students with severe disabilities in typical junior high school classes: The effects of class wide peer tutoring, multi-element curriculum, and accommodations. *Education and Treatment of Children, 24*(2), 141–160.

Menchetti, B. M., & Garcia, L. A. (2003). Personal and employment outcomes of person-centered career planning. *Education and Training in Developmental Disabilities, 38*(2), 145–156.

Meyer, L. H., Peck, C. A., & Brown, L. (1991). *Critical issues in the lives of people with severe disabilities.* Baltimore: Paul H. Brookes.

Miller, M. C., Cooke, N. L., Test, D. W., & White, R. (2003). Effects of friendship circles on the social interactions of elementary age students with mild disabilities. *Journal of Behavioral Education, 12*(3), 167–184.

Neubert, D. A., & Moon, M. S. (2006). Postsecondary settings and transition services for students with intellectual disabilities: Models and research. *Focus on Exceptional Children, 39*(4), 1–8.

Phelps, L. A., & Hanley-Maxwell, C. (1997). School-to-work transitions for youth with disabilities: A review of outcomes and practices. *Review of Educational Research, 67,* 197–226.

Rubin, K. H. (2004). Three things to know about friendship. *International Society for the Study of Behavioral Development Newsletter, 46*(2), 5–7.

Rusch, F. R., & Braddock, D. (2004). Adult day programs versus supported employment (1988–2002): Spending and service practices of mental retardation and developmental disabilities state agencies. *Research and Practice for Persons With Severe Disabilities, 29*(4), 237–242.

Rynders, J. E., Schleien, S. J., & Matson, S. L. (2003). Transition for children with Down Syndrome from school to community. *Focus on Exceptional Children, 36*(4), 1–8.

Schaller, J., Yang, N. K., & Chien-Huey Chang, S. (2004). Contemporary issues in rehabilitation counseling: Interface with and implications for special education. In A. M. Sorrells, H. J. Rieth, & P. T. Sindelar (Eds.), *Critical issues in special education: Access, diversity, and accountability* (pp. 226–242). Boston: Pearson Education.

Schwartz, A. A., Holburn, S. C., & Jacobson, J. W. (2000). Defining person-centeredness: Results of two consensus methods. *Education and Training in Mental Retardation and Developmental Disabilities, 35*(3), 235–249.

Stancliffe, R. J., Abery, B. H., & Smith, J. (2000). Personal control and the ecology of community living settings: Beyond living-unit size and type. *American Journal on Mental Retardation, 105*(6), 431–454.

Taylor, S. (1988). Caught in the continuum: A critical analysis of the principle of the Least Restrictive Environment. *Journal of the Association for Persons With Severe Handicaps, 13,* 41–53.

Terman, D. L., Larner, M. B., Stevenson, C. S., & Behrman, R. E. (1996). Special education for students with disabilities: Analysis and recommendations. *Future of Children, 6,* 4–24.

Test, D. W., Carver, T., Ewers, L., Haddad, J., & Person, J. (2000). Longitudinal job satisfaction of persons in supported employment. *Education and Training in Mental Retardation and Developmental Disabilities, 35*(4), 365–373.

Test, D. W., Mason, C., Hughes, C., Konrad, M., Neale, M., & Wood, W. M. (2004). Student involvement in individualized education program meetings. *Exceptional Children, 70*(4), 391–412.

University of Illinois at Chicago National Research and Training Center. (2003). *Self-determination framework for people with psychiatric disabilities.* Chicago, IL: Author. Retrieved May 20, 2003, from http://www.psych.uic.edu/UICNRTC/s dframework.pdf

Walker, P. (1999). From community presence to sense of place: Community experiences of adults with developmental disabilities. *Journal of the Association for Persons With Severe Handicaps, 24,* 23–32.

Wehman, P. (2006). Integrated employment: If not now, when? If not us, who? *Research and Practice for Persons With Severe Disabilities, 31*(2), 122–126.

Wehman, P., Revell, W. G., & Brooke, V. (2003). Competitive employment: Has it become the "first choice" yet? *Journal of Disability Policy Studies, 14*(3), 163–173.

Wehmeyer, M. L., & Schalock, R. L. (2001). Self-determination and quality of life: Implications for special education services and support. *Focus on Exceptional Children, 33*(8), 1–20.

West, M. D., Wehman, P. B., & Wehman, P. (2005). Competitive employment outcomes for persons with intellectual and developmental disabilities: The national impact of the Best Buddies Jobs Program. *Journal of Vocational Rehabilitation, 23,* 51–63.

White, J., & Weiner, J. S. (2004). Influence of least restrictive environment and community based training on integrated employment outcomes for transitioning students with severe disabilities. *Journal of Vocational Rehabilitation, 21,* 149–156.

Wood, W. M., Karvonen, M., Test, D. W., Browder, D., & Algozzine, B. (2004). Promoting student self-determination skills in IEP planning. *Teaching Exceptional Children, 36*(3), 8–16.

Chapter 3

Arnett, J. J. (2000). Emerging adulthood: A theory of development from the late teens through the twenties. *American Psychologist, 55,* 469–480.

Baer, R. M., Flexer, R. W., & Dennis, L. (2007). Examining the career paths and transition services of students with disabilities exiting high school. *Education and Training in Developmental Disabilities, 42*(3), 317–329.

Baker, E. T., Wang, M. C., & Walberg, H. J. (1994–1995). The effects of inclusion on learning. *Educational Leadership, 52,* 33–35.

Bambara, L. M., Wilson, B. A., & McKenzie, M. (2007). Transition and quality of life. In S. L. Odom, R. H. Horner, M. E. Snell, & J. Blacher (Eds.), *Handbook of developmental disabilities* (pp. 371–389). New York: Guilford.

Benz, M. R., Lindstrom, L., & Yovanoff, P. (2000). Improving graduation and employment outcomes of students with disabilities: Predictive factors and student perspectives. *Exceptional Children, 66,* 509–529.

Bouck, E. C. (2004). State of curriculum for secondary students with mild mental retardation. *Education and Training in Developmental Disabilities, 39,* 169–176.

Brolin, D. E. (1997). *Career education: A competency-based approach* (5th ed.). Balston, VA: Council for Exceptional Children.

Carter, E. W., & Hughes, C. (2005). Increasing social interaction among adolescents with intellectual disabilities and their general education peers: Effective interventions. *Research and Practice for Persons With Intellectual and Developmental Disabilities, 30*(4), 179–193.

Carter, E. W., & Hughes, C. (2006). Including high school students with intellectual and developmental disabilities in general education classes: Perspectives of general and special educators, paraprofessionals, and administrators. *Research and Practice for Persons With Intellectual and Developmental Disabilities, 31,* 174–185.

Carter, E. W., & Kennedy, C. H. (2006). Promoting access to the general curriculum using peer support strategies. *Research and Practice for Persons With Severe Disabilities, 31,* 284–292.

Certo, N. J., Mautz, D., Pumpian, I., Sax, C., Smalley, K., Wade, H. A., et al. (2003). Review and discussion of a model for seamless transition to adulthood. *Education and Training in Developmental Disabilities, 38*(1), 3–17.

Cole, C. M., Waldron, N., & Majd, M. (2004). Academic progress of students across inclusive and traditional settings. *Mental Retardation, 42,* 136–144.

Copeland, S. R., Hughes, C., Carter, E. W., Guth, C., Presley, J. A., Williams, C. R., & Fowler, S. E. (2004). Increasing access to general education: Perspectives of participants in a high school peer support program. *Remedial and Special Education, 25,* 342–352.

Darling-Hammond, L., Rustique-Forrester, E., & Pecheone, R. (2005). *Multiple measures approaches to high school graduation.* Stanford, CA: School Redesign Network.

DiMartino, J., & Castaneda, A. (2007). Assessing applied skills. *Educational Leadership, 64*(7), 38–42.

Downing, J. E. (2002). *Including students with intellectual and developmental and multiple disabilities in typical classrooms: Practical strategies for teachers* (2nd ed.). Baltimore: Paul H. Brookes.

Downing, J. E., & Peckham-Hardin, K. D. (2007). Inclusive education: What makes it a good education for students with severe intellectual and developmental disabilities? *Research and Practice for Persons With Intellectual and Developmental Disabilities, 32*(1), 16–30.

Field, S., & Hoffman, A. (2002). Preparing youth to exercise self-determination: Quality indicators for school environments that promote the acquisition of knowledge, skills, and beliefs related to self-determination. *Journal of Disability Policy Studies, 13,* 113–118.

Field, S., Martin, J., Miller, R., Ward, M., & Wehmeyer, M. (1998). *A practical guide for teaching self-determination.* Reston, VA: Council for Exceptional Children.

Fisher, M., & Meyer, L. H. (2002). Development and social competence after two years for students enrolled in inclusive and self-contained educational programs. *Research and Practice for Persons With Intellectual and Developmental Disabilities, 27*(3), 165–174.

Flexer, R. W., Simmons, T. J., Luft, P., & Baer, R. M. (2001). *Transition planning for secondary students with disabilities.* Upper Saddle River, NJ: Merrill/Prentice Hall.

Frank, A. R., & Sitlington, P. L. (2000). Young adults with mental disabilities: Does transition planning make a difference? *Education and Training in Mental Retardation and Developmental Disabilities, 35*(2), 119–134.

Grigal, M., Neubert, D. A., & Moon, S. M. (2002). Postsecondary options for students with significant disabilities. *Teaching Exceptional Children, 35*(2), 68–73.

Hardman, M. L., Drew, C. J., & Egan, M. W. (2007). *Human exceptionality: School, family, and community* (9th ed.). Boston: Houghton Mifflin.

Herman, J. (1997). Portfolios: Assumptions, tensions, and possibilities. *Theory and Research Into Practice, 36*(4), 196–204.

Hunt, P., & McDonnell, J. (2007). Inclusive education. In S. L. Odom, R. H. Horner, M. Snell, and J. Blacher (Eds.), *Handbook on developmental disabilities* (pp. 269–291). New York: Guilford.

Johnson, D. R., Thurlow, M. L., Cosio, A., & Bremer, C. D. (2005). Diploma options for students with disabilities. *National Center on Secondary Education and Transition Information Brief, 4*(1), 1–3. Retrieved April 27, 2008, from http://www.ncset.org/publications/info/NCSETInfoBrief_4.1.pdf

Johnson, D. R., Thurlow, M. L., & Stout, K. E. (2007). *Revisiting graduation requirements and diploma options for youth with disabilities: A national study* (Technical Report 49). Minneapolis, MN: University of Minnesota, National Center on Educational Outcomes.

Kohler, P. D., & Field, S. (2003). Transition-focused education: Foundation for the future. *The Journal of Special Education, 37*(3), 174–183.

Lewis, S. G., & Batts, K. (2005). How to implement differentiated instruction? Adjust, adjust, adjust. *Journal of Staff Development, 26*(4), 26–31.

Lichtenstein, S. (1998). Characteristics of youth and young adults. In F. R. Rusch & J. G. Chadsey (Eds.), *Beyond high school: Transition from school to work*. Belmont, CA: Wadsworth Publishing.

McDonnell, J. (2003). Secondary programs. In J. McDonnell, M. L. Hardman, & A. P. McDonnell (Eds.), *An introduction to persons with intellectual and developmental disabilities: Educational and social issues* (pp. 307–330). Boston: Allyn & Bacon.

McDonnell, J., Hardman, M., Hightower, J., & O'Donnell, R. (1991). Variables associated with in-school and after-school integration of secondary students with severe disabilities. *Education and Training in Mental Retardation, 26*, 243–257.

McDonnell, J., Hardman, M. L., & McGuire, J. (2007). Teaching and learning in secondary schools. In L. Florian (Ed.), *The handbook of special education* (pp. 378–389). London: Sage.

McDonnell, J., Johnson, J. W., & McQuivey, C. (2008). *Embedded instruction for students with developmental disabilities in general education classes*. Alexandria, VA: Division of Developmental Disabilities, Council for Exceptional Children.

McDonnell, J., Mathot-Buckner, C., & Ferguson, B. (1996). *Transition programs for students with moderate/severe disabilities*. Pacific Grove, CA: Brooks/Cole.

Miller, M. C., Cooke, N. L., Test, D. W., & White, R. (2003). Effects of friendship circles on the social interactions of elementary age students with mild disabilities. *Journal of Behavioral Education, 12*(3), 167–184.

Mortimer, J. T. (2003). *Working and growing up in America*. Cambridge, MA: Harvard University Press.

Neubert, D. A., & Moon, M. S. (2006). Postsecondary settings and transition services for students with intellectual disabilities: Models and research. *Focus on Exceptional Children, 39*(4), 1–8.

Neubert, D. A., Moon, M. S., & Grigal, M. (2002). Post-secondary education and transition services for students ages 18–21 with significant disabilities. *Focus on Exceptional Children, 34*(8), 1–11.

O'Neill, P. T. (2001). Special education and high stakes testing for high school graduation: An analysis of current law and policy. *Journal of Law and Education, 30*(2), 185–222.

Patton, J. R., Cronin, M. E., & Jarriels, V. (1997). Curricular implications of transition. *Remedial and Special Education, 18*, 294–306.

Phelps, L. A., & Hanley-Maxwell, C. (1997). School-to-work transitions for youth with disabilities: A review of outcomes and practices. *Review of Educational Research, 67*, 197–226.

Putnam, J. W. (1994). *Cooperative learning and strategies for inclusion: Celebrating diversity in the classroom*. Baltimore: Paul H. Brookes.

Riesen, T., McDonnell, J., Johnson, J. W., Polychronis, S., & Jameson, M. (2003). A comparison of constant time delay and simultaneous prompting within embedded instruction in general education classes with students with severe disabilities. *Journal of Behavioral Education, 12*(4), 241–259.

Rusch, F. R., & Millar, D. M. (1998). Emerging transition best practices. In F. R. Rusch & J. G. Chadsey (Eds.), *Beyond high school: Transition from school to work*. Belmont, CA: Wadsworth Publishing.

Salend, S. J., & Garrick-Duhaney, L. M. (1999). The impact of inclusion on students with and without disabilities and their educators. *Remedial and Special Education, 20,* 114–126.

Sapon-Shevin, M., Ayres, B. J., & Duncan, J. (1994). Cooperative learning and inclusion. In J. S. Thousand, R. A. Villa, & A. I. Nevin (Eds.), *Creativity and collaborative learning: A practical guide to empowering students and teachers* (2nd ed., pp. 45–58). Baltimore: Paul H. Brookes.

Sitlington, P. L., Clark, G. M., & Kolstoe, O. P. (2000). *Transition education and services for adolescents with disabilities* (3rd ed.). Needham Heights, MA: Allyn & Bacon.

Spooner, F., Dymond, S. K., Smith, A., & Kennedy, C. H. (2006). What we know and need to know about accessing the general curriculum for students with significant cognitive disabilities. *Research and Practice for Persons With Intellectual and Developmental Disabilities, 31*(4), 277–283.

Terman, D. L., Larner, M. B., Stevenson, C. S., & Behrman, R. E. (1996). Special education for students with disabilities: Analysis and recommendations. *Future of Children, 6,* 4–24.

Test, D. W., Mason, C., Hughes, C., Konrad, M., Neale, M., & Wood, W. M. (2004). Student involvement in individualized education program meetings. *Exceptional Children, 70*(4), 391–412.

Tomlinson, C. (1999). Mapping a route toward differentiated instruction. *Educational Leadership, 57*(1), 12–16.

Udvari-Solner, A., Villa, R. A., & Thousand, J. S. (2002). Access to the general education curriculum for all: The universal design process. In J. S. Thousand, R. A. Villa, & A. I. Nevin (Eds.), *Creativity and collaborative learning: The practical guide to empowering students, teachers, and families* (2nd ed., pp. 85–104). Baltimore: Paul H. Brookes.

Walker, P. (1999). From community presence to sense of place: Community experiences of adults with developmental disabilities. *Journal of the Association for the Severely Handicapped, 24,* 23–32.

Wehman, P. (2006a). Integrated employment: If not now, when? If not us, who? *Research and Practice for Persons With Intellectual and Developmental Disabilities, 31*(2), 122–126.

Wehman, P. (2006b). *Life beyond the classroom: Transition strategies for young people with disabilities* (4th ed.). Baltimore: Paul H. Brookes.

West, M. D., Wehman, P. B., & Wehman, P. (2005). Competitive employment outcomes for persons with intellectual and developmental disabilities: The national impact of the Best Buddies Jobs Program. *Journal of Vocational Rehabilitation, 23,* 51–63.

Williams, L. J., & Downing, J. E. (1998). Membership and belonging in inclusive classrooms: What do middle school students have to say? *Journal of the Association for the Severely Handicapped, 23*(2), 98–110.

Chapter 4

Bambara, L. M., Wilson, B. A., & McKenzie, M. (2007). Transition and quality of life. In S. L. Odom, R. H. Horner, M. E. Snell, & J. Blacher (Eds.), *Handbook of developmental disabilities* (pp. 371–389). New York: Guilford.

Bellamy, G. T., Wilcox, B., Rose, H., & McDonnell, J. (1985). Education and career preparation for youth with disabilities. *Journal of Adolescent Health Care, 6,* 125–135.

Bouck, E. C. (2004). State of curriculum for secondary students with mild mental retardation. *Education and Training in Developmental Disabilities, 39,* 169–176.

Browder, D. M., Ahlgrim-Delzell, L., Courtade-Little, G., & Snell, M. E. (2006). General curriculum access. In M. E. Snell & F. Brown (Eds.), *Instruction of students with severe disabilities* (6th ed., pp. 489–525). Upper Saddle River, NJ: Pearson.

Browder, D., Ahlgrim-Delzell, L., Flowers, C., Karvonen, M., Spooner, F., & Algozzine, R. (2005). How states implement alternate assessments for students with disabilities. *Journal of Disability Policy Studies, 15*(4), 209–220.

Browder, D., Flowers, C., Ahlgrim-Delzell, L. A., Karvonen, M., Spooner, F., & Algozzine, R. (2004). The alignment of alternate assessment content with academic and functional curricula. *The Journal of Special Education, 37,* 211–223.

Brown, L., Albright, K. Z., Rogan, P., York, J., Solner, A. U., Johnson, F., et al. (1988). An integrated curriculum model for transition. In B. L. Ludlow, A. P. Turnbull, & R. Luckasson (Eds.), *Transitions to adult life for people with mental retardation: Principles and practices* (pp. 67–84). Baltimore: Paul H. Brookes.

Brown, L., Branston, M. B., Hamre-Nietupski, S., Pumpian, I., Certo, N., & Gruenwalk, L. (1979). A strategy for developing chronologically-age-appropriate and functional curricular content for severely handicapped adolescents and young adults. *Journal of Special Education, 13,* 81–90.

Brown, L., Branston-McClean, M. B., Baumgart, D., Vincent, L., Falvey, M., & Schroder, J. (1979). Using the characteristics of current and subsequent least-restrictive environments in the development of curricular content for severely handicapped students. *AAESPH Review, 4,* 407–424.

Falvey, M. A. (1989). *Community-based curriculum: Instructional strategies for students with severe handicaps.* Baltimore: Paul H. Brookes.

Flowers, C., Browder, D., & Ahlgrim-Delzell, L. (2006). An analysis of three states' alignment between language arts and mathematics standards and alternate assessments. *Exceptional Children, 72,* 201–213.

Ford, A., Davern, L., & Schnorr, R. (2001). Learners with significant disabilities: Curricular relevance in an era of standards-based reform. *Remedial and Special Education, 22,* 214–222.

Ford, A., Schnorr, R., Meyer, L., Davern, L., Black, J., & Dempsey, P. (1989). *The Syracuse community-referenced curriculum guide for students with moderate and severe disabilities.* Baltimore: Paul H. Brookes.

Hasazi, S. B., Gordon, L. R., & Roe, C. A. (1985). Factors associated with the employment status of handicapped youth exiting high school from 1979 to 1983. *Exceptional Children, 57,* 455–469.

Horner, R. H., McDonnell, J., & Bellamy, G. T. (1986). Efficient instruction of generalized behaviors: General case programming in simulation and community settings. In R. H. Horner, L. H. Meyer, & H. D. Fredericks (Eds.), *Educating learners with severe handicaps: Exemplary service strategies* (pp. 289–314). Baltimore: Paul H. Brookes.

Hunt, P., & McDonnell, J. (2007). Inclusive education. In S. L. Odom, R. H. Horner, M. Snell, & J. Blacher (Eds.), *Handbook on developmental disabilities* (pp. 269–291). New York: Guilford.

Johnson, D. R., Stodden, R. A., Emanuel, E. J., Luecking, R., & Mack, M. (2002). Current challenges facing secondary education and transition services: What research tells us. *Exceptional Children, 68,* 519–531.

Keyes, M. W., & Owens-Johnson, L. (2003). Developing person-centered IEPs. *Intervention in School and Clinic, 38,* 145–152.

Kleinert, H. L., & Thurlow, M. L. (2001). An introduction to alternate assessment. In H. L. Kleinert & J. F. Kearns (Eds.), *Measuring outcomes and supports for students with disabilities* (pp. 1–15). Baltimore: Paul H. Brookes.

Kohl, F. L., McLaughlin, M. J., & Nagle, K. (2006). Alternate achievement standards and assessments: A descriptive investigation of 16 states. *Exceptional Children, 73,* 107–122.

Lowrey, K. A., Drasgow, E., Renzaglia, A., & Chezan, L. (2007). Impact of alternate assessments on curricula for students with severe disabilities: Purpose driven or process driven. *Assessment for Effective Intervention, 32,* 244–253.

McDonnell, J., Mathot-Buckner, C., & Ferguson, B. (1996). *Transition programs for students with moderate/severe disabilities.* Pacific Grove, CA: Brooks/Cole.

McDonnell, J., & Wilcox, B. (1987). Alternate performance strategies for individuals with severe disabilities. In B. Wilcox & G. T. Bellamy (Eds.), *A comprehensive guide to the activities catalog: An alternate curriculum for youth and adults with severe disabilities* (pp. 47–62). Baltimore: Paul H. Brookes.

McGregor, G. (2003). Standards-based reform and students with disabilities. In D. L. Ryndak & S. Alper (Eds.), *Curriculum and instruction for students with significant disabilities in inclusive settings* (pp. 32–50). Upper Saddle River, NJ: Allyn & Bacon.

McLaughlin, M. J., & Tilstone, C. (2000). Standards and curriculum: The core of educational reform. In M. Rouse & M. J. McLaughlin (Eds.), *Special education and school reform in the United States and Britain* (pp. 38–65). London: Routledge.

Neel, R. S., & Billingsley, F. F. (1989). *Impact: A functional curriculum handbook for students with moderate to severe disabilities.* Baltimore: Paul H. Brookes.

Nolette, V., & McLaughlin, M. (2005). *Accessing the general curriculum: Including students with disabilities in standards-based reform.* Thousand Oaks, CA: Corwin Press.

Patton, J. R., Cronin, M. E., & Jarriels, V. (1997). Curricular implications of transition. *Remedial and Special Education, 18,* 294–306.

Perske, R. (1972). The dignity of risk and the mentally retarded. *Mental Retardation, 10,* 24–27.

Rosenthal-Malek, A., & Bloom, A. (1998). Beyond acquisition: Teaching generalization for students with developmental disabilities. In A. Hilton & R. Ringlaben (Eds.), *Best and promising practices in developmental disabilities* (pp. 139–155). Austin, TX: Pro-Ed.

Sitlington, P. L. (2003). Postsecondary education: The other transition. *Exceptionality, 11,* 103–113.

Thompson, S. J., Quenemoen, R. F., Thurlow, M. L., & Ysseldyke, J. E. (2001). *Alternate assessment for students with disabilities.* Thousand Oaks, CA: Corwin Press.

U.S. Department of Education. (2005). *Alternate achievement standards for students with the most significant cognitive disabilities: Non-regulatory guidance.* Washington, DC: Author.

U.S. Department of Education. (2007a). *Modified academic achievement standards: Non-regulatory guidance.* Washington, DC: Author.

U.S. Department of Education. (2007b). *Standards and assessments peer review guide: Information and examples for meeting requirements of the No Child Left Behind Act of 2001.* Washington, DC: Author.

Wakeman, S. Y., Browder, D. M., Meier, I., & McColl, A. (2007). The implications of No Child Left Behind for students with developmental disabilities. *Mental Retardation and Developmental Disabilities Research Reviews, 13,* 143–150.

Wehman, P. (2001). *Life beyond the classroom: Transition strategies for young people with disabilities.* Baltimore: Paul H. Brookes.

Wilcox, B., & Bellamy, G. T. (1982). *Design of high school programs for severely handicapped students.* Baltimore: Paul H. Brookes.

Wilcox, B., & Bellamy, G. T. (1987). *The activities catalog: An alternative curriculum for youth adults with severe disabilities.* Baltimore: Paul H. Brookes.

Chapter 5

Abery, B., & Stancliffe, R. (1996). The ecology of self-determination. In D. J. Sands & M. L. Wehmeyer (Eds.), *Self-determination across the life-span: Independence and choice for people with disabilities* (pp. 111–146). Baltimore: Paul H. Brookes.

Aspel, N., Bettis, G., Quinn, P., Test, D. W., & Wood, W. W. (1999). A collaborative process for planning transition services for students with disabilities. *Career Development for Exceptional Individuals, 22,* 21–42.

Baer, R. (2008). Transition planning. In R. W. Flexer, R. M. Baer, P. Luft, & T. J. Simmons (Eds.), *Transition planning for students with disabilities* (pp. 317–339). Upper Saddle River, NJ: Pearson.

Benz, M. R., Lindstrom, L., & Yovanoff, P. (2000). Improving graduation and employment outcomes of students with disabilities: Predictive factors and student perspectives. *Exceptional Children, 66,* 509–529.

Benz, M. R., Yovanoff, P., & Doren, B. (1997). School-to-work components that predict postschool success for students with and without disabilities. *Exceptional Children, 63,* 151–166.

Blackorby, J., & Wagner, M. (1996). Longitudinal postschool outcomes of youth with disabilities: Findings from the National Longitudinal Transition Study. *Exceptional Children, 62*(5), 399–413.

Brolin, D. (1997). *Life-centered career education: A competency based approach* (5th ed.). Reston, VA: Council for Exceptional Children.

Browder, D. M. (2001). *Curriculum and assessment for students with moderate and severe disabilities.* New York: Guilford.

Brown, F., Snell, M. E., & Lehr, D. (2006). Meaningful assessment. In M. E. Snell & F. Brown (Eds.), *Instruction of students with severe disabilities* (pp. 71–112). Upper Saddle River, NJ: Pearson.

Chambers, C. R., Hughes, C., & Carter, E. W. (2004). Parent and sibling perspectives on adulthood. *Education and Training in Developmental Disabilities, 39,* 79–94.

Clark, G. M., & Patton, J. R. (2007). *Transition planning inventory.* Austin, TX: Pro-Ed.

Collet-Klingenberg, L. L. (1998). The reality of best practices in transition: A case study. *Exceptional Children, 65,* 67–78.

Cooney, B. F. (2002). Exploring perspectives on transition of youth with disabilities: Voices of young adults, parents, and professionals. *Mental Retardation, 40,* 425–435.

Craddock, G., & Scherer, M. J. (2002). Assessing individual needs for assistive technology. In C. L. Sax & C. A. Thoma (Eds.), *Transition assessment: Wise practices for quality lives* (pp. 87–101). Baltimore: Paul H. Brookes.

deFur, S. (1999). *Transition planning: A team effort.* NICHCY Publication No. TS10 (pp. 1–24). Washington, DC: National Information Center for Children and Youth With Disabilities.

deFur, S. H., Todd-Allen, M., & Getzel, E. E. (2001). Parent participation in the transition planning process. *Career Development for Exceptional Individuals, 24,* 19–36.

Etscheidt, S. K. (2006). Progress monitoring: Legal issues and recommendations for IEP teams. *Teaching Exceptional Children, 38*(3), 56–60.

Falvey, M. A., Forest, M., Pearpoint, J., & Rosenberg, R. L. (1993). *All my life's a circle: Using the tools of circles, MAPS and PATH.* Toronto: Inclusion Press.

Forest, M., Pearpoint, J., & Snow, J. (1992). *The inclusion papers.* Toronto: Inclusion Press.

Frank, A. R., & Sitlington, P. L. (2000). Young adults with mental disabilities: Does transition planning make a difference? *Education and Training in Mental Retardation and Developmental Disabilities, 35,* 119–134.

Grigal, M., Test, D. W., Beattie, J., & Wood, W. M. (1997). An evaluation of transition components of individualized education programs. *Exceptional Children, 63,* 357–372.

Halpern, A. S., Herr, C. M., Doren, B., & Wolf, N. H. (2000). *Next step: Student transition and educational planning.* Austin, TX: Pro-Ed.

Hasazi, S. B., Furney, K. S., & Destefano, L. (1999). Implementing the IDEA transition mandates. *Exceptional Children, 65,* 555–566.

Hunt, P., Soto, G., Maier, J., & Doering, K. (2003). Collaborative teaming to support students at risk and students with severe disabilities in general education classrooms. *Exceptional Children, 69*(3), 315–332.

Individuals with Disabilities Education Act of 2004, Public Law 108–446, 20 U.S.C. § 1414(d)(1)(A) (2004).

Johnson, D. R., & Sharpe, M. N. (2000). Results of a national survey on the implementation transition services requirements of IDEA of 1990. *Journal of Special Education Leadership, 13,* 5–26.

Johnson, D. R., Stodden, R. A., Emanuel, E. J., Lueking, R., & Mack, M. (2002). Current challenges facing secondary education and transition services: What the research tells us. *Exceptional Children, 68*(4), 519–531.

Johnson, L. J., Zorn, D., Tam, B. K. Y., LaMontagne, M., & Johnson, S. A. (2003). Stakeholders' views of factors that impact successful interagency collaboration. *Exceptional Children, 69*(2), 195–209.

Kim, K., & Morningstar, J. E. (2005). Transition planning involving culturally and linguistically diverse families. *Career Development for Exceptional Individuals, 29,* 92–103.

Kochhar-Bryant, C. A., & Izzo, M. V. (2006). Access to post-high school services: Transition assessment and the Summary of Performance. *Career Development for Exceptional Individuals, 29,* 70–89.

Kohler, P. D. (1993). Best practices in transition: Substantiated or implied? *Career Development for Exceptional Individuals, 16,* 107–121.

Lindstrom, L., Doren, B., Metheny, J., Johnson, P., & Zane, C. (2007). Transition to employment: Role of the family in career development. *Exceptional Children, 73*(3), 348–366.

McDonnell, J., Mathot-Buckner, C., & Ferguson, B. (1996). *Transition programs for students with moderate/severe disabilities.* Pacific Grove, CA: Brooks/Cole.

Merchant, D. J., & Gajar, A. (1997). A review of the literature on self-advocacy components in transition programs of students with learning disabilities. *Journal of Vocational Rehabilitation, 8,* 223–231.

Miller, R. J., Lombard, R. C., & Corbey, S. A. (2007). *Transition assessment: Planning transition and IEP development for youth with mild to moderate disabilities.* Boston: Pearson.

Miner, C. A., & Bates, P. E. (1997). The effect of person centered planning activities on the IEP/transition planning process. *Education and Training in Mental Retardation and Developmental Disabilities, 32,* 105–112.

Mount, B., & Zwernick, K. (1988). *It's never too early, it's never too late: A booklet about personal futures planning.* Minneapolis, MN: Metropolitan Council.

Murray School District. (2003). *The big picture planning process.* Murray, Utah: Author.

Phelps, L. A., & Hanley-Maxwell, C. (1997). School-to-work transitions for youth with disabilities: A review of outcomes and practices. *Review of Educational Research, 67,* 197–226.

Rainforth, B., & York-Barr, J. (1997). *Collaborative teams for students with severe disabilities: Integrating therapy and educational services* (2nd ed.). Baltimore: Paul H. Brookes.

Rueda, R., Monzo, L., Shapiro, J., Gomez, J., & Blacher, J. (2005). Cultural models of transition: Latina mothers of young adults with developmental disabilities. *Exceptional Children, 71,* 401–414.

Rusch, F. R., & Millar, D. M. (1998). Emerging transition best practices. In F. R. Rusch & J. G. Chadsey (Eds.), *Beyond high school: Transition from school to work* (pp. 36–59). Belmont, CA: Wadsworth.

Sitlington, P. L., Neubert, D., Begun, W., LeConte, W., & Lombard, R. (1996). *Assess for success: Handbook for transition assessment.* Reston, VA: Council for Exceptional Children.

Test, D. W., Mason, C., Hughes, C., Konrad, M., Neale, M., & Wood, W. M. (2004). Student involvement in individualized program meetings. *Exceptional Children, 70,* 391–412.

Thoma, C. A., Rogan, P., & Baker, S. R. (2001). Student involvement in transition planning: Unheard voices. *Education and Training in Mental Retardation and Developmental Disabilities, 36,* 16–29.

Thousand, J., & Villa, R. (2000). Collaborative teaming: A powerful tool for school restructuring. In R. A. Villa & J. S. Thousand (Eds.), *Restructuring for caring and effective education: Piecing the puzzle together* (2nd ed., pp. 254–291). Baltimore: Paul H. Brookes.

Trach, J., & Shelden, D. (2000). Meeting attendance and transition outcomes as reflected in students' individualized education programs. In D. R. Johnson & E. J. Emanuel (Eds.), *Issues influencing the future of transition programs and services in the United States* (pp. 137–152). Minneapolis: University of Minnesota.

Turnbull, A. P., & Turnbull, H. R. (2001). Self-determination for individuals with significant cognitive disabilities and their families. *Journal of the Association for Persons With Severe Handicaps, 26*(1), 56–62.

Vandercook, T., York, J., & Forest, M. (1989). The McGill Action Planning System (MAPS): A strategy for building the vision. *Journal of the Association for Persons With Severe Handicaps, 14,* 205–215.

Wagner, M., Newman, L., Cameto, R., & Levine, P. (2005). *Changes over time in the early postschool outcomes of youth with disabilities. A report of findings from the National Longitudinal Transition Study (NLTS) and the National Longitudinal Transition Study-2 (NLTS2).* Menlo Park, CA: SRI International. Available at www.nlts2.org/reports/2005_06/nlts2_report_2005_06_complete.pdf

Wehman, P. (2006). *Life beyond the classroom: Transition strategies for young people with disabilities* (4th ed.). Baltimore: Paul H. Brookes.

Williams, J. M., & O'Leary, E. (2001). What we've learned and where we go from here. *Career Development for Exceptional Individuals, 24*(1), 51–71.

Chapter 6

Agran, M., & Hughes, C. (2008). Asking student input: Students' opinions regarding their individualized education program involvement. *Career Development for Exceptional Individuals, 31,* 69–76.

Arndt, S., Konrad, M., & Test, D. (2006). Effects of the self-directed IEP on student participation in the planning meetings. *Remedial and Special Education, 27,* 194–207.

Field, S., Martin, J., Miller, R., Ward, M., & Wehmeyer, M. (1998). Self-determination for persons with disabilities: A position statement of the division of career development and transition. *Career Development for Exceptional Individuals, 21,* 113–128.

Izzo, M., & Lamb, P. (2002). *Self-determination and career development: Skills for successful transition to postsecondary education and employment.* Unpublished manuscript.

Konrad, M. (2008). 20 ways to involve students in the IEP process. *Intervention in School and Clinic, 43,* 236–239.

Langone, J., Clees, T., & Oxford, M. (1995). Acquisition and generalization of social skills by high school students with mild mental retardation. *Mental Retardation, 33,* 186–196.

Malian, I., & Nevin, A. (2002). A review of self-determination literature. *Remedial & Special Education, 23,* 9–19.

Martin, J., Marshall, L., Maxson, L., & Jerman, P. (1997). *Self-directed IEP.* Longmont, CO: Sopris West.

Martin, J., Van Dycke, J., Christensen, W., Greene, B., Gardner, J., & Lovett, D. (2006). Increasing student participation in IEP meetings: Establishing the Self-Directed IEP as an evidence-based practice. *Exceptional Children, 72,* 299–316.

Martin, J., Van Dycke, J., Greene, B., Gardner, J., Woods, L., & Lovett, D. (2006). Direct observation of teacher-directed IEP meetings: Establishing the need for student IEP meeting instruction. *Exceptional Children, 72,* 187–200.

Mason, C., Field, S., & Sawilowsky, S. (2004). Implementation of self-determination activities and student participation in IEPs. *Exceptional Children, 70,* 441–451.

Mason, C., McGahee-Kovac, M., & Johnson, L. (2004). How to help students lead their IEP meetings. *Teaching Exceptional Children, 36,* 18–24.

McGahee, M., Mason, C., Wallace, T., & Jones, J. (2001). *Student-led IEPs: A guide for student involvement.* Arlington, VA: Council for Exceptional Children.

Sands, S., & Wehmeyer, M. (1996). *Self-determination across the life span: Independence and choice for people with disabilities.* Baltimore: Paul H. Brookes.

Test, D., Fowler, C., Brewer, D., & Wood, E. (2005). A content and methodological review of self-advocacy intervention studies. *Exceptional Children, 72,* 101–125.

Test, D., Fowler, C., Wood, E., Brewer, D., & Eddy, S. (2005). A conceptual framework of self-advocacy for students with disabilities. *Remedial and Special Education, 26,* 43–54.

Wehmeyer, M., Agran, M., & Hughes, C. (1998). *Teaching self-determination to students with disabilities: Basic skills for successful transition.* Baltimore: Paul H. Brookes.

Wehmeyer, M., Kelchner, K., & Richards, S. (1996). Essential characteristics of self-determination behavior of individuals with mental retardation. *American Journal on Mental Retardation, 100,* 632–642.

Wehmeyer, M., & Palmer, S. (2003). Adult outcomes for students with cognitive disabilities three years after high school: The impact of self-determination. *Education and Training in Developmental Disabilities, 38,* 131–144.

Wehmeyer, M., Palmer, S., Agran, M., Mithaug, D., & Martin, J. (2000). Promoting causal agency: The Self-Determined Learning Model of Instruction. *Exceptional Children, 66,* 439–453.

Wehmeyer, M., Palmer, S., Soukup, J., Garner, N., & Lawrence, M. (2007). Self-determination and student transition planning knowledge and skills: Predicting involvement. *Exceptionality, 15,* 31–44.

Wood, W., Karvonen, M., Test, D., Browder, D., & Algozzine, B. (2004). Promoting student self-determination skills in IEP planning. *Teaching Exceptional Children, 36,* 8–15.

Chapter 7

Bailey, D. B., McWilliam, R. A., Darkes, L. A., Hebbeler, K., Simionsson, R. J., Spiker, D., et al. (1998). Family outcomes in early intervention: A framework for program evaluation and efficacy research. *Exceptional Children, 64*(3), 313–329.

Balli, S., Demo, D. H., & Wedman, J. F. (1998). Family involvement with children's homework: An intervention in the middle grades. *Family Relations, 47*(2), 149–157.

Barrera, I. (2000). Honoring differences: Essential features of appropriate ECSE services for young children from diverse sociocultural environments. *Young Exceptional Children, 3*(4), 17–24.

Barrera, I., & Corso, R. M. (with MacPherson, D.). (2003). *Skilled dialogue: Strategies for responding to cultural diversity in early childhood.* Baltimore: Paul H. Brookes.

Barrera, I., & Kramer, L. (1997). From monologues to skilled dialogues: Teaching the process of crafting culturally competent early childhood environments. In P. J. Winton, J. A. McCollum, & C. Catlett (Eds.), *Reforming personnel preparation in early intervention: Issues, models, and practical strategies* (pp. 217–251). Baltimore: Paul H. Brookes.

Beach Center on Disability. (2008). *How do I implement participant direction of funding and supports and services in my state or area?* Retrieved July 5, 2008, from http://www.beachcenter.org/resource_library/beach_resource_detail_page.aspx?ResourceID=1754&Type=tip

Blue-Banning, M., Summers, J. A., Frankland, H. C., Nelson, L. L., & Beegle, G. (2004). Dimensions of family and professional partnerships: Constructive guidelines for collaboration. *Exceptional Children, 70*(2), 167–184.

Buckley, J., Mank, D., & Sandow, D. (1990). Developing and implementing support strategies. In F. R. Rusch (Ed.), *Supported employment: Model, methods, and issues* (pp. 131–144). Sycamore, IL: Sycamore Publishing.

Butterworth, J., Hagner, D., Heikkinen, B., Farris, S., DeMello, S., & McDonough, K. (1993). *Whole life planning: A guide for organizers and facilitators.* Boston: Children's Hospital and University of Massachusetts.

Callahan, K., Rademacher, J. A., & Hildreth, B. K. (1998). The effect of parent participation in strategies to improve the homework performance of students who are at risk. *Remedial and Special Education, 19,* 131–141.

Chambers, C., Hughes, C., & Carter, E. (2004). Parent and sibling perspectives on the transition to adulthood. *Education and Training in Developmental Disabilities, 39,* 79–94.

Chavkin, N. F., Gonzalez, J., & Rader, R. (2002). A home-school program in Texas-Mexico border school: Voices from parents, students, and school staff. *School Community Journal, 10*(2), 127–137.

Cooney, B. (2002). Exploring perspective on transition of youth with disabilities: Voices of young adults, parents, and professionals. *Mental Retardation, 40,* 425–435.

Cooper, H. M., Lindsay, J. J., & Nye, B. (2000). Homework in the home: How student, family, and parenting-style differences relate to the homework process. *Contemporary Educational Psychology, 25*(4), 464–487.

Council for Exceptional Children. (2001). Improving family involvement in special education. *Research Connections in Special Education, 91,* 1.

Dehyle, D., & LeCompte, M. (1994). Cultural differences in child development: Navajo adolescents in middle school. *Theory Into Practice, 33*(3), 156–166.

Elliott, G., & Feldman, S. (1990). Capturing the adolescent experience. In S. Feldman & G. Elliott (Eds.), *At the threshold: The developing adolescent* (pp. 1–13). Cambridge, MA: Harvard University Press.

Falbo, T., Lein, L., & Amador, N. A. (2001). Parental involvement during the transition to high school. *Journal of Adolescent Research, 16,* 511–529.

Ferguson, P. M., & Ferguson, D. L. (2000). The promise of adulthood. In M. E. Snell & F. Brown (Eds.), *Instruction of students with severe disabilities* (5th ed., pp. 629–656). Upper Saddle River, NJ: Prentice Hall.

Ferguson, P. M., Ferguson, D. L., Jeanchild, L., Olson, D., & Lucyshyn, J. (1993). Angles of influence: Relationships among families, professionals, and adults with severe disabilities. *Journal of Vocational Rehabilitation, 3*(2), 14–22.

Finn, J. D. (1998). Parental engagement that makes a difference. *Educational Leadership, 55*(8), 20–24.

Giangreco, M. F., Cloninger, C. J., & Iverson, V. S. (1998). *COACH: Choosing Outcomes and Accommodations for Children: A guide to educational planning for students with disabilities* (2nd ed.). Baltimore: Paul H. Brookes.

Gollnick, D. M., & Chinn, P. C. (2002). *Multicultural education in a pluralistic society* (6th ed.). Upper Saddle River, NJ: Merrill/Prentice Hall.

Gonzalez, A. R. (2002). Parental involvement: Its contribution to high school students' motivation. *The Clearing House, 7*(3), 132–134.

Greene, G. (1996). Empowering culturally and linguistically diverse families in the transition planning process. *Journal for Vocational Special Needs Education, 19,* 26–30.

Hall, E. T. (1976). *Beyond culture.* Garden City, NY: Anchor Books.

Hanley-Maxwell, C., Pogoloff, S. M., & Whitney-Thomas, J. (1998). Families: The heart of transition. In F. R. Rusch & J. G. Chadsey, *Beyond high school: Transition from school to work* (pp. 234–263). Belmont, CA: Wadsworth.

Hanline, M. F. (1993). Facilitating integrated preschool service delivery transitions for children, families and professionals. In C. A. Peck, S. L. Odom, & D. D. Bricker (Eds.), *Integrating young children with disabilities into community programs* (pp. 133–146). Baltimore: Paul H. Brookes.

Harris, K. (2005). Guardianship is not self-determination. *TASH Connections, 31*(9/10), 1–3.

Harry, B. (1992). *Cultural diversity, families, and the special education system: Communication and empowerment.* New York: Teachers College Press.

Harry, B. (1997). Leaning forward or bending over backwards: Cultural reciprocity in working with families. *Journal of Early Intervention, 21,* 62–72.

Harry, B. (2008). Collaboration with culturally and linguistically diverse families: Ideal versus reality. *Exceptional Children, 74,* 372–388.

Hecht, M. L., Andersen, P. A., & Ribeau, S. A. (1989). The cultural dimensions of nonverbal communication. In M. K. Asante & W. B. Gudykunst (Eds.), *Handbook of international and intercultural communication* (pp. 163–185). Beverly Hills, CA: Sage.

Henderson, A. T., & Berla, N. (Eds.). (1994). *A new generation of evidence: The family is critical to student achievement.* Washington, DC: Center for Law and Education.

Hoyle, D. (2005). Eliminating the pervasiveness of guardianship. *TASH Connections 31*(9/10), 4–5.

Hutchins, M. P., & Renzaglia, A. (1998, March/April). Interviewing families for effective transition to employment. *Teaching Exceptional Children, 30*(4), 72–78.

Joe, J. R., & Malach, R. S. (2004). Families with American Indian roots. In E. W. Lynch & M. J. Hanson (Eds.), *Developing cross-cultural competence: A guide for working with children and their families* (3rd ed.). Baltimore: Paul H. Brookes.

Jordan, B., & Dunlap, G. (2001). Construction of adulthood and disability. *Mental Retardation, 39*(4), 286–296.

Kalyanpur, M., & Harry, B. (1999). *Culture in special education: Building reciprocal family-professional relationships.* Baltimore: Paul H. Brookes.

Keith, T. Z., Keith, P. B., Quirk, K. J., Sperduto, J., Santillo, S., & Killings, S. (1998). Longitudinal effects of parent involvement on high school grades: Similarities and differences across gender and ethnic groups. *Journal of School Psychology, 36,* 335–363.

Kim, K., & Turnbull, A. (2004). Transition to adulthood for students with severe intellectual disabilities: Shifting toward person-family interdependent planning. *Research and Practice for Persons With Severe Disabilities, 29,* 53–57.

Koenigsburg, J., Garet, M., & Rosenbaum, J. (1994). The effect of family on the job exits of young adults. *Work and Occupation, 21,* 33–63.

Kraemer, B. R., & Blacher, J. (2001). Transition for young adults with severe mental retardation: School preparation, parent expectations, and family involvement. *Mental Retardation, 39*(6), 423–435.

Lake, J. F., & Billingsley, B. S. (2000). An analysis of factors that contribute to parent-school conflict in special education. *Remedial and Special Education, 21*(4), 240–251.

Levinson, D., Darrow, C., Klein, E., Levinson, M., & McKee, B. (1978). *The seasons of a man's life.* New York: Alfred A. Knopf.

Lichtenstein, S. (1998). Characteristics of youth and young adults. In F. R. Rusch & J. G. Chadsey (Eds.), *Beyond high school: Transition from school to work* (pp. 3–35). Belmont, CA: Wadsworth.

Luft, P. (2008). Multicultural and collaborative competencies for working with families. In R. W. Flexor, R. M. Baser, P. Luft, & T. J. Simmons (Eds.), *Transition planning for secondary students with disabilities* (3rd ed., pp. 54–81). Columbus, OH: Pearson Merrill Prentice Hall.

Lynch, E. W. (1998). Developing cross-cultural competence. In E. W. Lynch & M. J. Hanson (Eds.), *Developing cross-cultural competence: A guide for working with children and their families* (2nd ed., pp. 23–46). Baltimore: Paul H. Brookes.

Lynch, E. W. (2004). Developing cross-cultural competence. In E. W. Lynch & M. J. Hanson (Eds.), *Developing cross-cultural competence: A guide for working with children and their families* (3rd ed., pp. 41–78). Baltimore: Paul H. Brookes.

Lynch, E. W., & Hanson, M. J. (1993). Changing demographics: Implications for training in early intervention. *Infants and Young Children, 6,* 50–55.

Lynch, E. W., & Hanson, M. J. (2004). *Developing cross-cultural competence: A guide for working with children and their families* (3rd ed.). Baltimore: Paul H. Brookes.

McDonnell, A. P., & Hardman, M. L. (2003). Multicultural and diversity issues. In J. J. McDonnell, M. L. Hardman, & A. P. McDonnell (Eds.), *An introduction to persons with moderate and severe disabilities: Emotional and social issues* (2nd ed., pp. 94–137). Boston: Allyn & Bacon.

McHugh, M. (2003). *Special siblings: Growing up with someone with a disability.* Baltimore: Paul H. Brookes.

Mount, B. (1992). *Person-centered planning: Finding directions for change using personal futures planning.* New York: Graphic Futures.

Mount, B. (1995). Benefits and limitations of personal futures planning. In V. Bradley, J. Ashbough, & B. Blaney (Eds.), *Creating individual supports for people with developmental disabilities* (pp. 97–108). Baltimore: Paul H. Brookes.

Nieto, S. (2000). *Affirming diversity: The sociopolitical context of multicultural education* (3rd ed.). New York: Longman.

O'Brien, J., & Lovett, H. (1992). *Finding a way toward everyday lives: The contribution of person centered planning.* Harrisburg: Pennsylvania Department of Public Welfare, Office of Mental Retardation.

O'Brien, J., & Lyle, C. (1987). *Framework for accomplishment.* Decatur, GA: Responsive Systems Associates.

Ohtake, Y., Santos, R. M., & Fowler, S. A. (2000). It's a three-way conversation: Families, service providers, and interpreters working together. *Young Exceptional Children, 4,* 12–18.

Pachter, L. M. (1994). Culture and clinical care: Folk illness beliefs and behaviors and their implications for health care delivery. *Journal of the American Medical Association, 271,* 690–694.

Payne-Christiansen, E. M., & Sitlington, P. L. (2008). Guardianship: Its role in the transition process for students with developmental disabilities. *Education and Training in Developmental Disabilities, 43,* 3–19.

Preto, N. G. (1999). Transformation of the family system during adolescence. In B. Carter & M. McGoldrick (Eds.), *The expanded family life cycle: Individual, family, and social perspectives* (3rd ed.). Needham Heights, MA: Allyn & Bacon.

Resource Foundation for Children with Challenges. (2000). *Guardianship for the adult child.* Accessed April 4, 2008, from http://www.specialchild.com/archives/ ia-025.html

Roberts, R. N., Barclay-McLaughlin, G., Cleveland, J., Colston, W., Malach, R., Mulvey, L., et al. (1990). *Developing culturally competent programs for families of children with special needs.* Logan: Utah State University, Early Intervention Research Institute, Developmental Center for Handicapped Persons. (Prepared by Georgetown University Child Development Center, Washington, DC.)

Saleebey, D. (1996). The strengths perspective in social work practice: Extensions and cautions. *Social Work, 41*(3), 296–306.

Salomone, P. R. (1996). Career counseling and job placement: Theory and practice. In E. M. Szymanski & R. M. Parkers (Eds.), *Work and disability: Issues and strategies in career development and job placement* (pp. 365–420). Austin, TX: Pro-Ed.

Santos, R. M., & Chan, S. (2004). In E. W. Lynch & M. J. Hanson (Eds.), *Developing cross-cultural competence: A guide for working with children and their families* (3rd ed., pp. 299–344). Baltimore: Paul H. Brookes.

Shaver, A. V., & Walls, R. T. (1998). Effect of Title I parent involvement on student reading and mathematics achievement. *Journal of Research and Development in Education, 31*(2), 90–97.

Sheehey, P. H., & Sheehey, P. E. (2007). Elements for successful parent-professional collaboration: The fundamental things apply as time goes by. *TEACHING Exceptional Children Plus, 4*(2), Article 3. Retrieved May 15, 2008, from http://escholarship.bc.edu/education/tecplus/vol4/iss2/art3

Smith, T. E. C., Gartin, B. C., Murdick, N. L., & Hilton, A. (2006). *Families and children with special needs: Professional and family partnerships.* Upper Saddle River, NJ: Pearson Merrill Prentice Hall.

SRI International. (2005). *Family involvement in the educational development of youth with disabilities: A special topic report of the findings from the National Longitudinal Transition Study-2 (NLTS2)* (report prepared for the Office of Special Education Programs, U.S. Department of Education). Menlo Park, CA: SRI International.

Steere, D. E., Rose, E., & Cavaiuolo, D. (2007). *Growing up: Transition to adult life for students with disabilities.* Boston: Pearson-Allyn & Bacon.

Sturm, L., & Gahagan, S. (1999). Cultural issues in provider-parent relationships. In D. B. Kessler & P. Dawson (Eds.), *Failure to thrive and pediatric undernutrition: A transdisciplinary approach* (pp. 351–374). Baltimore: Paul H. Brookes.

Thorin, E., Yovanoff, P., & Irvin, L. (1996). Dilemmas faced by families during their young adults' transitions to adulthood: A brief report. *Mental Retardation, 34,* 117–120.

Timmons, J., Whitney-Thomas, J., McIntyre, J., Butterworth, J., & Allen, D. (2004). Managing service delivery systems and the role of parents during their children's transitions. *Journal of Rehabilitation, 70,* 19–26.

Turnbull, A. P., Summers, J. A., & Brotherson, M. J. (1984). *Working with families with disabled members: A family systems approach.* Lawrence: University of Kansas, Kansas Affiliated Facility.

Turnbull, A. P., Summers, J. A., & Brotherson, M. J. (1986). Family life cycle: Theoretical and empirical implications and future directions for families with mentally retarded members. In J. J. Gallagher & P. M. Vietze (Eds.), *Families of handicapped persons: Research, programs, and policy issues* (pp. 25–44). Baltimore: Paul H. Brookes.

Turnbull, A. P., & Turnbull, H. R. (2001). Self-determination within a culturally responsive family systems perspective: Balancing the family mobile. In L. E. Powers, G. H. Singer, & J. A. Sowers (Eds.), *On the road to autonomy promoting self-competence among children and youth with disabilities* (pp. 195–200). Baltimore: Paul H. Brookes.

Turnbull, A., Turnbull, R., Erwin E. J., & Soodak, L. C. (2006). *Families, professionals, and exceptionality: Positive outcomes through partnerships, and trust* (5th ed.). Upper Saddle River, NJ: Merrill Prentice Hall.

U.S. Census Bureau. (2000). *Profile of general demographics.* Retrieved August 18, 2008, from http://www.census.gov/Press-Release/www/2002/demoprofiles.html

U.S. Census Bureau. (2004). *American community survey—race.* Washington, DC: U.S. Department of Commerce, U.S. Census Bureau.

Vandercock, T., York, J., & Forest, M. (1989). The McGill Action Planning System (MAPS): A strategy for building the vision. *Journal of the Association for Persons With Severe Handicaps, 23,* 5–16.

Varnet, T. (2006). *Guardianship.* Accessed April 4, 2008, from Tuberous Sclerosis Alliance Web site at http://www.tsalliance.org/pages.aspx?content=62

Vaughn, S., Bos, C. S., & Schumm, J. S. (1997). *Teaching mainstreamed, diverse, and at-risk students.* Boston: Allyn & Bacon.

Wehman, P. (1998). *Developing transition plans.* Austin, TX: Pro-Ed.

Wehmeyer, M. L., Morningstar, M., & Husted, D. (1999). *Family involvement in transition planning and implementation* (Transition Series). Austin, TX: Pro-Ed.

Wehmeyer, M. L., & Schalock, R. L. (2001). Self-determination and quality of life: Implications for special education services and supports. *Focus on Exceptional Children, 33*(8), 1–16.

Westling, D. L., & Fox, L. (2008). *Teaching students with severe disabilities* (4th ed.). Upper Saddle River, NJ: Merrill Prentice Hall.

Whitechurch, G. G., & Constantine, L. L. (1993). Systems theory. In P. G. Boss, W. J. Doherty, R. LaRossa, W. R. Schumm, & S. K. Steinmetz (Eds.), *Sourcebook of family theories and methods: A contextual approach* (pp. 325–352). New York: Plenum.

Chapter 8

Agran, M., Sinclair, T., Alper, S., Cavin, M., Wehmeyer, M., & Hughes, C. (2005). Using self-monitoring to increase following-direction skills of students with moderate to severe disabilities in general education. *Education and Training in Developmental Disabilities, 40,* 3–13.

Baker, E. T., Wang, M. C., & Walberg, H. J. (1994–1995). The effects of inclusion on learning. *Educational Leadership, 52,* 33–35.

Bambara, L. M., Wilson, B. A., & McKenzie, M. (2007). Transition and quality of life. In S. L. Odom, R. H. Horner, M. E. Snell, & J. Blacher (Eds.), *Handbook of developmental disabilities* (pp. 371–389). New York: Guilford.

Benz, M. R., Lindstrom, L., & Yovanoff, P. (2000). Improving graduation and employment outcomes of students with disabilities: Predictive factors and student perspectives. *Exceptional Children, 66,* 509–529.

Berry, R. A. W. (2006). Inclusion, power, and community: Teachers and students interpret the language of community in an inclusion classroom. *American Educational Research Journal, 43,* 489–529.

Broer, S. M., Doyle, M. B., & Giangreco, M. F. (2005). Perspectives of students with intellectual disabilities about the experiences with paraprofessional support. *Exceptional Children, 71,* 415–430.

Brown, L., Branston, M. B., Hamre-Nietupski, A., Pumpian, I., Certo, N., & Gruenwald, L. A. (1979). A strategy for developing chronological age-appropriate and functional curricular content for severely handicapped adolescents and young adults. *Journal of Special Education, 13,* 81–90.

Burnstein, N., Sears, S., Wilcoxen, A., Cbello, B., & Spagna, M. (2004). Moving toward inclusive practices. *Remedial and Special Education, 25,* 104–116.

Carter, E. W., Cushing, L. S., Clark, N. M., & Kennedy, C. H. (2005). Effects of peer support interventions on students' access to the general curriculum and social interactions. *Research and Practice for Persons With Severe Disabilities, 30,* 15–25.

Carter, E. W., Hughes, C., Copeland, S., & Breen, C. (2001). Differences between high school students who do and do not volunteer to participate in a peer interaction program. *Journal of the Association for Persons With Severe Handicaps, 26,* 229–239.

Carter, E. W., Hughes, C., Guth, C. B., & Copeland, S. R. (2005). Factors influencing social interaction among high school students with intellectual disabilities and their general education peers. *American Journal on Mental Retardation, 110,* 366–377.

Carter, E. W., & Kennedy, C. H. (2006). Promoting access to the general curriculum using peer support strategies. *Research and Practice for Persons With Severe Disabilities, 31,* 284–292.

Causton-Theoharis, J. N., & Malmgren, K. W. (2005). Increasing peer interactions for students with severe disabilities via paraprofessional training. *Exceptional Children, 71,* 431–444.

Chesley, G. M., & Calaluce, P. D. (2005). The deception of inclusion. In M. Byrnes (Ed.), *Taking sides: Clashing views on controversial issues in special education* (2nd ed., pp. 201–205). Dubuque, IA: McGraw-Hill/Dushkin.

Coots, J. J., Bishop, K. D., & Grenot-Scheyer, M. (1998). Supporting elementary age students with significant disabilities in general education classrooms: Personal perspectives on inclusion. *Education and Training in Mental Retardation and Developmental Disabilities, 33,* 317–330.

Cushing, L. S., & Kennedy, C. H. (2004). Facilitating social relationships in general education settings. In C. H. Kennedy & F. M. Horn (Eds.), *Including students with severe disabilities* (pp. 206–216). Boston: Allyn & Bacon.

Cushing, L. S., Kennedy, C. H., Shukla, S., Davis, J., & Meyer, K A. (1997). Disentangling the effects of curricular revision and social grouping within cooperative learning arrangements. *Focus on Autism and Other Developmental Disabilities, 12,* 231–240.

Cutts, S., & Sigafoos, J. (2001). Social competence and peer interactions of students with intellectual disability in an inclusive high school. *Journal of Intellectual and Developmental Disability, 26,* 127–141.

Devlin, P. (2005). Effects of continuous improvement training on student interaction and engagement. *Research and Practice for Persons With Severe Disabilities, 30,* 47–59.

Downing, J. E. (1996). *Including students with severe and multiple disabilities in typical classrooms: Practical strategies for teachers.* Baltimore: Paul H. Brookes.

Downing, J. E., Ryndak, D. L., & Clark, D. (2000). Paraeducators in inclusive classrooms: Their own perceptions. *Remedial and Special Education, 21,* 171–181.

Doyle, M. B. (2002). *The paraprofessional's guide to the inclusive classroom: Working as a team.* Baltimore: Paul H. Brookes.

Dugan, E., Kamps, D., Leonard, B., Watkins, N., Rheinberger, A., & Stackhaus, J. (1995). Effects of cooperative learning groups during social studies for students with autism and fourth-grade peers. *Journal of Applied Behavior Analysis, 28,* 175–188.

Dymond, S. K., Renzaglia, A., Rosenstein, A., Chun, E. J., Banks, R. A., Niswander, V., et al. (2006). Using participatory action research approach to create a universally designed inclusive high school science course: A case study. *Research and Practice for Persons With Severe Disabilities, 31,* 293–308.

Fisher, D., & Frey, N. (2001). Access to the core curriculum: Critical ingredients for student success. *Remedial and Special Education, 22,* 148–157.

Fisher, D., Sax, C., & Pumpian, I. (1999). *Inclusive high schools: Learning from contemporary classrooms.* Baltimore: Paul H. Brookes.

Ford, A., Schnorr, R., Meyer, L., Davern, L., Black, J., & Dempsey, P. (1989). *The Syracuse community-referenced curriculum guide for students with moderate and severe disabilities.* Baltimore: Paul H. Brookes.

Fredericks, H. D., Baldwin, V. L., Grove, D. N., Riggs, C., Furey, V., Moore, W., et al. (1975). *A data based classroom for the moderately and severely handicapped.* Monmouth, OR: Instructional Development Corporation.

French, N. (2003a). *Managing paraeducators in your school: How to hire, train, and supervise noncertified staff.* Thousand Oaks, CA: Corwin Press.

French, N. (2003b). Paraeducators in special education programs. *Focus on Exceptional Children, 36*(2), 1–16.

Giangreco, M. F., & Broer, S. M. (2005). Questionable utilization of paraprofessionals in inclusive schools: Are we addressing symptoms or causes? *Focus on Autism and Other Developmental Disabilities, 20,* 10–26.

Giangreco, M. F., & Broer, S. M. (2007). School-based screening to determine overreliance on paraprofessionals. *Focus on Autism and Other Developmental Disabilities, 22,* 149–158.

Giangreco, M. F., Broer, S. M., & Edelman, S. W. (2002). "That was then, this is now!" Paraprofessional supports for students with disabilities in general education classrooms. *Exceptionality, 10,* 47–64.

Giangreco, M. F., Cloninger, C. J., & Iverson, V. S. (1998). *Choosing outcomes and accommodations for children: A guide to educational planning for students with disabilities* (2nd ed.). Baltimore: Paul H. Brookes.

Giangreco, M. F., Edelman, S. W., Luiselli, T. E., & MacFarland, S. Z C. (1997). Helping or hovering? Effects of instructional assistance proximity on students with disabilities. *Exceptional Children, 64,* 7–18.

Giangreco, M. F., Edelman, S. W., & Nelson, C. (1998). Impact of planning for support services on students who are deaf-blind. *Journal of Visual Impairment and Blindness, 92,* 18–30.

Gilberts, G. H., Agran, M., Hughes, C., & Wehmeyer, M. (2001). The effects of peer delivered self-monitoring strategies on the participation of students with severe disabilities in general education classrooms. *Journal of the Association for Persons With Severe Handicaps, 26,* 25–36.

Guess, D., & Helmstetter, E. (1986). Skill cluster instruction and the Individualized Curriculum Sequencing model. In R. H. Horner, L. H. Meyer, & H. D. Fredericks (Eds.), *Educating learners with severe handicaps: Exemplary service strategies* (pp. 221–250). Baltimore: Paul H. Brookes.

Halvorsen, A. T., & Neary, T. (2001). *Building inclusive schools: Tools and strategies for success.* Boston: Allyn & Bacon.

Harper, G. F., Maheady, L., & Mallette, B. (1994). The power of peer-mediated instruction: How and why it promotes academic success for all students. In J. S. Thousand, R. A. Villa, & A. I. Nevin (Eds.), *Creativity and collaborative learning: A practical guide to empowering students and teachers* (pp. 229–242). Baltimore: Paul H. Brookes.

Harrower, J. (1999). Educational inclusion of children with severe disabilities. *Journal of Positive Behavioral Interventions, 1,* 215–230.

Horner, R. H., McDonnell, J., & Bellamy, G. T. (1986). Efficient instruction of generalized behaviors: General case programming in simulation and community settings. In R. H. Horner, L. H. Meyer, & H. D. Fredericks (Eds.), *Educating learners with severe handicaps: Exemplary service strategies* (pp. 289–314). Baltimore: Paul H. Brookes.

Hughes, C., & Carter, E. W. (2006). *Success for all students: Promoting inclusion in secondary schools through peer buddy systems.* Upper Saddle River, NJ: Allyn & Bacon.

Hughes, C., Copeland, S. R., Agran, M., Wehmeyer, M. L., Rodi, M. S., & Presley, J. A. (2002). Using self-monitoring to improve performance in general education high school classes. *Education and Training in Mental Retardation and Developmental Disabilities, 37,* 262–272.

Hunt, P., Doering, K., Hirose-Hatae, A., Maier, J., & Goetz, L. (2001). Across-program collaboration to support students with and without disabilities in general education classrooms. *Journal of the Association for Persons With Severe Handicaps, 26,* 240–256.

Hunt, P., & McDonnell, J. (2007). Inclusive education. In S. L. Odom, R. H. Horner, M. Snell, & J. Blacher (Eds.), *Handbook on developmental disabilities* (pp. 269–291). New York: Guilford.

Hunt, P., Soto, G., Maier, J., & Doering, K. (2003). Collaborative teaming to support students at risk and students with severe disabilities in general education classrooms. *Exceptional Children, 69*(3), 315–332.

Hunt, P., Soto, G., Maier, J., Muller, E., & Goetz, P. (2002). Collaborative teaming to support students with AAC needs in general education classrooms. *Augmentative and Alternate Communication, 18,* 20–35.

Hunt, P., Staub, D., Alwell, M., & Goetz, L. (1994). Achievement by all students within the context of learning groups. *Journal of the Association for Persons With Severe Handicaps, 19,* 290–301.

Jacques, N., Wilton, K., & Townsend, M. (1998). Cooperative learning and social acceptance of children with mild intellectual disabilities. *Journal of Intellectual Disability Research, 42,* 29–36.

Jameson, J. M., McDonnell, J., Polychronis, S., & Riesen, T. (2008). Training middle school peer tutors to embed constant time delay instruction for students with significant cognitive disabilities in inclusive middle school settings. *Intellectual and Developmental Disabilities, 46,* 346–365.

Janney, R., & Snell, M. E. (2000). *Modifying schoolwork.* Baltimore: Paul H. Brookes.

Janney, R. E., & Snell, M. E. (1997). How teachers include students with moderate and severe disabilities in elementary classes: The means and meaning of inclusion. *Journal of the Association for Persons With Severe Handicaps, 22,* 159–169.

Johnson, D. W., Johnson, R. T., & Holubec, E. J. (1993). *Circles of learning: Cooperation in the classroom* (4th ed.). Edina, MN: Interaction Book Company.

Jorgensen, C. M. (1998). *Restructuring high schools for all students: Taking inclusion to the next level.* Baltimore: Paul H. Brookes.

Kamps, D. M., Barbetta, P. M., Leonard, B. R., & Delquardri, J. (1994). Classwide peer tutoring: An integration strategy to improve reading skills and promote peer interactions among students with autism and general education peers. *Journal of Applied Behavior Analysis, 27,* 49–62.

Kamps, D. M., Leonard, B., Potucek, J., & Garrison-Harrell, L. (1995). Cooperative learning groups in reading: An integration strategy for students with autism and general classroom peers. *Behavioral Disorders, 21,* 80–109.

Kennedy, C. H., Cushing, L. S., & Itkonen, T. (1997). General education participation improves the social contacts and friendship networks of students with severe disabilities. *Journal of Behavior Education, 7,* 167–189.

Kennedy, C. H., Shukla, S., & Fryxell, D. (1997). Comparing the effects of educational placement on the social relationship of intermediate school students with severe disabilities. *Exceptional Children, 64,* 31–47.

King-Sears, M. E. (1999). Teacher and researcher co-design self-management content for an inclusive setting: Research training, intervention, and generalization effects on student performance. *Education and Training in Mental Retardation and Developmental Disabilities, 34,* 134–156.

Koegel, L. K., Harrower, J. K., & Koegel, R. L. (1999). Support for children with developmental disabilities in full inclusion classrooms through self-management. *Journal of Positive Behavioral Interventions, 1,* 26–34.

Lee, S. H., Amos, B. A., Gragoudas, S., Lee, Y., Shogren, K. A., Theoharis, R., et al. (2006). Curriculum augmentation and adaptation strategies to promote access to the general curriculum for students with intellectual and developmental disabilities. *Education and Training in Developmental Disabilities, 41,* 199–212.

Lipsky, D. K., & Gartner, A. (1997). *Inclusion and school reform: Transforming America's classrooms.* Baltimore: Paul H. Brookes.

Marks, S. U., Schrader, C., & Levine, M. (1999). Paraeducator experiences in inclusive settings: Helping, hovering, or holding their own? *Exceptional Children, 65,* 315–328.

McDonnell, J. (1998). Instruction for students with severe disabilities in general education settings. *Education and Training in Mental Retardation and Developmental Disabilities, 33,* 199–215.

McDonnell, J., Hardman, M. L., & McDonnell, A. P. (2003). *An introduction to persons with severe disabilities: Social and educational issues* (2nd ed.). Boston: Allyn & Bacon.

McDonnell, J., Johnson, J. W., & McQuivey, C. (2008). *Embedded instruction for students with developmental disabilities in general education classes.* Alexandria, VA: Division of Developmental Disabilities, Council for Exceptional Children.

McDonnell, J., Johnson, J. W., Polychronis, S., & Riesen, T. (2002). The effects of embedded instruction on students with moderate disabilities enrolled in general education classes. *Education and Training in Mental Retardation and Developmental Disabilities, 37,* 363–377.

McDonnell, J., Mathot-Buckner, C., Thorson, N., & Fister, S. (2001). Supporting the inclusion of students with severe disabilities in typical junior high school classes: The effects of class wide peer tutoring, multi-element curriculum, and accommodations. *Education and Treatment of Children, 24,* 141–160.

McDonnell, J., Thorson, N., Allen, C., & Mathot-Buckner, C. (2000). The effects of partner learning during spelling for students with severe disabilities and their peers. *Journal of Behavioral Education, 10,* 107–122.

McGuire, J. M., Scott, S. S., & Shaw, S. F. (2006). Universal design and its application in educational environments. *Remedial and Special Education, 27,* 166–175.

Moortweet, S. L., Utley, C. A., Walker, D., Dawson, H. L., Delquadri, J. C., Reddy, S. S., et al. (1999). Classwide peer tutoring: Teaching students with mild mental retardation in inclusive classrooms. *Exceptional Children, 65,* 524–536.

Neel, R. S., & Billingsley, F. F. (1989). *Impact: A functional curriculum handbook for students with moderate to severe disabilities.* Baltimore: Paul H. Brookes.

Park, H. S., Hoffman, S. A., Whaley, S., & Gonsier-Gerdin, J. (2001). Ted's story: Looking back and beyond. In M. Grenot-Scheyer, M. Fisher, & D. Staub (Eds.), *At the end of the day: Lessons learned in inclusive education* (pp. 151–162). Baltimore: Paul H. Brookes.

Phelps, L. A., & Hanley-Maxwell, C. (1997). School-to-work transitions for youth with disabilities: A review of outcomes and practices. *Review of Educational Research, 67,* 197–226.

Putnam, J. W. (1993). *Cooperative learning and strategies for inclusion: Celebrating diversity in the classroom.* Baltimore: Paul H. Brookes.

Rainforth, B., & England, J. (1997). Collaborations for inclusion. *Education and Treatment of Children, 20,* 85–104.

Renzaglia, A., Karvonen, M., Drasgow, E., & Stoxen, C. C. (2003). Promoting a lifetime of inclusion. *Focus on Autism and Other Developmental Disabilities, 18,* 140–149.

Roach, A. T., & Elliot, S. N. (2006). The influence of access to the general education curriculum on alternate assessment performance of students with significant cognitive disabilities. *Educational Evaluation and Policy Analysis, 28,* 181–194.

Rose, D., Meyer, A., & Hitchcock, C. (2005). *The universally designed classroom: Accessible curriculum and digital technologies.* Cambridge, MA: Harvard University Press.

Rule, S., Losardo, A., Dinnebeil, L., Kaiser, A., & Rowland, C. (1998). Translating research on naturalistic instruction into practice. *Journal of Early Intervention, 21,* 283–293.

Ryan, A. M. (2000). Peer groups as a context for the socialization of adolescents' motivation, engagement, and achievement in school. *Educational Psychologist, 35,* 101–111.

Ryndak, D. L., & Alper, S. (2003). *Curriculum and instruction for students with significant disabilities in inclusive settings.* Upper Saddle River, NJ: Allyn & Bacon.

Ryndak, D. L., Morrison, A. P., & Sommerstein, L. (1999). Literacy before and after inclusion in general education settings: A case study. *Journal of the Association for Persons With Severe Handicaps, 24,* 5–22.

Sailor, W., Halvorsen, A., Anderson, J., Goetz, L., Gee, K., Doering, K., et al. (1987). Community intensive instruction. In R. H. Horner, L. H. Meyer, & H. D. B. Fredericks (Eds.), *Education of learners with severe handicaps: Exemplary service strategies* (pp. 251–288). Baltimore: Paul H. Brookes.

Sailor, W., & Roger, B. (2005). Rethinking inclusion: Schoolwide applications. *Phi Delta Kappan, 86*(7), 503–509.

Salend, S. J., & Garrick-Duhaney, L. M. (1999). The impact of inclusion on students with and without disabilities and their educators. *Remedial and Special Education, 20,* 114–126.

Schepis, M. M., Reid, D. H., Ownbey, J., & Parsons, M. (2001). Training support staff to embed teaching within natural routines of young children with disabilities in an inclusive preschool. *Journal of Applied Behavior Analysis, 34,* 313–327.

Schumaker, J. B., & Deshler, D. D. (2006). Teaching adolescents to be strategic learners. In D. D. Deshler & J. B. Schumaker (Eds.), *Teaching adolescents with disabilities: Accessing the general education curriculum* (pp. 121–156). Thousand Oaks, CA: Corwin Press.

Schwartz, I. S., Staub, D., Peck, C. A., & Gallucci, C. (2006). Peer relationships. In M. E. Snell & F. Brown (Eds.), *Instruction of students with severe disabilities* (pp. 375–404). Upper Saddle River, NJ: Pearson.

Shapiro-Barnard, S., Tashie, C., Martin, J., Malloy, J., Schuh, J., Piet, J., et al. (2005). Petroglyphs: The writing on the wall. In M. Byrnes (Ed.), *Taking sides: Clashing views on controversial issues in special education* (2nd ed., pp. 196–200). Dubuque, IA: McGraw-Hill/Dushkin.

Shukla, S., Kennedy, C. H., & Cushing, L. S. (1998). Component analysis of peer support strategies: Adult influence on the participation of peers without disabilities. *Journal of Behavioral Education, 8,* 397–413.

Shukla, S., Kennedy, C. H., & Cushing, L. S. (1999). Intermediate school students with severe disabilities: Supporting their social participation in general education classrooms. *Journal of Positive Behavior Interventions, 1,* 130–140.

Slavin, R. E. (1995). *Cooperative learning: Theory, research, and practice* (2nd ed.). Boston: Allyn & Bacon.

Snell, M. E. (2007). Effective instructional practices. *TASH Connections, 33*(3/4), 8–11.

Snell, M. E., & Brown, F. (2006). *Instruction of students with severe disabilities.* Upper Saddle River, NJ: Pearson.

Stockall, N., & Gartin, B. (2002). The nature of inclusion in a Blue Ribbon school: A revelatory case. *Exceptionality, 10,* 171–188.

Udvari-Solner, A. (1996). Examining teacher thinking: Constructing a process to design curricular adaptations. *Remedial and Special Education, 17,* 245–254.

Villa, R. A., Thousand, J. A., Nevin, A., & Liston, A. (2005). Successful inclusive practices in middle and secondary schools. *American Secondary Education, 33,* 33–49.

Wagner, M., Newman, L., Cameto, R., Levine, P., & Marder, C. (2003). *Going to school: Instructional contexts, programs, and participation of secondary school students with disabilities.* Menlo Park, CA: SRI International.

Wallace, T., Anderson, A. R., & Bartholomay, T. (2002). Collaboration: An element associated with the success of four inclusive high schools. *Journal of Educational and Psychological Consultation, 13,* 349–381.

Wehmeyer, M. L. (2006). Universal design for learning, access to the general education curriculum and students with mild mental retardation. *Exceptionality, 14,* 225–235.

Wehmeyer, M. L., Field, S., Doren, B., Jones, B., & Mason, C. (2004). Self-determination and student involvement in standards-based reform. *Exceptional Children, 70,* 413–426.

Wehmeyer, M. L., Lattin, D. L., Lapp-Rincker, G., & Agran, M. (2003). Access to the general curriculum with middle school students with mental retardation: An observational study. *Remedial and Special Education, 24,* 262–272.

Wehmeyer, M., & Sailor, W. (2004). High school. In C. H. Kennedy & E. M. Horn (Eds.), *Including students with severe disabilities* (pp. 259–281). Upper Saddle River, NJ: Allyn & Bacon.

Wehmeyer, M. L., Yeager, D., Bolding, N., Agran, M., & Hughes, C. (2003). The effects of self-regulation strategies on goal attainment for students with developmental disabilities in general education classes. *Journal of Developmental and Physical Disabilities, 15,* 79–91.

Weiner, J. S. (2005). Peer-mediated conversational repair in students with moderate and severe disabilities. *Research and Practice for Persons With Severe Disabilities, 30,* 26–31.

Westling, D. L., & Fox, L. (2009). *Teaching students with severe disabilities.* Upper Saddle River, NJ: Merrill.

Wilcox, B., & Bellamy, G. T. (1982). *Design of high school programs for severely handicapped students.* Baltimore: Paul H. Brookes.

Wilcox, B., & Bellamy, G. T. (1987). *A comprehensive guide to the Activities Catalog: An alternative curriculum for youth and adults with severe disabilities.* Baltimore: Paul H. Brookes.

Wolery, M., Ault, M. J., & Doyle, P. M. (1992). *Teaching students with moderate to severe disabilities: Use of response prompting strategies.* New York: Longman.

Young, B., Simpson, R. L., Smith-Myles, B., & Kamps, D. M. (1997). An examination of paraprofessional involvement in supporting inclusion of students with autism. *Focus on Autism and Other Developmental Disabilities, 12,* 31–40.

Chapter 9

Albin, R., McDonnell, J., & Wilcox, B. (1987). Designing program interventions to meet activity goals. In G. T. Bellamy & B. Wilcox (Eds.), *The activities catalog: A community programming guide for youth and adults with severe disabilities* (pp. 63–88). Baltimore: Paul H. Brookes.

Albin, R. W., & Horner, R. H. (1988). Generalization with precision. In R. H. Horner, G. Dunlap, & R. L. Koegel (Eds.), *Generalization and maintenance: Life-style changes in applied settings* (pp. 99–120). Baltimore: Paul H. Brookes.

Ayres, K. M., Langone, J., Boon, J. T., & Norman, A. (2006). Computer-based instruction for purchasing skills. *Education and Training in Developmental Disabilities, 41,* 253–263.

Bambara, L. M., Wilson, B. A., & McKenzie, M. (2007). Transition and quality of life. In S. L. Odom, R. H. Horner, M. E. Snell, & J. Blacher (Eds.), *Handbook of developmental disabilities* (pp. 371–389). New York: Guilford.

Bates, P. (1980). The effectiveness of interpersonal skills training in the social skill acquisition of moderately and severely retarded adults. *The Journal of Applied Behavior Analysis, 13,* 237–248.

Baumgart, D., & Van Walleghem, J. (1986). Staffing strategies for implementing community-based instruction. *Journal of the Association for Persons With Severe Handicaps, 11,* 92–102.

Bennett, D. L., Gast, D. L., Wolery, M., & Schuster, J. (1986). Time delay and system of least prompts: A comparison in teaching manual sign production. *Education and Training of the Mentally Retarded, 21,* 117–129.

Billingsley, F. F., & Albertson, L. R. (1999). Finding a future for functional skills. *Journal of the Association for Persons With Severe Handicaps, 24,* 292–300.

Branham, R., Collins, B., Schuster, J. W., & Kleinert, H. (1999). Teaching community skills to students with moderate disabilities: Comparing combined techniques of classroom simulation, videotaped modeling, and community-based instruction. *Education and Training in Mental Retardation and Developmental Disabilities, 34,* 170–181.

Carnine, D. W., & Becker, W. C. (1982). Theory of instruction: Generalization issues. *Educational Psychology, 2,* 249–262.

Chadsey, J. (2007). Adult social relationships. In S. L. Odom, R. H. Horner, M. E. Snell, & J. Blacher (Eds.), *Handbook of developmental disabilities* (pp. 449–466). New York: Guilford.

Cihak, D. F., Alberto, P. A., Kessler, K. B., & Taber, T. A. (2004). An investigation of instructional scheduling arrangements for community-based instruction. *Research in Developmental Disabilities, 25,* 67–88.

Coon, M. E., Vogelsberg, R. T., & Williams, W. (1981). Effects of classroom public transportation instruction on generalization to the natural environment. *Journal of the Association for the Severely Handicapped, 6,* 46–53.

Cooper, J. O., Heron, T. E., & Heward, W. L. (2007). *Applied behavior analysis* (2nd ed.). Upper Saddle River, NJ: Pearson Education.

Darling-Hammond, L., Rustique-Forrester, E., & Pecheone, R. (2005). *Multiple measures approaches to high school graduation.* Stanford, CA: School Redesign Network.

DiMartino, J., & Castaneda, A. (2007). Assessing applied skills. *Educational Leadership, 64*(7), 38–42.

Ferguson, B., & McDonnell, J. (1991). A comparison of serial and concurrent sequencing strategies in teaching community activities to students with moderate handicaps. *Education and Training in Mental Retardation, 26,* 292–304.

Gaylord-Ross, R. J., Haring, T. G., Breen, C., & Pitts-Conway, V. (1984). The training and generalization of social interactions skills with autistic youth. *Journal of Applied Behavior Analysis, 17,* 229–248.

Herman, J. (1997). Portfolios: Assumptions, tensions, and possibilities. *Theory and Research Into Practice, 36*(4), 196–204.

Horner, R. H., Eberhardt, J., & Sheehan, M. R. (1986). Teaching generalized table bussing: The importance of negative examples. *Behavior Modification, 10,* 457–471.

Horner, R. H., Jones, D., & Williams, J. A. (1985). A functional approach to teaching generalized street crossing. *Journal of the Association for Persons With Severe Handicaps, 10,* 71–78.

Horner, R. H., McDonnell, J. J., & Bellamy, G. T. (1986). Teaching generalized skills: General case instruction in simulation and community settings. In R. H. Horner, L. H. Meyer, & H. D. Fredericks (Eds.), *Education of learners with severe handicaps: Exemplary service strategies* (pp. 289–314). Baltimore: Paul H. Brookes.

Horner, R. H., Sprague, J., & Wilcox, B. (1982). Constructing general case programs for community activities. In B. Wilcox & G. T. Bellamy (Eds.), *Design of high school programs for severely handicapped students* (pp. 61–98). Baltimore: Paul H. Brookes.

Horner, R. H., Williams, J. A., & Stevely, J. D. (1987). Acquisition of generalized telephone use by students with moderate and severe mental retardation. *Research in Developmental Disabilities, 8,* 229–247.

Hutcherson, K., Langone, J., Ayres, K., & Clees, T. (2004). Computer assisted instruction to item selection in grocery stores: An assessment of acquisition and generalization. *Journal of Special Education Technology, 19,* 33–42.

Kayser, J. E., Billingsley, F. F., & Neel, R. S. (1986). A comparison of in-context and traditional instructional approaches: Total task, single trial versus backward chaining, multiple trials. *Journal of the Association for Persons With Severe Handicaps, 11,* 28–38.

Marchetti, A. G., McCartney, J. R., Drain, S., Hopper, M., & Dix, J. (1983). Pedestrian skills training for mentally retarded adults: Comparison of training in two settings. *Mental Retardation, 21,* 107–110.

Marholin, D., O'Toole, K. M., Touchette, P. E., Berger, P. L., & Doyle, D. (1979). I'll have a Big Mac, large fry, large Coke, & an apple pie—or teaching community skills. *Behavior Therapy, 10,* 236–248.

McDonnell, J. (1987). The effects of time delay and increasing prompt hierarchy strategies on the acquisition of purchasing skills by students with severe handicaps. *Journal of the Association for Persons With Severe Handicaps, 12,* 227–236.

McDonnell, J., Hardman, M. L., Hightower, J., & Drew, C. J. (1993). Impact of community-based instruction on the development of adaptive behavior in secondary-level students with mental retardation. *American Journal on Mental Retardation, 97,* 575–586.

McDonnell, J., & Horner, R. H. (1985). Effects of in vivo versus simulation-plus-in vivo training on the acquisition and generalization of grocery item selection by high school students with severe handicaps. *Analysis and Intervention in Developmental Disabilities, 5,* 323–343.

McDonnell, J., Horner, R. H., & Williams, J. (1984). Comparison of three strategies for teaching generalized grocery purchasing to high school students with severe handicaps. *Journal of the Association for Persons With Severe Handicaps, 9,* 123–133.

McDonnell, J., & Laughlin, B. (1989). A comparison of backward and concurrent chaining strategies in teaching community skills. *Education and Training in Mental Retardation, 24,* 230–238.

McDonnell, J., Mathot-Buckner, C., & Ferguson, B. (1996). *Transition programs for students with moderate/severe disabilities.* Pacific Grove, CA: Brooks/Cole.

McDonnell, J., & McFarland, S. (1988). A comparison of forward and concurrent chaining strategies in teaching Laundromat skills to students with severe handicaps. *Research in Developmental Disabilities, 9,* 177–194.

McDonnell, J., & McGuire, J. (2007). Community-based instruction. In M. F. Giangreco & Mary Beth Doyle (Eds.), *Quick-guides to inclusion: Ideas for educating students with disabilities* (2nd ed., pp. 307–314). Baltimore: Paul H. Brookes.

Mechling, L. C. (2004). Effects of multimedia, computer-based instruction on grocery shopping fluency. *Journal of Special Education Technology, 19,* 23–34.

Mechling, L. C., & Cronin, B. (2006). Computer-based video instruction to teach use of augmentative and alternate communication devices for ordering at fast-food restaurants. *The Journal of Special Education, 39,* 234–245.

Mechling, L. C., Gast, D. L., & Barthold, S. (2003). Multimedia computer-based instruction to teach students with moderate intellectual disabilities to use a debit card to make purchases. *Exceptionality, 11,* 239–254.

Mechling, L. C., & Ortega-Hurndon, F. (2007). Computer-based video instruction to teach young adults with moderate intellectual disabilities to perform multistep, job tasks in a generalized setting. *Education and Training in Developmental Disabilities, 42,* 24–37.

Morrow, S. A., & Bates, P. E. (1987). The effectiveness of three sets of school-based instructional materials and community training on the acquisition and generalization of community laundry skills by students with severe handicaps. *Research in Developmental Disabilities, 8,* 113–136.

Nietupski, J., Clancy, P., Wehrmacher, L., & Parmer, C. (1985). Effects of minimal versus lengthy delay between simulated and in vivo instruction on community performance. *Education and Training of the Mentally Retarded, 20,* 190–195.

Nietupski, J., Hamre-Nietupski, S., Clancy, P., & Veerhusen, K. (1986). Guidelines for making simulation an effective adjunct to in vivo community instruction. *Journal of the Association for Persons With Severe Handicaps, 11,* 12–18.

Page, T. J., Iwata, B. A., & Neef, N. A. (1976). Teaching pedestrian skills to retarded persons: Generalization from the classroom to the natural environment. *Journal of Applied Behavior Analysis, 9,* 433–444.

Panyan, M. C., & Hall, R. V. (1978). Effect of serial versus concurrent task sequencing on acquisition, maintenance, and generalization. *Journal of Applied Behavior Analysis, 11,* 67–74.

Phelps, L. A., & Hanley-Maxwell, C. (1997). School-to-work transitions for youth with disabilities: A review of outcomes and practices. *Review of Educational Research, 67,* 197–226.

Rosenthal-Malek, A., & Bloom, A. (1998). Beyond acquisition: Teaching generalization for students with developmental disabilities. In A. Hilton & R. Ringlaben (Eds.), *Best and promising practices in developmental disabilities* (pp. 139–155). Austin, TX: Pro-Ed.

Sailor, W., Anderson, J. L., Halvorsen, A. T., Doering, K., Filler, J., & Goetz, L. (1989). *The comprehensive local school: Regular education for all students with disabilities.* Baltimore: Paul H. Brookes.

Sarber, R. E., & Cuvo, A. J. (1983). Teaching nutritional meal planning to developmentally disabled clients. *Behavior Modification, 7,* 503–530.

Sarber, R. E., Halasz, M. M., Messmer, M. C., Bickett, A. D., & Lutzker, J. R. (1983). Teaching menu planning and grocery shopping skills to a retarded mother. *Mental Retardation, 21,* 101–106.

Schuster, J. W., Morse, T. E., Ault, M. E., Doyle, P. M., Crawford, M. R., & Wolery, M. (1998). Constant time delay with chained tasks: A review of the literature. *Education and Treatment of Children, 21,* 74–106.

Snell, M. E., & Brown, F. (2006). *Instruction of students with severe disabilities* (6th ed.). Upper Saddle River, NJ: Pearson Education.

Spooner, F., Weber, L. H., & Spooner, D. (1983). The effects of backward and total task presentation on the acquisition of complex tasks by severely retarded adolescents and adults. *Education and Treatment of Children, 6,* 401–420.

Sprague, J. R., & Horner, R. H. (1984). The effects of single instance, multiple instance, and general case training on generalized vending machine use by moderately and severely handicapped students. *Journal of Applied Behavior Analysis, 17,* 273–278.

Tashie, C., Jorgensen, C., Shapiro-Barnard, S., Martin, J., & Schuh, M. (1996, September). High school inclusion strategies and barriers. *TASH Newsletter, 22*(9), 19–22.

van den Pol, K. A., Iwata, B. A., Ivancic, M. T., Page, T. J., Neef, N. A., & Whitley, F. P. (1981). Teaching the handicapped to eat in public places: Acquisition, generalization, and maintenance of restaurant skills. *Journal of Applied Behavior Analysis, 14,* 61–70.

Waldo, L., Guess, D., & Flanagan, B. (1982). Effects of concurrent and serial training on receptive language labeling by severely retarded individuals. *Journal of the Association for the Severely Handicapped, 6,* 56–65.

Wehman, P. (2006). *Life beyond the classroom: Transition strategies for young people with disabilities* (4th ed.). Baltimore: Paul H. Brookes.

Westling, D. L., & Fox, L. (2004). *Teaching students with severe disabilities* (3rd ed.). Upper Saddle River, NJ: Merrill.

Wissick, C. A., Gardner, J. E., & Langone, J. (1999). Video-based simulations: Considerations for teaching students with developmental disabilities. *Career Development for Exceptional Individuals, 22,* 233–249.

Wolery, M., Ault, M. J., & Doyle, P. M. (1992). *Teaching students with moderate to severe disabilities: Use of response prompting strategies.* New York: Longman.

Zane, T., Walls, R. T., & Thvedt, J. E. (1981). Prompting and fading guidance procedures: Their effect on chaining and whole task teaching strategies. *Education and Training of the Mentally Retarded, 16,* 125–135.

Chapter 10

Algozzine, K., O'Shea, D. J., & Algozzine, B. (2001). Working with families of adolescents. In D. J. O'Shea, L. J. O'Shea, R. Algozzine, & D. J. Hamitte (Eds.), *Families and teachers of individuals with disabilities* (pp. 179–204). Boston: Allyn & Bacon.

Beakley, B. A., & Yoder, S. L. (1998). Middle schoolers learn community skills. *Teaching Exceptional Children, 30*(3), 16–21.

Berry, J. O., & Hardman, M. L. (1998). *Lifespan perspective on the family and disability.* Boston: Allyn & Bacon.

Browder, D. M. (2001). *Curriculum and assessment for students with moderate and severe disabilities.* New York: Guilford.

Browder, D. M., Cooper, K. J., & Lim, L. (1998). Teaching adults with severe disabilities to express their choice for settings for leisure activities. *Education and Training in Mental Retardation and Developmental Disabilities, 33*(3), 228–238.

Browder, D. M., & Snell, M. E. (1993). Daily living and community skills. In M. E. Snell (Ed.), *Instruction of students with severe disabilities* (4th ed., pp. 480–525). New York: Merrill.

Calhoun, M. L., & Calhoun, L. G. (1993). Age appropriate activities: Effects on the social perceptions of adults with mental retardation. *Education and Training in Mental Retardation, 28,* 143–148.

Dunst, C. J. (2002). Family centered practices: Birth through high school. *The Journal of Special Education, 36,* 139–147.

Geenen, S., Powers, L. E., & Lopez-Vasquez, A. (2001). Multicultural aspects of parent involvement in transition. *Exceptional Children, 67*(2), 265–282.

Heal, L. W., Rubin, S. S., & Rusch, F. R. (1998). Residential independence of former special education high school students: A second look. *Research in Developmental Disabilities, 19,* 1–26.

Horner, R. H., McDonnell, J., & Bellamy, G. T. (1986). Teaching generalized skills: General case instruction in simulated and community settings. In R. H. Horner, L. H. Meyer, & H. D. Fredricks (Eds.), *Education of learners with severe handicaps: Exemplary service strategies* (pp. 289–314). Baltimore: Paul H. Brookes.

Hughes, C., Pitkin, S. E., & Lorden, S. W. (1998). Assessing preferences and choices of persons with severe and profound mental retardation. *Education and Training in Mental Retardation and Developmental Disabilities, 33*(4), 299–316.

Hunt, P., & McDonnell, J. (2007). Inclusive education. In S. L. Odom, R. H. Horner, M. Snell, & J. Blacher (Eds.), *Handbook on developmental disabilities* (pp. 269–291). New York: Guilford.

Kim, K., & Turnbull, A. (2004). Transition to adulthood for students with severe intellectual disabilities: Shifting toward person-family interdependent planning. *Research and Practices for Persons With Severe Disabilities, 29*(1), 53–57.

Lancioni, G. E. (1996). A review of choice research with people with severe and profound developmental disabilities. *Research in Developmental Disabilities, 17*(5), 391–411.

Logan, K., Jacobs, H. A., Gast, D. L., Murray, A. S., Daino, K., & Skala, C. (1998). The impact of typical peers on the perceived happiness of students with profound multiple disabilities. *The Journal for the Association for Persons With Severe Handicaps, 23*(4), 309–318.

McDonnell, J., Johnson, J. W., & McQuivey, C. (2008). *Embedded instruction for students with developmental disabilities in general education classrooms.* Arlington, VA: Council for Exceptional Children.

McDonnell, J. J., Mathot-Buckner, C., & Ferguson, B. (1996). *Transition programs for students with moderate/severe disabilities.* Pacific Grove, CA: Brooks/Cole.

McDonnell, J. J., Wilcox, B., & Hardman, M. L. (1991). *Secondary programs for students with developmental disabilities.* Boston: Allyn & Bacon.

Miner, C. A., & Bates, P. E. (1997). The effect of person centered planning activities on the IEP/transition planning process. *Education and Training in Mental Retardation and Developmental Disabilities, 32,* 105–112.

Nisbet, J., Clark, M., & Covert, S. (1991). Living it up! An analysis of research on community living. In L. H. Meyer, C. A. Peck, & L. Brown (Eds.), *Critical issues in the lives of people with severe disabilities* (pp. 115–144). Baltimore: Paul H. Brookes.

Rosenthal-Malek, A., & Bloom, A. (1998). Beyond acquisition: Teaching generalization for students with developmental disabilities. In A. Hilton & R. Ringlaben (Eds.), *Best and promising practices in developmental disabilities* (pp. 139–155). Austin, TX: Pro-Ed.

Schalock, R., & Lilley, M. A. (1986). Placement from community based mental retardation programs: How well do clients do after 8–10 years? *American Journal of Mental Deficiency, 90,* 669–676.

Schalock, R., Wolzen, B., Ross, I., Elliot, B., Werbel, G., & Peterson, K. (1986). Post-secondary community placement of handicapped students: A five year follow up. *Learning Disability Quarterly, 9,* 295–303.

Schwartzman, L., Martin, G. L., Yu, C. T., & Whiteley, J. (2004). Choice, degree of preference, and happiness indices with persons with intellectual disabilities: A surprising finding. *Education and Training in Developmental Disabilities, 39*(3), 265–269.

Smith, R. B., Morgan, M., & Davidson, J. (2005). Does the daily choice making of adults with intellectual disabilities meet the normalization principle? *Journal of Intellectual and Developmental Disability, 30*(4), 226–235.

Spooner, F., & Test, D. W. (1994). Domestic and community living skills. In E. C. Cipani & F. Spooner (Eds.), *Curricular and instructional approaches for persons with severe disabilities* (pp. 149–183). Boston: Allyn & Bacon.

Steere, D. E., & Cavaiuolo, D. (2002). Connecting outcomes, goals, and objectives in transition planning. *Teaching Exceptional Children, 34*(6), 54–59.

Turnbull, A. P., & Turnbull, H. R. (2001). Self determination for individuals with significant cognitive disabilities and their families. *Journal of the Association of Persons With Severe Handicaps, 26*(1), 56–62.

Turnbull, A. P., Turnbull, H. R., Shank, M., & Smith, S. J. (2004). *Exceptional lives: Special education in today's schools* (4th ed.). Upper Saddle River, NJ: Prentice Hall.

Turnbull, H. R., Beegle, G., & Stowe, M. S. (2001). The core concepts of disability policy affecting families who have children with disabilities. *Journal of Disability Policy Studies, 12*(3), 133–143.

Wehman, P. (2006). Integrated employment: If not now, when? If not us, who? *Research and Practice for Persons With Severe Disabilities, 31*(2), 122–126.

Wehmeyer, M., & Palmer, S. (2003). Adult outcomes for students with cognitive disabilities three years after high school: The impact of self-determination. *Education and Training in Developmental Disabilities, 38,* 131–144.

Wehmeyer, M., Palmer, S., Agran, M., Mithaug, D., & Martin, J. (2000). Promoting causal agency: The Self-Determined Learning Model of instruction. *Exceptional Children, 66,* 439–453.

Wilcox, B. (1988). Identifying programming goals for community participation. In B. L. Ludlow, A. P. Turnbull, & R. Luckasson (Eds.), *Transition to adult life for people with mental retardation: Principles and practices* (pp. 119–136). Baltimore: Paul H. Brookes.

Chapter 11

Americans with Disabilities Act of 1990 (ADA) 42 U.S.C. § 12101 *et seq.* (1990).

Argyle, M. (1996). *The sociology of leisure.* London: Penguin.

Ashton-Shaeffer, C., Johnson, D. E., & Bullock, C. C. (2000). A questionnaire of current practice of recreation as a related service. *Therapeutic Recreation Journal, 34*(4), 323–334.

Ashton-Shaeffer, C., Shelton, M., & Johnson, D. E. (1995). The social caterpillar and the wallflower: Two case studies of adolescents with disabilities in transition. *Therapeutic Recreation Journal, 29*(4), 324–336.

Bedini, L., Bullock, C., & Driscoll, L. (1993). The effects of leisure education on factors contributing to the successful transition of students with mental retardation. *Therapeutic Recreation Journal, 27*(2), 70–82.

Braun, K. V. N., Yeargin-Allsopp, M., & Lollar, D. (2006). Factors associated with leisure activity among adults with developmental disabilities. *Research in Developmental Disabilities, 27,* 567–583.

Browder, D. M., & Cooper, K. J. (1994). Inclusion of older adults with mental retardation in leisure opportunities. *Mental Retardation, 32,* 91–99.

Bullock, C. C., & Luken, K. (1994). Reintegration through recreation: A community-based rehabilitation model. In D. M. Compton & S. E. Iso-Ahola (Eds.), *Leisure and mental health* (Vol. 1, pp. 61–79). Park City, UT: Family Resources.

Bullock, C. C., & Mahon, M. J. (2001). *Introduction to recreation service for people with disabilities: A person-centered approach* (2nd ed.). Champaign, IL: Sagamore.

Carter, E. W., Cushing, L. S., Clark, N. M., & Kennedy, C. H. (2005). Effects for peers support interventions on student's access to general curriculum and social interactions. *Research and Practice for Persons With Severe Disabilities, 30*(1), 15–25.

Chen, S., Zhang, J., Lang, E., Miko, P., & Joseph, D. (2001). Progressive time procedures for teaching gross motor skills to adults with severe mental retardation. *Adaptive Physical Activity Quarterly, 18,* 35–48.

Cihak, D., Alberto, P., Kessler, K., & Taber, T. (2004). An investigation of instruction scheduling arrangements for community-based instruction. *Research in Developmental Disabilities, 25,* 67–88.

Cimera, R. E. (2007). Utilizing natural supports to lower cost of supported employment. *Research and Practice for Persons With Severe Disabilities, 32*(3), 184–189.

Collins, B., Hall, M., & Branson, T. (1997). Teaching leisure skills to adolescents with moderate disabilities. *Exceptional Children, 63,* 499–512.

Conyers, C., Doole, A., Vause, T., Harapiak, S., Yu, D., & Martin, G. L. (2002). Predicting the relative efficacy of three presentation methods for assessing preferences of persons with developmental disabilities. *Journal of Applied Behavior Analysis, 35*(1), 49–58.

Dattilo, J. (Ed.). (1999). *Leisure education and program planning.* State College, PA: Venture Publishing.

Dattilo, J., & Hoge, G. (1999). Effects of leisure education program on youth with mental retardation. *Education and Training in Mental Retardation, 34,* 20–34.

Dattilo, J., & St. Peter, S. (1991). A model for including leisure education in transition services for young adults with mental retardation. *Education and Training in Mental Retardation, 26,* 420–432.

Draheim, C., Williams, D., & McCubbin, J. (2002). Prevalence of physical inactivity and recommended physical activity in community-based adults with mental retardation. *Mental Retardation, 40,* 436–444.

Dunn, J. M. (1997). *Special physical education: Adapted, individualized, developmental* (7th ed.). Madison, WI: Brown & Benchmark Publishers.

Graham, A., & Reid, R. (2000). Physical fitness of adults with an intellectual disability: A 13-year follow-up study. *Research Quarterly for Exercise and Sport, 71*(2), 152–161.

Green, C. W., & Reid, D. H. (1996). Defining, validating, and increasing indices of happiness among people with profound disabilities. *Journal of Applied Behavior Analysis, 29,* 67–78.

Green, C. W., & Reid, D. H. (1999). A behavioral approach to identifying sources of happiness among people with profound multiple disabilities. *Behavior Modification, 23,* 280–293.

Halpern, A. S. (1993). Quality of life as a conceptual framework for evaluating transition outcomes. *Exceptional Children, 59*(6), 486–498.

Hawkins, B. A. (1997). Promoting quality of life through leisure and recreation. In R. L. Schalock (Ed.), *Quality of life Volume II: Application to persons with disabilities* (pp. 117–133). Washington, DC: American Association on Mental Retardation.

Heyne, L. A., & Schleien, S. J. (1996). Leisure education in the schools: A call to action. *Leisurability, 23*(3), 3–14.

Heyne, L. A., Schleien, S. J., & McAvoy, L. (1993). *Making friends: Using recreation activities to promote friendship between children with and without disabilities.* Minneapolis: Institute on Community Integration.

Heyne, L., Schleien, S. J., & Rynders, J. (1997). Promoting quality of life through recreation participation. In S. Ptiescliel & M. Sustrova (Eds.), *Adolescents with Down syndrome: Toward a more fulfilling life* (pp. 317–340). Baltimore: Paul H. Brookes.

Houston-Wilson, C., Lieberman, L., & Horton, M. (1997). Peer tutoring: A plan for instructing all abilities. *Journal of Physical Education, Recreation, and Dance, 68*, 39–44.

Individuals with Disabilities Education Improvement Act (IDEA) of 2004, 20 U.S.C.A. § 1400 *et seq.* (2004).

Johnson, M. (2003). *Make them go away: Clint Eastwood, Christopher Reeve, & the case against disability rights.* Louisville, KY: Advocado Press.

Kermeen, R. B. (1992). *Access to public recreation facilities and universal design.* USDA Forest Service Gen. Tech. Rep. PSW-132.

Krebs, P. L., & Block, M. E. (1992). Transition of students with disabilities into community recreation: The role of the adapted physical educator. *Adapted Physical Activity Quarterly, 9*(4), 305–315.

Krueger, D. L., DiRocco, P., & Felix, M. (2000). Obstacles adapted physical education specialists encounter when developing transition plans. *Adapted Physical Education Quarterly, 17*(2), 222–236.

Lanagan, D., & Dattilo, J. (1989). The effects of a leisure education program on individuals with mental retardation. *Therapeutic Recreation Journal, 23*(4), 62–72.

Lennox, N. G., Green, M., Diggens, J., & Ugoni, A. (2001). Audit and comprehensive health assessment programme in the primary healthcare system of adults with intellectual disability: A pilot study. *Journal of Intellectual Disability Research, 45*(3), 226–233.

Lieberman, L. J., Lytle, R. K., & Clarcq, J. A. (2008). Getting in right from the start: Employing universal design for learning approach to your curriculum. *Journal of Physical Education, Recreation, and Dance, 79*(2), 32–39.

Lieberman, L. J., & Stuart, M. (2002). Self-determined recreational and leisure choices of individuals with deaf-blindness. *Journal of Visual Impairment & Blindness, 96*(10), 724–736.

Mahon, M., & Bullock, C. (1992). Teaching adolescents with mild mental retardation to make decisions in leisure through the use of self-control techniques. *Therapeutic Recreation Journal, 26*(1), 9–26.

Mannell, R. C., & Kleiber, D. A. (1997). *A social psychology of leisure.* State College, PA: Venture.

Modell, S., & Valdez, L. (2002). Beyond bowling: Transition planning for students with disabilities. *Teaching Exceptional Children, 34*(6), 46–53.

Nietupski, J., Hamre-Nietupski, S., & Ayres, B. (1984). Review of task analytic leisure skill training efforts: Practitioner implications and future research needs. *Journal of the Association for the Severely Handicapped, 9,* 88–97.

Odem, S. L., Brantlinger, E., Gersten, R. H., Thompson, B., & Harris, K. R. (2005). Research in special education: Scientific methods and evidence-based practices. *Exceptional Children, 71,* 137–148.

Parsons, M. B., Harper, V. N., Jensen, J. M., & Reid, D. H. (1997). Assisting older adults with severe disabilities in expressing leisure preferences: A protocol for determining choice-making skills. *Research in Developmental Disabilities, 18*, 113–126.

Patton, J. R., Polloway, E. A., Smith, T. E., Edgar, E., Clark, G. M., & Lee, S. (1996). Individuals with mild mental retardation: Postsecondary outcomes and implications for educational policy. *Education and Training in Mental Retardation and Developmental Disabilities, 31*, 75–85.

Rimmer, J. H., Braddock, D., & Fujiura, G. (1993). Prevalence of obesity in adults with mental retardation: Implications for health promotion. *Mental Retardation, 31,* 105–110.

Rose, T., McDonnell, J., & Ellis, E. (2007). The impact of teacher beliefs on the provision of leisure and physical activity on curriculum decisions. *Teacher Education Special Education, 30*(3), 183–198.

Roth, K., Pyfer, J., & Huettig, C. (2007). Transition in physical recreation and students with cognitive disabilities: Graduate and parent perspectives. *Education and Training in Developmental Disabilities, 42*(1), 94–106.

Russell, R. (2002). *Pastimes: The context of contemporary leisure.* Champaign, IL: Sagamore Publishing.

Sands, D. J., & Kozleski, E. B. (1994). Quality of life differences between adults with and without disabilities. *Education and Training in Mental Retardation and Developmental Disabilities, 29,* 90–101.

Siperstein, G. N., Parker, R. C., Bardon, J. N., & Widaman, K. F. (2007). A national study of youth attitudes toward the inclusion of students with intellectual disabilities. *Exceptional Children, 73*(4), 435–455.

Smart, J. (2001). *Disability, society, and the individual.* Gaithersburg, MD: Aspen.

Sparrow, W. A., Shrinkfield, A. J., & Karnilowicz, W. (1993). Constraints on the participation of individuals with mental retardation in mainstream recreation. *Mental Retardation, 31,* 403–411.

Special Olympics. (2008). *Special Olympics: About us.* Retrieved on March 19, 2008, from http://www.specialolympics.org/Special+Olympics+Public+Website/English/About_Us/default.htm

Storey, K. (2004). The case against the Special Olympics. *Journal of Disability Policy Studies, 15*(1), 35–42.

Terman, D. L., Larner, M. B., Stevenson, C. S., & Behrman, R. E. (1996). Special education for students with disabilities: Analysis and recommendations. *The Future of Children, 6*(1), 4–24.

Tripp, A., Rizzo, T. L., & Webbert, L. (2007). Inclusion in physical education: Changing the culture. *Journal of Physical Education, Recreation, and Dance, 78*(2), 32–36.

U.S. Department of Health and Human Services. (1999). *Promoting physical activity.* Champaign, IL: Human Kinetics.

U.S. Department of Health and Human Services. (2000). *Healthy People 2010: Understanding and improving health* (2nd ed.). Washington, DC: U.S. Government Printing Office.

U.S. Department of Health and Human Services. (2005). *Dietary guidelines for Americans, 2005.* Washington, DC: U.S. Government Printing Office.

Vandercook, T. (1991). Leisure instruction outcomes: Criterion performance, positive interactions, and acceptance by typical high school peers. *The Journal of Special Education, 25*(3), 320–339.

Wall, M., & Gast, D. (1997). Caregivers' use of constant time delay to teach leisure skills to adolescents or young adults with moderate or severe intellectual disabilities. *Education and Training in Mental Retardation and Developmental Disabilities, 32*(4), 340–356.

Walter, M. G., & Harris, C. (2003). The relationship between fitness levels and employees' perceived productivity, job satisfaction, and absenteeism. *Journal of Exercise Physiology, 6*(1), 24–28.

Wehman, P., & Marchant, J. (1977). Developing gross motor recreational skills in children with severe behavior handicaps. *Therapeutic Recreation Journal, 11*(2), 18–31.

Weissinger, E., Caldwell, L., & Bandolos, D. (1992). Relationship between intrinsic motivation and boredom in leisure time. *Leisure Sciences, 14,* 317–325.

Werts, M. G., Wolery, M., Snyder, E. D., & Caldwell, N. (1996). Teachers' perceptions of the supports critical to the success of inclusion programs. *Journal of the Association for Persons With Severe Disabilities, 21,* 9–21.

Witman, J. P., & Munson, W. W. (1992). Leisure awareness and action: A program to enhance family effectiveness. *Journal of Physical Education, Recreation, and Dance, 63,* 41–43.

Wolery, M., Werts, M. G., Caldwell, N. K., Snyder, E. D., & Lisowski, L. (1995). Experienced teachers' perceptions of resources and supports for inclusion. *Education and Training in Mental Retardation and Developmental Disabilities, 30,* 15–26.

Yu, D. C. T., Spevack, S., Hiebert, R., Martin, T. L., Goodman, R., Martin, T. G., et al. (2002). Happiness indices among persons with profound and severe disabilities during leisure and work activities: A comparison. *Education and Training in Mental Retardation and Developmental Disabilities, 37*(4), 421–426.

Zhang, J., Cote, B., Chen, S., & Liu, J. (2004). The effect of a constant time delay procedure on teaching an adult with severe mental retardation a recreation bowling skill. *Physical Educator, 61*(2), 63–74.

Zhang, J., Gast, D., Horvat, M., & Dattilo, J. (1995). The effectiveness of a constant time delay procedure on teaching lifetime sport skills to adolescents with severe to profound intellectual disabilities. *Education and Training in Mental Retardation and Developmental Disabilities, 30,* 51–64.

Zoerink, D. A. (1988). Effects of a short-term leisure education program upon the leisure functioning of young people with spina bifida. *Therapeutic Recreation Journal, 22*(3), 44–52.

Zoerink, D. A., & Lauener, K. (1991). Effects of a leisure education program on adults with traumatic brain injury. *Therapeutic Recreation Journal, 25*(3), 19–28.

Chapter 12

Benz, M. R., Lindstrom, L., & Yovanoff, P. (2000). Improving graduation and employment outcomes of students with disabilities: Predictive factors and student perspectives. *Exceptional Children, 66,* 509–529.

Berryman, S. E. (1993). Learning in the workplace. In L. Darling-Hammond (Ed.), *Review of research in education* (pp. 341–404). Washington, DC: American Educational Research Association.

Blackorby, J., & Wagner, M. (1996). Longitudinal postschool outcomes of youth with disabilities: Findings from the National Longitudinal Transition Study. *Exceptional Children, 62*(5), 399–413.

Fair Labor Standards Act, 29 U.S.C. § 201 *et seq.* (1990).

Fisher, D., Sax, C., & Pumpian, I. (1999). *Inclusive high schools: Learning from contemporary classrooms.* Baltimore: Paul H. Brookes.

Hasazi, S., Johnson, D., Thurlow, M., Cobb, B., Trach, J., Stodden, B., et al. (2005). Transition from home and school to the roles and supports of adulthood. In K. C. Lakin & A. Turnbull (Eds.), *National goals and research for people with intellectual and developmental disabilities* (pp. 65–92). Washington, DC: American Association on Mental Retardation.

Hunt, P., & McDonnell, J. (2007). Inclusive education. In S. L. Odom, R. H. Horner, M. Snell, & J. Blacher (Eds.), *Handbook on developmental disabilities* (pp. 269–291). New York: Guilford.

Inge, K. J., & Moon, M. S. (2006). Vocational preparation and transition. In M. E. Snell & F. Brown (Eds.), *Instruction of students with severe disabilities* (pp. 569–609). Upper Saddle River, NJ: Pearson.

Izzo, M. V., Johnson, J. R., Levitz, M., & Aaron, J. H. (1998). Transition from school to adult life: New roles for educators. In P. Wehman & J. Kregel (Eds.), *More than a job: Securing satisfying careers for people with disabilities* (pp. 249–286). Baltimore: Paul H. Brookes.

Jorgensen, C. M. (1998). *Restructuring high schools for all students: Taking inclusion to the next level.* Baltimore: Paul H. Brookes.

Luft, P. (2008). Career development theories for transition planning. In R. W. Flexer, R. M. Baer, P. Luft, & T. J. Simmons (Eds.), *Transition planning for secondary students with disabilities* (pp. 82–100). Upper Saddle River, NJ: Pearson.

McDonnell, J., Mathot-Buckner, C., & Ferguson, B. (1996). *Transition programs for students with moderate/severe disabilities.* Pacific Grove, CA: Brooks/Cole.

Mortimer, J. T. (2003). *Working and growing up in America.* Cambridge, MA: Harvard University Press.

National Center on Secondary Education and Transition. (2005, February). *Handbook for implementing a comprehensive work-based learning program according to the Fair Labor Standards Act.* Minneapolis: University of Minnesota.

Phelps, L. A., & Hanley-Maxwell, C. (1997). School-to-work transitions for youth with disabilities: A review of outcomes and practices. *Review of Educational Research, 67,* 197–226.

Rusch, F. R., & Braddock, D. (2004). Adult day programs versus supported employment (1988–2002): Spending and services practices of mental retardation and developmental disabilities state agencies. *Research and Practice for Persons With Severe Disabilities, 29,* 237–242.

Simmons, T. J., & Flexer, R. W. (2008). Transition to employment. In R. W. Flexer, R. M. Baer, P. Luft, & T. J. Simmons (Eds.), *Transition planning for secondary students with disabilities* (pp. 230—257). Upper Saddle River, NJ: Pearson.

Sitlington, P. L. (2003). Postsecondary education: The other transition. *Exceptionality, 11,* 103–113.

Sowers, J. A., & Powers, L. (1991). *Vocational preparation and employment of students with physical and multiple disabilities.* Baltimore: Paul H. Brookes.

Steere, D. E., Rose, E., & Cavaiuolo, D. (2007). *Growing up: Transition to adult life for students with disabilities.* Boston: Pearson.

Szymanski, E. M. (1998). Career development, school-to-work transition, and diversity: An ecological approach. In F. R. Rusch & J. G. Chadsey (Eds.), *Beyond high school: Transition from school to work* (pp. 127–145). Belmont, CA: Wadsworth Publishing.

Szymanski, E. M., Ryan, C., Merz, M. A., Trevino, B., & Johnston-Rodriquez, S. (1996). Psychosocial and economic aspects of work: Implications for people with disabilities. In E. M. Szymanski & R. M. Parker (Eds.), *Work and disability: Issues and strategies in career development and job placement* (pp. 9–38). Austin, TX: Pro-Ed.

U.S. Department of Education, Office of Special Education. (1992). *OSEP memorandum 92-20: Guidelines for implementing community-based educational programs for students with disabilities.* Washington, DC: Author.

Wehman, P. (2006). *Life beyond the classroom: Transition strategies for young people with disabilities* (4th ed.). Baltimore: Paul H. Brookes.

Wehman, P., Inge, K. J., Revell, W. G., & Brooke, V. A. (2007). *Real work for real pay: Inclusive employment for people with disabilities.* Baltimore: Paul H. Brookes.

Chapter 13

Bellamy, G. T., Horner, R. H., & Inman, D. P. (1979). *Vocational rehabilitation of severely retarded adults.* Baltimore: University Park Press.

Benz, M. R., Lindstrom, L., & Yovanoff, P. (2000). Improving graduation and employment outcomes of students with disabilities: Predictive factors and student perspectives. *Exceptional Children, 66,* 509–529.

Blackorby, J., & Wagner, M. (1996). Longitudinal postschool outcomes of youth with disabilities: Findings from the National Longitudinal Transition Study. *Exceptional Children, 62*(5), 399–413.

Brooke, V., Wehman, P., Inge, K., & Parent, W. (1995). Toward a customer-driven approach of supported employment. *Education and Training in Mental Retardation and Developmental Disabilities, 30,* 308–320.

Butterworth, J., Hagner, D., Helm, D. T., & Whelley, T. A. (2000). Workplace culture, social interactions, and supports for transition-age young adults. *Mental Retardation, 38,* 342–353.

Callahan, M., & Condon, E. (2007). Discovery: The foundation of job development. In C. Griffin, D. Hammis, & T. Geary (Eds.), *The job developer's handbook: Practical tactics for customized employment* (pp. 23–34). Baltimore: Paul H. Brookes.

Chadsey, J. (2007). Adult social relationships. In S. L. Odom, R. H. Horner, M. E. Snell, & J. Blacher (Eds.), *Handbook of developmental disabilities* (pp. 449–466). New York: Guilford.

Chadsey, J., & Sheldon, D. (1998). Moving toward social inclusion in employment and postsecondary school settings. In F. R. Rusch & J. G. Chadsey (Eds.), *Beyond high school: Transition from school to work* (pp. 406–438). Belmont, CA: Wadsworth.

Cooper, J. O., Heron, T. E., & Heward, W. L. (2007). *Applied behavior analysis* (2nd ed.). Upper Saddle River, NJ: Pearson.

Flexer, R. W., Baer, R. M., Luft, P., & Simmons, T. J. (2008). *Transition planning for secondary students with disabilities.* Upper Saddle River, NJ: Pearson.

Green, J. H., Wehman, P., Luna, J. W., & Merkle, A. J. (2007). Current trends of partnerships with private enterprises. In P. Wehman, K. J. Inge, W. G. Revell, & V. A. Brooke (Eds.), *Real work for real pay: Inclusive employment for people with disabilities* (pp. 273–292). Baltimore: Paul H. Brookes.

Griffin, C., Hammis, D., & Geary, T. (2007). *The job developer's handbook: Practical tactics for customized employment.* Baltimore: Paul H. Brookes.

Grossi, T. A., & Heward, W. L. (1998). Using self-evaluation to improve the work productivity of trainees in a community-based restaurant training program. *Education and Training in Mental Retardation and Developmental Disabilities, 33,* 248–263.

Hagner, D. C. (1992). The social interactions and job supports of supported employees. In J. Nisbet (Ed.), *Natural supports in school, at work, and in the community for people with severe disabilities* (pp. 217–239). Baltimore: Paul H. Brookes.

Hasazi, S., Johnson, D., Thurlow, M., Cobb, B., Trach, J., Stodden, B., et al. (2005). Transition from home and school to the roles and supports of adulthood. In K. C. Lakin & A. Turnbull (Eds.), *National goals and research for people with intellectual and developmental disabilities* (pp. 65–92). Washington, DC: American Association on Mental Retardation.

Horner, R. H., Dunlap, G., & Koegel, R. L. (1988). *Generalization and maintenance: Life-style changes in applied settings.* Baltimore: Paul H. Brookes.

Inge, K., & Targett, P. (2006). Identifying job opportunities for individuals with disabilities. *Journal of Vocational Rehabilitation, 25,* 137–139.

Inge, K. J., Targett, P. S., & Armstrong, A. J. (2007). Person-centered planning: Facilitating inclusive employment outcomes. In P. Wehman, K. J. Inge, W. G. Revell, & V. A. Brooke (Eds.), *Real work for real pay: Inclusive employment for people with disabilities* (pp. 57–74). Baltimore: Paul H. Brookes.

Izzo, M. V., Johnson, J. R., Levitz, M., & Aaron, J. H. (1998). Transition from school to adult life: New roles for educators. In P. Wehman & J. Kregel (Eds.), *More than a job: Securing satisfying careers for people with disabilities* (pp. 249–286). Baltimore: Paul H. Brookes.

Mast, M., Sweeny, J., & West, M. (2001). Using presentation portfolios for effective job representation of individuals with disabilities. *Journal of Vocational Rehabilitation, 16,* 135–140.

Mautz, D., Storey, K., & Certo, N. (2001). Increasing integrated workplace social interactions: The effects of job modification, natural supports, adaptive community instruction, and job coach training. *Journal of the Association for Persons With Severe Handicaps, 26,* 257–269.

McDonnell, J., Mathot-Buckner, C., & Ferguson, B. (1996). *Transition programs for students with moderate/severe disabilities.* Pacific Grove, CA: Brooks/Cole.

McDonnell, J., Nofs, D., Hardman, M., & Chambless, C. (1989). An analysis of the procedural components of supported employment programs associated with worker outcomes. *Journal of Applied Behavior Analysis, 22,* 417–428.

Moon, M. S., Inge, K. J., Wehman, P., Brooke, V., & Barcus, J. M. (1990). *Helping persons with severe mental retardation get and keep employment: Supported employment issues and strategies.* Baltimore: Paul H. Brookes.

Office of Disability Employment Policy, U.S. Department of Labor. (2005). *Customized employment: Practical solutions for employment success.* Retrieved October 1, 2008, from www.dol.gov/odep/pubs/custom/index.htm

Owens-Johnson, L., & Hanley-Maxwell, C. (1999). Employer views on job development strategies for marketing supported employment. *Journal of Vocational Rehabilitation, 12,* 113–123.

Phelps, L. A., & Hanley-Maxwell, C. (1997). School-to-work transitions for youth with disabilities: A review of outcomes and practices. *Review of Educational Research, 67,* 197–226.

Riehle, J. E., & Datson, M. (2006). Deficit marketing: Good intentions, bad results. *Journal of Vocational Rehabilitation, 25,* 69–70.

Rusch, F. R., & Braddock, D. (2004). Adult day programs versus supported employment (1988–2002): Spending and services practices of mental retardation and developmental disabilities state agencies. *Research and Practice for Persons With Severe Disabilities, 29,* 237–242.

Rusch, F. R., & Mithaug, D. E. (1981). *Vocational training for mentally retarded adults: A behavior analytic approach.* Champaign, IL: Research Press.

Smith, K., Webber, L., Graffam, J., & Wilson, C. (2004). Employer satisfaction, job-match and future hiring intentions for employees with a disability. *Journal of Vocational Rehabilitation, 21,* 165–173.

Sowers, J., & Powers, L. (1991). *Vocational preparation and employment of students with physical and multiple disabilities.* Baltimore: Paul H. Brookes.

Storey, K. (2007). Review of research on self-management interventions in supported employment settings for employees with disabilities. *Career Development for Exceptional Individuals, 30,* 27–34.

Unger, D. (2007). Addressing employer personnel needs and improving employment training, job placement and retention for individuals with disabilities through public-private partnerships. *Journal of Vocational Rehabilitation, 26,* 39–48.

Wehman, P. (2006). *Life beyond the classroom: Transition strategies for young people with disabilities* (4th ed.). Baltimore: Paul H. Brookes.

Wehman, P., Inge, K. J., Revell, W. G., & Brooke, V. A. (2007). *Real work for real pay: Inclusive employment for people with disabilities.* Baltimore: Paul H. Brookes.

Wehman, P., & Moon, M. S. (1988). *Vocational rehabilitation and supported employment.* Baltimore: Paul H. Brookes.

Weiner, J. S., & Zivolich, S. (2003). A longitudinal report for three employees in a training consultant model of natural support. *Journal of Vocational Rehabilitation, 18,* 199–202.

Chapter 14

American Association on Intellectual and Developmental Disabilities. (n.d.). *Fact sheet: Home ownership.* Retrieved October 3, 2008, from the American Association on Intellectual and Developmental Disabilities Web site at http://www.aaidd.org/Policies/faq_home_ownership.shtml

Boles, S., Horner, R. H., & Bellamy, G. T. (1988). Implementing transition: Programs for supported living. In B. L. Ludlow, A. P. Turnbull, & R. Luckason (Eds.), *Transition to adult life for people with mental retardation: Principles and practices* (pp. 85–100). Baltimore: Paul H. Brookes.

Braddock, D., Rizzolo, M. C., Hemp, R., & Parish, S. L. (2005). Public spending for developmental disabilities in the United States: A historical-comparative perspective. In R. J. Stancliffe & C. K. Lakin (Eds.), *Costs and outcomes of community services for people with intellectual disabilities* (pp. 23–44). Baltimore: Paul H. Brookes.

Community Choice Act of 2007, S. 799, 110th Cong. (2007).

Dautel, P. J., & Frieden, L. (1999). *Consumer choice and control: Personal attendant services and supports in America. Report on the national blue ribbon panel on personal assistant services.* Houston: Independent Living Research Utilization.

Feinstien, C. S., Levine, R. M., Lemanowicz, J. A., Sedlak, W. C., Klien, J., & Hagner, D. (2006). Homeownership initiatives and outcomes for people with disabilities. *Journal of Community Development and Society, 37*(3), 1–7.

Gardern, J. F., & Carran, D. T. (2005). Attainment of personal outcomes by people with developmental disabilities. *Mental Retardation, 43,* 157–174.

Hagglund, K. J., Clark, M. J., Farmer, J. E., & Sherman, A. K. (2004). A comparison of consumer-directed and agency-directed personal assistant service programmes. *Disability and Rehabilitation, 26*(9), 518–527.

Harkin, T. (2007). Statement before the Senate Finance Committee on the Community Choice Act, 108th Cong.

Howe, J., Horner, R. H., & Newton, S. J. (1998). Comparison of supported living and traditional residential services in the state of Oregon. *Mental Retardation, 36*(1), 1–11.

Kaiser Commission on Medicaid and the Uninsured. (2004). *Olmstead v. L.C.: The interaction of the Americans with Disabilities Act and Medicaid.* Washington, DC: The Henry J. Kaiser Family Foundation. Available at http://www.kaiserfami lyfoundation.org/medicaid/upload/Olmstead-v-L-C-The-Interaction-of-the-Americans-with-Disabilities-Act-and-Medicaid.pdf

Kennedy, M. J. (2004). Living outside the system: The ups and downs of getting on with our lives. *Mental Retardation, 42*(3), 229–231.

Kim, S., Larson, S. A., & Lakin, K. C. (2001). Behavioural outcomes of deinstitutionalization for people with intellectual disability: A review of US studies conducted between 1980 and 1999. *Journal of Intellectual and Developmental Disabilities, 26*(1), 35–50.

Klien, J. (1992). Get me the hell out of here: Supporting people with disabilities to live in their own homes. In J. Nisbet (Ed.), *Natural supports in school, at work, and in the community for people with severe disabilities* (pp. 277–340). Baltimore: Paul H. Brookes.

Klien, J. (2000). The history and development of a national homeownership initiative. *Journal of Vocational Rehabilitation, 15,* 59–66.

Lakin, K. C., Braddock, D., & Smith, G. (2007). HCBS recipients are likely to live with parents or other relatives. *Intellectual and Developmental Disabilities, 45*(5), 359–361.

Lakin, K. C., Gardner, J., Larson, S., & Wheeler, B. (2005). Access and support for community lives, homes, and social roles. In K. C. Lakin & A. Turnbull (Eds.), *National goals and research for people with intellectual and developmental disabilities* (pp. 179–216). Washington, DC: American Association on Mental Retardation.

Lakin, K. C., Prouty, R., & Coucouvanis, K. (2006). Changing patterns in the size of residential settings for persons with intellectual and developmental disabilities, 1977–2005. *Mental Retardation, 44*(4), 306–309.

Lakin, K. C., & Stancliffe, R. J. (2007). Residential support for persons with intellectual and developmental disabilities. *Mental Retardation and Developmental Disabilities Research Review, 13,* 151–159.

Litvak, S., Zukas, H., & Heumann, J. (1987). *Attending to America: Personal assistance for independent living.* Berkeley, CA: World Institute on Disability.

Medicaid Community Attendant Services and Supports Act of 1999, S. 1935, 106th Cong. (1999).

Nisbet, J., Clark, M., & Covert, S. (1991). Living it up! An analysis of research on community living. In L. H. Meyer, C. A. Peck, & L. Brown (Eds.), *Critical issues in the lives of people with severe disabilities* (pp. 115–144). Baltimore: Paul H. Brookes.

O'Brien, J. (1994). Down stairs that are never your own: Supporting people with developmental disabilities in their own homes. *Mental Retardation, 32,* 1–6.

Prouty, R., Alba, K. M., Scott, N. L., & Lakin, K. C. (2008). Where people lived while receiving services and supports from state developmental disabilities programs in 2006. *Intellectual and Developmental Disabilities, 46,* 82–85.

Rehabilitation Act Amendments, 29 U.S.C. § 725, S. 799, 110th Cong. (2007).

Stancliffe, R. J., & Lakin, C. K. (2007). Independent living. In S. L. Odom, R. H. Horner, M. E. Snell, & J. Blacher (Eds.), *Handbook of developmental disabilities* (pp. 429–447). New York: Guilford.

Taylor, S. J. (2001). The continuum and current controversies in the USA. *Journal of Intellectual and Developmental Disabilities, 26*(1), 15–33.

Wagner, M., Newman, L., Cameto, R., Levine, P., & Marder, C. (2007). *Perceptions and expectations of youth with disabilities A special topic report of findings from the National Longitudinal Transition Study-2 (NLTS2).* Menlo Park, CA: SRI International. Available at http://ies.ed.gov/ncser/pdf/20073006.pdf

Walker, P. (1999). From community presence to sense of place: Community experiences for adults with developmental disabilities. *Journal of the Association for Persons With Severe Handicaps, 24,* 23–32.

Wieck, C., & Strully, J. L. (1991). What's wrong with the continuum? A metaphorical analysis. In L. H. Meyer, C. A. Peck, & L. Brown (Eds.), *Critical issues in the lives of people with severe disabilities* (pp. 229–234). Baltimore: Paul H. Brookes.

World Institute on Disability. (1991). *Resolution on personal assistance services.* Retrieved October 3, 2008, from the World Institute on Disability Web site at http://www.wid.org/publications/personal-assistance-services-a-new-millennium/resolution-on-personal-assistance-services

Chapter 15

Benz, M. R., Lindstrom, L., & Yovanoff, P. (2000). Improving graduation and employment outcomes of students with disabilities: Predictive factors and student perspectives. *Exceptional Children, 66,* 509–529.

Braddock, D., Rizzolo, M., & Hemp, R. (2004). Most employment services growth in developmental disabilities during 1988–2002 was in segregated services. *Mental Retardation, 42*(4), 317–320.

Brooke, V., Wehman, P., Inge, K., & Parent, W. (1995). Toward a consumer driven approach of supported employment. *Education and Training in Mental Retardation and Developmental Disabilities, 30,* 309–320.

Callahan, M., & Condon, E. (2007) Discovery: The foundation of job development. In C. Griffin, D. Hammis, & T. Geary (Eds.), *The job developer's handbook: Practical tactics for customized employment* (pp. 23–34). Baltimore: Paul H. Brookes.

Chambers, C. R., Hughes, C., & Carter, E. (2004). Parent and sibling perspective on transition to adulthood. *Education and Training in Developmental Disabilities, 39*(2), 79–94.

Elinson, L., & Frey, W. (2005). *Evaluation of disability employment policy demonstration programs: Task 10: Interim report on ODEP demonstration programs: Accomplishments and issues identified by the independent evaluation.* Maryland: WESTAT. Retrieved October 6, 2008, from the U.S. Department of Labor Web site at www.dol.gov/odep/categories/research/policy_programs.htm

Griffin, C. (1996). Job carving as a job development strategy. In D. Dileo & D. Langton (Eds.), *Facing the future: Best practices in supported employment* (pp. 36–38). St. Augustine, FL: TRN.

Griffin, C., Hammis, D., & Geary, T. (2007). Person-centered job development strategies: Finding the jobs behind the jobs. In C. Griffin, D. Hammis, & T. Geary, (Eds.) *The job developer's handbook: Practical tactics for customized employment* (pp. 49–72). Baltimore: Paul H. Brookes.

Horner, R. H., McDonnell, J. J., & Bellamy, G. T. (1986). Teaching generalized skills: General case instruction in simulation and community settings. In R. H. Horner, L. H. Meyer, & H. D. Fredericks (Eds.), *Education of learners with severe handicaps: Exemplary service strategies* (pp. 189–289). Baltimore: Paul H. Brookes.

Kennedy, M. J. (1988). *From sheltered workshops to supported employment.* Syracuse, NY: Syracuse University, Center on Human Policy. Retrieved February 12, 2008, from http://thechp.syr.edu/kdywork.htm

Kregel, J. (1998). Developing a career path: Applications of person-centered planning. In P. Wehman & J. Kregel, (Eds.), *More than a job: Securing satisfying careers for people with disabilities.* Baltimore: Paul H. Brookes.

Kregel, J., & Dean, D. H. (2002). Sheltered vs. supported employment: A direct comparison of long-term earnings outcomes for individuals with cognitive disabilities. In J. Kregel, D. H. Dean, & P. Wehman (Eds.), *Achievements and challenges in employment services for people with disabilities: The longitudinal impact of workplace supports monograph* (pp. 63–83). Richmond: Virginia Commonwealth University, Rehabilitation Research and Training Center on Supported Employment.

Kregel, J., Wehman, P., Revell, G., Hill, J., & Cimera, R. (2000). Supported employment benefit-cost analysis: Preliminary findings. *Journal of Vocational Rehabilitation, 14,* 153–161.

Luecking, D. M., Gumpman, P., Saeker, L., & Cihak, D. (2006). Perceived quality of life changes of job seekers with significant disabilities who participated in a customized employment process. *Journal of Applied Rehabilitation Counseling, 37*(4), 22–28.

Luecking, D. M., & Luecking, R. G. (2006). A descriptive study of customizing the employment process for job seekers with significant disabilities. *Journal of Applied Rehabilitation Counseling, 37*(4), 14–21.

Mank, D., Cioffi, A., & Yovanoff, P. (1997). Analysis of the typicalness of supported employment jobs, natural supports, and wage and integration outcomes. *Mental Retardation, 35*(3), 185–197.

Mank, D., Cioffi, A., & Yovanoff, P. (2000). Direct support in supported employment and its relationship to job typicalness, coworker involvement, and employment outcomes. *Mental Retardation, 38*(6), 506–516.

Mank, D., Cioffi, A., & Yovanoff, P. (2003). Supported employment outcomes across the decade: Is there evidence of improvement in quality implementation? *Mental Retardation, 41*(3), 188–197.

Martin, J. E., Marshal, L. H., & De Pry, R. L. (2005). Participatory decision making: Innovative practices that increase self-determination. In R. W. Flexer, T. J. Simmons, P. Luft, & R. Baer (Eds.), *Transition planning for students with disabilities* (pp. 246–275). Upper Saddle River, NJ: Pearson.

McDonnell, J., Mathot-Buckner, C., & Ferguson, B. (1996). *Transition programs for students with moderated/severe disabilities.* Baltimore: Paul H. Brookes.

McGlashing-Johnson, J., Agran, M., Sitlington, P., Cavin, M., & Wehmeyer, M. (2003). Enhancing the job performance of youth with moderate to severe cognitive disabilities using the self-determined model of instruction. *Research and Practice for Persons With Severe Disabilities, 28*(4), 194–204.

Mentally Retarded Citizens of Missouri, Inc. (n.d.). *Defense of sheltered workshops.* Retrieved February 12, 2008, from http://www.rcomo.org/whatisasw.htm# Defense

Migliore, A., Mank, D., Grossi, T., & Rogan, P. (2007). Integrated employment or sheltered workshops: Preferences of adults with disabilities, their families, and staff. *Journal of Vocational Rehabilitation, 26,* 5–19.

National Organization on Disability. (2004). Key indicators from the 2004 national organization on disability/Harris survey on Americans with disabilities. Retrieved October 8, 2008, from http://www.nod.org/index.cfm?fuseaction= Feature.showFeature&FeatureID=1422

Nietupski, J. A., & Hamre-Nietupski, S. (2000). A systematic process for carving supported employment for people with severe disabilities. *Journal of Developmental and Physical Disabilities, 12*(2), 103–119.

Nietupski, J. A., & Hamre-Nietupski, S. (2001). A business approach to finding and restructuring supported employment opportunities. In P. Wehman (Ed.), *Supported employment in business: Expanding the capacity of workers with disabilities* (pp. 59–74). St. Augustine, FL: TRN.

Nisbet, J., & Hagner, D. (1988). Natural supports in the workplace: A reexamination of supported employment. *Journal of the Association for Persons With Severe Handicaps, 13*(4), 260–267.

Office of Disability Employment Policy. (2005). *Customized employment: Practical solutions for employment success.* Retrieved October 6, 2008, from the U.S. Department of Labor Web site at www.dol.gov/odep/pubs/custom/index.htm

Rehabilitation Act Amendments of 1992, 29 U.S.C. § 705 (1992).

Rosenthal-Malek, A., & Bloom, A. (1998). Beyond acquisition: Teaching generalization for students with developmental disabilities. In A. Hilton & R. Ringlaben (Eds.), *Best and promising practices in developmental disabilities* (pp. 139–155). Austin, TX: Pro-Ed.

Rusch, F., & Braddock, D. (2004). Adult day programs versus supported employment (1988–2002): Spending and service practices of mental retardation and developmental disabilities state agencies. *Research and Practice for Persons With Severe Disabilities, 29*(4), 237–242.

Rusch, F., & Hughes, C. (1989). Overview of supported employment. *Journal of Applied Behavioral Analysis, 22*(4), 351–363.

Simmons, T., Flexer, R. W., & Bauder, D. (2005). Transition services. In R.W. Flexer, T. J. Simmons, P. Luft, & R. M. Baer (Eds.), *Transition planning for students with disabilities* (pp. 211–244). Upper Saddle River, NJ: Pearson.

Social Security Administration. (2007). *2007 red book: A summary guide to employment support for individuals with disabilities under the Social Security Disability Insurance and Supplemental Security Income programs.* SSA Pub. No. 64-030. Washington, DC: Author.

Storey, K. (2002). Strategies for increasing interactions in supported employment: An updated review. *Journal of Vocational Rehabilitation, 17,* 231–237.

U.S. Department of Labor, Office of Disability Employment Policy; Customized Employment Grants, 67 Fed. Reg. 43154 (2002). Available at http://frwebgate.access.gpo.gov/cgibin/getpage.cgi?position=all&page=43154&dbname=2002_register

Wagner, M., Newman, L., Cameto, R., Garza, N., & Levine, P. (2005). After high school: A first look at the postschool experiences of youth with disabilities. *A report from the National Longitudinal Transition Study-2.* Menlo Park, CA: SRI International. Available at http://www.nlts2.org/reports/2005_04/index.html

Wehman, P. (2003). Workplace inclusion: Persons with disabilities and coworkers working together. *Journal of Vocational Rehabilitation, 18,* 131–141.

Wehman, P., & Bricout, J. (2001). Supported employment: New directions for the new millennium. In P. Wehman (Ed.), *Supported employment in business: Expanding the capacity of workers with disabilities* (pp. 3–22). St Augustine, FL: TRN.

Wehman, P., Revell, W. G., & Brooke, V. (2003). Competitive employment: Has it become the "first choice" yet? *Journal of Disability Policy Studies, 14*(3), 163–167.

Wehman, P., Revell, W. G., & Kregel, J. (1998). Supported employment: A decade of rapid growth and impact. *American Rehabilitation, 24*(1), 31–44.

Wehmeyer, M. L., & Schwartz, M. (1998). The self-determination focus of transition goals for students with mental retardation. *Career Development for Exceptional Individuals, 21,* 75–86.

West, M. D., & Parent, W. S. (1992). Consumer choice and empowerment in supported employment services: Issues and strategies. *Journal of the Association for Persons With Severe Handicaps, 17*(1), 47–52.

West, M., Revell, G., & Wehman, P. (1998). Conversion for segregated services to supported employment: A continuing challenge to the VR service system. *Education and Training in Mental Retardation and Developmental Disabilities, 33*(3), 239–247.

Westling, D., & Fox, L. (2000). *Teaching students with severe disabilities.* Upper Saddle River, NJ: Merrill.

Zivolich, S. (1991). Free market strategies for improving employment services: Transitioning segregated day activity programs to integrated employment services. *Journal of Vocational Rehabilitation, 1*(4), 65–72.

Chapter 16

Adreon, D., & Durocher, J. S. (2007). Evaluating the college transition needs of individuals with high-functioning autism spectrum disorders. *Intervention in School and Clinic, 42,* 271–279.

Anderson-Inman, L., Knox-Quinn, C., & Szymanski, M. (1999). Computer supported studying: Stories of successful transition to postsecondary education. *Career Development for Exceptional Individuals, 22,* 185–212.

Babbitt, B. C., & White, C. M. (2002). R u reading? Helping students assess their readiness for postsecondary education. *Teaching Exceptional Children, 35,* 62–66.

Barnett, E., Gardner, D., & Bragg, D. (2004). *Dual credit in Illinois: Making it work.* Urbana-Champaign: University of Illinois, Office of Community College Research and Leadership.

Basset, D. S., & Smith, T. E. C. (1996). Transition in an era of reform. *Journal of Learning Disabilities, 29*(2), 161–166.

Baum, S., & Ma, J. (2007). *Education pays 2007: The benefits of higher education for individuals and society.* Retrieved January 20, 2008, from the College Board Web site at http://www .collegboard.com/prod_downloads/about/news_info/ yr2007.pdf

Baum, S., & Payea, K. (2005). *Education pays 2004: The benefits of higher education for individuals and society.* Retrieved January 20, 2008, from the College Board Web site at http://www .collegeboard.com/prod_downloads/press/cost04/educationpays2004.pdf

Benz, M. R., Yovanoff, P., & Doren, B. (1997). School-to-work components that predict postschool success for students with and without disabilities. *Exceptional Children, 63,* 151–165.

Black, R. S., & Ornelles, C. (2001). Assessment of social competence and social networks for transition. *Assessment for Effective Intervention, 26,* 23–39.

Blalock, G., & Patton, J. (1996). Transition and students with learning disabilities: Creating sound futures. *Journal of Learning Disabilities, 29*(1), 7–16.

Bouck, E. C. (2004). Exploring secondary special education for mild mental impairment: A program in search of its place. *Remedial and Special Education, 25,* 367–382.

Brinckerhoff, L. C. (1996). Making the transition to higher education: Opportunities for student empowerment. *Journal of Learning Disabilities, 29,* 118–136.

Brinckerhoff, L. C., McGuire, J. M., & Shaw, S. F. (2002). *Postsecondary education and transition for students with learning disabilitie*s (2nd ed.). Austin, TX: Pro-Ed.

Carnevale, A. P., & Fry, R. A. (2000). *Crossing the great divide: Can we achieve equity when generation Y goes to college?* Princeton, NJ: Educational Testing Service.

Chadsey, J. G., & Shelden, D. (1998). Moving toward social inclusion in employment and postsecondary school settings. In F. R. Rusch & J. G. Chadsey (Eds.), *Beyond high school: Transition from school to work* (pp. 406–438). Belmont, CA: Wadsworth.

Crist, C., Jacquart, M., & Shupe, D. A. (2002). Improving the performance of high school students: Focusing on connections and transitions taking place in Minnesota. *The Journal of Vocational Special Needs Education, 24,* 41–55.

Dohm, A., & Shniper, L. (2007, November). Occupational employment projects to 2016. *Monthly Labor Review, 130*(11), 86–125.

Dolyniuk, C. A., Kamens, M. W., Corman, H., Opipery DiNardo, P., Totaro, R. M., & Rockoff, J. C. (2002). Students with developmental disabilities go to college: Description of a collaborative transition project on a regular college campus. *Focus on Autism and Other Developmental Disabilities, 17,* 236–241.

Doyle, M. B. (2003). We want to go to college too: Support students with significant disabilities in higher education. In D. L. Ryndak & S. Alper (Eds.), *Curriculum and instruction for students with significant disabilities in inclusive settings* (pp. 307–322). Upper Saddle River, NJ: Allyn & Bacon.

Dunn, C. (1996). A status report on transition planning for individuals with learning disabilities. *Journal of Learning Disabilities, 29*(1), 17–30.

Durlak, C. M., Rose, E., & Bursuck, W. D. (1994). Preparing high school students with learning disabilities for the transition to postsecondary education: Teaching the skills of self-determination. *Journal of Learning Disabilities, 27,* 51–59.

Fisher, D., Sax, C., & Pumpian, I. (1999). *Inclusive high schools: Learning from contemporary classrooms.* Baltimore: Paul H. Brookes.

Gajar, A. (1998). Postsecondary education. In F. R. Rusch & J. G. Chadsey (Eds.), *Beyond high school: Transition from school to work* (pp. 383–405). Belmont, CA: Wadsworth.

Getzel, E. E., & Finn, D. E., Jr. (2005). Training university faculty and staff. In E. E. Getzel & P. Wehman (Eds.), *Going to college: Expanding opportunities for people with disabilities* (pp. 199–216). Baltimore: Paul H. Brookes.

Getzel, E. E., Stodden, R. A., & Briel, R. W. (2001). Pursuing postsecondary education opportunities for individuals with disabilities. In P. Wehman (Ed.), *Beyond high school: Transition strategies for young people with disabilities* (pp. 247–260). Baltimore: Paul H. Brookes.

Grigal, M., Neubert, D. A., & Moon, M. S. (2001). Public school programs for students with severe disabilities in postsecondary settings. *Education and Training in Mental Retardation and Developmental Disabilities, 36,* 244–254.

Hall, M., Kleinert, H. L., & Kearns, J. F. (2000). Going to college: Postsecondary programs for students with moderate and severe disabilities. *Teaching Exceptional Children, 32,* 58–65.

Halpern, A. S. (1994). The transition of youth with disabilities to adult life: A position statement of the Division on Career Development and Transition, The Council for Exceptional Children. *Career Development of Exceptional Individuals, 17,* 202–211.

Hart, D., Mele-McCarthy, J., Pasternack, R. H., Zimbrich, D., & Parker, D. R. (2004). Community college: A pathway to success for youth with learning, cognitive, and intellectual disabilities. *Education and Training in Developmental Disabilities, 39,* 54–66.

Hart, D., Zimbrich, K., & Parker, D. R. (2005). Dual enrollment as a postsecondary education option for students with intellectual disabilities. In E. E. Getzel & P. Wehman (Eds.), *Going to college: Expanding opportunities for people with disabilities* (pp. 253–270). Baltimore: Paul H. Brookes.

Hitchings, W. E., Luzzo, D. A., Ristow, R., Horvath, M., Retish, P., & Tanners, A. (2001). The career development needs of college students with learning disabilities: In their own words. *Learning Disabilities Research and Practice, 16,* 8–17.

Hoffman, N. (2005). *Add and subtract: Dual enrollment as a state strategy to increase postsecondary success for underrepresented students.* Boston: Jobs for the Future.

Janiga, S. J., & Costenbader, V. (2002). The transition from high school to postsecondary education for students with learning disabilities: A survey of college service coordinators. *Journal of Learning Disabilities, 35,* 462–479.

Jordan, W. J., Cavalluzzo, L., & Corallo, C. (2006). Community college and high school reform: Lessons from five case studies. *Community College Journal of Research and Practice, 30,* 729–749.

Kochhar-Bryant, C. A. (2002). Building transition capacity through personnel development: Analysis of 35 state improvement grants. *Career Development for Exceptional Individuals, 26,* 161–184.

Kochhar-Bryant, C. A., & Izzo, M. V. (2006). Access to post-high school services: Transition assessment and the summary of performance. *Career Development of Exceptional Individuals, 29,* 70–89.

Macabe, R. (2000). *No one to waste.* Washington, DC: Community College Press.

McDonnell, J., Ferguson, B., & Mathot-Buckner, C. (1992). Transition from school to work for students with severe disabilities: The Utah community-based employment project. In F. R. Rusch, L. Destefano, J. Chadsey-Rusch, L. A. Phelps, & E. Szymanski (Eds.), *Transition from school to adult life: Models, linkages, and policy* (pp. 33–50). Sycamore, IL: Sycamore Publishing.

McDonnell, J., Mathot-Buckner, C., & Ferguson, B. (1996). *Transition programs for students with moderate/severe disabilities.* Pacific Grove, CA: Brooks/Cole.

Mull, C. A., & Sitlington, P. L. (2003). The role of technology in the transition to postsecondary education of students with learning disabilities: A review of the literature. *The Journal of Special Education, 37,* 26–32.

Newman, L. (2005). Postsecondary education participation of youth with disabilities. In M. Wagner, L. Neman, R. Cameto, N. Garz, & P. Levine (Eds.), *After high school: A first look at the postschool experiences of youth with disabilities* (pp. 4-1–4-17). Menlo Park, CA: SRI International.

Oliver, C., Hecker, L., Klucken, J., & Westby, C. (2000). Language: The embedded curriculum in postsecondary education. *Topics in Language Disorders, 21,* 15–29.

Page, B., & Chadsey-Rusch, J. (1995). The community college experience for students with and without disabilities. *Career Development for Exceptional Individuals, 18,* 85–95.

Park, H. S., Hoffman, S. A., Whaley, S., & Gonsier-Gerdin, J. (2001). Ted's story: Looking back and beyond. In J. Grenot-Scheyer, J. Fisher, & D. Staub (Eds.), *Lessons learned in inclusive education: At the end of the day* (pp. 151–162). Baltimore: Paul H. Brookes.

Patton, J. R., Cronin, M. E., & Jarriels, V. (1997). Curricular implications of transition. *Remedial and Special Education, 18*, 294–306.

Patton, J. R., Polloway, E. A., Smith, T. E. C., Edgar, E., Clark, G., & Lee, S. (1996). Individuals with mild mental retardation: Postsecondary outcomes and implications for educational policy. *Education and Training in Mental Retardation and Developmental Disabilities, 31*, 75–85.

Pearman, E., Elliott, T., & Aborn, L. (2004). Transition services model: Partnerships for student success. *Education and Training in Developmental Disabilities, 39*, 26–34.

Phelps, L. A., & Hanley-Maxwell, C. (1997). School-to-work transitions for youth with disabilities: A review of outcomes and practices. *Review of Educational Research, 67*, 197–226.

The Rehabilitation Act, Section 504, 29 U.S.C. § 794 (1973).

Reis, S. M., McGuire, J. M., & Neu, T. W. (2000). Compensation strategies used by high-ability students with learning disabilities who succeed in college. *Gifted Child Quarterly, 44*, 123–134.

Siperstein, G. N. (1988). Students with learning disabilities in college: The need for programmatic approach to critical transitions. *Journal of Learning Disabilities, 21*, 431–436.

Sitlington, P. L. (2003). Postsecondary education: The other transition. *Exceptionality, 11,* 103–113.

Smith, T. E. C., & Puccini, I. K. (1995). Position statement: Secondary curriculum and policy issues for students with mental retardation. *Education and Training in Mental Retardation and Developmental Disabilities, 30*, 275–282.

Speckman, N. J., Goldberg, R. J., & Herman, H. L. (1992). Learning disabled children grow up: A search for factors related to success in young adult years. *Learning Disabilities Research Practice, 7,* 161–170.

Stodden, R. A., Conway, M. A., & Chang, K. (2003). Secondary school curricula issues: Impact on postsecondary students with disabilities. *Exceptional Children, 70*(1), 9–25.

Stodden, R. A., & Whelley, T. (2004). Postsecondary education and persons with intellectual disabilities: An introduction. *Education and Training in Developmental Disabilities, 39*, 6–15.

Tashie, C., Malloy, J. M., & Lichtenstein, S. J. (1998). Transition or graduation? Supporting all students to plan for the future. In C. M. Jorgensen (Ed.), *Restructuring all high schools for all students: Taking inclusion to the next level* (pp. 233–260). Baltimore: Paul H. Brookes.

U.S. Department of Education, Office for Civil Rights. (2005, May). *Students with disabilities preparing for postsecondary education: Know your rights and responsibilities.* Retrieved February 10, 2008, from the U.S. Department of Education Web site at http://www.ed.gov/about/offices/list/ocr/transition.html?exp=0

Wasburn-Moses, L. (2006). Obstacles to program effectiveness in secondary special education. *Preventing School Failure, 50*, 21–30.

Wehman, P. (2006). *Life beyond the classroom: Transition strategies for young people with disabilities* (4th ed.). Baltimore: Paul H. Brookes.

Weiss, S. (Ed.). (2005, May). *The progress of education reform 2005: Dual enrollment* (Vol. 6, No. 3). Denver: Education Commission of the States.

Zafft, C., Hart, D., & Zimbrich, K. (2004). College career connection: A study of youth with intellectual disabilities and the impact of postsecondary education. *Education and Training in Developmental Disabilities, 39,* 45–53.

Zafft, C., Kallenbach, S., & Spohn, J. (2006). *Transitioning adults to college: Adult basic education program models. A report from the National Center for the Study of Adult Learning and Literacy, National College Transition Network.* Boston: World Education, Inc.

Index